Shoulder to Shoulder

DAILY DEVOTIONALS FOR LEADERS & THEIR TEAMS

MARK QUEEN

Introduction

Many years ago, I took on the challenge to read through the entire Bible in one year. I have learned to love this activity and have adopted it as a daily practice. At some point, I accepted a challenge to write a daily prayer for forty days to grow in my faith. The success of that challenge led me to journal as I read through the Bible. I always included a written prayer with it. This practice has been meaningful to me and has become meaningful to others as well.

I have made it a practice to share the devotionals with others and know that God has used it many times for His good. When I considered how helpful these daily devotionals were in my personal life, I also recognized how beneficial they were for me in business. It was the inspiration for what you have now.

This book is the work of years of reflection on the impacts that faith has on one's business, family, world events, team, and customers. Our brains are designed to do one thing at a time. The term multitasking has become an acceptable extension of productivity, but we really aren't meant to operate that way. The history of entrepreneurs building their own companies is littered with examples of successes.

Unfortunately, many of those examples are accompanied by those that have succeeded in business and lost their marriages, families, and faith along the way. Profits have been achieved at the cost of people.

This is not true of all companies, but it is true that every company owner will be challenged to keep a balance. Lack of balanced focus isn't something anyone aspires to, but running a company can be consuming, diverting our focus from things that are also important.

This book is a tool that has been created to help the entrepreneur, the company, and its team achieve a balance. The book is laid out to be read as a devotional with a particular theme being addressed for each day. The themes are as follows and in no particular order.

- Inspiration
- Focus
- Leadership
- Limits
- Accountability
- Collaboration
- Attitude

Some might choose a reading every day or every week. Some might choose to focus on one specific theme each month or each quarter. How you use this tool for your own inspiration is completely up to you. It only matters that you use it so you can achieve balance and success in all aspects of your life.

Our quest is that this tool helps you to lead a life of significance. The business world, the faith world, if not the entire world, needs this book more than ever before.

We hope that you'll find strength and inspiration from its pages and share it with anyone whom you believe it might help.

JANUARY 1: BRING IN THE LIGHT AND THE NEW YEAR

In the beginning, there was darkness. There was no light, but God was there, and he brought the light. He called the time of light day and the time of darkness the night. So, it became that God created something out of matter that wasn't fully formed. He moved from the potential held in the darkness to that which is in the light. And that's how many of us operate when we have new ideas for creation and growth. Those ideas may not be fully realized. They may sit in the darkness, waiting to be fleshed out, but the potential is there if we simply shine a light upon it and direct our focus.

"Then God said, 'Let there be light,' and there was light."

GENESIS 1:3 NLT

January starts the new calendar year, something I consider a clean slate. It is a good day to recognize where we are, how far we have come, and where we need to go as we focus our intent. You possess endless amounts of potential, opportunity, and the determination to achieve your goals moving forward. How you'll achieve said goals is completely up to you. Will you give encouragement, leadership, and trust? Will you offer forgiveness, seek forgiveness, give more financially, or transform physically? If your thought processes encompass the idea that you can improve in all areas, then you probably have plenty of things you'd like to get started on, but the key is focus. What will you focus on first? The slate is clean, and you're starting anew. So I want you to jump into this headspace and walk about for a bit. Are you ready? Here are a few things you can dedicate yourself to and repeat as a heartfelt mantra. Please pick one to focus and reflect on.

I will be better at listening. I will value honesty and give honesty. I will accept constructive criticism as I know it helps me improve. I will be slow to anger. I will be quick to love. I will make kindness my mantra. I will work on my relationship with my team in professional and personal spheres. How can you continue to do this throughout the year? The sky-bound spotlights that I associate with Hollywood premiers just rotate without a real focus, but we can place our spotlight with purpose. So, what will you intentionally focus on and give purpose to? The spotlight is ready, but the choice is yours. Happy New Year! Welcome to the very best year of your life thus far.

Let us pray.

Heavenly Father, you made the darkness into light. A light that still shines to this day. Help us to leave the dark behind and to share in your light. Make the love of a new day and of Christ surround us to draw nearer to you. In Jesus' name, we pray. Amen.

JANUARY 2: THE NEXT SEVEN DAYS

The creation account in Genesis gives us a timeline of seven days. Have you ever wondered why it was seven days? It could have been any number of days, so why seven instead of fourteen? God evidently had a plan and a progression. Once He began His process of creation, he saw it through until it was time to rest. Day and night, land and sea, and rest all happened through his activities per his plan. So, did you wake up today and even remember any of your resolutions? I firmly believe that it is not the resolutions that are going to change you or make the world better.

If God had said, "I resolve to create the universe and man to be in relationship" and did not have any action with which to back it up, it would have been a tragedy for us all. The resolution was followed up by action. Action took place over that seven-day period. In the next seven days, what are you going to do about your personal relationship with God, your career, profession, business, finances, and even your health? I like to think about the next seven days as the present. It's what is on my mind and relevant to my given situation.

> "On the seventh day God had finished his work of creation, so he rested from all his work."
>
> GENESIS 2:2 NLT

As a leader, how will you encourage your team to assess the next seven days? Do you supervise and oversee monthly, or is it a shorter or longer time frame? Whichever approach you use, we know that our team operates the best when there is collaboration, and we must have deadlines.

If we are not staying in touch with one another often enough, our team might begin to break down or get disconnected.

I believe that disconnected teams are less effective in delivering value. If you are planning on collaborating on the same schedule as last year, you might expect the same results. Stepping up the level of accountability affects focus and productivity. Giving the power of accountability is simple, but it is not easy if we want it to be effective.

Giving authority to those that can help build collaboration will likely bring value, and focusing on seven days at a time is how you take a big-picture approach and then break that big picture up into smaller steps that are achievable.

What smaller steps can be identified and then acted upon? Because a simple resolution is not enough. God did not make resolutions. He made declarations, and we can do the same. Will you commit to something more with God, or will you be satisfied with making a resolution and leaving it at that? What is the first thing you can do in the next seven days?

Let us pray.

Heavenly Father, thank you for presenting to us the ability to be in relationship with you. Thank you for the blessings that you have bestowed upon us this past year, but we are prepared to move forward. We resolve and declare to make the next seven days into ones of accountability. Help us by holding us in the palm of your hand. Comfort us as we move forward through the present because change is difficult, and it can be fearful. Take us where you might guide us to be as we make small incremental changes in our behaviors. Move us to love one another better, forgive one another faster, and to give more freely of our resources. In Jesus' name, we pray. Amen.

JANUARY 3: WHAT LABEL WOULD BE APPROPRIATE THIS WEEK OR YEAR?

As a follower of Jesus Christ, in what four ways would those you respect describe you? I see this passage calling Jesus four things. Our self-worth is an important part of living out our relationship with Jesus and the rest of the world. What four ways would Christ use to describe you? The answer might be formerly lost sinner, forgiven child, disciple of mine, or claimed as he knows your name.

As leader of your team, how do people describe you? Do they portray you as an overbearing father or strict mother? Does the label corporate muck or recognition grabbing supervisor stick to you? One of the most challenging moments a leader might ever face is to ask how others, who are connected to your team, would describe you. What four ways or terms do you think your clients and team members might use?

> "For a child is born to us, a son is given to us. The government will rest on his shoulders. And he will be called: Wonderful Counselor, Mighty God, Everlasting Father, Prince of Peace."
>
> ISAIAH 9:6 NLT

Generous, value driven, client focused, compassionate, and caring might be spoken as well as those other labels. The labels probably will not be limited to one term when you work with a team, but we might expect to hear several. Those labels are indicative of the value we might be bringing to them in their opinions. Other's perceptions are their realities. Your value is important and worth the risk of asking those you respect for an honest reflective answer. Growing others includes tough conversations and tough conversations start with us.

During this holiday season and into the new year, perhaps we can put an emphasis on the labels that Christ would give us and to live them out. What is the first thing that you can do about it in the next seven days?

Let us pray.

Father God, on Christmas Day we gave thanks for the reason for this celebration which is our Lord and Savior Jesus. Make us draw near to your heart and love today. Guide us to unwrap the gift of our relationship with Jesus like the gifts we exchange. May the label on each package we share remind us of the labels Christ has for every name read. In Jesus' name, we pray. Amen.

JANUARY 4: VOTE, KING OF KINGS!

Have you ever been part of a group that has no formal leader? They function in chaos if they all stay together. Some of the original members will likely move away from the group. If no organization happens then value will be challenged. The remaining participants will likely get organized around a single value. The value approach does not have to be complicated, and it does not have to remain small.

A value approach might even have the best result if it stays simple. For example, let's establish a food bank in our community. Where in your groups are you being led by simplicity of value?

I have seen new leaders introduce simple value into chaotic situations quite often, and they manage to turn that chaos into order with a few common factors. The common factors within these groups might be that the leader changed the focus from self-interest, comfort, and keeping the status quo to finding and providing value.

Everyone has empty holes in their sphere of influence when it comes to value. We have places that we can capture and provide value. Upon examination, where might you have a gap? Perhaps our sphere of influence will help others when we ourselves put more emphasis on the value that we desire in our own lives.

As a believer in the resurrection of Jesus, one has faith that he was put on this Earth to be a savior. Not just a savior but The Savior. That was the value offered to us. That is the value God gives us day after day even if we can't see it.

"Locusts—they have no king, but they march in formation."

PROVERBS 30:27 NLT

I believe that Gods' values have been sent to us through Him. There is nothing that we can do to cancel Gods' love for us. We can make bad choices that remove ourselves from His love, but it is never canceled. Limitations on love from God do not exist. The King of kings does not change the laws of this world. He changes us.

Remember that there is always an election time because we have a choice every morning to wake up. Leaders and kings are still going to be appointed to run governments and countries. But that will not change the value and gift that God sent to the world. Let us celebrate the gift that continues to keep on giving by bringing value to others in our thoughts, love, words, and actions. Someone in your sphere of influence has an emptiness that needs filling. It might be you. What is the first thing that you can do to offer value to another within the next seven days?

Let us pray.

Heavenly Father, thank you for the gift of Jesus Christ. Help us to remember that He was born and died the King of kings. He provides us with value through an everlasting opportunity to experience our change of heart. Make our hate be changed to love and respect. Make all greed be moved towards compassion and may our hearts vote to accept your gift with a simple thank you. In Jesus' name, we pray. Amen.

JANUARY 5: WHICH SIDE OF THE BRAIN DO YOU FAVOR?

Which side of the brain do you use the most? Is it the limbic system or the neocortex? Is it the creative side or the logical side? The feelings and creative side do not seem to use much of the "it all adds up" side. It seems to use a process that flows into the feelings. Those feelings can be tricky things. Feelings are not necessarily true and trustworthy. Surely, we can get caught into errors, fall easier into the area of judgment of others, and fall into bad practices using this side of the brain. But the logical side is just as easily swayed. If two plus two is four, and four plus four is eight, then four plus eight is twelve. But who asked the question of what is four plus eight?

We can very easily insert our own then statements. Then statements in the real world with people are not necessarily true. I am not convinced that they are true most of the time. Our brain works down neural pathways for speed and those pathways miss millions of signals and pieces of information. It has many automatic assumptions. We have so much going on when it comes to information coming into our brains that it must filter some of it out. That is why magic works. We cannot pay attention to all the information that is being made available. Our brains look for some key indicators to help us move quickly towards a solution.

When a person is frustrated an interruption to frustration can be valuable. Any interruptions can begin the change process and often an effective interruption is to ask what assumptions are being made. Curiosity interrupts the path. Where might your team benefit by using an interruption?

Which side of the brain does God use the most? Maybe the answer to my question is that God is not using our brain at all, we are. Whose brain is it? It is our brain. It is our free will. It is us that uses one side or the other. I think where I find God most is when I use both sides. Blending both sides, so that my heart might have a say as well. Can I figure a way through my thoughts in my mind so as to share what my heart knows?

> "Lord Almighty, you who examine the righteous and probe the heart and mind, let me see your vengeance on them, for to you I have committed my cause."
>
> JEREMIAH 20:12 NIV

Our broken world and selfishness can become top priority. Do you remember when Abram in the Bible told his wife Sarai, that he would call her his sister. It was out of fear of himself being killed that he asked such a thing. You can find it in Genesis 12. It was a very logical thing to do, but I do not know how Sarai might have felt about it. I suspect that she might have been offended. Do you see the logic and feelings connecting here? I believe that what the heart knows is that it wants to know love, to share love and to be loved.

Today, maybe we can focus on the heart. Consider taking the focus off sin if that is where you are at. Take the focus off what is not loving and off judgment. I am asking that we consider that we leave logic behind sometimes. Let us think with our heart some today. What is the first thing on your calendar in the next seven days that could use more of your heart than your head? Perhaps there is someone on your calendar that needs more of your heart than your head?

Let us pray.

Father, your love is so great. You make the dew on the grass and the heatwaves that arise from the sand. You send to us the feelings of love through your Son, Jesus and it touches us. May we connect our hearts to your love so that we might forgive faster, love better and grow towards excellence today. When our brain is thinking, or worrying too much, may we simply return to you and your love. In Jesus' name, we pray. Amen.

JANUARY 6: ARE YOU HOT OR COLD?

As a leader, what are you excellent at? I ask not that you brag but really reflect what your life has allowed you to develop. Would others recognize you for this ability?

You might be so good, that when you are doing this, time evaporates from your perception. This activity does not even seem to use your energy or make you tired. In fact, it might create energy within you when you do it. When you are doing things like this, I call it a unique ability.

Dan Sullivan has written much about it. You are more than just competent or good in this realm. On the other side of the spectrum are things that, to be blunt, we are incompetent at. Being incompetent at something is not a bad thing although you might have learned or been exposed to the thought that it is bad. I remember in school that being incompetent or getting a failing grade was something that I was expected to work on. One could even be chastised and looked down upon when this occurred. But being incompetent is not necessarily a bad thing. You are not bad when this occurs. You are just incompetent at it.

Consider it in this way. Are you a really bad thief, so much so that you could be considered to be incompetent at it? Would you consider it a blessing to be a great thief? I hope you never become really good at being a thief. Can you identify what you excel at and what you may struggle with in your professional areas? Which will your team focus on this week? A unique ability or incompetence? It is not uncommon that we overlook the progress that can be made when we make steps forward by stopping what is merely good or changing incompetence. To do so might start with dropping the stigma associated with incompetence.

It seems to me that God can call us to bless others through our unique abilities. We can draw others as well as ourselves to him when we use those abilities. But what about our incompetence? Does God use those as well to glorify him? I think that he can, but it might just be that we as Christian brothers and sisters are called to help one another the most by sharing our unique abilities with one another. In many places in the Bible, spiritual gifts are discussed. We have been given these unique gifts, and to those that have discovered them, they are like the unique abilities discussed earlier.

My incompetence is someone else's unique ability. The shepherd boy David had the ability to use a sling like no other. The Bible is full of unique ability. Moses was not a great speaker, but Aaron came along to pick up that task. I think that God can work through them both. The Bible tells us in Genesis, that we will have planting and harvesting, summer and winter, warm and cold, and day and night. I think we have unique abilities and incompetence as well. They seem to be opposites. How might you plan to use the unique abilities more and the incompetence less in your faith journey? Who in your sphere of influence has an ability you are failing to use? Where can you acquire a resource to overcome this? What is the first thing that you can do about it in the next seven days?

Let us pray.

Jesus, I know you to be my Savior. You shared with the world the unique ability to take on our sins. You have the unique ability as well to share the love of the Father through miracles of the heart and of healing. We ask today that you help us to remove layers that have our abilities covered up. They can be hidden and buried to keep us from sharing our best for God's glory. Make this day be one of discovery and the week be one of finding your treasure in us. Launch us on a personal treasure hunt of gifts and abilities today. In Jesus' name, we pray. Amen.

JANUARY 7: WEARY FROM YOUR BURDENS

In the old west, at the end of a long cattle drive, cowboys were tired and weary from the task at hand. I can imagine the trail master telling the payroll clerk to settle up with them and to use an expression, "turn 'em loose." As leader of your team, family, or organization, how do you celebrate a job well done? It is not easy to provide constant value to others. It is work, and lots of it. But the results and rewards should be celebrated.

After the round up where the calves and new cattle are branded or tagged for a ranch, they must be worked. They are roped or contained so that they are handled carefully. The brands or tags or both are applied and then they are turned loose. They spring up from the ground and are quick afoot, ready to get out of the shoot or area. We can celebrate like calves when our value delivery system has worked.

Today might be the very best day to do that. What can you celebrate from the last year or even just the past ninety days? What has been inspirational to you and who might you want to share that with? Celebrations do not have to be kept a secret. In fact, when we celebrate how others have made a difference in our lives, we can show appreciation. Appreciation is one of the four central components we desire as humans. Celebrating and uplifting others can give us a boost as well. We can have a spring in our step like the calf springs up from the ground after being untied. I would bet those who celebrate those successes will see others walk with a spring in their step for a bit as well.

Do you recall the twelve days of Christmas song? There is a line that says, "Ten Lords a leaping." Perhaps there will be ten springing up because of you today. Will it be you and your team? You are the only one keeping it from happening. What will you do about it today?

> "But for you who fear my name, the Sun of Righteousness will rise with healing in his wings. And you will go free, leaping with joy like calves let out to pasture."
>
> MALACHI 4:2 NLT

As people who walk with faith, we too can celebrate. A life enhanced by a personal relationship with Jesus, The Lord, is not a promise of a life with no pain. But it is also a life that does not have to be focused on pain. Jesus suffered pain because of the cross. Christians know the joy, love, and teaching of the rest of His life and resurrection as well. What do you have to celebrate from the last ninety days in your faith? Go ahead. Get with your people. Leap like calves let out to pasture. Why not turn 'em loose? Our joy comes from the Lord that we celebrate. Perhaps you might be inspired to take twenty minutes and do an inventory of the last ninety days.

Get pen and paper or your technology if you prefer. Think back to October of last year and list ideas, events, scripture, gifts, worship services, prayers and people that have made a difference in your faith. Identify at least ten that you might celebrate and include others where possible. If you cannot find ten, find one and share it ten times. What is the first thing you can do about it in the next seven days?

Let us pray.

Heavenly Father, you are worth celebrating. We can be distracted by pain and fear, but we choose today to take time to celebrate you. Guide us to your pastures and places. Let us leap for joy and be inspired by your word and love. Help us to listen for your voice in the calm still moments. Find us by the streams, pastures, and meadows leaping for joy. Look for our faces as we smile because of you. In Jesus' name, we pray. Amen.

JANUARY 8: I AM SUGGESTING A NEW FORMULA

The new year has started, and I am sure that I have brought some of last year with me. As a leader, have you done the same? Only a few days have passed, but I am certain that I have already made some mistakes and my team has as well. Of the mistakes, one includes missed opportunities. Have you and your team done the same? Because we have been connected and providing value in some way in the past, we carry momentum with us into the future. That momentum can be identified if we look through the errors and into the opportunity. Opportunity came with us into the year as well. There are almost always two sides to a story. Almost every challenge is an opportunity. But our thought processes can sometimes be a trap.

With confidence, I can say that I have been unjust, unforgiving, unproductive, unfocused, and unloving at some moments. I have felt that unless someone else fixes their mistake that my world will be off. I might have even felt that until others address their errors that I cannot proceed in some way. Do you see the "un" in those words? Really, stop reading and look for the letters u and n put together as un. As a leader, our value might be found in looking at the "nu" (new) instead of the "un."

Where can we flip the letters and flip our attitude? By choosing to view an error, mistake, or challenge in a new way, we can reorganize and find more value. When one recognizes the "un" as in being uncomfortable or unsettled, we might benefit by simply recognizing it and stopping. Changing perception can start with an attitude of mitigating and reorganizing the "un" for something new. Will we choose to "undo" for something new? What is the first thing that you can do about it with your team?

Those can really be nonproductive in our walk with each other and in our faith. But if we do the attitude shift to reorganize what is new then we might see a new experience. It might be a new day for growth, progress, and love. It might be for something better, something towards that which God has prepared us for.

> "Therefore, if anyone is in Christ, the new creation has come: The old has gone, the new is here!"
>
> 2 CORINTHIANS 5:17 NIV

I believe that God sent his son for the greatest of the un words. That word is undone. I have messed up and not loved as God has asked me to love. Christ has undone that result through his sacrifice. I have felt that until my transgressors do me right, I am owed. Christ has undone that "until." We can throw that chip on our shoulder away and do something new about it that will glorify God. Perhaps it is undone when I forgive. When I am seeing others treated in an unjustified manner, maybe my words and actions can be of a healing and gathering attitude.

The shift in attitude is about me. I must accept responsibility to put my thoughts together to move away from the un and move me to a better new. Maybe something in the last year or last day or anytime this new year seems unjust. Has someone been unloving to you? Have you felt that until something happens you cannot move forward? Have you been looking underfoot? Our answer just might be in the heavens and in the "new" that Christ brought us many years ago. We can choose to stop being in the unsettled. May we make progress today and bring the "new "to life in us. Where do you choose to start in the next seven days?

Let us pray.

Jesus, thank you for your undoing. You came and brought miracles to undo the ramifications of the sins of the world for our brothers and sisters. You take the unjust and show the power of love. You take the unloved and bring them to a new relationship of love. Help us to move forward today holding onto the new. May we honor the undoing that you brought to the world. I pray that your comfort be with us as we act now to undo what we need to make new in our lives. In Jesus' name, we pray. Amen.

JANUARY 9: THE COMPETITIVE ADVANTAGE

As a leader, sometimes we can find our organization in competition with another organization. I remember the long-distance service telephone wars. Companies would call your phone and offer you money to switch your service to them as your carrier. They had to buy your business. The competition was not focused on providing value but achieving success in the easiest way possible. This does not seem like a viable way to run a value delivery type of business. I have never worked for the telephone industry. I am curious what the team members were required to do at that time? It seems like all that mattered was gathering new clients and it seemingly was at any cost, including paying them.

This approach can open the door to abuses and abandonment of some basic core values for the team. Competition can be won in a different way. How we lead our team and compete can be measured by love by looking for the right fit. Our role is to drive value. Our value does not always need to be called the best value but needs to meet the value of those we serve. A company like this can win long-term by consistently thinking about how to increase its value. This type of company tends to be a long-term industry leader when this approach is taken. They might even be thought of by the competition to compete unfairly. I would not call it unfair but would call it unique. It seemingly comes down to what actions we will or will not provide.

Are we looking inward towards our service delivery, team, and customers with love, respect, and value? If so, our actions will probably bear witness to it. Where do you have a unique competitive advantage because of value?

"But I say, love your enemies! Pray for those who persecute you!"

MATTHEW 5:44 NLT

As brothers and sisters in Christ, how do you love someone else on earth and God? To differentiate the two ways, we might think of the feeling of love differently than the actions of love. To be in love with someone might be all about us. I remember the emergent love that occurred while I developed my relationship with my wife. She held my hand and, physically, I could feel she loved me. We even occupied space and time together which made me aware of her love because she was present with me. But could God love us this way? It may be that our love for God is not so much about ourselves as it may be about us. It could be about our actions. We can exhibit our love of God by acting to show others our love.

We may not hold Jesus' hands, but we can hold the hand of our children as we walk them to school. We can hold the hand of the homeless and walk them to a table to serve them dinner. We can put our arms under others to support them when they are hurting and need assistance. I believe that a big part of our love of God is about actions. Our actions. You and I can both be in action towards others in unique ways. How might you act uniquely today to love God by loving others? What is the first thing that you can do about it in the next seven days?

Let us pray.

Heavenly Father, we understand that we do not have your knowledge. We know that You love us because you sent your Son to us to show us how to relate to you through our roles in this world. Help us today to be in love with You, to have the confidence to share your love for all through our actions. Touch us as you might. Send the Holy Spirit to guide us today with a step forward even though it might feel like a giant scary leap. Relieve all our fears except the fear of a world that would be without You. In Jesus' name, we pray. Amen.

JANUARY 10: CLINK, CRASH, OR WINK?

As a leader of a family, company, or organization, we are all on a journey. That includes the team members both internal and external. As we travel our separate paths, we are sometimes walking beside one another. At other times we cross paths. Sometimes we bump into one another and other times there are crashes. It seems that when crashes or bumps occur, we can move into judgment mode because progress on our path has been interrupted. But I want to think about another alternative. It could be a different move we make. It might simply and memorably be called the turn. I think that when our path is interrupted, all that is required is to take a turn.

A small adjustment to our desired course would help us to move closer or farther from the crash point. We will not likely see all the crashes coming, so they will sometimes occur. When this happens will we stay in the crash? Will we debate, discuss, point fingers, accuse, and make our points known or can we more quickly make another turn at that moment? Speed is often a root cause of the crash. We can be moving so fast that the need for a turn is not recognized in time to slow down and avoid it. If a turn might throw us into a tailspin and tumble us out of control, we could be going too fast. Speed is also the catalyst to avoiding bumps and crashes as well. Perhaps our speed of progress should be only as fast as our ability to make turns.

Where are those on your team bumping or crashing into one another? The leader is likely the one who has set the throttle to manipulate the speed up and down. Which way does it need to be moved so effective turns can help?

"Do not judge others, and you will not be judged."

MATTHEW 7:1 NLT

As a Christian, we need the turn as well. We know that Christ taught us to turn the other cheek. But a turn is a change, and we do not like change. But it is so easy to judge partly because it supports our desire to stay on our path. Why not just make the turn? When one has a crash, we might benefit by speeding up the turn and apologize for the crash as we did not avoid it ourselves. We have the ability to observe the paths that will connect with us. Is someone headed for a location with us as a crash point?

Why would we keep our speed at the same rate just to crash? And when one crashes, the time spent there can be spent judging, identifying, and projecting who is right and who is wrong. I almost wrote protecting who is right because our brains want ourselves to be right. We do the projecting that we are right.

As I write, I think about how much time I have spent in a crash. People work through their version of the details and others likely get involved as well. Think of an auto accident and the people involved. The police, the wreckers, the auto body repair people, the insurance companies, and all the other people are trying to still make progress on their path.

If we are stuck in judgment back at the crash, we are likely to miss God winking or speaking to us. That is why the turn is so critical. We can miss spending more time in love and with God when stuck in the crash. Making the turn quicker might help us to progress down the path where God is waiting on us to arrive. Just like a father or mother waiting for a child to return from a trip, God could be waiting for you to come into his presence. What is the first thing you can do to make a turn this week?

Let us pray.

Heavenly Father, thank you for the blessings of this world. Thank you for those that I bump or even crash into. We ask that you provide us comfort and hold us in the palm of your hands as we move through our situations. Through the bumps of life that obstruct our path, we ask that you help us to turn, to use less judgment where it is not needed. Turn us in your direction, Lord. Guide us through the times of trial and bring us safely home. In Jesus' name, we pray. Amen.

JANUARY 11: A TOOLBOX YOUR TEAM CAN SHARE

I grew up in a house built in the early 1900's. It was a unique childhood where I grew up with walls being knocked out through the remodeling process. It was very educational, and it took the appropriate tools.

As a leader, what tools are you using this year?

We have natural resources of strength, energy, and knowledge. We used them in the rebuilding and remodeling process. But we used tools to leverage them so that the home became something that was better than before. We were improved in the process and so was the house that those tools worked on.

Maybe the team you lead and the value you deliver could benefit by using some tools or different resources this year. Leading a life with a mindset that there is a bigger future in front of us can often be a catalyst for growth. New tools can often accomplish exponential growth.

Imagine using a rock and a wood plug to connect two pieces of lumber. Is it possible?

I believe this type of connecting occurred in ages past, but imagine the first impact of an iron nail being used to connect. Then imagine an iron hammer being used on the nail instead of a rock. Today there are air hammers of many sizes and nail guns for connecting. I know that there are some tried and true tools that we rely on. I also know that my shop has tools that are hanging on the peg board or in my toolbox that will probably never be used again because they are obsolete.

Maybe we should clean out the old toolbox and ask our team what new tools they would use if they had them. Perhaps we can even look to our peers for ideas of tools they are using.

What is the first thing that you can do in the next seven days to leverage some tools?

In Genesis 22, we read about the story of Abraham and Isaac going out to a sacrifice because of Abraham's obedience to God's call. That was an amazing act of obedience. But in that act, Abraham took along at least two things besides himself and Isaac: a stack of wood (natural resources) and a knife (a tool).

In our faith journey, we can often make a greater connection with the people of the world if we can remember to have some resources and tools along with us. Maybe the resource is a two-gallon gas container to fill someone's tank who has run out of gas. Maybe the resource is a positive attitude or the smile that we might be wearing.

My Bible, my Bible app, the mobile phone, a computer, a notebook, a study guide, a devotional, a challenging book, a pen, or a piece of paper are all tools in our modern world. Would God be okay with you using the tools in your toolbox to help someone who is hurting? What limit would God put on your tools if they would help you bring someone to Christ?

But being mindful of the tools we use and how we use them is important because some tools can be destructive when used in the wrong circumstances or with the wrong intent. Have we been using any tools in our faith to harm others intentionally?

As we make progress in our faith, our toolbox needs an occasional inventory done to consider what is being used, what is obsolete, and what might we consider new to help us love and grow.

Let us pray.

Heavenly Father, you have formed us so marvelously. Our minds and creativeness are unrestricted in your design, but we create barriers to how we put them into action. Help us today to recognize the tools that we have available. Put us into action with those tools. Take our resources and combine them with the tools that we have so that they might be used with leverage to show others our love. Inspire us to use them to share the life of Jesus. In Jesus' name, we pray. Amen.

JANUARY 12: THE CODES OF LEADERSHIP

As a leader, there are many decisions that we make that affect others. The circle of people that are on our team are as important to us as customers are to a business. That circle is large and might include friends, coworkers, employees, neighbors, family, peers, church members and even competitors at times. That circle impacts us and therefore can shape the way we treat others. Do you have a way to let your team know that you have been thinking about them? At work, is there a personal way other than an employee benefit program or writing a check? We affirm the different people in our lives in different ways. The neighbor may get a wave or personal invite to your backyard picnic. But if someone on your team lives in another state, working virtually, they likely are not coming for a picnic. The members of our circle want to be affirmed. Affirmation is one of the four things that is built in the brain as a desire. We all want to be affirmed at some level, and if we are not affirmed, it seems like it might leave a hole in us. We might never be fulfilled if those we are connected to miss affirmation in their lives.

Different circles of influence exist for everyone, and our ability to affirm will likely be different in those different areas. Regardless of the area you focus on, I believe affirmation is likely a magnet. Genuine affirmation has the power to pull people together when used, and if not used, it pushes people apart. The force is always present, and the closer the two subjects are, the more powerful it is. Which areas in your spheres of influence have you been neglecting to affirm? The power of the magnetism of affirmation is likely at work there in reverse. Want to pull a team together? Perhaps we can use curiosity today to consider how we might affirm our teams this week. In our faith, we can be asking God to have an impact in decisions that affect our circles.

In Genesis 24, Abraham sends his servant back to his relatives to seek a wife for his son Isaac. The servant wants to please the people in his circle and be successful so he asks God to have a secret signal so that he might do the right thing. That right thing was that he might find the right woman, a special woman for his masters' special son. That seems to be a very important decision. The purpose of the secret signal "I'll water your camels too" which Rachel uttered was so that he would know that he might be pleasing God. If God is pleased, then his circle is probably going to be pleased. He wanted to be affirmed and found a way for God to be able to do that clearly. What if we asked God to have a special signal to influence our relationships? Would our circle appreciate that we had specifically prayed and talked to God about them? Would you like to know that others have affirmed you to the Lord on a regular basis?

Is there anything more powerful for our circle, our community, than to relate to God and allow his influence to be recognized in our lives?To count on his wisdom and influence seems appropriate. Maybe we can think of a way to have an "I'll water your camels too" signal in our lives for each of our circle members.

Let us pray.

Heavenly Father, you sent Jesus to be our Savior, and He is in our sphere of influence. We are connected as a people through your love, and it is easy sometimes to get more involved with each other than with you. Bless us today with a connection with you first as we affirm you. May we look for your influence to lead us. Lead our families, friendships, communities, and our circles this day. In Jesus' name, we pray. Amen.

JANUARY 13: DON'T GO IT ALONE

As a leader, who helps you when things get tough? There are events in life that seem to grab us and wrestle us to the ground. When that happens, we might go through a grieving and recovery period. If people are one's greatest asset, then we might need people in our sphere of influence and organization to assist us in achieving a recovery.

In a corporation there is a board of directors. Their role is to create a management team to accomplish the business of the organization. As a leader, do you have a board of directors that works with you? I prefer the use of this term, my "board of effectors". These are people that help me make changes in myself as well as for the benefit of my team. They have a different perspective that is not judgmental during those troubling times, which helps me to work through issues to become stronger.

On a board, there is generally a chairperson. My chairperson has a direct role with me as leader. Regardless of the size of the business, organization, or team, that position of chair on a board of effectors can be an ally to reflect with the leader. What issues are ahead of you in the next ninety days? One does not have to handle it by themselves. Being able to tag team in a wrestling match allows for recovery, observation, and creativity of strategy and tactic. What effecters can you tag to recover faster? If you are missing these types of people in your life, what effecters can you reach out to now, to start the process of becoming one? If you already have them, does your board need to be expanded? Perhaps someone should have an expanded role. Who is the chair and are you meeting them often enough?

The work of leadership does not require one to carry the weight of the world. Effecters help one to distribute and discard the weight. As Christians, we have troubling times in our lives as well. But acting as a part of the church, we can be effectors. In Genesis, we read that Isaac, the chosen son of Abraham, had the privilege of having God select a wife for him. A bride from his father's family from a faraway place. We know that she was a special person in his life just because of the way they were brought together.

But the Bible also says that she was a great relief for him after his mother Sarah died. Isaac was the leader, but Rebekah was an effector for him, even though she herself was struggling with the issue of bearing children. That was a large concern in her eyes because of the lineage of Abraham being foretold. But she still affected Isaac.

I am not sure that anyone has a right or responsibility to solve my problems. However, I do want to be around those that can affect my outcomes as much as I can by myself? Maybe the first and most diligently pursued right we can practice in our lives is a right to go to God. He is the ultimate effector. Another right we could consider is to go to the people of the church to help to affect our progress and outcome.

What is the first thing you can do about it in the next seven days?

Let us pray.

Dearest Jesus, today I want to pray for all those that are in close relationships. May our spouses and friends know that you want their help as your church. We ask you to help us. Touch our lives in large and little ways. Guide us to love others when they might feel unloved. Remind us to know that you want us to bring forgiveness when we might think that something is unforgivable. Cast out any unbelief so that we know that in our relationships, a place is reserved for you and your church. In Jesus' name, we pray. Amen.

JANUARY 14: WOULD JESUS USE A CELL PHONE?

As a leader, what communication improvements are you planning to make this year? Communication or a lack of communication is a large part of our confrontations and challenges in this world. Lack of communication can be like speaking on a call when the signal drops. It might be that you are calling the wrong number.

It can occur because you could be expecting the call when the other party is expecting the call from you as well. Whether a breakdown is large or small, most can be resolved when a clear and open line of communication is established. But even when an open line is available, we sometimes allow judgment to creep in and destroy the quality of the call.

Judgment can be like the static or garbling that can occur on the call. It may take us away from clarity and into an inappropriate and unhelpful perspective. We often seek to blame or judge the result instead of addressing the communication and perspectives.

Have you been ineffective at times to keep the line clear? I know that I have for sure. For some fun, ask all those you know to see who had to use a party line. Even more judgment could occur with those and there are likely stories to be shared. What can you do to reestablish any of your lines and drop less calls?

In Genesis 27, we hear about how Jacob steals Esau's blessing. How did it occur? Rebekah interrupted the line of communication by faking the entire communication line. Isaac is laying there on his near-death bed; he obviously cannot see or hear too well. Jacob comes in to ask for the blessing and Isaac is fooled by the communication Jacob gives him. He says the right words, wears the right lambskins, and even smells the part of his brother. Isaac is not sure that he is even hearing correctly. Jacob totally interrupts the lines of communication. Isaac is fooled and the rest is history.

Where are we challenged today with our lines of communication?

The person giving the signal needs to start by having a clear message. Focusing on losing little of it to static and judgment will help as well. The person giving the signal needs to have the attention of the receiver as well. If the receiver is blocked, for whatever reason, even the clearest of messages will not be received.

There are many obstacles that can block a receiver. Their attention to the items in their world is first. Second is our ability to stop what we can of our distractions and get their attention. Do we have the correct destination of where we want our signal to go? There are many possibilities for communication failure. It is a wonder that we get any messages through at all. We can work at getting better communication going on in our world.

If we do not improve, the cost is likely to be very high. We do not want anything keeping us from communicating our love of God to him or to others. What is the first thing that you can do about it in the next seven days?

Let us pray.

Father God, help us this day, to be better communicators regardless of whether we are sending the signals or receiving them. Help us to avoid the damaging effects like what happened to Isaac and his sons. Our relationships are too valuable to our hearts and souls. Remind us that the most important message is Jesus. Jesus, the Son of God, and Son of Man, is the one that carried the cost of our sins to the cross. Keep the lines of communication open and may our calls never drop with him. Let us share our love through our actions and communicate. In Jesus' name, we pray. Amen.

JANUARY 15: PONY PILE OR JOYFUL SMILE?

As the leader of a team like a family, a company or organization, how are you mitigating risks? The first step of risk mitigation is to look for risks in the first place. Our daily decisions may need to recognize those risks to choose how to act. If we ignore that we have areas of risks, then we are open to the risk and an attitude of victimhood. Victimhood is an attitude that does not promote value. If we are mitigating risks, we can reduce victimhood, and reducing victimhood leads to increases in value.

Victimhood gives one permission to stay broken and to stay where someone else puts them. One might stay in that place longer and almost certainly with less joy and love. Finding a way forward faster may be about deciding what actions we can create for ourselves, which results in the beginning of solving problems.

Casting blame or judgment to others just keeps the attitude lingering. It can be like a wheel spinning in the mud, digging deeper and deeper into the slop. How might you be able to transform an attitude of victimhood on your team? It might start with the statement; I might do this differently. Maybe we could use the statement, I might think about how to do it differently. When the team is empty of victimhood attitude, the team will likely begin to collaborate at a higher level. One might even be able to trust and to ask others for opinions without fear or judgment.

In Genesis 2, there is a double wedding story. A man named Jacob left his family under duress and found his uncle Laban. Jacob goes to work for seven years to marry Laban's daughter, Rachel. He was really enamored by her looks, as we are told she had a sparkle in her eye. But Jacob woke up from the wedding bedroom with the sister Leah! He was tricked. Was Jacob a victim? One might think yes, but the answer might also be maybe.

Consider this, did he carry a victim attitude? Not really.

He lodged his complaint and Laban shared that one cannot marry the youngest daughter first. Jacob did not do a very good job of understanding the cultural rules about weddings when he proposed. Notice how we might begin to defend Jacobs' right to be a victim. Even though he marries Leah, Jacob also receives Rachel as his wife. It happened in just seven days because he agreed to a new arrangement. He works another seven years to marry Rachel. His adjustment of his attitude must be done right away, or it could risk his future with Rachel.

In our walk with Christ, do we choose to find a new position of focus instead of feeling like a victim? We can look for the positive in everything. I recall a story of two boys who are placed in different rooms of a warehouse for an experiment on their birthdays. Each boy's attention is grabbed when the overhead garage door opens. Each excitedly retreats to a corner of their room while a truck backs into their room. The sound systems play happy birthday over the loudspeaker. The hiss of the brakes spew as the trucks stop, and each lift on the bed rises.

The back gates slide open, and manure begins to slide out filling each room. The first boy begins to sob and cry. He looks around with his sad eyes. This is not what he wanted for his birthday. The second boy runs to his pile and digs into it with gusto. He throws manure to the left and right. He is knee deep and covered head to toe when the scientist running the experiment enters and asks what he is doing. The boy responds, "Wherever there is this much horse manure, there must be a pony on a boy's birthday." Pony focus beats manure focus on your birthday, but a Christ focus helps every day.

Let us pray.

Heavenly Father, today we know that everything is not going to go our way. But we can still love you and we can still love one another. Help us to look for you in the places where we might not be looking. Help us to find our joy, in you, all day today. Let our smiles populate the world so that your love might be known. In Jesus' name, we pray. Amen.

JANUARY 16: WHY WISDOM IS NOT SPELLED WHYSDOM

As a leader of your team, why will you lead today? When you allow the question "why?" to start a decision, you get to the core of the beginning. You can get problems out in the open faster and begin to connect with others better.

There is a great book titled *Start with Why* by Simon Sinek. Businesses might be classified down to just two categories of commodity based or value based. If you do not know your why then your business likely leans towards being a commodity. Want to see the importance of why?

Think right now, whose opinion would you seek out today if you were in a tough spot? Is that person a commodity or do you think of them as valuable, as having some wisdom? That question gets one to the why, I think.

We would seek out a person because in some area of their life they have some wisdom that you might benefit from. That is the reason I like to transform the word wisdom and spell it a new way as "Whysdom." There are times when our businesses are challenged to enhance profits, reduce expenses, and reward team members. When this happens, we might benefit by examining our why again. It might be one of the easiest ways to find and deliver more value to both the internal team and the external team as well.

Where might you bring honor and value by doing a better task of defining your why this week? The book of Psalms has many verses written about wisdom. Check out Psalms 111:1-10 for a brief example if you like. But the book of Psalms itself is spelled uniquely. Have you ever wondered why the P starts off the word Psalms? Why don't you go to the ocean and catch psalmon?

That "why?" question takes us to our most important wants. Knowing why the p is not in front of the word salmon will not likely change your life and bring significance to it. But the quest of why you want God in your life just might help one to find significance. Why will you love one another? Why will you hate someone, be rude, or take advantage of one another?

Answer these questions of why and behavior will likely change over time. When we question why about hate, rudeness, and injuring others we will learn about ourselves. We will begin to grow more away from our independent needs of ourselves and grow to our bigger self and bigger future. Why has very few words that are more powerful than it. I choose to spell wisdom today as whysdom. What "why?" do you need to answer in your faith walk? What is the first thing that you can do about it in the next seven days?

Let us pray.

Heavenly Father, sometimes we get our lives entangled. One decision leads to that another. I need you in my life because I am a sinful being. Why do you love us so much that you sent your son? It is beyond my comprehension, but we believe that you did. That is why I will have confidence to go out into the world. I will love others better, pray for others more, and seek to be in relationship with Christ because you are my why. Help us to obtain wisdom by using whysdom as a tool. In Jesus' name, we pray. Amen.

JANUARY 17: SOMETHING WORTHY OF HOT PURSUIT

As a leader of a team, how much can you get done today? We all have limiting factors that keep us from achieving something. Some of those many limiting factors are resources of our physical and mental energy, our financial resources, our talents, our gifts, our education and so on. For most of us, the largest limiting factor is probably ourselves. Think of something that requires you to change your normal morning routine.

Maybe it is a flight somewhere for a vacation. You set the alarm clock an hour early. You jump out of bed and get around with just a little quicker pace and make the event happen. You know why the alarm must be just a little earlier. Knowing why it must happen allows how it will happen to fall into place. The why is the vacation, so where did those limiting factors go?

When we understand that we have our own limiting factors and viewpoints in place, we can choose which ones to address for the successes we want to experience in life. One powerful limiting factor for most is that our subconscious mind is still focusing on the basic element of survival. It wants to avoid pain and seek comfort. The subconscious brain believes that a big piece of comfort is staying in the status quo. No change needed. It wants to avoid change and that is no surprise.

But when we operate with a mindset that my survival is not threatened, our minds and behaviors can adopt something new. That means we are willing to reset the alarm clock or anything else for that matter. What is your biggest possibility for this year? How will you get around the biggest limiting factor, yourself?

In Genesis 31, Jacob takes his family and flocks and leaves to go back to his own home place. He does so without saying goodbye ,though, to the people that he was in relationships with for the last twenty years! It is three days after they depart before Laban, his father-in-law, finds out about it. Do you remember what Laban does? He gathers his remaining relatives and goes after Jacob and his daughters and grandchildren in hot pursuit. I can understand why he did as it seems reasonable to me that if my family was taken away secretly that I would likely want to find them. I bet you would also.

But wait a second, what happened to Laban's limiting factors? He was not chasing and then suddenly, he was chasing in a big way. He catches up to the departed group after just seven days from their leaving. Hot pursuit is a great description, but think of all the people that went. How many limiting factors were overcome? Read the passages and think of how many people were involved in the chase after Jacob and his clan. But the pursuers knew why they were going, and that made the "how" possible.

Do you want to be connected to Christ more? Why? Is it because you want to feel closer, to experience his love more, find comfort in places where you have pain, seek forgiveness where you do not believe you deserve it, or maybe it is to improve yourself through the great teacher? If you know why you want it, then how to make it happen is much easier.

If you want to know Christ more, then maybe you might read the New Testament and his stories more. If you want to read the stories more, then you need a Bible and some dedicated time to read it. In the next seven days, what is the first thing you can do to obtain it?

Let us pray.

Heavenly Father, in seven of your days, you created the world. You taught us that it happened day by day and that it was good. We can learn much from your story and ask that you hold us in the palm of your hands as we are uncomfortable with changing. Help us to set for ourselves the achievements we want with you instead of chasing after what others want. Move among us so that we might love the unlovable, love ourselves as well, and walk with you more. In Jesus' name, we pray. Together, Amen.

JANUARY 18: WOULD YOU DOUBLE PARK IF NECESSARY?

As a leader, how do you greet the day? Imagine the scene of the arrival doors at the airport. In your mind's eye, can you see the slow-moving traffic and the incredible excitement in the atmosphere? There are smiles, anticipation, hugs, and waves. Overall, it is a happy place and people are excited. Makes me realize that every day is an opportunity to choose what attitude we greet the day with.Can you relate to that feeling of the anticipated arrival that the people have waiting on loved ones coming home?

Do we meet every morning like we meet the arrivals at the airport? What would our teams be able to do with a little extra quickness in our step? Can we find the next face, shoot them a smile and a generous wave like a father receiving a son or daughter returning for their first Christmas break from college? That sounds like a great way to greet our teams at the house, office, store, or plant. That sounds like a great way to greet those around us as we awaken and move from place to place. The gates at the airport have that excitement the entire day. It never stops as the travelers continue to arrive. Will we stop with our attitude before the day is over? Our teams look to us to set the tone. How will you choose to greet the day?

As Christians, this might help us to imagine what it was like at the feeding of the five thousand in the Bible. In Matthew 14:13-21, we read about the event. Can you imagine the excitement as Christ arrived?

If this happened in today's world, do you think that people would double park, maybe even triple park if they knew that Christ was about to arrive any minute? I think that they would be jockeying around one another to get close and find him. When they did, would they wear a frown or be excited?

I have news about an arrival, but this one is not going to be at the airport or bus terminal necessarily! Christ is coming. His arrival could be any minute, but if we do not see him in the next minute, he has sent his love and example for us until that time. We can choose.

Will we do as he asked us to do and show an attitude of love towards ourselves and one another? Will we shoot smiles at one another with a generous wave, or will we continue to shoot bullets in the form of words of hate, or even actual bullets and wave weapons of destruction?

Brothers and sisters, choose and choose wisely today for the airplane has departed and is on the way. We have received the information about the departure and now the question is, how are we going to meet the plane? What is the first thing you can do about it in the next seven days?

Let us pray.

Jesus, you came and taught us why God loves us. Not only did you teach us the why of God, but you showed us how to love one another. We pray today that we make this day a day of arrival. A day where we greet others in love. A day where we begin to make a generous wave the norm and not the exception. A day where the smiles outnumber the frowns. A day where we take comfort in the palm of God's hands instead of what we think comforts us here in the world. In Jesus' name, we pray. Amen.

JANUARY 19: IS A GROUP ALWAYS RIGHT?

As a leader, how do you group? In business, it is common to group customers into an idea of a target market. Companies might group their team members into departments, by location, or by product as well as others not mentioned. Associations group the companies of an industry. Churches group themselves according to their prescribed beliefs.

When we group, it seems that there is going to be a comparison that will soon be made. Researchers have proven that we like to be around people like ourselves. That makes it a group. By grouping we can focus resources and potentially maximize our efforts. Seems like a smart move and it might even simplify.

However, by grouping, it can be easy to find ourselves in judgment. A common result of judgment is that it can lead to strife, anger, and resentment. By starting with grouping, we might be going down the path of commoditization.

Commoditization is a path where your value offered gets restricted. When we start with why we do what we do, we can avoid or delay the strife, anger, and resentment. Some might even be able to avoid grouping altogether. It might seem that a flow chart about value might end with a consumer or recipient and be traceable back to why the team exists in the first place.

Where is your team grouping before it thinks about why? If you cannot find a grouping, then an audit of what groups you are not serving might expose it. Exposed groups represent potential. Potential in finding new team members, new services, new markets, and new valued relationships. What is the first thing you can do about it in the next seven days?

"In this new life, it does not matter if you are a Jew or a Gentile, circumcised or uncircumcised, barbaric, uncivilized, slave, or free. Christ is all that matters, and he lives in all of us."

COLOSSIANS 3:11 NLT

As brothers and sisters in Christ, where are we grouping? In Colossians, we are reminded that once we accept Christ our old selves die. We must be careful when our culture begins to break out the grouping concept. When we say that there are the haves and have nots, the black and the white, the Protestants and the Catholics, the Democrats, and the Republicans, we have created a group. Let us do a better job of living where we find Christ. When we live where Christ lives with us, we will change the way we look at groups.

The world's problems will not likely be solved by big government or big corporations who are great about grouping. They will likely be solved when individuals find a way to provide value to the world. When we do this Christ is likely to see us loving others regardless of the group that they might be able to be in. Christ values only one grouping. Those that know him and those that do not. What grouping have we aligned ourselves with that is keeping us from drawing nearer to Christ?

Let us pray.

Heavenly Father, you sent your son to us to show the example of love. We have the Old Testament to show the comparison of what it is to follow the law. We have the Old Testament to show us how people grouped, judged, compared, and warred. Inspire us to have the knowledge and wisdom to understand the no. Join us, so that our yes is in Christ and a reflection of his love for all. In Jesus' name, we pray. Amen.

JANUARY 20: I HAVE OPTIONS?

As a leader, what do you pay attention to as your tank empties? Think of an automobile vehicle and say that your fuel tank is full at eighteen gallons. You go driving for a while and the tank is down to only one gallon left. One might think that the tank is nowhere near full and stress would likely set in. One would start looking for a refilling station. Concerns over finances might even enter your mind, thinking that one place is more cost effective than another to replace the fuel.

If you have been consumed with other thoughts or distracted, you might even find yourself afraid that you are going to get stuck along the side of the road. But the tank is not actually empty. While it is true that it only has one gallon of fuel, the other seventeen gallons are filled with air.

That air is important because it shows that we always have capacity. It is a natural law that the space or capacity will be filled, so what will you fill it with?

It probably gets filled with the easiest and least energy absorbing effort. The easiest neural pathway can be fear. However, fear is not the interruption that leads to value. We do not need to trust our feeling of fear as I quote a line from a song title, "Fear is a liar."

When your tank is empty as leader, a different interruption than fear can serve the team more effectively. Sometimes the best interruption as leader is to simply stop what you are doing and let that serve as the interruption. Changing our thought patterns and thinking about the air we have in the tank will change the chemicals in our brains. It can free up creativity as the cortisol release subsides in our brains. We cannot stop natural laws, but we can do an intervention against the way we react to them. What capacity do you need to capture?

Look for fear and frustration and know that there is capacity behind their curtains. Our teams look for us to find a new action to fill what might have been emptied. Fear, interrupt, and find action to fulfill capacity. That just might be the equation to fill capacity.

What is the first thing that you can interrupt as leader today?

As brothers and sisters of faith, we are never full. We live with the perception that we are being emptied. It is important to recognize that we are going to get filled back up whether we want to or not. If you empty yourself of love, joy, or pride and hate, then something will take its place. What will you have to take its place?

In the book of Matthew 12:43-45, Jesus teaches about an evil spirit leaving someone. That person's life is put in order and swept clean. He also taught in the same story that the bad spirit will come back, finding it neat and tidy. The evil spirit gets seven other spirits to come live with it. If that was me, I was probably full enough with just one evil spirit. I certainly did not want any more. But this lesson teaches us that we have more capacity. The story also tells us that the seven new spirits are more evil than the first. This might teach us that choosing what we refill in those places is critical.

If there is capacity for evil, then there is capacity for good as well. With Christ, we have the capacity to choose to fill this void by the decisions that we make with things aligned with him. Let us choose today to fill any of those voids that we have with those things that honor Christ. Just as we use the gas and energy in our automobiles, we need fuel in our faith walk. Many times, the fuel for us is the decisions that we make. We can choose what air and space will be filled within our relationship with Jesus. Do you feel that your tank is empty? Then you will likely have some space available.

What is the first thing that you can do about it in the next seven days?

Let us pray.

Heavenly Father, prepare us for the season of Lent. This year, as we think about a sacrifice that we might make, help us to think about what we might replace. Encourage us to find more peace, love, and joy. Inspire us to read the Bible more, write to others often, and give words of encouragement. In Jesus' name, we pray. Amen.

JANUARY 21: TO SHARPEN A BLADE

The question of the day is, "Who sharpens you?" As a leader, who helped you to become better last week, last month, or in the last year? We have a choice to make today. Will we share more time with them next week, next month, next quarter?

As a leader, you might have a role to do that for your teams that you lead. As an effective leader, you sharpen your team. But as leader, it is appropriate to question who sharpens you. The natural world will wear on us and allow us to become dull over time. It takes an intervention, a change, to stay sharp. When an instrument gets dull the effectiveness of the cut becomes degraded.

I use a chainsaw regularly. I can clear a lot of material with a sharp blade and the saw handles with ease. When I allow the saw to get dull over time or hit the blade against a hard object like a nail or rock the ease of handling vanishes. The saw grinds instead of cuts. The friction of the chain is now what is doing the damage to the tree and it slows down. The bar gets hot and the work drags on to an annoying slow pace.

Abraham Lincoln is known to have said, "Give me six hours to cut down a tree and I'll spend the first four sharpening the axe."

Where do you need to be sharpened? Who can help to sharpen you? What tools might you use? There is no time like the present to start the process. When the leader gets sharpened, the organization and team will be sharper as well. We can often find moments of inspiration in our faith walk when we allow ourselves to spend time with those that God has influenced. The little and the large distractions of life can keep us from those moments. They can dull our edge and reduce our ability to be focused on God. Our edge needs to be sharp. We want as little distraction as possible when it comes to God.

> "And now, dear brothers and sisters, one final thing. Fix your thoughts on what is true, and honorable, and right, and pure, and lovely, and admirable. Think about things that are excellent and worthy of praise."
>
> PHILIPPIANS 4:8

That applies to the people in our lives as well. Whoever is true, noble, right, pure, lovely, admirable- those that are praiseworthy- think about such things, spend time with them. Just as our sins may dull us, we live in grace and forgiveness which may sharpen us to be in a stronger relationship with our Lord. Let us break out our wet stone or our sharpening file and allow Christ to sharpen us. Perhaps we can put our differences aside and come together to sharpen each other as iron sharpens iron.

What is the first thing that you can do to allow Christ to sharpen you in the next seven days?

Let us pray.

Heavenly Father, life on this earth can dull us. It can put chips in our blade and keep us out of balance. Rub us together as you will, as we want to be sharp and in relationship with you. Join us today as we think of and thank those that help us to be sharp. Keep those near to us if they carry your wet stone and can sharpen us. Remind us of our experiences to draw nearer to you in the present and the future. Make the dulling moments of the past be a thing of the past as you sharpen us today. In Jesus' name, we pray. Amen.

JANUARY 22: MULTIPLYING YOUR GIFTS

We hopefully all arrive at the table today to gather nutrients to fuel our bodies and minds. The energy that we receive is what allows us to return something as we depart from the table as well. As leaders, I ask today what is it that we will give? Will we choose guidance, training, or praise? Could it be appreciation, affirmation or maybe a raise or bonus?

We have the power to give every day. I suspect that it is a power that we often fail to exercise as we might. When you consider it, our gift can be one of the least expensive items to share with others. Regardless of our station in life, we all have been given much from those that have come before us. Some chose to receive the gifts of the past and retain it for themselves. Others receive the gift of the past and only give it forward when demanded. When you reflect on the previous ninety days, where did you receive the most value from someone else? What is it that they gave?

As we look forward to the next ninety days, we might receive the most if our focus is on what it is that we can give as leaders. If there is a quarter of the year that could affect the others the most, it just might be this one. What is the first thing you might do to reinvest your gifts of talent, skill, and wisdom for the benefit of your team?

> "And he gave each of them new clothes—but to Benjamin he gave five changes of clothes and three hundred pieces of silver. He also sent his father ten male donkeys loaded with the finest products of Egypt, and ten female donkeys loaded with grain and bread and other supplies he would need on his journey."
>
> GENESIS 45:22-23 NLT

As brothers and sisters in Christ, we have received the gift of grace. The scripture in Genesis 45 shows us that Joseph received power, influence, and wealth from the Pharaoh of Egypt. He sends gifts instead of a demand of justice against his brothers who made him an outcast in the first place. Here are four ideas to focus on for giving. Will we give love? There are many around us that are hurting and do not have people in their lives to support them with love. Love is the most valuable asset that we can have. It is an asset that grows the most when we give it away.

Will we give trust? Giving trust is about relationships. The process of being in relationship with another is bound to ask you to give your trust to the other person. God asked us to trust in his gift to reconcile us. We will fall away from the close relationship he wants with us by withholding our trust. Will we give our resources? We have been blessed with many resources. Those resources include our earthly things like money, our time, talents, and wisdom. A life filled with resources kept to oneself is like sharing them with a mirror.

How long would it take looking in the mirror to realize that it is lonely there? A mirror will not celebrate your life like the relationships we can build on this earth. Will we give forgiveness? In our broken world, we have the opportunity every day to forgive. The choice we get to make is will we keep our damaged and broken world or will we move to the forgiven world. A reconciled world can bring growth and a stronger relationship. Let us share and give love, trust, resources, and forgiveness.

Let us pray.

Heavenly Father, your blessings are so bountiful that they are beyond measure. They are like the grains that Joseph gathered in the Bible prior to the seven-year drought of Egypt. You give so much that records cannot be kept. Give us confidence in those blessings, envisioned like massive piles of grain waiting to be shared. Encourage us to give to those that we think are not worthy, as much as to those that we think are deserving. Soften our hearts to give to the unloved and to the loved. Move among us Lord. In Jesus' name, we pray. Amen.

JANUARY 23: BE WHO YOU WANT TO BECOME

As leader of your family, organization or company, choices can be tough. There is no doubt about it. Some of the most difficult times in our lives are entangled into those moments of choice. But to be the leader we are called to be requires us to act. What will we choose to be regarding the choices placed in front of us this day and this year?

Will we look back over the year and see that we were deceitful or insightful, encouraging, or unengaged? Will we have listened more or talked more? If you were to ask your team which of these you exhibited in the last year, how would they respond to the question?

Be, is an action word and that fits into the role of the leader. As a leader we recognize that we have faults. We will make decisions that will, upon review, appear to have not maximized value. The mistakes of the past do not define us. Looking backwards to who you have been does not determine who you will be. Unless, that is, if we do not choose to be something better. Talk about a serious choice. That might be the most important choice we have. Shall we remain the leader we were or become the leader we can be? The day is before us, what will you be today, and who will you be three years from now?

> "Furthermore, we have seen with our own eyes and now testify that the Father sent his Son to be the Savior of the world."
>
> 1 JOHN 4:14

As Christians, we are called to be the church, to be the people of Christ. What does Christ call me to be this year? Will I be a witness? Will I be honest? Will I be listening? Will I be in and among the people of the church? These are important questions because there is power in the action of the being. By placing our attention on these acts of being we might see where God is wanting us to be more.

But instincts trump intentions. Those instincts are not good or bad, they just are. We must do an intervention to be what we are called to be. Being intentional and stopping the old behaviors that keep us from drawing nearer is up to us. Becoming who we were meant to be might start with our attitude about who we were before we were following Jesus. The attitude will be required for change to occur. What is keeping you from being what it is that you are called to be? What is the first thing that you can do about it today?

Let us pray.

Heavenly Father, you are. The words that we read in the Bible have described Jesus as using the words "I am." We are people who want to know the great "I am." We want to know you. But in our world of sin, we fall so short of who you have called us to be. Send us your Holy Spirit to assist us when we can be more than we are today. Help us to act to be closer to you. Help us to be your witness, to be honest in its simplest form, to be listening to others as well as for you, and to be your church. In Jesus' name, we pray. Amen.

JANUARY 24: WHAT YOU DO AND DON'T DO

If there were not so many distractions, I could keep my focus better. How about you? As a leader, do you get distracted easily? A contributing factor to distraction can be because we want to give our teams the attention they need. But can we set appropriate limits to help us achieve focus and give attention to the team? It seems as if those shiny objects can get our attention. I remember people in a group meeting one time calling out "squirrel." They said it was because the conversation had bounced around like a squirrel does when on the ground scampering about. The conversation had gotten lost at one point and just continued to scamper about losing effectiveness. A leader can get temporarily distracted and not focused on what they want or on what they might do. Are we being productive in those moments? What can we do to be more intentional with our activities as leaders? One idea is to do a time audit by building a journal of your activities. A financial audit is important to track and investigate for validation of what has occurred. It does not change that past, it just puts a perspective on it. Putting a reflective perspective on how much we get distracted will expose some of the causes. When you diagnose the cause, it can be mitigated. If we can do it as a leader, I think that our team just might follow our lead.

What is the first thing you can do about it this week to achieve a better level of focus for you and the team? We have a great example in the disciple Peter for a distraction story. It occurs in the story as Jesus is walking on the water. In Matthew 14:28 NLT, Peter left the boat to meet Jesus, but as soon he got distracted by the wind and the waves, down he went. Notice the set of conditions here. Focused: walked on water with miraculous effect. Distracted: sinking and "save me" cry. Jesus taught us to focus. That focus challenges us to do. What will be your focus this year, and what are you doing about it this week? I would suggest that we might consider avoiding distraction by praying. Perhaps you will join me in the prayer below to increase your ability to focus.

Let us pray.

Heavenly Father, we want our eyes and heart focused on Jesus. But sometimes we get distracted. Help us to enhance our connection with you by offering our prayers. We know that having a state of doing in our lives can bring us closer. May the act of prayer be one of intentional focus. Make it the focus we need today to lead us to you. In Jesus' name, we pray. Amen.

JANUARY 25: MONEY OR AFFIRMATION?

As a leader, how do you affirm your team? It is one of the most important activities we lead in. If we do not spend any effort affirming our team, then either our team will get affirmation from another source, or they will not get it at all. Which of those alternatives sounds most valuable to you?

Affirming them ourselves is more valuable than the other approaches. We can enhance the value of being on our teams by doing the affirming. Will you affirm only once this year at an employee review? Is it your plan to affirm on a birthday when others might be doing it also? Are you going to make it only your responsibility to affirm, or can we shape our entire organization to do the affirming?

What would an organization look like that was leveraging and multiplying affirmation across the entire spectrum of the entity?

As you think about that question, you might ask yourself if your organizations are doing it? Affirmation is something learned and therefore must be taught. In my experience, not everyone has been taught about the power of affirmation, and hence, they may not be proficient at it. If we want more affirmation, then we might need to create a training system to promote it among our team. What is the first step that you might take this week to improve the quantity and quality of your affirmation status?

"For where two or three gather together as my followers, I am there among them."

MATTHEW 18:20 NLT

As Christians, why do we attend worship? Is it for the companionship of other people who might be able to share in our pain or suffering? It could be that we want to celebrate joy that we have experienced. Maybe we attend worship to learn. For some, the only place that they have been exposed to the word of God in the Bible is in a worship. Perhaps we go to be moved by music and singing. Could we go to God in worship to praise him for his gifts? It could be that we go to express our anger with God, or it might be that we go to ask his forgiveness. Could it be that we go to be encouraged by being with others who we share at least one thing in common? I think that the answer is yes.

Yes, to all the above as reasons we attend worship.

Regardless of our reason to do it, we know that wherever two of us are gathered, Christ will be there also. You might go to worship for a reason today that is different than that of the person you might sit next to. I think that is ok, but we have gathered with Christ when we do so. That is the most important part of worship. It is us being there, doing worship to be with Jesus. The rest of the reasons take you there and make you a part of the community. If that is why we attend worship, we might consider worship to be a priority. If it is a priority, then you decide how often to do it.

We can affirm in our life the relationship by the time we spend doing it. What can you do to increase your time in worship in each quarter of the year? What is the first thing you can do about it in the next seven days?

Let us pray.

Heavenly Father, we know that wherever two of us gather, that Christ is with us. Thank you for your gifts of joy and laughter, of companionship and forgiveness. May our voices be lifted on high praising your name. It matters not whether it is to a hymn created in the psalms or to a drumbeat with an electric guitar as backup. May we gather in worship to glorify and praise you today and tomorrow. In Jesus' name, we pray. Amen.

JANUARY 26: FUMBLE AND BE HUMBLE

As a leader, I believe that your teams probably accomplish some very valuable results. I use the term teams because we likely have more than one team. Regardless of the team, our focus on value can be at the core of its success. If value is at your core, it is probably your why you do what it is that your team does. But how are you achieving it? I would like to offer that attitude matters when we carry out value. What attitude helps us to continue exuding value? Is it pride or humbleness? I think that an attitude of humbleness is more aligned with value than pride. There is always something bigger than us or even bigger than our team. It is our teams that succeed, so let us approach our success every day with humbleness and be glad to serve on the team.

Sometimes the role of leadership requires us to hand the baton to someone else on the team. Is our attitude ready to hand off, cheer on others, run another leg of the race if needed, and pick up the baton if it falls? As a leader, if we bumble or fumble this one attitude of humbleness, our value might be harmed. There are so many things in our lives to be proud of. We might enhance our wisdom by watching for the mixed messages that we share that tend to move us away from humbleness.

I would bet that the reader can probably identify people from the present and past that had their pride distract or destroy value. Think about if you had a board balancing on a pivot and pride and humbleness where on the opposite ends. Where are you and your team on the board right now? What is the first thing that you can do about it in the next seven days?

> "Jesus turned to Peter and said, 'Get away from me, Satan! You are a dangerous trap to me. You are seeing things merely from a human point of view, not from God's.'"
>
> MATTHEW 16:23 NLT

In Matthew 16, Peter had just been blessed by Jesus, and now he is telling Jesus what to do. That does not seem like a humble attitude, and Jesus tells him that it is the wrong point of view. I had a great reminder of being humble in the years past. I got the flu. It really zapped me of my energy, my desires, my plans, and my activities. I was pretty much stripped mentally to a shell and did not really have anything but Christ. But the teams that I am a part of continued to do what they do without me. Let us do everything with humility. When it all seems to fall apart, Christ will be there. Our spheres of influence, including the sphere of influence of our faith, will be there. Let us remember that when it all seems to come together, Christ will be there also. Have you been challenged recently regarding your humbleness? What is the first thing you can do about it in the next seven days?

Let us pray.

Heavenly Father, you are the great I Am. You created the world, and we are but a sparkle in your eye. Those sparkles are full of love. That sparkle is all we need. May all the opportunities and successes of our world be made known through you. We thank you for the gifts you have bestowed upon us. We thank you for the talents and skills that have allowed us to grow. May we use all that we have humbly to do all that might bring you glory. In Jesus' name, we pray. Amen.

JANUARY 27: COLLABORATING IN A HIGH-PERFORMANCE ZONE

As a leader, what is your mindset as you start the day? Do you have a practice or habit that you use to set it daily? Our mindset is important, and our focus on it is difficult to maintain. As an example, you have probably heard that athletes can be in the zone. Does that sound like a mindset to you?

Their performance seems to be enhanced because of the zone. Somehow, they were better in that moment than at other times because of the mind. But we know that we do not hold that zone mindset continuously or else there would be no zone identified. Could it really be that simple that we can be a better leader and have better team results just by setting our mind?

Research shows that the answer is a resounding yes. We might want to perform a mindset intervention for ourselves and for our teams. I have a project that I take groups through to show the power of mindset.

In it, the participants see the power of an intentional mindset versus one that is distracted. Without a proper mindset, activities can likely fail to be completed efficiently or even at all. It can take over ten times the amount of time to complete an activity just because of the mindset. Without an "intention mindset" we might be caught up with fires and activities that will somehow seek us out.

What are your mindset tools you have used in the past? What are you using now? How might you and your team benefit by having an intentional mindset in the next seven days? Do you remember in the book of Matthew of the Bible, that Jesus was asked by the disciples why they could not heal the boy?

"You do not have enough faith," Jesus told them. "I tell you the truth, if you had faith even as small as a mustard seed, you could say to this mountain, 'Move from here to there,' and it would move. Nothing would be impossible."

MATTHEW 17:20 NLT

Sounds to me like their mindset was not correct. Let us be aware today, to have the mindset of possibilities in place of expectations. How do we improve our ability to be in the zone with Christ? How awesome would it be for the church and its people to be in the zone? We are capable of being in the zone with Jesus when we have claimed to follow Him. What is the first thing that you can do to get there and maybe bring someone there with you?

Let us pray.

Jesus, we want to walk with you. We want to be your faithful followers, but we allow our sin to get in the way. Our distractions move us away from you, but we recognize that it is we who allow it to happen. Help us today to learn how we might improve our ability to stay in the Jesus zone. It is the connection zone we want with you because we know that we can love deeper, forgive sooner, and glorify the Father through our word, actions, and love. In Jesus' name, we pray. Amen.

JANUARY 28: RESCHEDULED AND CANCELED

As a leader, how do you lead when something is lost? Imagine that you have lost an important file on your computer or an envelope with $1,000 cash. What would you or your team do? Human behavior will have you spend time looking for what is lost. Why? Because our minds want the status quo. We are more concerned with what we have and have had than what we might gain by doing something new.

The brain likes being comfortable, and it does not want our situation to change. That is how compelling a loss is. We will ignore the potential of what we could accomplish by looking for that which we lost. But that is totally unreasonable when our focus should be on growth and value for others.

"If a man has a hundred sheep and one of them wanders away, what will he do? Will not he leave the ninety-nine others on the hills and go out to search for the one that is lost?"

MATTHEW 18:12 NLT

The fact is the other ninety-nine sheep have much more potential. The flock is going to produce several more lambs in the spring. But off we go, chasing the lost, and then when we find it what does he say we will do? We hold a celebration for the recovered one and for the status quo.

But he states after the celebration that God's will is that the little children do not perish. What keeps those children from perishing is God's concern. A challenge then is will you and I have the courage to look the other way, to lead, when we lose something?

Will we look forward from our sin of this morning to draw closer to Christ this afternoon or will we wallow in fear, shame, and regret of how we lost our closeness to our Savior? The opportunity of growth in Christian love and living is here and so is the desire of keeping the status quo. That battle is the tough part. This is one of the reasons that being in a community of believers is important. It can help us so that we can stand up for one another and gently prod each other along. We can be moving forward to what could be, not staying focused on what was. What is the first thing you can do about it in the next seven days?

Let us pray.

Heavenly Father, life with you is a bounty. Our minds' eye cannot comprehend all the ways that you love us. We are trapped in this world for now, but thank you for giving us Christ as an example of your love. Guide us to love Him, to love others, and not to be focused on loving the past or the status quo. Encourage us along our path of personal growth with Christ. Send your Holy Spirit to move us, to move your church, and to move our small communities that encourage each of us. Help us, as the flock, following the great Shepherd, to move towards a deeper relationship with Him. May the lost in our path be found where the Shepherd is leading us. In Jesus' name, we pray. Amen.

JANUARY 29: WHERE DO YOU KEEP THE GOOD SOIL?

In the Midwest of the United States, there is some of the best soil in the world. It is called the breadbasket of the world because so much grain is grown there. To be a successful farmer, you must start with the soil. As a leader of your teams, what do you start with? What is your soil? What is the one thing that you believe your team can come together in delivering value?

The Ag producer balances inputs, equipment, human and computer capital with the elements of nature. Eventually, a crop comes forth when it is successful. But if you just focus on these items without understanding the soil, the crop is likely to fail. Your team balances many items as well, but what can you state is your soil? Can you state it simply? Can your team state it simply? Without an intentional understanding of what the soil of your business or organization is, the focus will mistakenly be placed on the other areas.

If an agricultural producer focuses on technology only, he finds that the soil will not produce what was desired. When you know the soil, everything else can get aligned to work effectively and efficiently with it. Obstacles can be overcome, and damage can be avoided. Where can you improve your soil today?

As Christian brothers and sisters, the soil to the farmer is what our experiences are to our growth in our relationship with Jesus. Our experiences, or lack of them in our lives, shape us. Some bring us to a state of joy and celebration while others bring us to fear and sometimes panic. But when we take a minute to think about them, we can begin to transform our current condition.

We can start to see where the Holy Spirit is at work in our lives. We can share in the experiences of others as well. Thinking about someone else's condition of poverty might make you feel blessed about your current condition, enhance our attitudes of humbleness, and lead us to express feelings of appreciation. Thinking about events like weddings or funerals can bring about those experiences of joy or even pain.

All those experiences give us a base, like soil, that can be arranged so that we may grow nearer to Christ. In the book of Exodus, we read about the experiences of Moses.

The next time we are not feeling confident, maybe we might consider the experiences of the Bible to help us regain our confidence in Christ.

Let us think about our soil and begin to transform it to make sure that our faith is ready for spring planting and growth. What is the first thing you can do about it in the next seven days?

Let us pray.

Heavenly Father, it is easy for us as humans to be selfish and live out what is best for us. We thank you for the many experiences that you have shared with us in our lives. We thank you for the people of yesterday and today who share with us. We thank you for the experiences shared in the Bible. We thank you for the connections of experience we have through our neighborhoods and churches, our coworkers and our vendors, our governments, and our leaders. May you mix our experiences in our minds like a gardener turns the soil today. Make us ready for amazing growth. We want to witness a wonderful harvest. In Jesus' name, we pray. Amen.

JANUARY 30: HOW MANY NO'S FOR A YES?

As a leader, how do we handle the answer no? As we lead and direct our teams, the answer of no can lead to disappointment, frustration and sometimes even anger. But an authentic no really means that a value proposition has not met the satisfaction of those that were offered the ability to make a decision. Sometimes a no is transformed when the proposition is shared a different way.

"Can I have a piece of candy?" asks a child.

"No," says the mother.

Perhaps please might have transformed the next response. You might remember making that request as a child. It could be that you have been in that exchange at a store with a child where the conversation goes on and on. We have been in places where the questions keep coming and the answer is still no.

Why does it take so many no's to stop a barrage of requests? Persistence, desire, and tenacity can keep the questions coming, but without a transformation the answer might stay the same. I have heard the question before, "How many times do I have to tell you no?"

Maybe the answer for our teams when we hear no is to focus on our value proposition and communicate it in a different way. Even the child knows that he can reshape the question by going to ask dad or another person. The value proposition is more important and provides more value than a piece of candy to a child. An audit of the no's of the past might be a place to find value.

In the book of Exodus, God sent Moses to Pharaoh for a request. He sent him to ask Pharaoh to let the people of Israel go. God certainly took the opportunity to show his power and authority when the no kept coming from Pharaoh. As the one making the decision, Pharaoh failed to modify his behavior from his no answers he gave. Sometimes we do not listen or study when we experience a no.

I think that I can get into the same mindset that Pharaoh had with Moses in the passage. My mindset can be that it is my way, or I have done it this way in the past. I can say, "It is my right, or I have the authority."

Are we listening for God in those moments and responding with something other than a no? It seems reasonable when I am saying no that God might be desiring a yes. He might want my heart to soften some to honor His way, the way Christ taught. By what authority and perspective will we listen and react? Will it be the authority of our sinful self, or will it be the authority given as a new people, saved through the sacrifice of Christ?

Let us pray.

Heavenly Father, our life is a continuous battle of no and to know. Thank you for your gift today of Jesus. We want to focus on knowing we are in a relationship. We want your love. Guide us today so that we might see where you have asked, and we have responded no. Thank you for sharing your love and for turning us towards the yes. Help us to transform the questions and answers that honor you. In Jesus' name, we pray. Amen.

JANUARY 31: STICK WITH THE CHOSEN SEEDS

Winter is still here in the Midwest of the United States, but spring is around the corner. That means that gardeners and farmers will set their minds to the flowers, plants, and crops of the season. They will be laying out the plans of what gets planted where and will envision what they will look like when they grow.

As a leader, what plans have you made for the remaining eleven months? Yes, the first month is gone. For farmers and gardeners, seed selection is critical. If you pick the wrong seeds, then one might expect that the original goal will not match the harvest. If you choose dandelion seeds to plant but are expecting sunflowers, the results will not match, and time will slip away. You might miss the planting season.

If one chooses either in error, then chances are you will be disappointed if you do not catch the opportunity to make a correction early. As a leader, does your team know what harvest is going to happen and have you selected the appropriate seeds?

The end of January is a great time to do an audit to make sure that the rest of the year brings value. Where have you grown your team, expanded your offerings, and brought more value? What adjustments can you make now that could increase your harvest by double or even ten times? The only thing that is keeping your team from such an accomplishment is likely your own adjustments. Measuring and monitoring allow us to take the opportunity to have laser precise focus. What is the first thing that you can do about it in the next seven days?

The scriptures of the Bible may be the seeds God chooses to help us grow in his love. The stories and messages are meant to be planted in us to digest, ferment, and grow. If we take the time to read, listen and live with those scriptures, the garden that God plants within us will match his plan for the harvest.

What seeds will you allow to be planted in you? Societies around the world will choose seeds for you if you do not make the choices yourself. Will we allow entertainment, maybe the television, perhaps a book like Harry Potter or maybe seeds of the money tree to be planted in us? What harvest will we reap and what might we expect to bloom with those seeds?

When we live with intention, we might keep our garden to the design that God has for us. There are plenty of weeds willing to sprout up and choke out God's seeds if we do not keep watch. January is gone. If you were reading through the Bible on a one-year planner model, you would already be through the book of Genesis. Where do you need to do some gardening in your faith?

Let us pray.

Heavenly Father, you are the Creator of the most beautiful garden. You started with the garden of Eden and now you garden in us. This year, inspire us to be moved by the seeds you plant within us. Inspire us with the words of the Bible. Help us to eliminate the weeds in our garden. Open our eyes to do some gardening and farming so that we may grow in your love. In Jesus' name, we pray. Amen.

FEBRUARY 1: SOUVENIR BALLS OR JERSEYS?

As a leader, the team you lead might have significant moments or milestones that happen. We want the recipients of our value proposal to celebrate and be raving fans. We want our interaction with our team and clients to be souvenir worthy. As a leader, are your team members collecting souvenirs of your leadership?

The prized possession from a professional baseball game is a homerun ball that one of the home team players hit. But if you are not in the outfield seats, that is unlikely to happen. The concessions stand and gift shop will be sure to make you an offer, though. If sitting behind the dugout, by chance, you might get a foul ball as well. You do not have to leave the stadium without a souvenir. But what are we doing for our team and our clients to remind them of the value we deliver?

Is our value important enough that we should consider being intentional about remembering its value and finding a way to symbolize it? If we allow our value to be remembered by chance, it is likely that our members will not get that foul ball, let alone a homerun ball. What is worse is being in the stands and having the ball hit you on the head.

Leaders, I call out "batter up." What can you do to celebrate this week?

As brothers and sisters in Christ, where are our souvenirs that remind us of the most important person in our lives, Jesus Christ? Do we have reminders of our significant moments with Christ that shape us and give value and meaning to our lives? Do we remember them with as much emphasis as we put on the treasured home run or foul ball? The odds that Christ will make a positive impact on your life are one hundred percent if you follow him and participate in his events.

In Matthew 21, we read about Jesus riding into Jerusalem on a donkey. It says that most of the crowd put their garments on the ground and others laid palm branches before his path. Would you have put down your garment for the donkey to walk over? That would probably be a garment worth remembering, but Jesus would want us to do more than just remember. He has asked that we put on the garment and go do His work. I ask us to consider, are we ready to do His work this year, or are we busy looking at mantels of souvenirs of the things of this world? Let us pray.

Heavenly Father, there is nothing more important in our lives than your love for us. We often move away from your love, though. It is easy to get distracted by the people, places, and events which we might call the souvenirs of this world. We ask today that you send us your Holy Spirit to move among us to focus on you. May our mantels be more concerned with displaying our Lord Jesus Christ than with foul balls. May we remember his gifts of service, his lessons as written in the Bible, and his miracles that he shared with the crowds and the disciples. Let us remember, but more importantly, help us to live out his calling and mission. In Jesus' name we pray, Amen.

FEBRUARY 2: THE WALL IN WEST GERMANY

Leaders, what walls have you built for your team? They get put up to build the structures of the homes we live in, the structures that we shop in, and the businesses we serve from. Walls are structures of support, and we build strategic walls in organizations as well. Walls are unique structures because we build them in our minds as well as physical ones. Some of them are strong, too strong. Some physical walls we make are made of concrete, studs, and wall board while others are built in nature by mountains or water.

Have you ever thought that the lack of air is a form of a wall?

You must do some very specific things to live behind a wall that has no air. We can erect mental walls in our minds that restrict whom we serve, when we serve, and how we serve. While walls give us structure, they also restrict. Have you known anyone with walls that offended you? Think about prejudice or exclusionary practices. Those are walls.

Our value can be enhanced by looking where a wall of our own might need to be dismantled. Some of our walls could be enhanced and strengthened. I am curious where your team might say your organization has walls that are restricting your value and service. Perhaps some strategic growth can occur because of moving a wall or taking one down.

The greatest walls ever built were talked about in Exodus chapter 14. They were the walls that God built in the Red Sea. Between those walls of water, God provided a path where the nation of Israel took to safety. Those walls created a very specific pathway. It was not a passable pathway until the wind dried it. That wind was channeled by the walls. They provided a very valuable, life granting path. But we put walls up to harm people sometimes.

The story talks about how God intended to finally teach Pharaoh about his power. He specifically brought the people back to the place that the sea walls were built so that the Egyptians' hearts would again be hardened. They came running as they saw the Israelites stopped at the shoreline. When the Egyptians of the story entered the walled area, they found their ending when God brought the walls down. Not a survivor was to be found.

So, what are your walls? As brothers and sisters in Christ, do we have walls up that keep us from loving others? Have I erected walls so that I do not have to be in relationship with others; the homeless, the sick, the dying, the elderly, criminals or gangs? Have I separated myself from others out of hate or disrespect or for a difference of opinion?

Let us look for our own walls today and make sure that they are not walls intended to harm. If we have built a wall, it might have become bigger and stronger as time has passed. But it is within our power to deconstruct the wall. Even if it must come down stone by stone, brick by brick, or by block and stud. Let us tear down those walls and find the path set out for us by Christ.

What is the first thing you can do about it in the next seven days?

Let us pray.

Jesus, you came and showed us a different way. Show us where love can take the place of hate. Help us today to tear down the walls that keep us in our place today and keep us from going down a better path with you. Let the Holy Spirit be the foreman for the deconstruction job. In Jesus' name, we pray. Amen.

FEBRUARY 3: MAKING RESERVATIONS

I greet you today by saying Happy New Year, Happy Birthday, and Happy Anniversary! One thing in common here is that parties can be the focus of these celebrations. It takes planning to prepare for the party. Entertainment is engaged, decorations are designed and deployed, the venue is prepared, and the party is set up. It is a lot of work and there also should be an invitation.

How are you doing as a leader when it comes to inviting others? It takes a compelling invitation today to get a person to a party it seems. Much like our attention span, the RSVP process, and the window for responding has gotten shorter. Are we as leaders capturing the attention of our team with our value proposition? Everyone needs to know the theme, the time, the place, and it needs to be known if there is anything to bring. One does not want to show up to a wedding without a wedding gift. We do not want our team showing up to deliver value and to be empty handed either.

Where might you do a better job of inviting and submitting your RSVP?

In Matthew 22:2, Jesus told the parable of the wedding feast held for the King's son. We know that two sets of people were invited. The first were the people the King initially invited and who ignored the invitation. The second was everyone else. The invitations were to the same party. But some are not going to be at the party. Of those that are going to it, they should make an RSVP as should we. The sooner we make our RSVP's the better our lives will be. By doing so, we can live in the possibility of what the party is going to be like and prepare ourselves to go to it. We can decide whether to show up dressed for the occasion and come bearing the correct gifts or not. Christ has called us to follow him and I suspect that when a new follower gives his life to Christ, there is a party held in heaven.

As brothers and sisters, are we inviting others to the party? Have we made RSVP'd that we are coming? How many are you bringing to the party? I hope it is more than just yourself. What is the first thing you can do about it in the next seven days?

Let us pray.

Heavenly Father, you have sent us an invitation. The information is complete, and we know your expectations. Because of your plan, not ours, we can attend a great banquet. Prepare us for such an event as we have never seen before. Help us to prepare our minds now for what is to come. May we share the love that we have been given through you. Encourage us to take the opportunity to invite other guests to come with us as you described in the invitation. Abundantly send our treasures and gifts ahead so that they will be at the party when we arrive. In Jesus' name, we pray. Amen.

FEBRUARY 4: TRIANGLE, SQUARE, OR STAR?

Do you remember the hard plastic expandable ball/case that is a childhood toy? You take the triangle, square, or star object and push it through the exact matching cutout in the case. Once you fit in all the pieces, you just grip the handles and expand the ball to let the pieces fall out and do it again. That developmental toy is the actual embodiment of the saying "you cannot put a round peg in a square hole".

We need different pegs or objects in our lives for the different holes that we need filled. As leader, you are part of a team. You and I are part of a team somewhere. Maybe it is as a member of a family, or a company or a church but we are part of a team. We belong to that roundish toy case that I mentioned earlier. Our role as an oval, rectangle or half-moon is important as it is our design to fill exactly that. Being part of a unique ability team asks us to be the very best triangle, circle, or square that we can be.

Let the star be the best star that it can be. It does not require any judgment, envy, or praise just because it is a star. We need all the pieces to complete the case or project which will advance our mission. So, what is your role and where have you been trying to be a rectangle instead of being the star that you are?

In Exodus, Moses met with his father-in-law Jethro, after leading the people out of

Egypt. Jethro taught Moses that he needed a team because he was trying to do it all himself. God could do much more with him if he were to put his energies into the team instead of just himself. Just because we can be a great star in one area does not mean that a star performance is needed in the triangle time of life. Moses understood that and began to work with a better team. It became a unique ability team. That is a modern term, not a biblical one.

He gathered the triangles, squares, and circles. They were wise advisers who were put in place so that the effect of the whole system was much more than the cumulative sum of the parts. It is powerful to focus on our valuable contribution. But we must work on putting ourselves in the right holes to bring our value to God's creation. When we try to force ourselves into the wrong space, we will likely waste energy, create frustration, and potentially hurt others or us.

Where can you shift your efforts so that you might find a better fit for your talents?

Let us pray.

Heavenly Father, you have created us in your own image. Each of us is uniquely designed and built so we have our shape. Inspire us to use the insights and wisdom of our shape to bring value to others. Help us to be true to your design and trust in it to bring value to your world. Make us to be the round peg for your will today so that we can fill the round holes that you might put in front of us. May Christ be the first shape that we put into our case every day. In the name of Jesus, we pray. Amen.

FEBRUARY 5: NO FILTERS!

As a leader, stop and think how many filters are around. Some might have a colander for kitchen use. It washes your food, removing the particles that you do not want. Your fuel filter on transportation vehicles keeps particles from entering your combustion chambers, prolonging their usefulness. Many water systems have filters on them to purify the water that you use for drinking or everyday use. They are all around us. All people have logic and mental filters as well. These filters are much subtler than a kitchen colander but certainly more powerful.

Our mind uses some without even thinking about them. You do not have to think about breathing to do it. We are built with a filter in place that allows that to happen without our consciousness. I suspect that your organization has some filters in it whether you know it or not.

Where might you build some filters to help your team? If an area seems to be breaking down or is worn out it just might be that you need a new filter. We could also have a filter that just needs changing. What is the first thing you can do to change your filters?

As brothers and sisters in Christ, we also build filters based on our experiences and thought processes. Sometimes those filters are not productive towards our connection with Christ, and we are not aware of it. We might not realize that what can be filtered out are some of the critical elements that we want in our lives.

> "Blind guides! You strain your water so you will not accidentally swallow a gnat, but you swallow a camel!"
>
> MATTHEW 23:24 NLT

Jesus told about the religious leaders filtering their water so that even a gnat was kept from their drinking water. We must be very careful of the filters that we create. They can keep us from loving Christ and from loving one another.

What is not in your life today? It just might be that if you are missing it, that you have a filter in place keeping you from it. Filters that do not connect us with Christ are not needed when we become a new person by accepting him. Many of us have left in place those filters of our previous self and it can be difficult to remove them. What is the first thing that you can do about it in the next seven days?

Let us pray.

Heavenly Father, you have told us "Ask and it shall be given." You are the Creator and can do anything. But we realize that if we have a filter in the way, when you send what we ask for, our filter will keep us from receiving it. Help us to build honorable filters that keep out hate, envy, and jealousy. Remove the unnecessary filters that we have that keep us from loving you, loving ourselves, and loving our neighbors. In Jesus' name, we pray. Amen.

FEBRUARY 6: YOU WILL NOT SAY?

Have you heard the expression, "You don't say?" I have heard it used before when someone was confirming what they did hear. Did you hear that there was an accident on the highway? You don't say? It is a request for another confirming statement.

As a leader, there is a lot of communication that occurs by what we do not say. How engaged are we really being when we do not say? When we keep the words in our minds are we helping the situations where value is not being brought forth? How do we fully bring resources and value to our team and customers if we do not say? We often bring judgment instead of value and are willing to tell others about it. Perhaps as a leader we can be careful not to bring judgment on others as the way to start our conversations.

Is that what we are used to having been brought to us? Maybe we are setting the example for it. Maybe it is because we are the ones who are not communicating an emphasis on value. Maybe it is a filter that we have. But remember, not all our filters were built correctly. Filters need to change like we change in our leadership growth and capability. So, what do you say? Where can you verbalize your value today?

In Matthew 23 and 24, we can see Christ sharing his words with us. I cite these chapters because the words are very intentional. They are shared, communicated, and given away to us as gifts to hear and lock in our hearts and minds. There is not much left unsaid here. We do not remember Christ for what he did not say but what he did say. It was a life that he taught and showed but not about what he kept it to himself. So, what is trapped in your mind or heart that you are not letting out?

One of our largest assets as followers of Christ could possibly be that we can approach others and be approachable. We can speak without judgment but with curiosity and love. The tongue may be the most powerful muscle in the human body. I think we should use that muscle to speak as Jesus taught us. The cultures around the world could use a little more talk that would follow those parameters. All those cultures' words could start with one person sharing a kind word. I think that may be a variant of the golden rule. Let us pray.

Heavenly Father, you say and speak to us throughout the Bible and through the Holy Spirit. You have let it be known how to love. Sometimes we allow the unspoken to dominate our thoughts and behaviors. Help us today to respond to one another in a respectful and loving relationship first. Let us put our judgment of the sin aside and be able to love the sinner. In the name of Jesus, we pray. Amen.

FEBRUARY 7: OVERCOME AN ATTITUDE

It is hiring time. An employer somewhere is looking for someone to join their organization. The person will have certain duties to perform, will need to work with others, and ultimately help the organization to provide value to others. It does not matter if you are hiring or looking to be hired. This entire process is about being ready to provide value. As a leader, do you bring someone on the team for talent and skill or do you hire for attitude? I think that attitude has much more to do with value than talent and skill. The concept of value is something that is really determined in the eyes of the beholder. To prove this, all you must do is look at the different value propositions in the travel world.

On an airplane, there are more expensive seats available in first class and less expensive tickets in coach. If you want an exit row or a seat near the front, then you must pay more. The plane will get from point A to B either way. The customer is going to decide what is of value. We need our teams to be focused on delivering value. We need them to be ready at any minute to enhance that value with a smile or a kind tone of voice. The people that serve on your team are going to influence our customers' perspectives more than the seat position. Where is the attitude holding back value on your team?

In Matthew 24: 2-51, we read about being ready. The people in our organizations need to be ready. Time is short. When a customer wants to make a purchase, the team must be ready to assist. They may not get a second chance. Not only must employees be ready, but so do we, the members of the church. There may not be time to go downstairs to get your things as it states in the story. We know that it makes sense that where one is ready another might not be. This is not about skill or talent; it is about attitude.

As members of organizations, and as members of the body of the church, maybe our focus could be on attitude first. When someone comes to your church or small group meeting it will be the attitude of the people that might overcome any other obstacle that a new person might see. As leaders of organizations, let us be prepared with our attitudes as well. The leader will set an example of attitude. What is the first thing you can do about it in the next seven days?

Let us pray.

Heavenly Father, you have blessed us beyond measure. The opportunities are endless before us because of you. Ease our many anxieties as we place those cares with you today. We ask that you might send your Holy Spirit to us to help discern the attitudes of the people that want to be part of our organizations. Make our attitudes be ones that reflect our intent to be ready. Encourage us as we share with our teams in a way that honors you. In Jesus' name, we pray. Amen.

FEBRUARY 8: THE REST SHOULD NOT WAIT

There is much to get done. It can be easy to forget about a Sabbath day of rest when you are a business owner. Many businesses are open on Sunday, and they must be staffed. Sales will occur and closing for a day might be the difference between profit and loss. Staff will show up and sometimes staff will be sick and need to be replaced. So, where is the Sabbath or the rest? The mission can be selling and service, just like the wash and rinse cycle on a washing machine, again and again it happens all for the benefit of a profit. But we can choose to focus on the result, value, profit, and rest.

As leaders, the challenge can be to put the most important piece of our week first. Will we put a Sabbath spot of rest in our weekly calendar and then keep it? I think that our team and employees want rest and rejuvenation. If they do not spend some time recharging their batteries their productivity will collapse. You might have heard that some people are lacking in work ethic and that it is hard to find quality workers. That might be true, but it might be true that it is also difficult to find leaders and owners who have a strong leadership ethic.

A leadership principle is that as the leader gets better, everyone gets better. So, if a team is not getting better, the work might need to start with the leader. If our leaders are not as sharp as they once were, let us consider looking to the recharge habits being used or the concept of Sabbath. We cannot make others honor the intent of a Sabbath as it is their time away from work. We can as leaders though schedule them for the team and for ourselves. When was the last time you had a true 24 hours without thinking about your business?

In Matthew, we read about the meal where the woman takes the expensive oil and pours it on Jesus' head. Some complained that it could have been sold and the money given to the poor. They were complaining that the resources were not maximized for the kingdom. While true, Jesus submits to them that he is only here with them for a little while. Let us not be obsessed with the result or profit so much that we place it as priority over being with Christ on our Sabbath. Let us place the Sabbath on our agenda, on our calendar first.

Good idea? If so, how about putting it in practice? Thanks to businesses like Hobby Lobby and others for showing us that it can be done. Not only can it be done, but it can be done profitably. If a business can set up a Sabbath for its team and even its customers, then what is keeping you from taking a Sabbath? What is the first thing you can do about it in the next seven days?

Let us pray.

Heavenly Father, today we can take the opportunity to make you our first priority. Help us to connect with you, to honor you with our time and our worship. May we be part of an organization that makes room for all to take a Sabbath. Guide us to build a schedule that provides us rest and connection with you. In the name of Jesus, we pray. Amen.

FEBRUARY 9: THE RISING AND SETTING OF THE SUN

How about that sun? It just keeps going and going and going. It has been there every morning whether you saw it rise in the sky or not. The clouds might hide it where you are in the world today or you might not have been awake, but it is there. Your father saw the sun and his father saw it before that. Your grandmother's great grandmother saw it.

As a leader of a family, an organization or an entrepreneurial team, the value we provide can be like the sun. It can always be present. If we allow ourselves to get distracted, stop measuring, and lose focus the value will likely decrease. That would be like the sun not showing up today. What would happen to the world without the rays of the sun? Imagine a life of darkness where plant life would cease, and our food supply would vanish. Could we survive? Maybe, but is our family worth gambling on a maybe?

Is your business worth betting on by ignoring our value proposition? As leaders, let us make sure value always gets center stage like the sun always gets a rise and a sunset. I think that the sun is to our world as Jesus is to our faith. We need Jesus of the past to help shape our present. While we do not want to live in the past, our Christ moves us from the past into the present in a relevant manner.

> "The sun rises at one end of the heavens and follows its course to the other end. Nothing can hide from its heat."
>
> PSALMS 1:6 NLT

The sun is a constant in our world. In our faith, Jesus is the constant where our fears get reduced, and our trespasses get forgiven. He helps us to grow so we do not keep starting over at ground zero every day, week, month, or year. What are you doing daily to stay connected to Christ? Regardless of our activities today, we do not ever have to let him leave our heart. Why would we ever allow the sun of the sky to interrupt its path? That would likely have catastrophic results on the earth and for other planets. Why would we allow our Savior, the Son of God, to be removed from our day? What is the first thing you can do about it in the next seven days?

Let us pray.

Heavenly Father, you have set the world spinning and made the sun rise daily. Let us be mindful of the traditions that help us to grow in our faith with Christ. Show us where our traditions might be enhanced. Expose our world to your love and compassion and encourage us to express it. Thank you for the blessings of Jesus on our walks. Guide our feet along this journey we take on the earth. Remind us that we are not home yet. Protect us, connect us, and let the sunlight shine in my soul. In the name of Jesus, we pray. Amen.

FEBRUARY 10: IS IT WISE TO GO THERE?

I like the word "before." I like what it implies to you and me. It might be that if I only knew before something happened that I might be able to have a more positive influence on the outcome. Maybe if I knew before, then some tragedy might be able to be averted. There was once a television program that was based on people knowing that a crime was going to occur in the future. The show spent their time developing the work around for the issue. Sometimes they were successful and sometimes they were not.

We have business plans, marketing plans and employee schedules that are put together before anything is sold or any service given. We put those items and offers together before an outcome occurs for a two-way result picture. The two-way result is we think of both the positive, to enhance it and the negative, to avoid those results.

The master of the before is God. Before an idol was ever created by us, there was God. Before the earth, sky and seas were in existence, there was God. In Psalms 31, the Psalmist shares with us that all that we say, do, and think happens before our God. In Proverbs 8, we are again reminded that he was here well before we were. We might be well served to think about his actions that came before us as we begin to be responsible for ours.

Almost everything happens twice. It happens in front of us and then it happens in our minds. We can also see things in our minds before we take action. The time of before can be very short or it can be stretched out. Either way, we can connect with others to bring God's love. Our emotions, pains, and fears can get in the way, but they are constructs that are really about the past.

We are working on the present and the future when we think of something before it occurs. If you can do something in your mind first and then experience it, you have experienced a "before" moment. Perhaps we can seek the opportunity before it comes to us and remember that God will see the "before" moment first. He might even meet us there. That inspires me to go there and see if we can connect.

Are you willing to try it this week, and if so, is there someone you might take with you?

Let us pray.

Heavenly Father, you were and always will be before. You will be here after as well. Help us to remember that you came first and that it makes a difference. May your guidance affect us by influencing our thoughts, our words, and our actions before we do them. Thank you for so many blessings that you have placed in our lives and the opportunities that exist for us because you are here before us. Let us remember that we make our decisions in front of you. In the name of Jesus, we pray. Amen.

FEBRUARY 11: GOT MILK, MESSES, OR MEMORIALS?

We are all born into this world through a process that we call birth. Every business has its own birth as well. As a leader, you might have started many things. But when we leave this world, we call it a death, and every business that I know of will probably have a death as well. It is a different process for a business to expire in many ways.

There are many businesses that have been around for the length of time that I have been on this earth. But they too will die someday in the future. We do not know when they will fail, though. The process of growing and of ending can be messy and even painful sometimes. It does not normally come at a time that is convenient and it generally requires some cleanup as well.

The good news is that there are people who remain loyal to us during that process. They help us through those transition points of time. I am thankful for those people. Sometimes those people can help us become renewed or even reborn. It requires resources and refocusing to become a new leader or a new business.

The history of the world has plenty of evidence of successes that have died. Some reading this article will remember Radio Shack and some will not. We can ask ourselves, "Where is our team in decay, where is our team experiencing the dying process?"

If it is a planned decay, congrats to you as a leader for accelerating it so that something else can be created. If it is not planned, then as leader what is next? At a minimum, we might thank those that have been part of our team. There is always an opportunity when decay or death begins. What is the first thing that you can do about it in the next seven days?

As Christians, the reality is we are either growing or decaying both mentally and physically. We can have an impact on the process especially when we allow those who are loyal to us to help. There is no one more loyal to us than the trinity. The Father, Son: Jesus Christ, and the Holy Spirit are all ready to help us to continue our path of growth. They will do it regardless of our physical state and what our body and minds might think are our limitations. Sometimes we just need to count on those that are loyal to us when things get messy.

"I am not overstating it when I say that the man who caused all the trouble hurt all of you more than he hurt me."

2 CORINTHIANS 2:5 NLT

When we get hurt and when the messes come, let us step back. Let us take ten and think about those times where those that are part of our team have been loyal. Those that are loyal share their love. Love in the home is effective and works. Love in the church works. Love in the workplace works as well. Love is what can transform decay into something else.

It is by love that Christ made his sacrifice on the cross. It is by that same love that our ultimate decay of our worldly bodies will have the opportunity for heavenly transformation. Let us bring heaven to earth now by finding those in decay and bring them a new opportunity.

Let us pray.

Heavenly Father, there are many messes. Endings can be especially messy, but we know that you hold the power to resurrect. Help us to turn to you when our lives and businesses get that way. Let us find you and the still small voice that you send to us. May we keep our ears, hearts, and minds open for your Holy Spirit to come to us in this place. In the name of Jesus, we pray. Amen.

FEBRUARY 12: THE POWER OF A SHIP'S RUDDER

What can you get done today for your family, for your business, your team of employees and the customers? Now think about how much more you can get done with a partner. We have partnerships just about anywhere we have a relationship. Often, we are tempted to think that it is all about us. Have you ever known an entrepreneur that did not think that they could not get the job done? But one of the most difficult things to do is to delegate effectively.

There are areas that we just do not function as well as a partner can. I think about my former hunting partner Brownie, a German Shorthaired Pointer, without whom, I would hardly ever find the birds. I would walk aimlessly about ,but with him, he brought his skills and talents, and they complemented mine in the field.

We were not perfect together, but we were better together than without one another. Working in partnership with others allows us the possibility to work towards a single goal and value purpose. The key is to create those partnerships with resources of different strengths. Working with a mirror is a restrictive partnership. All that would reflect would be your energies. Where might you need to improve a current partnership and where do you need to add one?

"The LORD replied, 'I will personally go with you, Moses, and I will give you rest —everything will be fine for you.'"

EXODUS 33:14 NLT

Moses is in partnership with God. We also read about Moses and Aaron's partnership. There are countless other examples of the partnerships and the challenges to those partnerships in the Bible. Sometimes the partnerships come under duress. I think that should be normal because we become stressed ourselves. Why would they be any different about stress when most partnerships are made up of people? We are the creators of stress. But the strongest partnerships look through stress, to the results they desire and communicate how to move forward.

They are focused on the value of the "ship" because a ship without a rudder is like driftwood. Would adding a rudder enhance or even multiply value? Where do you need to let others know that you appreciate their collaborative energies? That might be like adding some grease to a rudder that seems to have gotten a little sticky. What is the first thing that you can do about it in the next seven days?

Let us pray.

Jesus, you are our most influential partner in our lives. You complete us. Where we are not filled, you fill. Where we come up short, you complete us. When we sin, you provide forgiveness and have made the sacrifice for us. Help us to be in strong partnerships with others here on the earth. May we help others find you to be in partnership. May the greatest rudder of all time guide us. In Jesus' name, we pray. Amen.

FEBRUARY 13: ARE YOU READY TO CROSS THE BORDER?

Are you in the import and export business? Perhaps you travel to other countries for business or pleasure. If you are, then you are familiar with the customs organization that controls what comes into and out of a country over borders. There are rules and laws that must be enforced because countries do not necessarily agree on what should and should not be allowed. But there is another concept of customs. Those events or habits repeated on a recurring basis become our customs. The customs will become powerful mind constructs that we will learn to obey. We will not cross them, and our subconscious mind will be the enforcer.

What customs are you keeping in your business and personal life that are preventing your business from growing, your team expanding, and limiting your relationships? This is the time of year where New Year's resolutions for many are a thing of the past. Those resolutions were made about forty-five days or so ago, and it has been that long for many since they were in people's minds. A new custom to consider might be to look at this time of year to see or measure how we are doing with those enhancements.

Perhaps it could be associated with Valentine's Day as a reminder. Serious resolutions are thought on and reflected, determining if they were worthy when we established them. How powerful of an effect could following through on our resolutions be? That is a custom that would make a difference to your entire family, your team, and your clients. Making sure that you grow in relationships, team impact, and value for clients is an expression of love. What is the first thing that you can do about it in the next twenty-four hours?

> "Now it was the governor's custom each year during the Passover celebration to release one prisoner to the crowd—anyone they wanted."
>
> MATTHEW 27:15 NLT

What a celebration for the released! Imagine the feeling. They had been found guilty and imprisoned, and then the governor comes, and you happen to be the one that the crowd requests to be released. That would be liberating, freeing, and change one's perspective. Do you have a yearly custom to forgive and release someone from their past issues with you? Could that be for a customer, a vendor, or an employee? What if it were a son or daughter, maybe an ex-spouse, a neighbor, a pastor or maybe just a totally undeserving person? When we give thought to our customs, we can shape new thoughts to enhance and not to harm. If we are enhancing, we are building, not tearing down. We are called to be building up. Where might we be able to build this year? Perhaps it can become a new custom that we might be deliberate about by this time annually. What is the first thing you can do about it in the next seven days??

Let us pray.

Heavenly Father, your love is never ending. Neither are our human failures. We thank you for the forgiveness that you have extended to us, again, and again, and again. Your custom of forgiveness is an example to me of how to love and enhance others. Help us to shape customs in our lives and businesses that honor and glorify you. In Jesus' name, we pray. Amen.

FEBRUARY 14: GREAT STARTS WITH GOOD

Every successful business does some good things that customers do not really place value on. It seems that resources are being used up, raising the end user price. But they are good things, and they must be in place. Examples are things like accounting services, the utilities for the workspace, the internet access, and web hosting services. These good things are in place so that the service and product experience is not halted or interrupted. They must be done, or the business will probably suffer and sputter along with limited success at best.

The harvest will not be very good when they break down. Many activities must be planted before a crop ever comes to fruition. On our teams, we might provide more value if we build up those with unique abilities to do their respective part. No one person needs to deliver every part of a system. But it can be difficult to let things go even if we are not that good at doing them. Perhaps we can celebrate individual capability by assembling it skillfully and strategically.

We are better together, and the sum is greater than the addition of the parts. Who can you encourage this week to be great at the good? We might be able to multiply capability by offering to take something off their plate. What is the first thing you can do about it in the next seven days?

> "So let us not get tired of doing what is good. At just the right time we will reap a harvest of blessing if we do not give up."
>
> GALATIANS 6:6-10 NLT

The setup or foundation of a business, a local church, or family is critical. The basics must be in place or what you build is likely to need repairs and maintenance quicker. The structure might not even last for a normal lifetime. In business, some might call foundational pieces the overhead. With our people and relationships, it is what I see as the basic good of the team. What is the good you provide that comes easy to you to give? We can see this ability in those around us as well. Who on your team could you encourage to give more of their good?

Our good can be our unique ability. Let us remember that we are part of that good regardless of our role. It does not matter whether we are the CEO, the volunteer, the pastor, the singer in the choir, the janitor or the temporary employee just filling in for a short time. Never tire of doing what is good. What is the first thing you can do in the next seven days to step up the good? Starting with ourselves and bringing along others might show love and honor God.

Let us pray.

Heavenly Father, your grace is enough. You have given us the most wonderful base to run our lives from. Sometimes we find ourselves tired. We find that we overlook the everyday routine and take for granted the basic good you have given as a gift. Empower us to stop ourselves from complaining, criticizing, and reacting without compassion. Guide and steer us closer to you. Highlight the path to excellence every day and show us what might seem ordinary to be the good. In the name of Jesus, we pray. Amen.

FEBRUARY 15: AS SIMPLE AS ONE, TWO, THREE?

In business, does a wait staff clapping and singing say to you, thank you, we appreciate you, and we want you back? Or is it the smiles, the cheers, and sincerity of the action? What is it that you do as a leader to fully express that you appreciate your customers and team? You appreciate them, but they need to know it.

Perhaps we might share that if they need to be redeemed for some reason that we are ready to do it? Maybe we can share our thanks, sincerity, and our birthday wishes for our team members by celebrating for three days instead of one. What will you do for your team this year, and will it be the same as in the past? Will you shout Happy Birthday? Will it be a surprise party that gets thrown for someone's work anniversary?

There might be a banner or some decorations that might be displayed. The most valuable of all assets to a family or team or organization are the people. The main reason to come to a party is to show that you care. It is not about the presents. It is about showing them that if they ever needed to be redeemed, that you would. Think about a team member that could not collaborate or participate with you unless you redeemed them somehow.

What would you willingly do to redeem them which would express how important they are to you? How might you share with your team in the next seven days?

I remember in the Bible many verses about God requesting the first of everything. The first and best of the grains at harvest, the first of those born to the flock or herd, and the first born of the family. If you had a first-born son, you were to dedicate the son to God, but you did not sacrifice them on the altar, you redeemed them. You made an offering to God to purchase them back. A great example to follow is that God loves us so much, that he sent a gift for us. It is a gift wrapped around a cross, then it was put in storage, until it was brought out three days later.

I like that I will be redeemed when I pass away because I know that Christ was resurrected, redeemed, and I claim him as Savior. Perhaps we might think about birthdays that way. That we can let others know that we would redeem them if they ever needed it. That until God redeems them, being in relationship with others makes it our responsibility to one another to share in our lives, to celebrate it and to share Christ. What is the first thing that you can do about it in the next seven days?

Let us pray.

Heavenly Father, you have recognized that each one of us is worthy of your love. Every birthday is a gift of life. Every life is worth redeeming so you have sent a gift to all of us. Embolden us to share that message and to celebrate it, especially on birthdays. In the name of Jesus, we pray. Amen.

FEBRUARY 16: CHANGE IN FORTY DAYS

Are you ready? Have all preparations been put in place? Entrepreneurs and leaders do not just get ready to get ready. They do not just talk about getting ready because, ultimately, results matter. Leaders are part of the team. The team operates with systems and processes that make things happen. Therefore, actions are required so that value might be provided to the team and others. They put their plans together and then results appear. Grand openings occur and people are fed.

These are all results of a leader and team working together. There are times though that the planning and research can drag on endlessly. To keep our situation exactly as is means that the leader is failing. It has been said that if you are not growing then you are decaying. Is anyone on your team just getting ready to get ready? This activity results in delaying value delivery. The world is always ready for value, but our fear of loss can hold us back. Often, that fear of loss can keep a team in the think it over loop. This is just a means of being stuck. There is no magic formula for how much planning and activity is needed but accountability can help a leader and the team move forward faster. Where might you be stuck in a ready cycle? Ask yourself this question. Where am I not being accountable?

There are many Bible passages about getting ready and making plans. I want to highlight two. The first is the story told about the construction and making of the Tabernacle. The design was given, the people put in place, the funding was achieved, and then it all came together. The altar, the lamp stands, the connecting rings, the stands for the pillars were all made. The Israelites were ready to worship.

The other story is found at the beginning of the book of Mark. Jesus was baptized by John, and then he went into the wilderness for forty days! I like to think of those forty days as his preparation for what was about to begin. I like to think about him being in thought about how the people were going to be offered a new way of life. I like to think that Jesus was thinking about, well, about you and me. He took time to prepare. The season of lent will soon be upon us. Let us use our time of lent to prepare as well because Easter is coming. Action is required to avoid the decay, so get your plans put together now.

What can you do in your life for lent this season? What project can you launch in your business in the next forty days? Jesus prepared for the changing of the world in just forty days. What one thing will you do to change yourself, your world, your business, or your family?

Let us pray.

Heavenly Father, Jesus went into the wilderness for forty days and we know you were there. He was tempted, but we also know he came out of the wilderness and launched the greatest story ever told. We ask for your guidance as we prepare ourselves for a journey of our own forty days. Open our eyes to a project that will help us to connect to you, grow in our relationships, and to serve others. In the name of Jesus, we pray. Amen.

FEBRUARY 17: HOW IMPORTANT IS BEING FIRST?

Who is up first today? You might not have read this first thing when you woke from your sleep today. Think back and reflect upon who or what was first on your mind as you started the day. Was it the first meeting that you intended to have?

It might have been your household members or perhaps the loud neighbor in an upstairs apartment. The first person up from rest is the one who gets the day moving and begins the thinking of the day. The first person out of bed is taking the baton of leadership whether they realize it or not. That person begins in the role of leadership. Leaders need time for themselves but also put energy into thinking about their teams and the value they lead.

We know that leaders must pass the baton among their team members. Does everyone in your household see themselves as a leader when they arise? Everyone gets better when the leader gets better. Everyone is a leader. That would mean that we all can be improving and finding a way to deliver value to others. I like to think that it is the leaders who think of themselves as the first to move the value proposition. For most people, a healthy mind and body means that they get plenty of rest.

To be the first one to rise implies that the same person is probably the one who needs to be first to bed. So many times, leaders can be sleep deprived which will cause leadership to slip. Perhaps the baton needs to be passed more effectively so that all leaders know their role for the day, and all can be rested and ready for peak performance in life and at work. Who is the first person that comes to mind to enhance some self-care leadership?

In the Bible, Mark 1:35 shares a story about Jesus being the first one awake. Everyone else got a later start. We then see that he began to heal people and that the crowds began to come. There was a buzz in the community. It was not long before he could not go anywhere without the crowd limiting where he might be able to walk to. People wanted to see him so much that they did extravagant things to get close. But he started early, and he brought value.

Where might your team need to start a little earlier? Where do you as a leader need to start a little earlier? Do you remember the story of how the men dug a hole through the roof to lower their friend to Jesus to be healed? It comes right after this early start of Jesus in Mark 1. As brothers and sisters in Christ, when was the last time you made a hole in a roof to do something? As a leader, you know you have something of value to give when people are finding new ways to get to you. Maybe today we can be a little more creative and think about how to open new introductions to our faith. When we do, I think that others might come running and they will bring their friends with them.

For us, what are we so passionate about getting to, that we are finding a new path to get there? If we are not that excited to find a new path, or to be first, then maybe we do not have that passion yet. What is the first thing you can do about it in the next seven days?

Let us pray.

Heavenly Father, thank you for this day. Thank you for the people that we get to share our lives with and the differences that we have. Thank you for helping us to find similarities and ways to worship you together. Thank you for those that decide to first glorify you, to create a buzz for you, and for those that have decided to live passionately for you. Guide us as we explore our worlds with you. May you be as important in our walk as the air we breathe. In the name of Jesus, we pray. Amen.

FEBRUARY 18: ROBIN AND "MAT"BAN

As leaders, are we aligned with a purpose today? There is a pretty good chance that if you have ever heard of Batman and Robin then the title today annoyed you. Our judgment filters and need to be right make us want to fix things. When they cannot be fixed the frustration gap occurs. I can think of times when a value offer has been perceived as annoying because it was not aligned correctly. It could be the extra suggestive sale proposition that a salesperson asks you after the first sale. "Would you like a milkshake with that?"

Sometimes I appreciate them and at other times I really wonder why they asked. This can be an issue of being aligned with our why. The restaurant industry tends to get the concept, or they do not. Would you like a piece of pie and ice cream to go with your salad, steamed vegetables, and grilled chicken breast? That is an example of a restaurant or server that is missing the point of the order in the first place.

If I had been offered a low-calorie Jell-O dessert with fruit, I just might have jumped at the offer. But the offer just did not fit the situation as it was out of alignment with my purpose of the order. When a business is making an offer to its customer, we need to have our purposes align. That takes us to a point of awareness with one another. As leaders, we serve better when our team is aligned as well. Think of that wobbly wheel at the base of the grocery market shopping cart. When the cart's wheels are not in alignment it changes the experience so much that customers might abandon the cart. That means that our team members might leave as well. Where might you or your team be out of alignment with values? Hoping that team members will tolerate the wobbly wheel is likely to lead to disappointment and decreased value. Who can help you find alignment?

We are taught in the book of Mark in the Bible, a great example that correlates. Jesus was quoted in chapter 2:27 as saying, "The Sabbath was made to meet the needs of the people, and not people to meet the requirements of the Sabbath." Are our businesses and relationships made to meet the needs of our customers and employees?

It could be that we have made our business to be for our needs first and everyone else, a distant second. That might be characterized as providing you an income instead of creating a value-based business serving others. That can be a very lonely and detached situation. In the same way, we must pay attention to the church and the value that it offers. Where might we be out of alignment as followers or as Christ's church? Let us put as much energy into meeting the needs of others as we might for the requirements of ourselves. Ultimately, we are the ones that are to align things even when we receive offers that are not aligned. At your church organization, is the trinity, the leaders, the members, and those you seek to serve in alignment? What is the first thing that you can do about it in the next seven days?

Let us pray.

Heavenly Father, today we will have the opportunity to give our love and service to benefit others. May our blessings that you bestow on us be enough every day. May our love for your world be served with a smile. May we start our day with a focus on your "why." In Jesus' name we pray. Amen.

FEBRUARY 19: WHERE'S THE FIRE?

As leaders, what is the one thing that you will do every day this year? Is that a scary thought? To decide so intently that you commit to do it every day, regardless of what comes, is a big deal. You might go on a vacation, get sick and not feel well, or maybe a tragedy will strike in your sphere of influence. All of these interruptions might put stress on your world and your habits. Can we and should we commit to a daily activity this focused?

If we can learn how to go from being committed for a week to forty days, maybe we can then move to a commitment for the entire year. As an entrepreneur, how would your company benefit from doing one thing, for sure, no excuses, for forty days? It might be that you greet at least three employees a day with a smile. It might be that you treat an employee to an extra break during the day to spend time with you, sharing ideas. Maybe a better service or something more valuable could result.

If there was a fire started in your physical place, would someone react and put it out to prevent the damage from spreading? Would you put the fire out if it happened every day? I will bet that you would. Then we can be intentional about what we can do every day for the benefit of our team, ourselves, and those we serve. What is your "fire" and what can you do about it in the next week?

We find in Leviticus 6:13, instructions to the Levites to always keep the altar fire burning. This is speaking about the altar fire where the sacrifices were burned. The instruction is that the fire must never go out. Every day, every week, every month, and every year they were to keep the fire going. They were given no excuses for letting it go out. Rain or shine, hurricane or beautiful day, would not be acceptable reasons to allow it to falter. They had to keep it going. Christ's example lives before us in the New Testament. He taught us how to live and treat one another.

As a believer, how would your life change if you did one thing, for sure, no excuses, for forty days that would honor Christ? What is your "fire" that you might make happen? Life giving habits can be formed by us being intentional. Setting our priorities is only up to us when it comes to growing our relationship with him. What is the first thing you can do about it in the next seven days?

Let us pray.

Heavenly Father, you are the father and fire of creation. You have made us in your image in a world that has sin. We ask today that we might connect with you in a special way for the next forty days. Each of us can be dedicated to a purpose for forty days. We ask that you walk with us to assist us in being successful with our commitments. Help us to keep our fire burning daily and shape the days so that you might be honored and glorified. Make the joy of your love be like hot coals to our fire. In Jesus' name, we pray. Amen.

FEBRUARY 20: SEASON HAVE REASONS

What season are you in right now in your life? What season is your business or team in? As our lives change our activities change as well. In my life, when I was an active athlete, I believed that meant that I was to compete. I needed an athletic coach to help that happen. The coach scheduled the competitions, organized the whole team, ran practices, kept everyone coordinated and communicated with me. He did not play for me, though. I showed up and did my part so that the team could accomplish victory. I also learned that the best teams had discussions to define what victory meant. When someone joined the team for social purposes and it was a competitive team, it did not take long for them to realize that they were on the wrong team. Our businesses are that way also. We have different seasons, different purposes, and focuses at different times.

Startups focus on survival and on transactions, lots of transactions. But mature companies deepen relationships, and they need transactions as well. Do those companies need the same coach? The correct answer is that it is possible they do not. Many entrepreneurs miss the value of having a coach as there is no legal requirement to have one. Where might we be missing a coach? How successful would a professional athlete be if their attitude was, I do not need a coach? If we have a coach, where do we need to evaluate the coaching method or to change the plays the team is running?

What season are you in on your faith walk? Are you at one of those joyous places or are you walking through a valley of darkness? There is different work to be done and different coaches might be needed.

> "A wise youth harvests during the summer, but one who sleeps during harvest is a disgrace."
>
> PROVERBS 10:5

What would the coach be saying to those sleeping youths? I think he might say, "Okay ladies and gentlemen, it is time to take the field. Get out there and show them what you have prepared to do." That grain is there for the taking, let us get out there and show them that our training, our teamwork, and our talent has been refined. That means we are here to compete. When the coach speaks to you, then we go get it done. What are you waiting for?

If you do not have a coach that you count on to help you grow in your relationship with Christ, then you might consider getting one. If your business has moved to a different level, or you want a different level and you are not obtaining it, then you probably need a new coach. We are told that we all make up the body of the church and that we need every part. Coaches, mentors, advisors, and players are all needed on the field. The harvest is plentiful. What is the first thing you can do about it in the next seven days?

Let us pray.

Heavenly Father, you have provided so many opportunities by putting others on our path with us. Give me a fresh perspective about the season that I am in right now. May the coming days of Lent help me to see where others might help me to grow. May they show me where I might help others as well. May the words of our mouths and actions of our heart be those that bring others to you. In Jesus' name, we pray. Amen.

FEBRUARY 21: ARE YOU PLANNING A TEN-CITY TOUR?

As a leader, when you think of your habits, and the habits of your team, do you think of the positive ones or the negative ones? Pause on that thought. The interesting thing that we have just done when you assign a good or bad label to the habit is to express your perception. The habit is, well, just a habit. It is a repeated set of behaviors that you do almost without thought. It is something that becomes routine and gets ingrained into your normal behaviors.

The challenge of habits is that they will take you, when combined with your activities in the world, to a plateau. Many businesses end up getting stagnant, and they seem to struggle to be more successful. Moving from success to significance requires work and a different set of habits. What you did to get where you are now is probably not going to be what you must do to get you up to the next level of growth. This applies to our teams as well. We need to look at our habits constantly to really progress to where we want to go.

Where might you and your team benefit from a habit change?

Do you remember the story of the evil spirit and the pigs? You can find it in the book of Mark 5:13. The spirits are cast out by Christ. The spirits take over a herd of pigs and they go off a cliff. The people of the area tell Christ to leave. They are not happy and want Christ out of there. The man from whom the spirits were cast out wants to go with Christ. This is a very smart idea because the man was about to go back to the city that he had tormented. He had bothered those citizens for years, and now he was to stay but could not defend himself like he had done when the evil spirit was in him. He was going to have to change his behavior immediately. He needed a new set of habits.

Changing our old ways is difficult at best. It takes energy and it takes vision. Our faith faces this every week. Can we move more towards the next step in our progress with Jesus or will we remain with the status quo? Most people will stay in the status quo because we do not want change. People do not actually fear change. They fear loss.

Take a step and define what your next level of progression looks like because change does not have to be a giant leap. You do not have to go on a ten-city tour like the formerly possessed man did, but you can if that is the step you define for yourself. Jesus told the man to go and simply tell people how God had been merciful to him. Scary? Yes, but very doable one step and one city at a time. Can you do that for yourself and your team? Remember, you do not have to do it alone. If you have not started purposefully moving from success to significance the process starts with you.

What is the first change you can do in the next seven days to start the process of reaching it?

Let us pray.

Heavenly Father, we can sometimes get stuck in our ways, not yours. We do things that make us comfortable and that are not seeking out the discomfort of your call. Help us to grow towards a more perfect love with you. We are stewards of our time, talents, gifts, and service. May we be willing to change how we assemble all of those to honor you. Let us come to the comfort of the palm of your hands when we get scared of the new step in our progression. Guide our thoughts and activities as we take up our own ten-city tours. Help us to answer these questions and to support one another. In Jesus' name, we pray. Amen.

FEBRUARY 22: IS IT TIME FOR A HOMETOWN VISIT?

It can be uncomfortable to be somewhere and have others not recognize you for who you have become. We can get used to our old notion of who people were and then keep that image. Unless you have a reason to update or reboot your perspective, it stays with the old perspective. We tend to believe what our minds tell us about the people in our past. But the past is not the present. We can be in the present, but it is up to us to bring the focus there. It can be tough in business to keep the past, and especially its successes, in the past. We bring the past systems, the past people, and the past inventory into the present with us. But the challenge for some is to come to the present and to acknowledge what the value is now.

Where is our business and its people now? This is the first step towards a future that is bigger than the present. How can we be of value now and move that value even bigger into the present of tomorrow? We might start by realizing that what got us here will not likely be that which will get us to where we want to be. A new destination will require something better. What is the first area of your sphere of influence that you would make bigger? What is the first step you can take towards it in the next seven days?

In Mark 6:1-6, we hear about Christ going back to his hometown. He shares himself in the present of the moment. He shared what he had become, as announced by John the Baptist, but the townspeople were stuck in the past. They saw him perform some healing, but they did not accept who he had become. He did not perform any miracles while with them. Christ knew his ministry and found their unbelief amazing. But the unbelief did not keep him from moving forward. Their unbelief did not define, deter, or derail who he was, what he was, or who he would become on the cross.

If you are living your life as his disciple, then we can follow in the same pattern. We can move past the fears and from the questions of self-doubt that sometimes arise for everyone. Where are we stuck in the past and not accepting where we have come to? If you can only believe in miracles in the past or future, I think we should choose to believe in them in our future. What miracles are we keeping from occurring because of our beliefs and perceptions? What is the first thing you can do about it in the next seven days?

Let us pray.

Heavenly Father, we need your miracles in our lives. We can remain in our places of comfort very easily but that does not necessarily allow us to experience your miracles. We want your miracles in our lives now. Help us to reflect upon the past and to see opportunities to grow with you. We want your miracles in our future. Help us to live fully. We want you in our lives. In Jesus' name, we pray. Amen.

FEBRUARY 23: IF YOU REMOVE A STOP SIGN WILL PEOPLE STILL STOP?

You have probably heard the saying if you think you can or cannot, then you're right. Our minds are powerful. They are either being restrictive, which keeps us where we are, or they are not. When not restricted, we can grow differently. If you can think it, or think of it, just as if it were already here, it can probably be done. In business, we use our planning capabilities to think about what can be done. What will make the future a better place and provide more value?

We focus on the value even if our product or service is about a negative result that people encounter. Take a flood for example. The flood waters eventually recede and then the building begins again. Some areas wind up building their homes using stilts. That is forward thinking and making the best of a possibly bad situation. But to be the messenger can be difficult. If some suggestion is not the old way, what is normally done, that kind of message can be difficult to give and to receive.

It may seem strange but sometimes our brain is comfortable staying stuck. It may stay focused on the negative and focused on what was. How do you share a message of yes, we can do something new? It takes a different kind of approach and attitude to bring others along.

In Mark 6:30-56, we read two stories about positive thinking, and I highlight one here. The first was Jesus' first feeding story in Mark. As Jesus and the disciples approach the shore and get out, they are met by a large crowd. The disciples believe and think it is too late in the day to do anything, so they want Jesus to dismiss the crowd. He advises them, however, to feed the crowd. He gives them instructions on how to do it by breaking down the crowd into groups and then assigning tasks.

The seemingly impossible mission is accomplished with only five loaves of bread and two fish. The disciples' thinking, their assumptions, and beliefs were challenged. This was not the first time that Jesus had shared a transformation of what can be. They were shown that if you think it can be, you are probably right. The path of transformation rarely looks the way that we envision it in a stuck perspective. A pit of quicksand looks differently when you are stuck in the middle of it as opposed to standing safely on the edge.

When are we allowing thoughts of what cannot be to keep us from making progress for our faith, families, our businesses, and for our personal growth? Would you change the first "cannot" in your business or faith? What is the first step you can take in the next seven days?

Let us pray.

Heavenly Father, you are the Creator. Anything that you want to bless, you will, and that includes those things which we think cannot be blessed. May the "cannot" of this world be transformed to a blessing of can. May the unforgivable be forgiven. May the unreliable be reliable. May the unlovable be loved. May the unmovable be moved. Send your transforming spirit to guide us so that we might draw closer to you. In Jesus' name, we pray. Amen.

FEBRUARY 24: YOUR COMPANY, FAMILY, OR CHURCH NAME

Every day we have things that come into our realm and leave our realm or sphere of influence. In our businesses, it is resources in, then we apply more resources and then a product or service goes out. In our lives, it is the same thing. We use resources and then the results or byproducts of those processes are used, sold, or disposed of. But the impact of what is going to be accomplished with that process of transforming resources is determined by our purpose or "why bother" statement.

Why is it that a business, like a legal service, exists? Is it going to help people to manipulate the law, a jury, or a judge? Would it be helping people to get what they do not deserve? That does not sound like the type of firm that I would want representing me. Why would you take the resources of people and use them in the practice of law? I would want my attorney to uphold the intent of the law in my legal matters. I want to be a law-abiding citizen not a manipulating citizen.

Maybe if we consider our present situation, we might find a picture of our own unique why. Do your employees in your company know the company's purpose? How can we deliver a consistent value if it is not known? The vision of our why should provide clarity to our business. What is the first thing you can do this week to confirm that you know your why?

Our ability to define our why helps to shape our lives. We are all different, so our why's are not going to be the same. That is an exciting element but so is the fact that although we are different, we will share some of the same in our why's as people of faith.

Christ taught in the Bible in Mark 7:18 what I like to consider to be a "why" lesson. He begins to tell the leaders of the time that their rituals of eating certain foods are not what defiles you. It is the matters of the heart that defile us. A few matters of the heart that he mentioned were greed, envy, slander, pride, deceit, and theft. These matters are issues of "why."

If we are using our resources of time, labor, and those of employees to deceive others then our actions are not honoring Christ. If we allow our businesses to deceive then they will not honor Christ either. We, as a people of faith, are moving away in our relationship with Christ Jesus if our actions are not consistent with the why that he taught. How might you want to realign your actions with the "why" of Christ's message. What is the first thing you can do about it in the next seven days?

Let us pray.

Heavenly Father, you know our why's. Sometimes we have allowed our hearts to realign the why almost daily. You know when they are consistent with the call to love that you have given. We know and you know that we fall short so many times as we sin, but we ask that your Holy Spirit help to guide us. Share with us when our why has become distorted. Keep the people strong in our lives that can support us to live out the why of Christ. In Jesus' name, we pray. Amen.

FEBRUARY 25: DO NOT GET ME STARTED!

We all have probably had awkward moments where we sometimes get caught off guard and can respond verbally in ways that are not appropriate. Inappropriate might be where we talk too much. You have probably heard the phrase do not get me started. People say it because if they get started then they know that they will not be able to stop. Passion or emotional investment for the cause is driving the behavior.

Entrepreneurs and leaders can do that as well as anyone can. There are many issues that they know and are passionate about. We have employee related issues, financial matters, clients, regulations, marketing, and other professional relationships as only a partial list of issues. A passionate discussion can occur around any of those topics. But a better result of a passionate conversation might be to build stronger relationships instead of just talking. Those conversations have a more purpose focus than passion focus. It seems reasonable that having both is a better way to build relationships.

How might a purpose question have changed the results in your last thirty days? Questions that ask why, and what has to happen, start us down that stronger path. These can build relationships. Which relationship would reap big rewards by you using the purpose driven question in the next seven days?

As followers of Christ, we have that same issue of having important conversations. We have much to talk about. We have Bible studies, small groups, causes and volunteer work, the people of the church, the staff and so on. We could talk for hours if not days, about these topics. But talking does not necessarily indicate or build loving relationships. We draw closer to others by being in relationship with them at a deeper level, asking questions that connect us.

Christ asked us to follow him. He did not just talk about it.

"Too much talk leads to sin. Be sensible and keep your mouth shut."

PROVERBS 10:1

Sometimes the best thing to do is ask a question and then hold our tongue in silence. This week, I would like to believe that the opportunity will present itself. We can be in a relationship and the best action we might take is to ask questions. Let us ask those deep questions that will contribute to our relationship. If those we are talking with do not actually say "I like your questions," you might not be asking them enough.

What is the first question you believe you need to ask someone this week? What is the first thing you can do to make sure that you ask it?

Let us pray.

Father God, we thank you for giving us two ears and one mouth. We cannot listen for your still small voice if we are talking all the time. Come to us this week when we call out with questions and then keep ourselves quiet to hear you. Help us to listen to others this week who need someone to care and love them through listening. May we grow with our relationships listening and loving others. In Jesus' name, we pray. Amen.

FEBRUARY 26: WHEN THE WORDS DO NOT COME

Awkward moments happen. When they occur, we can be tempted to speak when we do not really know what it is that we want to say. Why is being speechless such an awkward feeling? Entrepreneurs and leaders are not immune to this phenomenon. What is it that you would say if a customer came to you with an awkward moment? What is your current answer that you might give to an associate or an employee who presents an awkward moment?

Your current response may not be the response you want to give. We might give a great answer, or the answer might be harmful. If we do not have a response, we are leaving our reactions to the exposure of emotions and a lack of confidence. We all want confidence in our world. Maybe we can think about the awkward places from our past.

Those spaces in our minds and hearts could be the answer to the awkwardness of the future. Can we develop a repeatable phrase that can provide us some time to think in those moments? I am curious where you might start. Curiosity is an amazingly powerful attitude. How might your phrase use it? What is a thought phrase you might use before it is needed? Saying the right thing at the right time may start with us thinking about it right now.

In the book of Mark, we read about the disciple Peter who got caught in an awkward moment.

> "Rabbi, it's wonderful for us to be here! Let's make three shelters as memorials-one for you, one for Moses, and one for Elijah."
>
> MARK 9:5-6 NLT

We are told that his response was given because he really did not know what else to say.

As an entrepreneur or leader, we might serve better by knowing how to lead in these awkward moments. In our walks of faith, we might follow Jesus by thinking of our responses to awkward moments as well. Why do you believe the stories of the Bible? Why do you go to church? Do you really believe that Jesus Christ arose from the dead?

If we do think forward, we have a better chance to bring value, show compassion and share the love of Christ. We all want confidence in our world and confidence in Christ. Our thoughtful reflection does not devalue our response in the future. I am not suggesting that we have a canned response either. I am suggesting that our hearts and minds will be better prepared to hold a space for the Holy Spirit by thoughtfully reflecting on moments that are yet to be. Has someone else had a response ready to your question of faith. Did it have an impact on you? I would bet that if someone has not had a response that it impacted you. What awkward question are you ready to reflect on in the next seven days?

Let us pray.

Heavenly Father, your response has always been of love, but we get caught in awkward moments. Help us prepare for the multiple awkward moments that will come upon us. May our responses that we share with family, associates, and people be those that glorify you. Draw us close and help us to share your love. In Jesus' name, we pray. Amen.

FEBRUARY 27: EVERYONE GETS A BONUS!

As a leader, what do you do when you are granted something extra? I think that is an excellent question to pose to ourselves and to our team. What do you expect your team to do with a bonus of some kind? A bonus does not have to be cash or monetary currency. It might be an extra piece of technology, maybe it is more memory for a new computer, or maybe it is time off to enjoy their families. It is simply something extra. Let today be declared bonus day.

How can you put a focus on a bonus to make a significant difference in someone's life? How will you use the new focus? Will it just be another day, added to the daily grind, or will you choose to use it in a special way? If you use a bonus attitude today, you might find it useful to include a bonus day on a regular basis. It might be that you could create a tradition unique to your team and your value proposition. What separates us from others makes us unique and adds value to our internal and external spheres of influence. Is a bonus idea something valuable for you to ponder? I'm curious what your team and family would think of the idea of a bonus.

As brothers and sisters in Christ, what would you consider to be a bonus in your faith? I like to think of a bonus in my faith walk as a blessing. Do you agree or see the perception that a bonus is a blessing?

> "Then he took the children in his arms and placed his hands on their heads and blessed them."
>
> MARK 10:16 NLT

There is no more viable blessing in my life than those that Christ presents to us. Some calendar years are leap years. On a leap day, what might you do to honor your relationship with Christ? It truly is a unique day. There is nothing more unique in our lives than our relationship with Christ. Maybe we could just give it the correct attention by making sure to put an emphasis on our Christ. What is the first thing you are going to do about it in the next seven days??

Let us pray.

Heavenly Father, you have provided us so many blessings that they are not countable. Today, we want to honor our Christ Jesus. Help us to celebrate the love and sacrifice that he shared for us. We recognize it as more than a unique gift that comes every four years. It is a gift that came only once but gives forever and ever. In Jesus' name, we pray. Amen.

FEBRUARY 28: GOT A SPHERE?

What and who is going to influence your day today? That sphere of influence will impact you in many ways. It seems that we allow ourselves to be influenced by that sphere. There is more than just our own interpretation to it though. Our team will be influenced by it also. We are exposed to the influences of this world and then we react. Those reactions are subject to our brains' limbic and neocortex systems. Once they are engaged, off we go into our mannerisms and feelings.

I think that there might be some significant insight to thinking in between the two systems though. Maybe it is maturity or our personal development, but both seem to come with some wisdom. We can understand that our reactions to both systems are important. Our reactions can be more than just these two systems if we choose to make them so. But we must do an intervention for ourselves and choose.

Will we spend our time complaining instead of focusing on results? Will we choose to be upset at someone else's attitude or performance when we as leaders are supposed to lead? Where have you or your team missed making a choice in between the two systems? Why would we choose that way again when more value is to be gained using the wisdom in between? Between the two systems there is an interval or gap. It is that gap that gives us the opportunity to focus on something that we choose. What will you choose today?

As brothers and sisters in Christ, how can we choose in the next seven days to be influenced in a positive manner? We could choose to spend our time with someone we respect. We could choose to learn something new or listen to another. Our sphere of influence can be very defining for us. Choose that sphere purposefully.

> "But now you have tossed us aside in dishonor. You no longer lead our armies to battle."
>
> PSALMS 44:9 NLT

We find example after example of the writer sharing from their heart but notice how the person is describing how they have been influenced. In between the lines is where we find the wisdom and grace granted from the Father. Where have you exhibited an attitude or behavior that did not honor Jesus? What is on your calendar in the next seven days that might influence you in a way that does not honor God? By stopping in the interval now, we can change that sphere for one that can honor Jesus. By choosing on purpose, we can give purpose and intentionality to our sphere. What is the first thing you can do about it in the next seven days?

Let us pray.

Father God, you have sent us Christ to be a positive influence for our lives. Our daily lives are influenced by the worldly perspective. Help us to see your influence upon all things and may we be reflective of that influence. Take us from where we are to where you want us to be. In Jesus' name, we pray. Amen.

MARCH 1: SUBTLE CHANGES HAVE DRAMATIC RESULTS

In our businesses and organizations, we have team members, employees, and customers to be in a relationship with. When others need something of value in their lives, we need to be able to look at the small and large changes that might make it easier to deliver value to them. The people that are willing to grow the most are the ones that need us to be of value in a new way. Those people might include our friends and families that are growing and developing as well. If we are stuck, delivering the same things as when they were new to us, it is likely that they will need or want us to grow also.

When we get stuck, our value will decrease to them, and our relationship will decrease as well. We need to grow ourselves and that requires us to leave some of the old behind and to acquire new habits. What might you need to leave behind? Are we growing and changing to serve others with a better value? Because of our potential to serve so many others, including team members and employees, it is critical to make the changes needed for a bigger future. Sometimes the changes will be very subtle but subtle changes will indeed change things. What do you think your employees and team might need from you at this point? What will they need tomorrow? What is it that you can do to lead the change in yourself to make it happen? What is it that you can do in the next seven days?

In the Bible there is a passage in the book of Mark 10:52 about Jesus healing a blind beggar. The beggar was calling out on the road and Jesus was passing by. This is not the only blind man that Jesus ever healed. What is different about this healing is that it did not require anything but Jesus to command. No laying on of hands that we are told about. No spittle or mud for this healing. Just words.

Although several blind people are spoken about being healed in the Bible, they were healed in different ways. Jesus healed in different ways. He changed his methods, and he was a great example to us. How might we venture out into the world and be willing to change as well? If Jesus changed his ways, showing that there is more than one option to address personal challenges and issues, it might be a great example for us to follow. When we continue to expect others to change, perhaps the change we need to explore is the one in ourselves.

What recurring issue continues to come around again and again in your life? I am curious. What could be a small change you could implement in the next seven days?

Let us pray.

Heavenly Father, change is difficult for us. But you have changed the world again and again. Regardless of the changes we experience, you have given us Christ and the Holy Spirit. They have not changed. They remain a constant in our lives, but we are the ones that wind up moving away from you. When we move away, give us insight to know that we need to be changed. May we help one another in a loving way to recognize how we might be able to draw nearer to you. Bless us as we begin to change. In Jesus' name, we pray. Amen,

MARCH 2: STIR THE SOUP OR SET THE TABLE?

Occasionally, things really get stirred up in our companies, culture, and country. The status quo gets challenged. It could be that we believe items or issues are out of our control like the weather. A massive snowstorm could dump a huge covering of snow on your city. A tornado or hurricane could wreak havoc which would destroy property and potentially kill others. It could be that someone's health takes a dive for the worse. But what is more important than the havoc is that we control our behaviors to the challenges that are presented to us.

As leader, you decide what you expect your employees or team to do in these situations. You set the table with expectations for them which dictates alternative behaviors as opposed to just stirring the pot. Just stirring the pot keeps everything contained and seemingly moving. But when you stop stirring, the ingredients will still taste the same although in a potentially different order. Do we stay at home and complain about the snow, or do we encourage our team to go out to remove snow for ourselves and an elderly neighbor? Do we wait for a diagnosis for someone that is ill, or do we go to their side and build relationships before it happens?

What is the first thing to do in the next seven days to answer the challenge to the status quo in your sphere?

In Mark 11:15, we read about Jesus clearing the temple of the money changers. This is a great example of the status quo being changed. Imagine this Jesus man shows up one morning and you are setting up your normal day to day business. You have the pigeons and doves ready, different currencies, and maybe you have checked the going exchange rate. Then bam, everything is upside down. Some might even have run away from the person tearing up the place. The status quo is no more.

So, what did they do? Did they listen to Jesus' message? Some of the money exchangers might have been focused on gathering their supplies and setting back up just as soon as they could. Some of the people in the temple that day might have decided to follow Christ. May we be that bold to follow Jesus in the face of challenges like tables being overturned.

Where are you being challenged right now? Is it in your faith, your relationships, your work or maybe it is your family? Was the table set prior to the challenge or can you stop the fear and set it right now in a way that honors Jesus? What is the first thing that you can do about it in the next seven days?

Let us pray.

Father God, you challenged our sinful nature by sending us your son. Now it is up to us to decide how we will modify our behavior. Let us think anew for we are born again. Be with us today as we answer the call to the challenges of the status quo. In Jesus' name, we pray. Amen.

MARCH 3: WHAT IS IMPORTANT?

It seems like the concern or question of what is the "most important" has been around forever. It is not a unique question or concern to just you or me. Time has been very good to this question, which means to me that we should be looking at it in our own lives. So, what is the most important thing to you today?

As an employer, it would serve us well to think about what the most important thing is today. We need to give our focused energy to something today. Let us make it a very intensive purpose. Jumping from one thing to another, every three minutes, is probably not as effective as spending ninety minutes really working on the one thing that can bring value to our employees.

After ninety minutes, we can take a break and work through some other issue.

We might give some time to others, stretch our legs or mind somehow. Then back to a ninety-minute sprint of focus on the one thing we can bring to our customers.

How would that change your day today? What is the first thing you can do to work on the most important issue in the next seven days? As a follower of Christ, we can answer a very similar question. What is the one thing you can do today to share the love of Christ?

> "'What is the most important commandment?' Jesus responded, 'Listen, O Israel! The Lord our God is the one and only Lord. And you must love the Lord your God with all your heart, all your soul, all your mind, and all your strength.'"
>
> MARK 12:28-34

Whether we are thinking about the most important issues for our companies, families or walk with Christ, we would benefit by reflecting upon the answer and acting. To know what is most important and fail to act does not provide value. It also does not provide love.

What will you do today about it?

Let us pray.

Heavenly Father, you have created the laws of the universe and the laws of relationship. Help us to focus on what is important today. Use our energy to glorify your love. Help us in the areas that support our most important efforts. Send your Holy Spirit to make our focus time be impactful. Be with those who are sick and suffering today. May they especially know your love today. In Jesus' name, we pray. Amen.

MARCH 4: SOME TASKS REQUIRE ENDURANCE

There is an expression in the running world of hitting the wall. It happens when the body has been pushed to a point when passed, it begins to shut down its normal operations. It is tough to walk, let alone run when you hit the wall.

What makes any progress occur past the wall is really our mind through our focus. The mind shapes our ability to do the physical. We hit lots of walls in our life, and some of the hardest walls to get through are the ones that are not physical, they are mental.

Entrepreneurs have lots of mental and logical walls to overcome. There are employee relationships, training, and retention issues. There is the struggle to keep business and personal relationships in balance. I do not believe that people who start businesses do so with the intention of making sure the business survives regardless of the cost to their family. These two areas do not even address the financial, faith, or fitness walls that entrepreneurs face.

Only one of the areas directly impacts the physical walls of running performance and that is the fitness area. As an entrepreneur, what is the largest wall you are facing today mentally in the next seven days? You probably have several.

If you want to make a list right now, do it. Who can you collaborate with to knock down or break through the wall? Most importantly, what one small thing can you do to begin getting past that wall?

Can you do it in the next seven days? Pull out your calendar and schedule it right now. As Christians, we hit our walls as well. We are told in the Bible that things are going to be tough. Christ tells us that we will suffer. But in Christ, we can endure and have hope.

"But the one who endures to the end will be saved."

MARK 13:13 NLT

When you hit the wall today or tomorrow, remember that you have brothers and sisters in Christ. Some of them can probably be of support to help you with your wall. We know that if we can move mountains with Christ, he can surely help us to dig under, go over, travel around or break down walls. Sometimes we just have to ask. If collaboration was an asset listed on your balance sheet how much would be listed there? What is the first thing you can do right now to take on one of your walls?

Let us pray.

Father God, you are, and you know. You know the walls that restrict us, and you know where we believe that we cannot challenge those walls. Provide vision for us to see the cracks in the wall. Give us the confidence in you to challenge them. Make our path to be littered with rubble from the walls that you help us to break down. Strengthen and beautify us by turning walls that were brought down into relationships with those that helped us to destroy them. May the actions of destroying those walls glorify you. In Jesus' name, we pray. Amen.

MARCH 5: IS CONTINUOUS BUILDUP COUNTERPRODUCTIVE?

There are times when reserves are a good thing. In business, we keep some financial reserves, and some employers even keep reserves in the employment pool. Employees tend to store their vacation and sick pay as well. These are examples of some of the ways that we keep reserves. But they can also hold us back. Where might we be keeping reserves that are no longer needed in the old ways? Does your business really need six months of revenue to cover payroll anymore? That reserve of capital means that it is capital not at work. You might have a line of credit now that you did not have when you started your business.

Why not deploy the capital into people which can deliver more value to others? No matter what type of reserve we keep, reserves sometimes hold us back. What are three of the largest reserves that you are keeping today? Are any of them too big and how would you redeploy those reserves in a valuable way? There might be strategic projects or products you could launch. What is the first thing you can do to address your reserves?

In the book of Mark 13:14-18 NLT, Jesus spoke about the time to flee. When it occurs, people are to leave whatever they are doing immediately. If you are on the deck of the house, you do not pack but go directly downstairs and leave. There is no call to go get your extra bag. No luggage needed. You just go. How often is our automatic reaction to count on our reserves instead of counting on God? If your shelter was just at the start of catching on fire but not containable, we might be tempted to grab something before running out of or away from the fire. Many might be tempted to even run back in and grab something. We like that which we have obtained in the past. But sometimes when we go forward, we will need both hands free to catch and accept what is about to be encountered.

If our hands are full, how can you catch what is coming? I suppose you could try to catch something with your teeth. I have seen people in my past that got hit with an issue that seemingly smacked them in the face. It is difficult to catch things with your teeth or face, and it is generally going to result in pain and damage. Where can we reduce our reliance on the things of this world? They are the reserves of the world we think we control. God intends us to catch his gifts in our hearts, not with our face. I believe God has a bigger use for you. What is the first thing that you can do about lowering our worldly reserves and accept the gifts that God has in store?

Let us pray.

God you can provide everything we need. Help us to count on you more. Let us engage and lean into our relationship with you and on our reserves less. Help us to look past our worldly reserves. Open our eyes to put our reserves into action for your will as we surrender to the comfort of the palms of your hands. Nothing compares to the palms of your hands. In Jesus' name, we pray. Amen.

MARCH 6: PREFERRED ATTITUDES FOR TEENAGERS

In business, the term target market speaks identifying the type of business or person that needs or wants a business's product or service. If you know your target market, you can then begin to shape your offerings to them specifically. Businesses do not advertise denture adhesives to school children. However, a denture adhesive manufacturer does serve two markets which are female and male identified. How well do you know the markets you serve?

We might serve more than one market, but do you know how many you and your team serve? Our attitudes make a difference to our markets. If a passenger on an airplane does not keep an attitude consistent with safety, the passenger will not be tolerated on the plane. If they smoke in the lavatory or fail to comply with the buckle of your seatbelt request, they can be deplaned. Attitudes matter to your markets, so it is logical to know them and your most important attitudes. If we do not know the markets clearly then we might not be serving them clearly either.

This is especially important when we realize that the internal team you work closely with are also a target market. They are people that we serve and collaborate with. If we do not recognize them as a market, then we might miss providing them with what they want and need. One might also misalign the attitudes we need to collaborate with them effectively. Misalignment with a market or with an attitude will cause friction and frustration. Where are you misaligned, and what is the first thing you can do about it today?

In our Christian life, we are given a new life when we accept Christ. We have been forgiven of the past and come into a new life with Christ. One challenge we face is figuring out which target our behaviors are trying to satisfy? Are we satisfying what our egos need from our old selves or are we satisfying the new life of following Jesus?

> "Against you, and you alone, have I sinned; I have done what is evil in your sight. You will be proved right in what you say, and your judgment against me is just."
>
> PSALMS 51:4

Are we serving Christ, ourselves, or the world? Those are three different targets. We might question if our behaviors in one market are consistent with another market. The attitudes that we have towards our target matters as well. Answering the question in the title of today's devotion affirms it.

What attitudes do you want a teenager to hold? A parent of a teenager will likely have a different answer than an eighty-year-old childless couple. But Jesus wants us to align with his most important attitudes regardless of our station or circumstances in life. What is the most productive thing we can do this week to think and act in our most important market? What is the first thing you can do about it in the next seven days?

Let us pray.

Heavenly Father, we live in a world of past, present, and future. These times are demanding. It is you that we desire but we are pulled. The attractions of this world continue to pull on us, and we continue to be pulled from our relationship with you. Thank you for your gifts. Gather us back to you and help us to keep you first. Empower us to allow all other requests to be secondary to yours. In Jesus' name, we pray. Amen.

MARCH 7: ARE YOU INSIDE, OUTSIDE, OR BOTH?

No matter how big a business organization is, the leader needs help. We do not know everything, and we cannot do everything. As a leader, we can accept the challenge to recognize where we need that help. Once you know where you need help, you can deploy and delegate for enhanced value. There are two teams to consider leading. Those teams are the internal team and the external team. Some of the team members are people that are within your day-to-day activity of leadership and management. Those might be employees or volunteers of the team.

The other team members are the external team which are those that provide business to business or organizational support. Both teams help to deliver the organization's mission as well as products and services. Asking yourself what you would do with your time if you had a clone of yourself can help. A clone replicating what you do would give you time to do more.

What is missing from your internal team that a clone could do? One can look at the external team as well. What is the most important component you could add to your external team? It might be a coach or maybe even a new member of your board. This focus can have an exponential effect on an organization and its members. What can you do about it in the next seven days?

As followers of Christ, we need help as well. An inner circle level of relationship can help us follow Christ. Those friends in the inner circle can understand the struggles we deal with, and they support us.

> "They said to all the people of Israel, 'The land we traveled through and explored is a wonderful land!'"
>
> NUMBERS 14:7 NLT

These are the words from Joshua and Caleb. They were supporting the inner circle of Moses even when the other ten tribes did not. Our inner circle does not act for us, but they can share their perspective and lift us up when we feel that we cannot get up. They will not be our salvation. They are not responsible for doing the work that I am called to do. My inner circle of friends will not justify me before God on judgment day. I cannot save others, as a friend. That is where Jesus comes in.

He is the Savior who died on the cross. I need the Savior in my life, and I need the members of God's church who are in my inner circle to support me on my walk with Jesus. We are not designed to walk alone. What is the first thing you can do today to connect with the Savior Jesus? Who is in your inner circle? What might be the first thing you need to do this week to help your circle that would honor Christ??

Let us pray.

Heavenly Father, Jesus suffered for me, and I want him in my life. We thank you for your gifts and for sending Christ. Help me to be in a relationship with the church. Grow our inner circle of people to support one other. Make our unique talents and skills be used to lift one another. Make healing occur and relationships built, all to honor and glorify you. In Jesus' name, we pray. Amen.

MARCH 8: LEADERSHIP CONSIDERS OTHER PERSPECTIVES

The business world is fast-paced, and things are changing all the time. Fads come and go, advertising and slogans are constantly moving, and we are always looking for the next move. Think of how many products and services have become new and improved. They make promises to get the whites whiter and the brights brighter. But sometimes our motions forward are just wrong. They do not fit our business "why." We can miss the messages or warning signals that we might encounter before we move down that path. When we make those errors, we wind up paying the price for them. They can cost profits, reputation and sometimes cause personal damage to people and relationships.

If there was an area where you might be going down a path you suspect to be wrong, how would you know? Could it be in the technology field? Maybe it is in your accounting or your relationships with your team. Being able to discern if you are adjusting while still staying true to purpose is critical. Sometimes an independent perspective can help the discerning process. What is the first thing you can do today to audit your purpose and adjustments that need evaluating? Who might you be able to reach out to for a discussion?

In our walk to follow Christ, we can be tempted in the same way. We think that we know our way to be the correct way. It is like we believe that our interpretation of the facts and history must be right, and so we begin acting out according to our interpretation. It is challenging to consider where our actions and beliefs might not be as loving as Christ wants us to be. Where do you know you are right? Think how your light might not be exhibiting love. If your light shines into a darkroom that is developing film, the light is not being loving. If that is the case, how can you show more love?

We read in the Bible that the nation of Israel was on the march and moving toward the land flowing with milk and honey. God had promised them the land. Twelve men were sent to scout the land. They brought their knowledge back and told the people what they believed to be right. Only two of the twelve were reminding the people what God had said about the land and encouraged them to take it. The crowd chooses the people's way, the way of the majority.

In the New Testament, Jesus told Peter that he would deny him three times before the rooster crowed twice. Peter said no way. But we know that Jesus was correct. How confident do you think Peter was? Where in your faith walk do you know you are right? Leadership can require us to take a different perspective. We might ask ourselves if we are using an attitude of love. What is the first thing you can do about it before the rooster crows twice today?

Let us pray.

Jesus, you showed so many miracles while you were on the earth. You shared parables and taught us how to love. But here we are, continuing to act like the generations before us. When our actions are not bringing us closer to you, we know that they cannot be right. Help us to bring you close. May our thoughts of what is right be measured through your example and by your measuring stick, not ours. Help us to measure twice and cut once, your way. Help us to heal the broken relationships where we have not drawn close to you. In Jesus' name, we pray. Amen.

MARCH 9: THE DIFFERENCE BETWEEN SCARED AND SCARRED

Sometimes when injury occurs, mistakes are made, and people or entities can be scarred. You can probably think of a business that was scarred by an error they might have caused. You might even be thinking about an event that you were a part of. Think of your luggage being lost. Think of the customer service representative who handled a complaint in a very cursory manner. You might have gotten the wrong order at a fast-food restaurant. These have the potential to scar the business and the client or customer. A scar is a process on the human body that shows it has been recovered and ready to function again. But the event that caused the scar can initiate fear, resentment, and avoidance of situations that caused the damage in the first place.

The scars can serve as a reminder to us of what happened, or it can serve another purpose as well. Will we use scars to help us to do things in a different manner the next time? It is our perception that can transform. That is like the power of the letter r in words. It totally changes the meaning and eventual result. We can allow negative events to help shape a more positive future. What are the three biggest scars of the last ninety days? What are the three most positive things that can happen because you know of a scar? What will you do about it in the next seven days?

In Mark 15:15, we begin to read about the physical injury that would surely have scarred Christ if he would have been allowed to recover. The flogging, the crown of thorns, and the crucifixion injured him. As Christians, our hearts are filled with joy knowing that Christ was resurrected three days later. But let us not forget the wounds that he suffered. These wounds remind us that Christ suffered. That suffering was for you and for me. But notice that his wounds did not have a chance to become scars.

For us, we can use the wounds of Christ's injuries to make a difference in our attitudes and behaviors. Will we allow ourselves to be scarred or just mentally wounded? Consider if we really need to complain about our injuries. Will the complaining heal us any faster or bring us to a stronger relationship with others or Jesus? I do not believe that trying to show that my scars are deeper or more harmful than yours is a way to honor Christ.

What injuries caused scars that you might be holding onto? Where can we allow the wounds of Christ to allow us to transform the scars? How we choose to think about wounds and scars matters. A comparison of our scars to Christ's wounds might be enlightened and lifting. What is the first thing you can do about it in the next seven days?

Let us pray.

Father God, thank you for giving us Christ. In our minds, we avoid scars and injury, but you have used the wounds of your Son to let us know how much you love us. Help us to remember that our scars are the result of a healing process. Let your Holy Spirit be upon us this week as we think how the scars may be a useful reminder. Make us to be in stronger relationships, relate to others better, and fully serve your world. May our thoughts and actions glorify your Holy name. In Jesus' name, we pray. Amen.

MARCH 10: ROLLING STONES DAILY

Sometimes the past can be a powerful tool. We might define the last ninety days as our immediate past. Those last ninety days can be very telling of your strengths. To focus on the strengths and successes can really help us shape the next seven days, which is what I like to think of as the present. Viewing the next seven days as our present is a powerful concept because we know that we are going to run into challenges in the next seven days. It could be that a natural disaster might hit your business, or an employee might have to call in sick. Things are going to change, and if our brains will allow us to be the best we can be, we can make the most of the opportunities before us.

Can we see the opportunities in the challenges before us in the present? Can we ask ourselves what would you like the result to look like if we were on the other side of the challenge? Many times, our brain will want to merely survive a change as we fear loss during change. But connecting with others who have a different perspective is one manner of changing perspective from fear to past and present comparison.

We read the resurrection story in the Bible and see that the women prepared to go to the tomb after the Sabbath. It starts in Mark 16:1 NLT. They had witnessed the cross, the death, and even went and acquired the spices needed for the tomb. The old pattern of what happens for a funeral was just processing along. It says they thought, "How will we move the stone?" They show up and the stone does not need to be rolled away. That started a major change. They see someone or something at the tomb and they are told to go tell the disciples what they saw! How about that for a change?

As Christians, we need to be the best we can by being in the here and now. What opportunities or challenges are in front of you right now? Remove the fear for a moment and think about your biggest challenge. Maybe that change is like a stone rolled away for you. If Jesus were to move the stone away from your biggest challenge, how would life change for you? Christ offers us the ability to bend towards his way of life. How might we question ourselves about the changes we could make if we allow Jesus to be more present in the next seven days? Today is a great day to collaborate with Christ. What opportunity or challenge will you allow him to assist you with?

Let us pray.

Heavenly Father, your birds are somewhere singing this morning. They sing their songs of joy and of warnings. May we recognize the joy and the challenges that this day presents us. Open our eyes that we might see the stones rolled away as an opportunity to see Christ in our lives. Help us to be what you have called us to be. Make the fears that come upon us today be remolded into actions that bring you glory. In Jesus' name, we pray. Amen.

MARCH 11: THE DIFFERENT HATS WE WEAR

Being an entrepreneur and leader requires many different things. We mitigate risks but also capture opportunities. We advance our ideas and employ others to help us move them into value propositions. Putting all that together and balancing our personal life and family needs, while growing our faith and financial desires is difficult. It can be easier if we have coaches and mentors to help us reflect upon those issues where we might get off track. Therapists help repair and restore us like helping someone after a fall on a bicycle ride. Mentors and consultants help you improve the bike that you ride. But a coach helps you ride the bicycle faster, more efficiently, and for as long as you want to ride it.

As an entrepreneur or leader, how many mentors have helped to shape you and your business? If you are on the successful end of being in business for yourself, is being a mentor on your radar? If you can answer questions and ask questions you might have what it takes to add value to a younger leader. What is the first thing you can do in the next seven days to thank a mentor of the past or to start a new mentorship opportunity within your triangle of influence?

As Christians, we need to be in fellowship and have mentors as well. The disciples had Christ. The Bible tells in the New Testament how Christ sent the followers out in two's as well. We learned that Mary, the mother of Jesus, went to Elizabeth for six months while they were both pregnant. You can find that in Luke 1:26-39 NLT. These verses show the value of being in relationship with others. Others can help us with our struggles and celebrations. When we allow others to be in relationship with us, we do not have to have the same perspectives, but we agree to share them. Being authentically curious helps in any relationship because it does not focus on being right. We have pastors, Sunday school classmates, elders, and others in the church to help us.

If you do not have a mentoring relationship, do you think that you could benefit by having one? If you are growing in your faith, you might be of value to another in a mentoring relationship. Where is the first place you would go for help to be mentored or to become a mentor? What is the first thing you can do to grow or become involved in a mentorship in the next seven days?

Let us pray.

Heavenly Father, you have given us one another and each with so many strengths. We can lift one another when we are in a relationship. Many are looking to grow their relationship with you and to be accountable to a mentor. Help those that want to become part of a mentoring relationship to find compatible participants. Help both people to grow closer to you and bring you glory. In Jesus' name, we pray. Amen.

MARCH 12: MOUNTAIN TOP OR VALLEY LOW

Defining moments occur. For some businesses, they treat many aspects of their businesses as defining moments while other businesses allow most of their tasks to become mundane. But a great business can be shaped by defining moments. One example can occur when a customer of your product or service becomes a raving fan. You know you have achieved a defining moment for the customer when that occurs. The defining moments can be separated into two basic types. I like to call them challenges and open opportunities.

Challenges get our attention because they have at least a little fear associated with them. Some challenges are when something has not lived up to the expectations of the customer. Our open opportunities might be about the growth of the business or its team. What are the immediate challenges your business has seen in the last ninety days? Both open opportunities and challenges can be transformed by anyone on the team. It takes a transitional moment to move into action is all. A mountain top experience does not occur unless you take the time to look and experience it. Our brain has five times the neural receptors for the low points, so they are likely to be experienced without much energy to look for them. What can you do in the next seven days to transform either perspective into a positive defining moment for a bigger future?

In the book of Luke, we read the story of how the baby who became John the

Baptist was named. His father, Zechariah, experienced a vision. It happened in his and his wife's old age. In that vision he is told the baby is special, but there will be another born who is more special than him. His son will bring people to God and prepare the way of the Christ. He is to name his son John regardless of the tradition to name the first born after the father. I see this as a defining moment. It was an open opportunity for Zechariah to follow or abandon course. He chose to follow the instructions and treat it as the defining moment it was. It shaped the future.

As followers of Christ, we have had at least one defining moment, the moment we decided to give our hearts to Christ. In the next seven days, we can watch and be ready for more defining moments. The decision now is how will you decide to recognize the defining moments of today? Today, I will decide and define, what about you?

Let us pray.

Heavenly Father, you have defined forgiveness. There is no other gift greater than you forgiving us for the many shortcomings that we have here in our world. Work on our hearts to look for those moments in our lives that can be defining. Shape our understandings and our misunderstandings so that we might serve you more. In Jesus' name, we pray. Amen.

MARCH 13: STUCK VS. STUBBORNLY STUCK

Markets change, technologies change, and competitors arise from nowhere it seems. How does your company innovate to stay unique? Are you doing the same thing over and over without thought of innovation? If we are not innovating and thinking about the future, we are likely to become part of the past. Blockbuster and RadioShack are company names that went out of business in 2010 and 2015. There are elementary school children that will not know those names if you ask them. Will our companies, teams and families be like that? Will your company be like that? We must think differently about the future or we might become viewed as stubbornly holding onto the past.

I can imagine a child being told no and giving the international symbol of arms crossed, eye burrowed into a frown, and standing rigid in defiance. The stance does not change reality. It only shows the perception of those willing to defy and ignore. In what way are you stubbornly holding onto the past? What is the first thing you can do to think about those areas? Who is the first person you trust to ask their opinion about the matter? Can you ask and be curious for that opinion in the next seven days and not be judgmental about the person who gave it?

King Balak in the Old Testament, Numbers 22-24, is known for his stubbornness. At least three different times he tried to get Balaam to place a curse on the people of Israel. Each time he was rebuffed, and not only did God not curse but he put a blessing on the people. Each time Balak changed the offer just a little as he tried to carry his own idea of success out. But to no avail, he was rebuffed again and again. How many times are we stuck stubbornly in our ways not doing what Jesus has asked us to do? What have you been asked to do over the last ninety days that you have ignored? Anything at all? It could be that if you have not stood in defiance that you might not be listening to the still small voice of the Holy Spirit.

When God asks us to move it most likely will be uncomfortable. But getting comfortable being a little uncomfortable is part of God's plan. What is the first thing that you can do about your stubbornness in the next seven days?

Let us pray.

Jesus, you came as our Savior into the world. You brought us love and great miracles of forgiveness. Come work in our minds and hearts to forgive the unforgivable of our minds and hearts. You brought us healing where no answers of healing were believed possible. May we bring healing through your power and inspiration in our times today. Remove the mud from our eyes which we have stubbornly refused to wash away. In Jesus' name, we pray. Amen.

MARCH 14: LIFE IS NOT A RACE, IT'S A RELAY

Have you ever heard that life is a relay? Business owners need others to partner with them to achieve success. Leaders need a team that will follow and provide value. When life is a relay, we pass the baton forward. Finding the right people to be on your team to pass the baton to is important. If we are not aligned with one another, the baton will swing wildly and the handoff will likely drop. We learn to run in the same lane as we will cause disqualification when we fail to do so. Sometimes the baton will fail to even get passed when out of alignment.

Our hands need to come together and come together at the right time. We must learn to let go at the right time as well. We need people with great attitudes and competent talents. We must learn to work together and be trained in our collaborative efforts. But we also need some people to have leadership capabilities. Someone must assemble the team, get them trained, and be ready to focus when the starting pistol sound rings in the air. How many have you chosen to be a leader at your company? If you have not chosen them yourself then others might be appointing a leader for you. Why would one expect followers to stay in your lane if we are not focused on how to serve them and lead them in our lane? What can you do in the next seven days to choose or confirm a leader?

Moses' run was a great one. One of the biggest stories in the Bible. He was a leader but even the biggest runs come to an end. Who are we choosing and how do we choose the leaders in our lives? Are we allowing God to use his still small voice to guide the way or are we doing it our way? Moses had Joshua as his replacement, and he was well prepared. Being prepared can be accomplished on a dual tract.

A leader can be engaged in training those that will serve in their place someday. Wisdom, valuable insight, intellectual knowledge, and life experiences can be shared. Maybe God has placed someone in your life already who might be a candidate to follow you. Who might they be? Perhaps you might grow in your faith by discipling with someone else who has leadership qualities that appeal to your stage of life. Without a focus on who can help us grow or who we can help grow, growth is likely stunted. Jesus had twelve disciples he asked to follow him. Who are your closest twelve? What could you do in the next seven days to locate your leaders and grow them or thank them?

Let us pray.

Heavenly Father, you are the ultimate leader and guide. Bring us together and help us to know those that trust in you. Place your blessing upon those that lead your people as well as those who follow you with their whole hearts. In Jesus' name, we pray. Amen.

MARCH 15: A VALENTINE'S OR ST. PATRICK'S DAY GIFT?

Do you ever get stuck and cannot seem to come up with a way to express your love for someone on Valentine's Day? If that is true, then one might really get stuck on what type of gift you give on St. Patrick's Day? Does that holiday require a gift? There are a lot of activities happening in our world on holidays. It is a nice little boom for restaurants and retailers. Valentine's Day is one of the most important days of the year if you are a chocolate seller or florist. Whatever your business might be, we are all able to think about others and how we will provide value.

The workspace does not have to eliminate love. I believe that we all want to be appreciated and affirmed, so why not give away love with our product or service? As entrepreneurs, we have many demands that we place on ourselves. We willingly accept risks for the benefit of ourselves, our families, employees, and customers. At the end of the day, it is not the risks that get the most valuable rewards but the love you give. It is not about us but how we can serve others and create value for them. As a leader, is your value proposition for others greater than your reward. How might you enhance your value today?

As a Christian leader, how do you celebrate holidays? In America, Valentine's Day is looked on as a day to celebrate love. There have been many gifts to express love. Flowers, chocolates, and balloons are all common on that holiday. To get extravagant, some people go way beyond this and give surprise travel gifts, cars, or diamonds. But the best gift of love ever given was the gift of Christ given to us from God. On this St. Patrick's Day, how will you experience the greatest gift of love ever shown, our Savior and Lord, Jesus Christ? If our leadership on our foundation of faith is ignored, we might get distracted and think that green is the most important aspect of the day. To experience and give love, no sale is needed, green is not required, and no parade must take place. The ultimate sacrifice has been paid for us. How can you lead with love as you celebrate for the next seven days?

Let us pray.

Heavenly Father, this week our society thinks of the Irish. When we think of love, we think of you and your example. Thank you for loving us first. Thank you for showing us your love. Guide us to show our love for you by loving others. Empower us to love them more deeply and more authentically. In Jesus' name, we pray. Amen.

MARCH 16: MATCHING OR CONNECTING IS NOT ALWAYS HONORABLE

Sometimes as an entrepreneur or leader we put systems in place. We need the systems for delivery of consistency. There are systems for payroll, software, and security. Think of as many systems as you can that you have helped influence. It is intriguing to realize that we are tempted by our logical processes to have those systems match and connect. First things must be first, and then another system completes follow through. Each system connects to the next one so that a complete loop is created. Sounds reasonable enough. Systems can be designed to honor other things such as profits, people, or destruction. But in the end, what we might want is for our products and services to be honoring value.

When this mindset is used, it will likely mean the product or service is honorable. Most products and services are not created to hurt or harm people. Part of the honor of your product includes a reasonable profit. Another part is for our companies and people to be a part of a progressing community. Where might we have built systems more concerned with matching than with a focus on honor? If we have not used a mindset of honor in building the systems, we have some hidden limits. Discovering our limits can uncover value. How does your service or product honor your customer and advance them? What is the first thing you can do to improve your systems to honor your relationships with your customers?

I was reading in the book of Numbers 2:12 NLT one day when I came across a passage about one of the many festivals that the nation of Israel holds. I found it odd that the first day of activities started with a sacrifice of many things, but it included 13 bulls. Every day the bull count went down and stopped with seven. Seven, why seven? My brain wanted the numbers to coincide with the event. Start with thirteen bulls and end with one bull. That makes more sense to me, maybe it does to you too. But the purpose of the festival is to honor God. It is not to make my brain satisfied with how the system works!

How often do we get caught up on how we are doing something? Many times, we are consuming our energy with a focus on what activity we are choosing to do. Other times, we focus on how others are choosing to do something. When we can look to see why we are doing something we may find misalignment occurring. Where am I missing the why today and because of it failing to honor the sacrifice of Christ? Where might you be missing the why in your life because of the systems you have put in place? We might do well to remember that others have put systems in place as well and they may not be honoring Christ. Breaking through our limits for Jesus is an honorable thing to do.

What is the first thing that you can do to begin getting yourself aligned in the next seven days?

Let us pray.

Jesus, you taught us why we are to be in relationship with you. It is the Father in heaven that established the why. He gave us you to remember that. Help us in our worldly struggle of the how's and what's. Deliver to us today the confidence to see our misalignment with your why. In Jesus' name, we pray. Amen.

MARCH 17: JUST ONE OF THOSE DAYS

Have you ever had a bad day? Companies and teams have bad days too. We all do. You might be a father or mother, a business owner or employee, a team leader, or a team member when it happens. But we are best served to meet the challenge of bad days with optimism. One way to keep up that optimism is to remember the value that we deliver on a regular basis. We know what happens on the front stage for our clients. That is the place where our customers engage us for the product.

We know what happens backstage as well. Customers do not see behind the curtain, so it is easier for them to get nearsighted. But our focus on the value of the front and backstage will affect our optimism. It may help us to remember how both stages operate. Those stages have a different perspective. When a sale is not closed, the salesperson has a perspective of lost commissions, but the accounting team may not even see that it happened. A new perspective is all that is needed sometimes to find optimism. On the other side of that bad day is the good day. The choice might be as simple as deciding to transition to a good day. Good days are where companies and customers are aligned, and great value is had by all. The next time a bad day happens, who might you be able to align with to find some optimism because their perspective is different?

For Christians, we have bad days as well. Those days might be where God seems so far off, and we might feel lonely and removed. There are days where airplanes get delayed and where the people we love suffer tragedies. But we can recall the gift of Christ and his sacrifice. That can give us hope. In Luke 4:16-30, we read where Christ returned to his hometown in Galilee. He spoke in the synagogue on the sabbath right before his hometown folks ran him off. That would not be a very good day for me in my opinion. But Christ had the ability to remind us of a Godly perspective. He did not have to change perspective because of who He was.

We get trapped very easily in our own perspectives. Imagine this, you are planning to travel on a flight and your flight is delayed. What if the delay gave you the opportunity to meet as many people as possible during that time? Instantly our focus, attitude, and demeanor would be changed. Those new connections might be the start of a loving relationship, a new friendship, a new client, and at least a new shift of perspective. Bad days can happen to the best of us.

So, the question is, what will you do in the next seven days to turn the next bad day around? It can start with thinking about how to collaborate with others to change perspective. If you do not have a bad day this week, what can you do to help others turn their bad days around? The Holy Spirit can move in our lives to collaborate with us. Perhaps we can switch our perspective to focus on the optimism of Christ. It can be as simple as collaborating in prayer. What will you do about it today?

Let us pray.

Heavenly Father, we are called to be a people of optimism. We have a Christ that has given His all for us. His sacrifice takes care of us on the best of days and on the worst of days. Help us when the worst of days become relevant to us and those around us. May your love be of comfort to the ailing and the mourning. Draw us near when it seems that everything else might be so far away. In Jesus' name, we pray. Amen.

MARCH 18: ACTIONS SPEAK LOUDER THAN WORDS

What actions are we taking today? Just like our body language or our words, our actions speak as well. Our actions are very important because others see them, and if others do not see them that speaks also. Entrepreneurs and leaders might need to be very conscious of this because they have at least three different sets of people watching. We have families, team members or employees, and customers at a minimum.

Ralph Waldo Emerson said, "Your actions speak so loudly, that I cannot hear what you are saying." Have you given some directions to a family member or employee and acted in a manner that is not consistent with your request? I believe that we might meet with some resistance from our teams when that happens. Where might you find a conflict in your actions this week with the words you have spoken? This is one way to do an accountability audit on yourself. What is the first thing that you can do in the next seven days to bring your words and actions together?

In the book of Numbers 32:1 NLT, the tribe of Reuben asked for an exception to the normal allotment of land that was planned. Their business was that of taking care of flocks and herds. Before they crossed the river Jordan, they saw Jazer and Gilead which were ideally suited for their livestock. That meant their business would certainly thrive it seemed. Why should they do anything else and risk their lives and miss this opportunity? Let us stay here, they thought.

But Moses and the other leaders knew that their actions would cause dissension. The leaders came up with a different plan so that the actions of the Reubenites would be seen by the rest of the tribes in a positive manner. It appears that they were not aware of how God was going to lay out the plan of how they were to divide the land. We must be careful when we come up with our own plans where God might have laid it out for us. We must also be careful to remember that our actions speak louder than our words.

Are your actions speaking for you in a manner that is inconsistent with your words? Are we claiming to be Christians to the world and then not attending worship because of our desire to golf, travel, or watch our favorite team on Sunday? Are we saying we love God, but our checkbook register shows little activity to expand his love with the treasures we hold? What can you do in the next seven days to bring one of your actions in alignment with your words?

Let us pray.

Heavenly Father, thank you for your gifts and forgiveness. The world we react and act in is full of us sinners. You know our hearts and how we love you, but our actions fall short. Although you know of our sins you have sent Christ to forgive us. We want to draw nearer to you. Help us align our words and our actions this week. May your love be more important to us than the enjoyment of entertainment. May your wisdom be more important than our quest for knowledge. May our treasure in heaven be greater than our treasure here on earth. In Jesus' name, we pray. Amen.

MARCH 19: WHO WILL CARRY YOU?

In business and life, we are better as part of a team. We are blessed with different unique attitudes, abilities, talents, and skills. It is when we put together the right people, for the right effort, that we can achieve amazing results. When we try to make things happen all on our own, we can struggle to even make the journey start. We can have great intentions but sometimes do not know the first action to take. We can know what result we are looking for but not have the stamina to get there.

A team can complement us. When we struggle to start, someone on the team can push us just a little or maybe they might even make the first step and pull us along. When we have a great new product or idea someone else on the team might have a resource or idea to bring it to the market quicker. We can use the energy of a team to assist each other, making our stamina last longer. Who is missing from your team that might help you do things faster, better, and less expensively with more confidence? What can you do in the next seven days to start to remedy the situation?

In Luke 5:18, we read about the four men that carry a man on a mat, taking him to Christ. The team knew the result they were looking for. The ailing man was ready to be healed. The carriers of the mat knew where Jesus was, so off they went. But the crowd was thick, so much so, that they could not get to Jesus. So, what happens next? They get the idea to go up. They go onto the roof, they remove the roof tiles, and lower him down. It is here that the opportunity met with the possibility of a miracle and Christ performs the miracle. That is a great example to us of teamwork! Who is on your team this week?

What can you do to express your appreciation to them for their sometimes-heroic efforts? How might you thank them for their uniqueness that is simply them? Is your team ready to climb to the top of the roof, remove tiles, and risk dropping a member to bring about the results needed? If our teams are not ready to do that, then our teams need work. What is the first thing you need to do this week to serve Christ with your team?

Let us pray.

Heavenly Father, sometimes we tend to think that we can do it ourselves. We think that we can do everything we need. But we acknowledge that it all starts with you. You have given us all that we have. Let us work together today to bring your message of love to others. Help us to build our teams so that your name might be glorified. Make our heroic efforts be done every day to bring people to you so that the Holy Spirit might work within them. Encourage us to rise to the challenges that seem to be above us, even on rooftops. Guide us and strengthen us as we work on our teams to bring ourselves closer to you. In Jesus' name, we pray. Amen.

MARCH 20: HAVE YOU FORGOT ABOUT YOUR TOOLS?

In business, industries have different tools used to provide products and services. But today I want to challenge us about the tools we use to build and advance our teams. The internet helps us to gather information. Phones help us to communicate as do electronic letters called emails. The written letter is almost a foregone tool of antiquity. We have personality tests that help us to know how others relate to one another. We have cognitive tests to understand how people get their work done. As a leader of a team, where do you keep a list of the tools you use to advance your team? I would be curious to know what tools the industry leader in your market uses as compared to what tools you are using now. Do we have all the tools we need?

How would we know if we have not considered doing an audit and searching for new tools? What tool do you use in your company to help yourself and your team members adjust their attitudes? My actual toolbox for mechanical fixes has over one hundred different pieces in it. I can almost guarantee you that many toolboxes have tools that are not used daily. The mechanic with a toolbox will also likely be able to tell you the most recently added tool. In your toolbox, what tool have you not used on yourself as the leader? Why not? Leaders need occasional maintenance just as our team does. What is the first thing that you can do about it in the next seven days?

In Numbers 25: 1-10, we read the story of Phinehas and how he runs a spear through a man and a woman to stop a plague against the nation of Israel. This is an example of a recurring theme in the Old Testament. God gave laws and then the people broke them to which God then sends his judgment. But we learn in the New Testament about Jesus' most powerful tool, love. As Christian brothers and sisters, which tools are we using the most? Love or hate, envy and jealousy, or compassion and generosity are all choices. Our toolbox of how to treat people is full of different tools and some can be destructive. Some of the tools are being used by us more often than others, while some of them are rusty and not being used at all. Tools might lay in the bottom of our box and simply take up space where another tool could be.

One challenge for us is to look in our heart which is the toolbox of our soul. What is down there that we have not been using very much lately? What tool is in your heart that is no longer needed? Perhaps the tools of bitterness, anxiety, or revenge are there. Maybe it is a good time during this season of Lent to pull out the toolbox and do an inventory. Maybe even throwing out some tools that are outdated and no longer helping us grow can draw us closer to God. I might think that our attitudes towards one another change when we do that inventory.

Let us pray.

Heavenly Father, we need you. Our attention gets drawn to the concerns and pains of this world so easily. Give us the ability to focus on you. Employ the tools of love, forgiveness, and compassion upon our hardened and cluttered hearts. Shine your light of hope in the recesses of our minds so that we might grow together to honor you. In Jesus' name, we pray. Amen.

MARCH 21: TWO SPECIALS ARE NOT ALWAYS IDEAL

Have you ever heard that phrase, too much information? It is used when someone hears something that they thought was inappropriate to be shared. But we have too much information all the time. It is so much information that our brain filters out the stimuli so that just what it believes is needed comes through. This highlights the importance of deciding what to give our attention to so that we have the most positive result. As entrepreneurs and leaders, we must learn to pick one, not two. Can we limit ourselves to one activity to occupy our mind? The distractions and information will continue to chase and pursue us like an important paper being dropped accidentally in the wind.

We can easily jump from one focus to another within areas of our families, finances, faith or our different business activities, and personal development. The list goes on and on. But for this moment, can I purpose myself for the next hour and a half, to be focused on only one thing? After ninety minutes I can rest and handle some distractions, but then back to focus. What is the one thing that you can do in the next seven days that would be valuable to your organization? What is the first thing you can do to give it your entire focus for ninety minutes? Just how productive might this concept make us for the day or week?

As a Christian, we have examples in the Bible of God picking one. In the Old Testament, we know of Moses' leadership. God picked Moses; Moses picked Aaron. Leaders have successors. Joshua was picked as Moses' replacement. God gave us Jesus Christ. He is the example that we are to follow.

I see lots of successors with a purpose. John the Baptist was not the Savior, he knew it and that was okay, but John still was able to focus on his work to progress the message. That was his part, so what is yours? This book is written so that our theme of Sunday is focus. The reason is because we are called to take a Sabbath day and to do that which requires focus. To rest in the comfort of God's hands for a day can be difficult for many people.

I suspect that many have never experienced a full day of resting with God. It is certainly a worthy objective to pursue. Are we willing to pursue it like we chase after that important document we might have dropped in the wind? Could it be we have the attitude that the wind is just blowing too fast, and it would be impossible to catch that document as it darts from one spot to another?

Perhaps that ability to focus for an entire day of rest can be accomplished by achieving one small step of just ninety minutes to begin with. What is the one thing you can do in the next seven days to draw closer to Jesus? What is the first thing you can do to make that happen? Our relationship with Christ is not a pick-two special at a restaurant. Jesus wants us wholly, not divided between the two.

Let us pray.

Jesus, we recognize your single sacrifice you made for us. We have made the single most important decision in our life which is to follow you. We are conflicted by the information that we are exposed to on a minute-by-minute basis. We do not need a pick-two special to have an impact for you. Help us to draw nearer to you today. We pick you. Help us as we focus on the one thing that will draw us to you today. In Jesus' name, we pray. Amen.

MARCH 22: IS IT TIME TO GET SMALL?

Sometimes it seems like I should be moving towards something bigger. Do you ever feel that way? I think that there can be both a pull of a bigger future and a pull of your past. It is like there is more than I have or am now, but it can lack definition as it is unknown. There are many places in our lives as an entrepreneur, parent, spouse, and leader that I know that the pull happens. It is that question of why that seems to matter the most about the pull at the beginning. The how I get there is important and what I do to get there makes a difference as well. But to get there, I really need to be brought back from the big of the future to the small of the moment.

I know why I exist, why our services and products exist, and why I am in relationship with my family. But to have an impact in my why, I need to get small. I need to work in the now. How about you? What will you do today, just today? Are we going to be purposeful with our impact in the present, which will shape our future? The why and the impact are not removed from one another but directly linked in an exponential manner. If we are not in the now, we are reducing the exponential effect on our future. What can you do today that will bring value and will bring stronger relationships? These both will serve a bigger future. How do we lead if we fail to keep our ability to do both? What is the first thing to do about it in the next seven days?

As a man of faith, I am called to be present as well. What about you? Am I being present in the relationships that I am in? Am I listening, loving, and leading those that need my leadership? Will I be faithful and follow in the footsteps of Christ who leads me? He is the Christ that leads us. Our present actions in our Christian journey can have an impact just as they can in our personal and professional worlds. They set the stage for exponential growth. I like the idea of exponential growth of my relationship with Jesus. Would you like to have ten times your net worth today or ten times the closeness of your relationship with Christ?

I am not speaking against one versus the other but drawing attention to the fact that we need to be present, in the here and now to make either happen. What are we doing in the next seven days to set the stage for that exponential growth of our relationship with Christ? In Luke, we read a section of scripture called the Beatitudes. When I read them, I feel that Christ is speaking directly to me. He challenges me right where I am, in the here and now. What am I going to do when He speaks to me? What are you going to do in the here and now? If you want to challenge yourself, find your Bible and read Luke 6:20-23. Digest it and see what is in store for you today. What is the first thing that you can do about it in the next seven days?

Let us pray.

Heavenly Father, today is the day the Lord has made. Today, that is where we want to be. Help to guide me today. Make the future hold the growth of my actions which occur right now. Bring me into focus for what my impact needs to be with those that I am in relationship with. Move those as you desire that I might need to be in a relationship with. Let me be listening and insightful so that I know how to serve them. Make the words of my mouth and the actions from my heart be acceptable in your sight. In Jesus' name, we pray. Amen.

MARCH 23: DEPLOY, DELEGATE, OR DELAY?

Companies are about building teams. Business owners know this. They take a service or product idea and build systems and processes around them. Those processes are deployed by people throughout the organization. But that organization is not done in a haphazard way. There is some very important thinking involved about how to best get it done. And then there is the delegation of the tasks and responsibilities that the company's teams put in place to make it happen. Sales and marketing work with the advertising team. Production works with logistics to get items to the right place in the right shape at the right time.

The management team works through all those systems and delegates responsibilities to bring it all together for the value to be received by the customer. Where are you missing the opportunity to delegate and work with a team? As a business owner and leader, we might consider looking at the least likely place and think how we might be able to delegate just a part of that task.

In Luke 7:1 NLT, we read about Jesus when he is in Capernaum. A Roman officer had a member of his entourage who was deathly ill. The officer had heard of Jesus' miraculous healing and sent word for Christ to save his person. Even the Jewish elders supported the request as they knew of the support the officer had given to them. The officer had supported the building of a synagogue for them. But as Jesus approached the place of the sick, the officer sent word that he was not worthy of Christ's presence. He need not bother himself with coming. All Christ needed to do was to command it. The officer understood delegation as he received it from his superiors and gave it to his troops that he commanded.

When Jesus heard of the officer's request, he was amazed. Christ had not yet seen faith of someone like this in all of Israel. What has Christ asked you to do, and you have not followed through with that delegation? Where has your faith been weak and therefore you believe that you are the only one that can take care of something? Is it time to get it done? In the name of Christ, who might be able to step in and accept the invitation to collaborate with you? What can you get done in the next seven days that you have been asked to delegate but you have been putting off?

Let us pray.

Heavenly Father, we are weak and scared many times during our lives. We believe sometimes that we are so strong that no one else can do something. It might keep us from you Lord. Help us to recognize where we might be able to answer the call where Christ has delegated a task for us to do that might honor you. May we accomplish it with your guidance now. Help us to delegate, deploy, and avoid delay. In Jesus' name, we pray. Amen.

MARCH 24: LINEAR FORMULAS DO NOT MOVE US EXPONENTIALLY

What are we doing that is a linear progression in our business? When a business designs systems so that they allow only step-by-step progression, the likely result is going to be linear. It is possible for systems to be focused on methods which are exponential. This kind of growth, value, and result is what can fuel rapid change. Our systems can be either of the two. Challenges and opportunities can also be linear or exponential. When we meet a challenge that is linear it does not require us to solve it in a linear way.

Think of a need for simple shade desired to provide people relief in a hot climate. One could plant a tree to grow tall and provide shade. But one could just as easily consider a tree that rapidly reproduces so that a forest might soon appear. Opportunities can be captured to benefit our own teams or even a specific team member. But why not consider how an opportunity could be solved exponentially and help hundreds or thousands of teams or people. Where are we moving our businesses in just a linear manner? What can we do to consider transformation of the issue exponentially? Is it worthy of your attention in the next seven days?

As people who are limited by our perceptions, we might tend to think linear as well in our faith. Where am I falling short and need forgiveness? That is a one stop idea. But what if the thought is changed to where do I need to extend forgiveness? Could I be causing others to not be as close to God as possible? That is an exponential question. The verse in 2 Thessalonians 11:1 shows an example of how we might grow. We are told that the people of the church are being prayed for which is linear. We also see that by God's power, he may fulfill every good purpose of yours and every act prompted by your faith. That fulfillment by God is exponential.

The exponential power of God is available to us by the Holy Spirit. Where are we being linear in our faith and actions? Jesus did not die on the cross for just the generation that He walked the earth with. He died for generation after generation of believers which is exponential. How will we act so that the good news can grow exponentially through us collaborating with the Holy Spirit? What is the first thing that you can do today to grow exponentially?

Let us pray.

Jesus, thank you for your linear relationship with me. You are direct and there is nothing between you and me. You have called us to be part of an exponential expression of love. You want every ounce of our being to be called to you to move. Let us love others exponentially. Let your love cover the earth and the people in it. Remove the barriers that limit us and especially remove those linear thoughts where we might be comfortable. Please use multiplication in our lives instead of us using addition. In Jesus' name, we pray. Amen.

MARCH 25: CHECKMATE AND CHECK IN CHESS AND LIFE

What are the biggest opportunities that exist in your organization or company? It does not matter if you own an organization or whether you work for one, it is wise for all to be concerned about this answer. What is the largest challenge at your organization? It is easier to be concerned about the smaller issues because they make us fear less. There is generally less risk associated with smaller issues. But the rewards are less as well. In the game of chess, when your opponent places your king in jeopardy, it is called being put in check. That is what fear can do to us. It can put you in check. But the game of chess is won when you put a king in jeopardy that cannot be avoided. It is called checkmate.

We tend to want our world to remain status quo, but the rewards of being in business for yourself can make a significant difference in our families, team, and customers' lives. When we turn ourselves around and face fear and the biggest challenges, we are likely to see them as opportunities. When we do this, I think we can call it checkmate as well. The danger and fear cannot win against us when we transform it into an opportunity which is a winning move. What is the first step you can do to capture a great opportunity or to mitigate your greatest danger?

As Christians, we tend to address the small challenges while the larger risks and dangers lurk in the background. Our fear of change may paralyze us. We miss some of the greatest opportunities in our lives as well. How can we shake the fear? The answer is in facing it. That requires us to meet it right where it comes at us. We can challenge it and send it packing.

Christ taught a lesson beginning in Luke 7:41. This is a parable about two people who had loans. One had a loan of fifty pieces and another person had a loan of five hundred pieces. Both people defaulted on their loans, but the person owed the money forgave their debts completely. The question from Christ was who was happier about the action of forgiveness. The one forgiven the most, the larger debtor was the answer. Why then are we scared to capture the biggest opportunities, forgive the biggest trespasses, and fear the biggest problems? It is time to follow Christ. Let us go big with Christ. Fear puts us in check, but Christ is the checkmate. If we cannot go big, why are we going at all? He does not want just some of our hearts. He wants it all. It is the Easter season, so it is a great time to step up and step out. What is the first thing you can do about it in the next seven days?

Let us pray.

Heavenly Father, you are so great. You have given us so much potential, but we tend to listen to our fears. We can avoid the bigger challenges in our lives by holding onto the comforts of what we have. We often trust in ourselves instead of in you. Help us to help others by looking for larger challenges and opportunities. Make the glory of our successes highlight the love we have for you. Guide us and help us to move forward, whether it is to step up to a challenge or to grab hold of an opportunity. In Jesus' name, we pray. Amen.

MARCH 26: YOUR TRIANGLE OF INFLUENCE

Who are the people in your present? What I mean by that is that you have friends, family, business associates, employees, employers, and you also are a customer somehow. Who are these people in your life? We are either serving them, in relationship with them, or being served by them. We bring value to one another in some manner. That value proposition is important because it is very likely that most of the relationships will change in some way. We can be asking ourselves every week how we might be in better relationships. I suspect that a better relationship with anyone starts with us.

If that seems reasonable to you then we might also stretch to think about how to bring more value to them. If our attitude is set to think how to bring more to others, we are more likely to do exactly that. We all have a desire to be comfortable. When others bring us comfort and provide value, we welcome them. We want to see them and be engaged more deeply with them. As a business owner, a father or mother, who are the top three people for you to build upon your relationships with in the next seven days?

There is a passage in the Bible found in Luke 8:19-21. I can recall thinking at my first reading of it that it was very strange. In the passage, we find Jesus with the disciples and a crowd gathered when Jesus' family comes to see him. The crowd is large enough that the family is not able to walk right up to Christ and therefore their arrival is told to Christ. But Christ states, "My mother and brothers are those that hear God's word and obey it." That is it. It seems that maybe he will not see the family. That he will not even recognize them.

Do you read it that way? I think that this may challenge our view of what we want from our relationships. We do not want change because we fear loss. Christ has shown that our relationships will change but that it does not have to imply or require loss. Our relationship with him itself is a change. We put our old ways out for a new life in him. Let us cherish our relationships that we have with others. Let us build upon them while we have them. Our family members will become more than just family members. They will become spouses, parents, colleagues, and members of our communities. What can we do to build on the relationships we have today? Christ chose twelve men to be his close group of disciples. Do you have twelve people that you are in close relationship with? What is the first thing that you can do about it in the next seven days?

Let us pray.

Heavenly Father, the only relationship that we will always have is with you. Bless our relationships as people will come in and out of our lives. Bring your comfort and love as we grow in our relationships that we have now. Help us to find new relationships as well. Help us to bring others in relationship to you. Guide us Lord. In Jesus' name, we pray. Amen.

MARCH 27: A LACK OF CURIOSITY

As a leader, will we miss the important questions and mindsets of the week? This week will be full of transactions. People will be running to the store for groceries, gas stations will pump gas, insurance premiums will be due and paid, and the bank will be open. I expect that there will be a few challenges. There will be questions about the satisfaction of service that we receive and provide. Somewhere this week, somebody is not going to get what they thought they were paying for. When they do not, how will we respond to their question of how we can resolve the difference between the expected and the actual?

There is always the opportunity to be amazed after a question is asked. These are times that leaders, organizations, and businesses can set themselves apart. There are times where raving fans can be created. It is difficult to create raving fans sometimes because of the attitude we might have. One way to address it is to identify the goal of your attitude right now for the coming seven days. How do you want your mindset to be if someone challenges you with a hard question?

I can see at least three options to consider. The first is to not care. They have a problem, so it is all on them. Sometimes life has bad apples so deal with it, and this is one of those times. Mindset two is to be curious to expect that we can amaze them. Your solution and answer to the question could far exceed their expectations. A curiosity and amazement mindset can move people emotionally so they will not be able to stop talking about it. Your solution might even make national news, or a video of the answer could go viral. Option three is to do as little as possible to meet their expectations. Which attitude is your team carrying? Which mindset will you choose in the next seven days?

We have an example of a mindset in Luke: 8:22-26. We find the story of the disciples and Jesus in another boat. This time they incur stormy seas so heavy that the disciples wake up Jesus and explain that they are frightened. Jesus rebukes the storm, and it ceases. Jesus then immediately questions the disciples. He asks, "Where is your faith?" to which they have no response to Christ. Who is this man who can even tell the weather what to do? What was their mindset? Were they prepared with a mindset of curiosity and amazement when the storm arose and threatened their lives? It might be that their fear of drowning, of the storm and rocky seas had overtaken an attitude of amazement.

As Christians, followers of our Savior, Jesus Christ, we are called to have attitudes of amazement. We believe in the resurrection of the Savior of the world. Prepare to be amazed. What is the first thing you can do today to set your mind for amazement in the next seven days?

Let us pray.

Heavenly Father, thank you for the gifts of the day. We enter the world today ready for you. We know that you can amaze us. We ask today that you help us to have an attitude that shares and prepares us for your amazing capabilities. We know that it is difficult to love the unlovable but through you, we can do it. We know it is difficult to forgive the unforgivable, but that is an opportunity for amazing energy and effort as well. May our attitudes today, especially today, be prepared to be amazing through you. We ask in Jesus' name, and in his name, it is possible to be amazed. Amen.

MARCH 28: MOVING A MESSAGE

Businesses of all sizes might hope to achieve success by moving through several tipping points. Think of a balancing scale where you add weights until the scale moves into balance. All the work up until the scale moves can seem tiring and monotonous. Building up to and through a tipping point is not required. But to achieve a high level of success we might have to look for them and search them out. The book, *The Tipping Point* is a good one. That desired future level of success might be just where the people of the company, the value proposition, and message movers have gotten aligned.

If any of the three are out of alignment, the tipping point might not happen. Who are the message movers of your team's value? Those are the people that believe in a company's values and services enough to share it with others. Who are your message movers for your company? Are employee's message movers, or what about your customers?

I am not sure that you must be one of these two classifications in every team or organization. There could be others in your value proposition. Another good question is who is not being a good message mover. What keeps someone on your team from moving the message? Could it be attitude, confidence, or training? If the message is not being moved, then a tipping point is possible with that one individual. Tipping is important for each of us, but it can demand our focus. If you have one tipping area identified, what can you do about it this week?

The Christian faith has been built and shared throughout history by message movers. In Luke, we are told about Jesus sending his twelve disciples out to share his message and to heal the sick. I think those twelve disciples would certainly qualify as message movers. When Jesus sent them out that was a tipping point, in my opinion. The message was still his message, but he authorized others to move it. As believers and followers of the faith, we too are called to be messages movers. How well are you doing in moving the message?

It is a challenge to live life as a Christian. Many of us can get tied up in the struggles of living beyond ourselves in a worldly viewpoint. To live according to the example of Christ is part of our challenge though. We are to be sharing our journey by our voice and by our example. What can you do this week to be a message mover? Could there be a better week to consider doing it than this? For me, I think it is a good week to pray for guidance, courage, and strength to be a better message mover. What is the first thing you can do about being a better message mover in the next seven days?

Let us pray.

Jesus, you gave us miracles, signs, and wonderful words to live by. But you asked us to move your message as well. Help us as we move between the message and the living. May you help us to combine our efforts but to be distinct as well. Help us to share the words that might be able to be moved by the Holy Spirit. Let our words be heard. Empower us to share the words and let you do the moving. In Jesus' name, we pray. Amen.

MARCH 29: MEASURE TWICE, CUT ONCE, ACTIVATE, REVIEW

Why and what do you measure? A carpenter measures pieces for cutting. The optometrist measures the weakness of the eyes to create a prescription for corrective lenses. The electric company measures the meter on the house to charge an appropriate fee for usage of the electricity. It should be clear that things are measured so that something can get created. My examples show a piece of furniture, a set of eyeglasses, and a bill getting created. But the creation of the measurement itself is valuable even before the creation gets delivered and deployed with others. It is a three-part system; establish some measurements, activate and create, then deploy and discuss.

The most useful systems measure and then deploy and discuss. This allows for continual improvement and value creation. Where can your company improve its measurements or its deployment and discussion? What you measure matters. If a leader wants its team to improve, there are some measurements that should be in place for both the leader and the team. How many times did you use the words "I promise" last week? How many times did you tell each of your team members thank you, appreciate them, or affirm them? Many companies put an emphasis on measuring financial items and that is important. How many measurements do you have that reflect the value of your relationships? What is the most important measurement that you could improve in the next seven days?

As Christians, we can be in relationship with one another to spread the word and the works of our faith. Are we measuring as a leader might? Are we deploying and discussing how to have a better impact for God's love in our world? In the Bible, we read about Jesus sending out the disciples to heal the sick and spread the message. In Luke 10, we read about the disciples returning from one of their mission trips. The first thing Jesus does is listen to them about the trip. They shared everything they had done. They slipped quietly away right after this. Seems like it was just as important to have a debrief when they returned as it was to give them clear instructions to go. Where are you measuring to know how you want to grow in your faith this week, month or quarter? With whom are you sharing what happened to be accountable?

Without the measurements and the accountability, our impact for the Kingdom of God is likely to fall short of the potential that has been put in us. We do not measure to achieve because we must earn our way to eternity. Spending eternity with Jesus is a gift of grace once you accept Christ. We measure if we choose to be intentional about growing. What is the first thing you can do this week to improve your measurement mentality? How might you install a new debrief idea? Maybe you need to schedule one.

Let us pray.

Heavenly Father, you have shared with us the old and the new. We have Christ in our hearts. We are in relationship with him, the church, and the world. Help us to have impactful measurements for ourselves and our teams. Let us further your kingdom here on earth by working in relationship together. Help us to share how we can walk closer to you by looking at our actions. Let us share words that show we have reflected on your love for us so that the Holy Spirit can work within us. Let us set standards for ourselves to improve and find mentors and accountability partners to help us grow in our faith. In Jesus' name, we pray. Amen.

MARCH 30: WHAT CAN CHANGE OUR PERSPECTIVE?

When you think you know, the answer could really be no you don't. As entrepreneurs, we build teams, coordinate our resources, and build systems. We do so to deliver value for our customers. Those systems and teams are going to be challenged by extreme situations though. Instead of an ownership transition taking place over a five-year period, it might take place over five days. A piece of technology could be developed to help the world more efficiently and cost effectively and it might result in your company's value being cut in half. Someone could decide to sell a product to keep the long-term average price up. That decision could force your business to lay off half of its team if the product price plummets afterwards.

Where are we the most comfortable today? That just might be the very place that is about to be challenged tomorrow. What strategy do you have in place today to deal with changes? Do you have people outside of your company you can count on to come to your aid? Or will you ignore even thinking today about this question? If so, that might be one of your biggest obstacles to your success and amazing growth of the future. What is the first thing you can do to challenge your perspective?

The story of the disciple Peter, denying Christ three times, is a commonly known story as it is part of the Easter journey. But roosters are a common thing as well. Roosters pretty much do the same thing around the world. They crow with their unique sounds, and even children can recognize what they are, regardless of their country of origin or language they speak. Cock a doodle dooooo! You've probably read these words and made the real sound in your head. Reflect on what you think Peter's attitude and comfort level was on the day before Jesus held the last supper and was taken away? Do you think that he might have felt fairly comfortable?

He had left his old life to walk the earth with Christ, the Messiah. He watched Him perform miracles. Jesus had told Peter that he would do miracles and he had been sent out to the world in mission trips to do exactly that. He had been in conferences with Christ. He even watched people be raised from the dead. Would you feel that you were in a very good place in your life if you were Peter? And then BAM, the world changed. The end of the beginning was happening, and the world was never the same.

Everything that Peter lived: the team, its leader, their systems, their message, their perspective, and value proposition was about to change. And he denied having anything to do with it. Where are you comfortable in your walk with Christ? Are you ready to accept the changes in your life and make the best of it? What is changing today that you can take a different perspective on? Cock a doodle dooo! It is time for another perspective change. What is the first thing you can do in the next seven days to make a smoother transition?

Let us pray.

Jesus, you are the most talked about human being that has ever existed on the earth. You are the son of God, the Messiah, the Savior of those that accept you as sent from God himself. I choose to accept that you are my personal Savior. I have changed my life and my perspective because of you. Walk with me today and help me to remember that my first reaction to change might be the one of my former life. It was a life prior to knowing and loving you. I want a perspective of us, the two of us. Open my eyes to look at changes and what they mean to me and my Savior. Help us to know you, not to deny you or say no. In Jesus' name, we pray. Amen.

MARCH 31: IN OR OUT?

Most businesses require capital. Whether you want to purchase a franchise store like a McDonalds or bootstrap a website for $100, you need some capital. From the capital investment and the contributions of a team, we hope to recognize some reward or income. The better we are at assembling the team as leaders and entrepreneurs, the better the rewards. But in business, you constantly must deal with the decision of what to do with any income. Do you take it into the personal side of financial net worth or put it back in as capital to the company?

Businesses can get comfortable just like people. When this happens, we tend to challenge ourselves less. We sometimes stop measuring the core values and looking at what will help us to grow in the future the most. What if we were challenged to think about the revenue generated this year and to do it right now? If your business generates more net revenue than you take to run your household, how do you expect to deploy the capital?

Go ahead, dream about the revenue being the largest it has ever been. What amount of income would be intimidating for you to think about? What would you do with it? When you have an answer, ask yourself why. Why will you do it that way and why would that amount intimidate you? Ask that question three times to yourself and share your answer with your team. I bet that you just might be surprised at the conversation.

As a Christian, have we ever reflected on the idea of the capital that Jesus invested into his thirty-three years here on the earth? He invested every drop of capital of His life's work into His value proposition. The rewards of His efforts were exclusively for the Father and put back into the organization. People received His message, and the reward was put into the people. The glory was given to God. People were the recipients of miraculous healing, and they took the reward and shared the message that God had sent the Messiah. They did it even if they were told not to tell anyone. So today, we have the decision of what we will choose to do with the reward of His message.

It is possible that we might need to keep it and grow it some because we do not have enough capital, enough of Jesus, in us. Then again, maybe we are capitalized enough that we have the confidence to share 10% of the reward we receive, at least for this week. Will we share the message, the love, the forgiveness, the smiles, the compassion or even the net income from today or this week? Maybe we can pour most of this week's capital back into the relationship we have with Christ. It could be for some that they need the capital personally for their well-being because they are hurting or suffering.

How might your life be improved this week by making a conscious decision to put back in the capital you have? I bet that the rewards will be significant. What is the first thing that you can do about it in the next seven days? Will you be accountable to make the decision?

Let us pray.

Heavenly Father, we thank you for the blessings of this week. You are an awesome God. We have the beauty of the earth, the joy of time to invest, and the pleasure of your heart-warming love. Help us to recognize the opportunities this week to put our rewards into our relationship with Jesus. May our ears and eyes be open to the opportunities. Guide us to put in some capital this week. Help us to capture the opportunity. In Jesus' name, we pray. Amen.

APRIL 1: WHEN DO COMPETITORS COLLABORATE?

Take a minute and think of some respected companies. Is being in business about the pursuit of competing in the marketplace or is it about the pursuit of delivering value? Delivering value does not mean that you do not compete, but the mindset of a company makes a difference to customers and clients. If a business is focused only on competing, the energy might get geared towards costs instead of value. That could result in manufacturing with substandard materials, skip processes, or hiring non-qualified people. If competition is the goal, profitability might be the focus without concern for loyalty of customers or reputation of the company as a societal contributor. These seem like tenuous issues for a business if you do not want to be a commodity. If our focus is on value, the viewpoint must be different.

Profits and costs are still evaluated but they are not the top or only focus. Our focus could be more about delivering an adequate product, through a great delivery model, and with a conscious effort of how to continuously improve. This type of attitude is what some businesses do and why they might wind up shaping industries. It requires them to be accountable to their value construct. Their product and delivery systems become the model for others to follow. But the need to be first is not the focus. It very well might be the result. What is your company going to do this week to focus on value? What is the one thing you can do in the next seven days to improve the value to your customers and employees?

As a people of faith, we can sometimes get askew in our relationship with Christ because of worldly competitive focus. We can get narrowed into a point of view of facts and figures. A viewpoint can be concentrated on what I have or what is in it for me. But these viewpoints are limiting and competitive instead of loving and valuable based on Christ as our Savior. The parable of the good Samaritan teaches this well. Find the parable in Luke 10:30 NLT. Samaritans were despised by the Jews. That sounds like a competitive viewpoint to me. But the parable teaches that the Jewish victim of the robbery is helped not by his fellow Jewish people but the Samaritan.

Where is the competition and where is the love and compassion in the story? It appears that the competition was between the religious Jewish leaders while the Samaritan was more focused on value for others. I know that I have been in a competitive focus at times, and you probably have too. Where might our competitive focus be keeping us from delivering value to our family, friends and walk of faith? It seems that collaborating brings us closer than competition might. What is one area that you can see improving in the next seven days?

Let us pray.

Jesus, you walked and talked about the value of a life lived with you. You showed us why to live this way, how to live this way, and what to do. Help us, we pray, to put our competitive nature into the secondary concerns. May our first concerns of this world be about how to be of value to your kingdom. Send your Holy Spirit to be with us and remove the temptations. I do not want to be concerned with counting the lashes on a robber so that the limit of forty is not broken. I want more to be in a relationship with Christ and my neighbor. Eliminate the need to rob others. Walk with us. In Jesus' name, we pray. Amen.

APRIL 2: BEING HERE DOES NOT MEAN BEING PRESENT

Businesses are full of people. We have many titles like manager, board members, employees, and customers to name a few. But regardless of one's title, we need to be present when we are talking to each other. It is disrespectful to look past or ignore a speaker when being spoken with, but it also disengages others when they notice it. To ignore or not engage the other person means that we, ourselves, are not engaged. We have not accepted our responsibility, at that moment, to work with our team members. We are focused on our task only and are not being respectful enough to ourselves or the other participants when this occurs. It takes practice to learn how to be present. Where might you not have been present in the last week? I suspect that you have witnessed someone who failed to be present with you when you needed them to be. It is a behavior that stunts growth, communication, and progress.

There are at least three levels of being present. One is to be able to speak and hear one another. The second level is to empathize, interpret, and feel the conversation. The third level can recognize the energy of the environment of the room or atmosphere where the conversation is happening. Who might you only be engaged with at level one? What would happen in your relationships if you could move to a deeper level? Try it today and this weekend and see how others react. I suspect that both the speaker and the listener will be surprised. Who do you know who you can be more present with in the next seven days?

Think about your schedule this week. How might it be set up so that it does not really help you to be present? Distractions can move us away from others. Lacking clear priorities for the day might get a dozen unimportant issues handled while important ones are left unattended. Answering the call to be like Christ includes a call to be present. It asks us to help those that are hurting right now. We are to be compassionate to those that we are in relationship with. We must be present to do this. It does not mean that we cannot think about the future or do planning. But wherever two of us are gathered, Christ is there as well. Let us be present.

A great example of being present is the story of Mary and Martha as hosts. You can find it in the book of Luke 10:38, NLT. It was Mary who sat at the feet of Jesus and learned as he taught while Martha prepared the dinner. Martha certainly could have been in the room learning in the presence of Jesus. Dinner could certainly wait. Perhaps it was her habit of preparing a meal that took her away. Perhaps it was her hunger. Perhaps it was her desire to please others. Regardless, it was her decision not to be present with Christ. Where might we be less than present in our walk? Think now of who we will be spending time with in the next three days. Perhaps we can bring the focus on being present with them and Jesus?

Let us pray.

Jesus, help us to recognize when we are not being present. Bring the opportunity to share your love with others by being with them. If others are ignored, let us address it immediately. Allow us to be present, and through us, the opportunity to know you. In Jesus' name, we pray. Amen.

APRIL 3: THAT MUST BE A FOUL!

There is no question, when you are a business owner, people are going to harm you or your business. It might seem that this is a ridiculous statement, but it happens. How are businesses harmed? Let us start with theft. People shoplift or take items from a business without paying for them. In the service business, people steal services as well. I have lived in a college town where I know of trash businesses that have dumpsters which are exploited by non-paying customers when semester ends.

The businesses know that their dumpsters were filled by non-paying customers because of the normal patterns they see, and the type of materials being dumped. Businesses can be victims of vandalism, rioting, and then there is also employee theft, including where productivity is stolen by not working their shift fully. How much time is spent on social media during work hours? Would anyone ever be caught looking at sports brackets in March? What about those funny viral video clips on YouTube?

An entrepreneur can get frustrated and disappointed when this happens. Sometimes they get angry or depressed. But how do the customers want them to react? Do clients want them to close their doors and stop operating to deliver value? I do not think so. I think that they want the businesses to be focused on delivering value. The more time a business must spend on addressing shrinkage issues is time they cannot be focused on direct value for clients. That is costly because it is a 180-degree swing in thought from what helps the raving fans of the business. I want our customers and the members of our teams to be raving fans.

When we are in the wrong mindset, it can be better to get ourselves quickly to the other. One way to get there quicker is to forgive. The process can start there. Is there some event in your professional life that forgiveness might help you move more people into a raving fan mode? What is the first thing you might need to forgive somebody for at your business?

As a Christian, have you earned all your forgiveness yet? A better question for ourselves might be, is there someone in our lives that has not earned our forgiveness yet? These could be the people that have harmed you. They are the ones that have not made what you believe restitution should be. They have not returned the rake they borrowed. It could be that they have not reciprocated an invitation or have not paid you back what they owed. We might ask if they are sorry. We might have been withholding forgiveness until we have been made whole. Then, and only then, do we forgive them? Maybe we have taken our eyes off the prize of our forgiveness that we have in Jesus when that happens.

Forgiveness from Jesus is not earned. You cannot pay for the best forgiveness from him, and you cannot earn it. All debts of forgiveness have already been paid on the cross by Jesus. Now our actions are about the value proposition of a life which follows Christ. That too, is a 180 degree turn of attitude. Like rocks carried in a backpack, the weight of carrying those acts which can be forgiven, weighs us down. They might constantly remind us as the shoulder straps cut into our shoulders. As the rocks shift from side to side in the pack, so do our minds as they keep us from loving fully in our relationships. Could today be the day that we drop a few rocks from our packs? What is the first thing that you can do about it in the next seven days?

Let us pray.

Jesus, we have done nothing worthy of the sacrifice that you paid for us. We cannot earn it with our words or thoughts or actions. What we can do is be in relationship with you. Help us to reflect on our own ability to forgive others this week. May we draw closer to you as you soften our hearts where they have been hardened. In Jesus' name, we pray. Amen.

APRIL 4: ONE WORRY OR THREE?

As a leader, what do you want at the heart of your team? Remember that a heart has a couple of chambers and one purpose. I like to think that our teams might be most effective if we can narrow our scope to three overarching behaviors that support our value proposition. Do you have three? I can think of many behaviors that we exhibit both to our customers and our team members. Here is a list of possibilities I will call the "be" list. Be: kind, pleasant, welcoming, open, conversant, communicative, warm, effective, focused, customer oriented, smiley, trustworthy, efficient, on-time, scheduled, organized…we can go on. But this list is too large.

What three behaviors would you value for your team the most? If we have not established those three behaviors, our leadership might be lacking. How can you recruit team members who are strong in those behaviors if you do not know them? Are we training our team with these behaviors in mind? Our own accountability to the behaviors might be weak as well. If we cannot focus the list down to three, we likely are doing a poor job of measuring how well we are doing them. What is the first thing that you can do about it in the next seven days?

> "But Jesus told him, 'Anyone who puts a hand to the plow and then looks back is not fit for the Kingdom of God.'"
>
> LUKE 9:62 NLT

There is a clear expectation set here about looking backwards. That is a behavior that we are being cautioned about doing. In our walk in this world, we are asked to do many behaviors. Often, they are not for our own benefit, nor are they for the benefit of the mission of Jesus Christ. It can be tempting to look back at those behaviors, but I challenge us to look forward today.

What is on your schedule this week that you know to be something that will cause stress, frustration and might even involve a little anger? By looking forward, we can set a different set of expectations. Could a focus on being humble, forgiving, and loving be a possible way to continue to advance your week? Maybe you have a different set of three behaviors that fit your week better if you look forward to them. It is possible that we spend our week looking back at all that was. Will we decide to spend our time being and looking forward and serving Christ? Where is your focus this week? What is the first thing you can do to develop and deploy them?

Let us pray.

Heavenly Father, you only need one behavior from us and that is love. Your greatest example of your love is Jesus. We pray this day for that love. Make the most powerful behaviors we present this week be in conjunction with that love. Bring them to the top of our mind and the tip of our tongues. In Jesus' name, we pray. Amen.

APRIL 5: HOW LONG ARE PRINCIPLES AND PROMISES GOOD FOR?

How long is a promise for? Do we promise or even expect that when a business is started that it will last for a year, a decade, or possibly even beyond one's lifetime? Although we operate in the present, our concern and thought of the immediate and distant future is relevant. It is relevant because if you are expecting to be providing value for a long time, we need to have a set of principles to subscribe to. Although our products and services will probably change over time, our principles probably will not.

What principles are you operating with today? Do you have them listed? Chances are, if you do not know what they are, or have them listed, then your employees, team, and customers do not know them either. As a result of not having them listed, customer loyalty is probably low, as well as employee or team loyalty. When we have our principles identified we can then make promises and fulfill them.

If one begins to experience costs that are no longer bearable, promises will stop happening. Businesses and teams will cease operations when that cost becomes so high as to destroy the equity of the team. Teams will disband and members will leave your organization when we break promises. But team members will leave as well when other teams make promises to them that they believe can be met. Why would you collaborate with others who fail to deliver on the promises they make? What is the first thing you can do to communicate your principles?

At Moses' legacy talk, before he passed away, he shared the history of the nation of Israel. You can find it in Deuteronomy. In doing so, he shared the importance of recognizing the time element of promises and their intentionality. He told Israel that God had them wander forty years as a punishment for not doing what he instructed. But he also shared that the covenant to enter the land would be measured for all the generations to come. The covenant would apply generation after generation. This was a call to a way of life. It was a call to a set of principles for them to live by.

By the time that Jesus roamed the earth the principles had become a mindset of rules to enforce instead of principles to live. We are the people of a resurrected Christ, a people of love and respect. We are a people who embrace a new life and a new promise. Where might a lack of a known set of principles be harming us individually, our families and our communities? What can we do to make sure to have that set of principles? If you do not have one written or developed, I would bet that you cannot communicate it clearly.

The more clarity we have of our principles, as a follower of Christ, the more we will follow his example. We might expect to fall short at times of His perfection so we can be thankful for his sacrifice and grace. But I want to walk closer with my Savior Jesus, how about you? What is the first thing you can do to live a principled life following Christ? What is your manifesto of principles today? I promise, if you do not have a manifesto of principles, then starting with identifying just one or two could be a powerful way to begin developing one.

Let us pray.

Heavenly Father, you are the Creator, and you still have secrets that you may share with us. Today, we are on a path walking with Jesus. Help us to know your desires in our hearts, so that we are empowered to live a principled life. Make your directions and covenants be honored with our words, thoughts, and actions. Jesus taught us how to live, using parables and miracles. Open our eyes to see, our ears to hear, and our hearts to feel and love your principles. Make them a reflection of our love for you in our principled lives for today, tomorrow, and the generations to come. In Jesus' name, we pray. Amen.

APRIL 6: MORALS OR MORELS?

It is almost a given that when a subject comes up, you really have two thoughts to explore; gross or net, sales or profits, advertising, or sales, hire or fire, and talent or skill. What about moral character or...wait, hold that thought. I am not sure that I have heard moral character compared to anything. Maybe that is a standalone issue to address and to reflect on. Maybe our moral character is only to be compared with a lack of moral character.

In our businesses, we want all our relationships to be relationships strong in moral character. We want equitable trade, reasonable profits, and value for all parties in our exchanges. In fact, when there is a breakdown in our organizations, it could be because there was a breakdown in the moral character. We would like to think that it is a temporary breakdown and not a systemic breakdown. But systemic breakdown can be a dangerous cavern in our organization.

For example, how do you have clarity when it comes to the moral character of a potential new employee? Do we take the time to really get to know candidates at this level? What about our customers, do we know their moral character? I like the idea of pairs, and it is at the top of my mind today. Pairs is how we started this thought today. What are two important components of moral character that you value in your organization? These moral characteristics are limits for our team. Does your team know that you value these two components? It might grow your organization to have your team reflect on those two components more than they do now. What is the first thing you can do to begin shaping it so that it happens?

Be strong and courageous. I would wager that you have heard that before. It is a phrase throughout the Bible. It has been in songs throughout culture during my life. These are words that reflect values of moral character. They reflect values that relate to the convictions in our lives. Moses instructed Joshua to be strong and courageous going forward into the new territory. Joshua was going to need his moral character because he was going to be challenged. The people were going to fall away from God. Moses knew it and he shared that with Joshua, so Joshua knew it. Moses affirmed the need for Joshua to be prepared, to always be strong and courageous. That is a challenge that speaks to me today as well. How about you? I can say that there are times in my week where I feel anything but strong and courageous. We can remember though that many have sacrificed before us.

Others have paid a significant price, some on a cross, others suffered persecution during life and then an ugly death. Where might we start living a stronger and more courageous life? I am sure that we can all find a place that will build the kingdom by living with a stronger and more courageous character. Being stronger does not mean bullying or pushing others around. Sometimes being stronger means to be vulnerable or approachable. What is the first thing you can do about it in the next seven days?

Let us pray.

Heavenly Father, you need no strength or courage, and we are thankful for that. You have created us in your image, but we live on an earth which challenges us. We face challenges and sometimes are weak. We fail to resist and sometimes submit when it does not glorify your name. Help us this week to be strong and courageous regardless of whether we are addressing a weak spot in our character or adding strength to a stronghold. Guide us we pray, embolden us to grow in your love and shape us into your people. In Jesus' name, we pray. Amen.

APRIL 7: PARTLY CLOUDY?

The weather forecast is a helpful tool for leaders of organizations, families, and companies. We make decisions around it. We close our businesses when threatened by hurricanes and typhoons. We bend our manufacturing of products and services sometimes to meet the demands of the weather. Our schedules certainly get modified by the weather as well. When a heat wave hits in the summer, construction and roofing crews commonly adjust the start of their day. They start during the very early cool of the morning so to stop before the intense heat occurs in the afternoon. But where does the weather forecast not help us? We cannot interpret many things about our business with the accuracy of a weather forecast. The pop-up thunderstorms of the summer still are not accurately predicted.

Ask a weatherman where a tornado will be three days from now. You will not get an accurate prediction. We cannot forecast when our employees are not going to perform in a superior fashion or just plain fail. We do not know when they, their family members or ourselves are going to become ill. Those events will affect our business. Where are we believing and having confidence in a forecast that might be far from reality? Relying on a forecast could be dangerous if leaders, team members, employees cannot show up for the tasks assigned to them? How will your clients be damaged or harmed when those failed tasks occur? What is the first thing we can do to have an emergency or contingency plan to address the risks?

This passage was written a long time ago and is forewarning us as believers about interpretations.

> "You fools! You know how to interpret the weather signs of the earth and sky, but you do not know how to interpret the present times."
>
> LUKE 12: 56 NLT

How true does that relate to your life today? It is possible that we might be looking at the weather forecast and receiving a false hope in our ability to predict our activities that we should do. We plan to stay inside when the forecast is for rain. We run to the grocery store for food and stocking up when the heavy snow is predicted. We can place false hope in other things as well because of forecasts.

Where might the media companies be serving us their interpretations? I believe that a media report is just one perspective. When we begin to allow others to interpret for us, we might be spending less time asking God for his interpretation. I think that I would trust the interpretation of Jesus more than anyone else. Maybe we can try to trust Jesus' interpretation this week. Today seems like a pretty good place to start. It may help us to be accountable to valuing another perception. What is the first thing that you can do about it in the next seven days?

Let us pray.

Dear Jesus, thank you for your sacrifice. It was the most important event ever forecasted by the prophets. Guide us to listen to your forecast and to act based on it. Let us consider every other forecast second. Walk with us and let the Holy Spirit cast confidence among us to love and live with you. In Jesus' name, we pray. Amen.

APRIL 8: TO BORROW OR NOT TO BORROW

Do we borrow in our businesses? I believe that we do, but what is it that we borrow? We borrow capital to purchase and deploy resources. We buy equipment, real estate and buildings, and create operating capital. That is all easy enough to identify, but there are other items we have borrowed as well. Two of the most important items we are borrowing are words and time. Let us focus on the time. We are all on borrowed time. We know that life is short. Even the ownership of our businesses might be short in the big scheme of things. It is challenging to think about your enterprises and begin to have the perspective that your management and direction of the enterprise is just on borrowed time.

What do you want to do while you have it? Evaluating how we are borrowing time and words will likely require us to collaborate with others in new ways. The rewards might be more valuable than you can imagine. As Christians, one may believe that our physical presence here on earth is not necessarily what it will be in heaven. That makes this body we maintain something borrowed. How we treat it matters.

In fact, we do not know exactly what heaven will be like. Maybe our minds and bodies are borrowed things as well. Luke 13:6 begins the parable of the fruitless fig tree. It gets to live on some borrowed time. It was fruitless for three years and was about to be destroyed. The gardener begs the owner for just one more year of growth and opportunity. We are living on borrowed time here on this earth. Christ showed us an example of how to make the best of it.

If you knew that this was the last seven days on the earth for yourself, what would you do to connect with Christ this week? Would you spend more time with the television or talking with a friend or relative? Make the best of the next seven days. Remember, they are borrowed. You might want to return them better than you received them. It is up to you.

Let us pray.

Heavenly Father, thank you for the gift of the day. The flowers are blooming somewhere, the gentle rains will fall, and the sun will rise. Help us to live fully in the borrowed time we have. May we return the day to you in the best manner possible. Provide your comforts to those that need them. In Jesus' name, we pray. Amen.

APRIL 9: ROSES, GELATIN, AND SKUNK

What is the purpose of your organization? I remember hearing that Bill Gates' purpose was to put a computer in every home. I do not personally know Bill Gates, but it sounds reasonable. I have heard that McDonalds' purpose is to have everyone in some areas of the world to be within four miles of a restaurant. That is a very clear purpose that permeates their marketplaces. Their purpose is so clearly known that it can deeply be shared with their team members and the market.

The purpose fills the internal and external members' minds like smoke can fill a room. Think about how a scented candle saturates the room that it burns in. There is no getting away from it. If you step into the area, the smell is going to be there. When we have this level of clarity about the purpose of our team, they can really become powerful to provide value. If the purpose is designed to be destructive, it can be devastating as well. But when we do not have clarity, we might think of fifteen scented candles of different varieties burning in the same room.

What smell would you encounter? It would be a mixture of aromas that would not be discernible, and I expect that it would not be very pleasant. The smells would be lost in all the confusion. We can apply this concept of fifteen aromas to our daily walk. How many distractions will we encounter today? It might be worthwhile to reduce the number of candles you are burning. Does your purpose of the organization you belong to include growing your people? If your purpose were to include growing people, how attractive would it be to the marketplace of employees and future team members? I like that smell, and I bet employees and team members would find it attractive also.

I read a scripture and saw a word that resonated with me. The word was "permeate" in the passage from Luke 13:20-21. The idea that heaven can permeate every part of our lives is a big idea. Why do we keep heaven out of our business dealings, our checking accounts, or on the highway when others cut us off in traffic? We allow the aromas of life and sin to distract us, and when it happens life can stink. Sometimes we choose or allow others to choose the aroma of gelatin for ourselves. There is no smell, no aroma, which is like having no love and no joy in our lives. I do not object to eating gelatin, but I never choose it for the aroma because it does not have any. It is a choice, though.

Heaven can permeate our lives like the scent of a candle if we allow it. It requires us to be inspired to do it, though. We have a choice. We can choose to find God in everything. The yeast permeates the entire batch of dough, and it does not have a choice. The baker simply mixes it in, and the chemical reaction of the natural world takes over. I refuse to believe that God's design of the world requires me to keep heaven and the love that permeates it away from my every minute of existence.

I think of that skunk that lies on the roadway. Will I choose to run through the remains and live with the smell into the future, or will I choose to adjust my route? We make a choice of what we will give our attention to. On this day, will we choose to allow more of heaven's love to be part of our day or will we decide on something else. I vote for the smell of heaven over that of gelatin or that of the skunk. Choose wisely today.

Let us pray.

Heavenly Father, your grace is always enough. Help us to see through the lens that shows love and not hate. Remove our blinders that hide us from either of the two. Empower us to live fully in you and not only in the smell of the world. Guide us, Lord. In Jesus' name, we pray. Amen.

APRIL 10: AUTHORITY FOR THE DAY

As a leader there are times when it is important that we have authority. It is just as important to give away authority. Do we only get or give away authority, or could it be that it is lost, taken, sold, or stolen? I suspect that no one is excited about the idea of having their authority stolen. Someone else using your authority without your permission is stealing authority. Losing your authority can happen because we are being careless with it. Carelessness with authority can mean that one has begun to not value it. Celebrities sell their authority when they do endorsements for products and services. When businesses sell to new owners, there is certainly some authority to transact business with the old customers. The transferability of authority is important in the leadership arena.

For our people to grow over time we are likely going to reach a point where giving some authority will be critical. We might think of authority in the metaphor of a vineyard. Do you give someone fruit authority? That could be a combination of authority to harvest, eat or sell the fruit. We might give leaf authority. If you have leaf authority, you collect the light for photosynthesis. Losing one leaf will not destroy the vine. You might give pruning authority which changes where the leaves grow and what part of the vine will be allowed to flourish.

Not every available shoot of the vine is important to keep. Excess vines rob the main system of energy and nutrients. Then there is the root authority. These decisions made with this level of authority are those that can kill the vine. We can grant authority at any of these levels. The more we can give and grow authority towards the fruit the better our teams and families will perform. What is an authority that you believe you need to be given? What is an area of authority that you could benefit from by giving away?

As a follower of Jesus, we have been granted authority in many ways. We have received authority to love others when we feel like they are an enemy. We have received it to love others as much as we love ourselves. We have received it to use our unique talents and gifts to glorify God and build His kingdom here on earth. Are we using it to share the kingdom with those that do not know Him? These might be areas that come to the top of our minds when thinking about authority. But where are we not being intentional with authority.

In Joshua 2:1, we read about Joshua sending out two scouts to bring back information about the land of Canaan. The scouts wind up being pursued and rescued by a woman named Rahab. She hides them but does so only after negotiating with the scouts for her protection when they come back to conquer their land. I wonder if the scouts had the authority to grant this. As a leader, had Joshua given them the authority to do anything to help themselves survive capture?

Our leadership in our journey of faith will influence others. That includes encouraging them and empowering them to use the authority that Jesus has given them. The authority that Christ has given is power that we all have to remind one another to use. What authority are you failing to exercise because it might be a little uncomfortable to do so? Perhaps it is only your attitude that is keeping you from doing so. Just for today, consider being a little uncomfortable and share some of the authority Jesus has given you.

Let us pray.

Jesus, thank you for the authority you have given us. We accept the baton of authority as you have handed it to us. When our hands are full of authority in this world, we ask you to help to discard them if they distract us from you. Grant us new authority to glorify the Father. In Jesus' name, we pray. Amen.

APRIL 11: ASKING TOO MANY TIMES

I was at a business conference where I heard Les Brown. I heard his story of overcoming the large obstacles and hurdles throughout his life. He challenged the audience to always ask at least seven times to advance towards your biggest goals. Often things can happen easily when the ask is mundane. But for our largest goals, it is more difficult. Not only can entrepreneurs fail to advance towards the loftiest goals, but so can their teams. Where has your team stopped advancing? It just might be that they have given up and deemed the task unobtainable. But these challenges might be conquered by requiring us to simply count.

Have we looked at the challenge seven different ways? Have we asked how we can overcome seven different times? I can imagine that most teams make it past the second "ask" and maybe the third. But seven times seems unreasonable because we do not like rejection, so we seek easier tasks where we can get a yes. But the seventh yes is much more rewarding. Where have you or your team stopped short of the seventh ask? What will you do about advancing that goal in the next seven days?

Jesus was asked how many times one is to forgive. Was it seven? No, it was seventy times seven. We read that in Matthew 18:22 NLT. But I ask myself, "Have I forgiven even the first seven people that might have harmed me?" Can I say that I am not holding a grudge against another for more than seven hours, seven days or seven months? Can I say that I have forgiven someone seven different times? I am the one that continues to fall short of what Christ asked of me. Who am I to keep from forgiving even once? As brothers and sisters in Christ, it is always time to reach the seemingly magical power of forgiveness even if we must ask seven times.

Let us walk with our Lord seven times this week and maybe our focus can be on the opportunity to forgive the first seven times. Who can you forgive this week? Can you do it every day for seven days? If so, I will celebrate with you, and you can celebrate with me as well. Let us put a focus on forgiveness today and see what joy we might have when our head hits the pillow tonight. What is the first thing you can do about it in the next seven days?

Let us pray.

Jesus, come. Come today and help to soften my heart, especially on this day. May I feel the Holy Spirit with us, not once, but seven times. I ask for the blessings of forgiveness with my brothers and sisters no less than seven times. Like the sun will rise and set seven times in the next week, I want the joy of reaffirming love through forgiveness. Let us have an addition of love through the subtraction of forgiveness. Take it away, Lord, take it away. In Jesus' name, we pray. Amen.

APRIL 12: ONE SECRET TO KEEP AND ONE TO SHARE

Do you have trade secrets? Some businesses have an unfair competitive advantage, and they might call it a secret. These advantages are normally short lived, but many businesses strive to obtain them, to develop them and they can wind up shaping industries because of them. What does your team do to develop an unfair competitive advantage? If you are not working on that advantage, then you are closer to being a commodity than you might think. Few companies want their business products to become commoditized because then the product is about nothing more than price.

Whoever can deliver the product at the lowest price can wear you out quickly! But keep in mind that a secret which is based on harm is what I would call an illegal secret. An example would be stealing someone's idea or property. You have damaged or hurt another on purpose to get an advantage. That is not ethical. We define an unfair competitive advantage as a positive effect of your teams' synergies and intellectual capacity. It is not a result of harming others. Where can your team work on having an unfair competitive advantage? You might already have one and just not be using it effectively. I hope that you do have one and that your perspective has changed. What can you do in the next seven days to identify any unfair competitive advantage you might have?

In Luke 16:1-18, there is a great parable about serving two masters. Will we, as brothers and sisters in Christ, expect to develop our relationship with Christ first or will it be anything else? Will we seek an unfair competitive advantage which is Christ? When our secret advantage is Christ, we can grow our relationship without keeping it a secret. If we are growing anything else, it might be that there are activities involved that do not honor Christ. We want to move away from those secrets or activities. Those other secrets involve the world and our sin. They might even carry with them guilt and shame. Let us leave those others behind to only serve one master. Let that advantage be the guide to direct the rest of our worldly work. What is one area that you can change your leadership that will place Christ as Master? The week is before us, and we can shape a secret to share with those that we encounter. How can you do that this week?

Let us pray.

Heavenly Father, you know all and see all. You will be waiting for us at your heavenly gates and want nothing more than to share your love forever with us. Let us honor you today with our thoughts, words, and actions. May we love better, speak kinder, and be attentive to you first. You provide us with true comfort. May we rest in the palm of your hand, especially as we cast aside anything that we held as more important than you. Send your Holy Spirit to help move us forward. You are our unfair competitive advantage in dealing with the world. In Jesus' name, we pray. Amen.

APRIL 13: DO YOU HAVE A JOB DESCRIPTION?

Job descriptions are meaningful for employees and employers. Without a description, one can wander about an organization looking for activity without purpose. Is our purpose more important than a description of duties? I think we want our support teams to know why we make up a team and keep it working. We are less effective if isolated into a silo of activity without connection to a purpose. When we know the purpose, our job description is more likely to be amended. We are more flexible to the purpose instead of being set in our ways, and only our ways. If you are the owner or leader of an organization today, what is your purpose? It might not be the same as it was when you started your company. If you do not have your purpose identified with clarity, maybe others in your organization are struggling because of it. Regardless of whether you are an owner or not, what is the first thing you can do to create clarity with your purpose and your job description? What can you do today about that?

Jesus shared the parable of the rich man and Lazarus in Luke 16:19-31. The parable closes by sharing that if the people would not follow Moses and the prophets, that they will not even follow someone that rises from the dead. Maybe the parable is teaching us that as human beings, we can be stubborn. Our minds can get set upon what we experience, read, and are told. It can be difficult in this world to define our purpose because we have the old way and the new reborn way. Which purpose will we live out? As Christians, if we allow ourselves to only be defined by a job description, by what we experience, by what we read or are told, we will probably lead a shallow life. But our purpose has been shown by Christ. It is to follow him first and foremost.

That is our purpose. When we have that clearly set in our way of being, we can then fulfill, with great joy, the job descriptions of this world. Let us not allow what we read or experience to limit us with our purpose. Where might you believe you are limited in your faith because of a job description? Where have you limited others because of a job description you have placed on them? What is your larger purpose? How might you begin to reshape, with the help of others, what your limits are this week?

Let us pray.

Heavenly Father, you are limitless. We thank you for the blessings of this world and for our experiences. But we ask today that you help us to remove the limitations that we have placed on ourselves. Sometimes we set expectations before setting or checking our purpose first. When that happens, we can put the world and its priorities first instead of placing you first. Help us to lead a purposeful life. As brothers and sisters in Christ, might we help one another with Christian love. In Jesus' name, we pray. Amen.

APRIL 14: CAN YOU GIVE TEN?

We all like to be appreciated. That is what a thank you is at its deepest level. It is used as a part of our culture as a common courtesy though. Its value can easily be overlooked. A thank you is something that we can aim and strive for in business. As a leader, what do you think is your ratio of thank you's? What I mean to ask is a twofold question. The two questions are how many thank you's are our teams giving, and the other question is how many we are receiving. If our service and products are delivered in the most spectacular manner, we might have a very high ratio of customers giving us thanks. But there might be a correlation between the number that we are actually giving.

How many thank you's are we giving to our customers and to our teams? Those two answers create the thank you ratio. What is your thank you ratio for your entire organization? My organizations are better when we are increasing the ratio toward the giving side. Would your organization be a better, stronger, more attractive organization if the ratio were higher? What is the first thing you might do to increase that ratio?

On his way to Jerusalem, Luke tells us in chapter 17, that Jesus saw ten lepers standing at a distance. They were crying out to him, "Jesus, Master, have mercy on us!" Jesus reacted by healing them and sent them on to the priests where rituals of Jewish law would need to be followed. One of the lepers, after seeing he was healed, came back to Jesus, and fell at his feet thanking him for what he had done. Did you see the thank you ratio? It was one of ten? It is interesting to me that only 10% thanked Jesus for this miraculous healing.

As followers of Christ, we are saved from our sins. We have all the reasons in the world, that is all our sins, to be thankful for Christ's sacrifice. When we awaken in the morning, are we thankful and appreciative of the day? When the sun has crossed the sky and we lay our heads to rest, will we close the day with thanks again? Will we choose to be with the nine lepers that chose not to thank God for the miracles of the day? What are you thankful for today? Maybe we can improve our personal ratio of thankfulness. What is the first thing you can do to make that improvement?

Let us pray.

Heavenly Father, we thank you for the creation of the world and for our ability to be in relationship with each other. Jesus, we thank you for your sacrifice on the cross to be in relationship with us. Holy Spirit, we are thankful that you touch us here in our world with the breath of God. May our relationships with one another be full of thanks. We thank you as we grow with you through the difficulties of this world. Guide us, Lord. In Jesus' name, we pray. Amen.

APRIL 15: CAN CURIOSITY KILL COMPLACENCY?

Curiosity kills complacency, not cats. As a leader or entrepreneur, your team probably has routines and systems that it uses. The use of them quickly creates habits as our brains create neural networks as we learn. But as valuable as these habits are, they are also restrictive. They hold our value proposition where it is set today. They do not advance or grow future value. A farmer who plants a field will experience a crop because of how much water, sun, and nutrients the plants can use. The repetition from year to year will get the same result which is a crop. But to have exponential growth there must be an intervention. There must be a point where we stop to be curious about what is normal.

Normal is the habit. It is the past. It is the commodity approach. But curiosity is the intervention. It has a future based impact. It is the exponential growth approach. To accelerate collaboration, we can use curiosity to explore possibilities for the leader and the team. Where might you be stuck in the past as a leader with habits? The results of those habits could be just what your team might be putting value on and be delivering. Changing the habit's results is a change of value. Where might it be time to challenge yourself this week by being curious?

As Christians, we live life with our habits as well. Some of our habits help us to draw closer to Jesus while others do not. But our set of habits will draw us to different depths. We are susceptible to the same limitations of habits in our faith as other areas of life.

> "Yes, it will be 'business as usual' right up to the day when the Son of Man is revealed."
>
> LUKE 17:30 NLT

We have the power today to be curious now. Being curious in our faith journey might allow us to study the Bible more, read a devotion, or attend worship without any excuse. It takes an intervention though. Where do you want to grow this year? Maybe all we need to do is to be curious for a little bit to break the cycle. I would bet that if Jesus came today, it would get our attention and our sense of curiosity would allow us to change the pattern of our activity. So why wait? I am curious. How would you answer the question, "I wonder how one could enhance their prayer life for just one day?" The only thing stopping us from doing something new is ourselves. Something new can start with a session of curiosity. What is the first thing that you can do in the next seven days?

Let us pray.

Heavenly Father, your wonders are shared with us on your terms. It is often that we do not hear the small still voice. Sometimes we can miss the obvious lightening and thunderous moments of our life in Christ. Help us to be able to step aside for a moment and be curious about Christ. Let us be curious as to how to be more compassionate, more loving, and how to grow our relationships with him. Thank you for giving us a sense of curiosity. May we use our curiosity to glorify your name. I wonder how you will touch me and my sphere of influence today? We pray that you do so. In Jesus' name, we pray. Amen.

APRIL 16: THERE IS A FREEDOM FORMULA

There are times in business that we must stop. Campaigns run their course; they stop. Products are no longer in demand, so we must stop stocking them. Technology advances and old technology becomes irrelevant; we stop using it. If you have a fleet of vehicles in your business, it is possible that you have fuel storage. Imagine if you changed the vehicles from gas to diesel fuel. If your fuel supplier continued to deliver gasoline, I imagine that you might say STOP. But how often do we really take a deep look at our activities to determine their effectiveness?

We get comfortable with our systems and ways of doing business. When that happens, we begin to let the market control us. There might be larger value where we decide we should stop. Successful companies usually are the ones that constantly look at themselves and determine where they need to stop something. When was the last time your business stopped something? When was the last time your team stopped something? Did the market force the stop? Did a competitor cause you to stop? Was it legislation that caused the stop? Why? Where might an area exist that could be vulnerable because you have not specifically looked? It is better that you look at it yourself instead of the market making you look at it. Who can help you to look at that and bring objectivity? Want to experience some freedom and opportunity, consider what you might stop.

As a Christian, we always have an answer to count on, our Savior and Lord Christ Jesus. As we live our lives there are areas where we will sin. We know it is best to stop. But just like companies and teams, we can find it difficult to stop. Often, we must have some outside factor or influence to cause the interruption to our activity. The compulsive gambler might have to go bankrupt before admitting he has a problem. The alcoholic might have a third driving under the influence infraction before they seek counseling. But there is an idea just as important as the stop idea. It is the idea to never stop.

In Luke 18, Jesus tells the story to the disciples to never stop praying. Never. When things are good, we pray. When things do not look so good, we pray. When things are terrible, we pray. The parable is about a persistent woman seeking justice from a judge. It is almost like she whines and whines and whines until the judge finally gives in. But our Father in heaven does not want our whining, he wants our hearts and souls. He wants us to pour it all out, the good and the bad, all of it in prayer. He wants it all at the foot of the cross. Where do you need to take something and lay it at the feet of the Lord? Where do you need to yell at the top of your lungs, I surrender? Where do you need to give it up, finally, once and for all? It can start right now. The cross is waiting so would you like to lay something there today? Go ahead, there is room at the foot of the cross. Freedom will find you there.

Let us pray.

Jesus, at your feet we bow our heads. We come to praise you and thank you for the compassion you have for us. We thank you for the cross and the sacrifice that you have given to us. We have not and never will earn it. Jesus, in the good and bad, we want to find nothing else but you. We come to sing your name and glorify the gifts that you have shared with so many. We come as well to cry. We come to scream and yell at the top of our lungs. We want you to be the one to take away our pains, our fears, and our troubles. We pray for them to stop! In Jesus' name, we pray. Amen.

APRIL 17: WHO IS YELLING? YOU OR THE TEAM?

I once knew of a story about a blind man. It goes like this. A blind man goes to a dentist to get his sight repaired, and he leaves with a cavity filled. I do not believe that is good service. But how would a blind man go to a dentist in the first place? It might have been that the dentist's message going out to the world was not the right message. If we do not have the right message being delivered, it is likely to miss the right audience we want to do business with. This can happen as easily with internal messages with employees as it can with our audience of potential clients and customers. Where have your messages been unclear in the last week or month? Look for areas of frustration as a clue. It might be that it was your message or the communication link.

When frustration occurs, the attitudes we wish to employ can get hijacked. Although the desired attitudes are available, they are not used because of the hijacked status that frustration has achieved. Curiousness can remove some of the power of the hijacker. I wonder what would remove our frustration the quickest. Developing a clear message to the right audience is a great way to avoid the frustration in the first place. What can you do to remove an old message completely and start a new, more effective one today?

There are many stories in the Bible of miraculous hearings. Did Jesus just walk around the earth and anything that he could place His eyes on was healed? Was He like a superhero from a comic book? Jesus sees something, puts His hands out, points and says be healed? That was not the norm as we know it. It might have happened sometimes. But I want us to focus on the story of the blind man who is healed as Jesus is on His way to Judah. He tells the disciples they are headed to Judah.

A crowd is surely with them. As they are on the trip, a blind man hears the people passing. He asks what is going on and is told that Jesus of Nazareth is coming. It is time for the most important message of his life. The blind beggar needs to have a clear message with this audience. He needs to be heard so he begins to yell. He is hushed by the crowd, but he will not allow his message to be stopped, so he continues yelling.

In Like 18:43 NLT we read, "Son of David, have mercy on me!" Jesus stopped and began to be in relationship with him. "What do you want?" he asked, and the blind man said, "I want to see." He was healed and followed Jesus immediately.

Where has your message in your witness to others not been clear? Where in your relationships have you been receiving unclear messages and working with frustration because of it? Let us work on our messages for the next seven days and leave some of the frustration we cause behind. What is the first message you need to clean up and can you deliver a new one in the next seven days?

Let us pray.

Heavenly Father, I thank you for the rain that falls to the earth and the scent of renewal. Today I will praise your Holy name and live in wonder. I pray that the messages that I deliver this week will be as clear as those that the beggar spoke to Jesus along the road. May we be strong enough in our relationships to validate the messages we receive which are not clear. Help us in our efforts to obey your message to follow you. Comfort us, Lord, as we stretch to do our best. In Jesus' name, we pray. Amen.

APRIL 18: WHAT ARE YOU WILLING TO TRIPLE PARK FOR?

As a leader, how do you greet the day? Imagine the scene of the arrival doors at the airport. In your mind's eye, you can see the slow-moving traffic and the incredible excitement in the atmosphere. There are smiles, anticipation, hugs, and waves. Overall, it is a happy place and people are excited. Makes me realize that every day is an opportunity to choose. Can you relate to that feeling of the anticipated arrival? Do we meet every morning like we meet the arrivals at the airport? What would our teams be able to do with a little extra quickness in our step?

What will they feel as they see our face, and we shoot them a smile with a generous wave? That sounds like a great way to greet our teams at the house, office, store, or plant. That sounds like a great way to greet those around us as we awaken and as we move from place to place. How will you choose to greet the day? Our focus can start the day and finish it, but it might start with our choice. What will you choose to start the week?

As Christians, this arrival gate excitement might help us to imagine what it was like at the feeding of the five thousand. In Matthew 14:13-21, we read about the event. Can you imagine the excitement as Christ arrived? Do you think that people would double park, maybe even triple park, if they knew that Christ was about to arrive any minute? I think that they would be jockeying around one another to get close and find him. When they did, would they have a frown or a face of excitement?

The absolute truth is that I have news about an arrival! Christ is coming. His arrival could be at any minute, but if we do not see Him in the next minute, He has sent His love and example for us until that time. So, we get to choose. Will we do as He asked us to do and show an attitude of love towards ourselves and one another? Will we shoot smiles to one another with a generous wave? Will we continue to shoot bullets in the form of words of hate, or even actual bullets and wave weapons of destruction?

Brothers and sisters, choose and choose wisely today, for the airplane has departed and is on the way. We have received the information about the departure, and the question now is whether we are going to meet the plane. What is the focus you will start the week with? How will you carry it through in the next seven days?

Let us pray.

Jesus, you came and taught us why God loves us. Not only did you teach us the why of God, but you showed us how to love one another. We pray today that we make this day a day of arrival. A day where we greet others in love. A day where we begin to make a generous wave the norm and not the exception. A day where the smiles outnumber the frowns. A day where we take comfort in the palm of God's hands and compassion instead of what we think comforts us here in the world. In Jesus' name, we pray. Amen.

APRIL 19: DO YOU WANT YOUR KEYS BACK?

Keys lock and unlock things. They are security for us. We have keys to secure things in certain places so upon our return we will know where everything is. At your place of business, I bet that you have at least one key. A physical retailer like my hometown hardware store locks the doors at closing, for example. The next day someone shows up and unlocks the front door with a key so customers can walk in to transact business. They unlock the gates to the lumber storage. They unlock the ice chest out front of the store. They unlock the safe where the petty cash is held, and they unlock the computer with their password keys.

But we are better as part of a team. I ask you who have you given keys to? Are you the only one with a key to something, or are you sharing your keys with others? If you have something so valuable that you are the only one with a key, I challenge you to ask yourself just how valuable it is if you cannot share it. If you are the only one with access, it means you are limiting its value. Keeping it to yourself carries a cost of not sharing. That means it has a price. Why not share it so that it might become priceless? Where might you be holding onto a key tightly? Could it be that your grip is causing pain and fatigue? It very well could restrict the growth of your business, your team, and your value proposition. What key will you release your grip on this week?

Do you remember Zacchaeus from the story in Luke 1:1 NLT? "You come down now" is what I think might be going through your mind right now. But I want to focus on his keys—but not his keys to his door or lock box. You see he had a very tight grip on his wealth key. He was known as a sinner among the people. He was a tax collector who we assume took more than what he was to collect, and he kept the overage. Maybe he believed he had to pay for medical care or maybe he needed a bigger house, a fancier robe, or stronger mule, horse, or donkey. Maybe he just wanted the best sandals that his wealth could buy.

So, he gripped his money key tightly and he locked it up securely. But as he took his perch in the tree to see the Nazarene pass by, Jesus called him down and they went to dinner. They broke bread together at Zacchaeus' house regardless of what everyone else was thinking. And what happened was a miracle. Zacchaeus loosened his grip on his key because Christ shared his key, the security of eternal life with him. When we unlock our grip, and we share the keys, we give the opportunity to be in relationship with others to unlock their doors. We give them the opportunity to share what it is that they believe is valuable. We give them a chance to create something priceless.

What key are you holding onto so tightly that you have not shared it with anyone in your faith journey? Maybe it could be that it is time to share your keys with someone else in your life. If you think Christ doesn't know about it, you are probably wrong. Maybe the first person to share our most valuable keys with is Christ. What key will you share in the next seven days?

Let us pray.

Heavenly Father, you have provided to us the keys to heaven by giving us your Son, Jesus, the Christ. Help us to share the keys that we hold so dearly. Unlock us so that others might experience love, joy, and compassion. Make our keys more valuable when we share them with others. Hold us from harm as we do so. In Jesus' name, we pray. Amen.

APRIL 20: THE LIMIT OF INEXPERIENCE AND WISDOM

Most businesses and organizations are made up of teams. Many teams that have experienced members have the benefit of wisdom on their side. That wisdom can be of unmeasurable benefit when delivering value to your customers and clientele. Think about your teams and put those people in your mind's eye. We appreciate what they bring to our teams and especially the wisdom. But now I want to ask you to go to the other spectrum. Who are those without experience on your teams? Teams that have both the fresh perspective of inexperience and the wisdom of experience have many perspectives to share. Many times, holding wisdom or sharing it only with others that are wise does not maximize the use of wisdom. Where in your company might you have restricted the use of your intellectual wisdom by isolating those that hold wisdom from the inexperienced?

What is the first thing that might bring value to your organization by reorganizing the wisdom? Wisdom is not like salt that can be spread on a snow-covered sidewalk. It is limited in its ability to spread. One does not just grab some and throw it out. Spreading wisdom requires intentionality. What can you do in the next seven days to spread the wisdom of your team members?

If you needed to get a task done today that involved using a donkey, would you use a young one or an old one? It seems to me that an older donkey would be wiser and have more training to be able to help. I think of the reputation of donkeys as being stubborn and correlate that to the idea of a younger donkey. A young donkey that has not been trained or broken, to use a cowboy term, might be rambunctious. It might tend to do what it wants and not the task that needs accomplished. Do you recall which kind of donkey Jesus sent the disciples to get for his ride into Jerusalem? Are you thinking of a young one? In Mark 11:7, Jesus told them that they would find a young donkey and they were to bring it. Are you kidding me?

Jesus is going to make his triumphant ride on an untrained, maybe never been broken animal of stubborn character! Then again, Jesus knows how to use the wisdom of the Father and bring love to the world. Why not use the inexperienced, the lowest and least to make a difference in the world? That is what he does with me, and that is what he does with you. We do not deserve to be used by him. We do not and cannot do anything to make us so that we have earned his love and compassion because it is offered and given by him regardless.

We do not have to be trained for the trail or the ride, we just have to be willing to come along. We must be willing to believe and follow the directions that he is giving. Where might you consider yourself to have been stubborn in the last month? Where might we allow ourselves to be led in the next seven days? Will we allow the wisdom of others to blend in with our inexperience?

Let us pray.

Jesus, you rode in on the back of the inexperienced. You spent your time with the sick, the hurting, the lacking, the needy. We ask today that you help us by bringing those with wisdom to us. Help us to be in relationships in our world with those that are different from ourselves. Make us at times be your servants who lack wisdom but know your love. At other times, make us to be the ones who have the wisdom to share with someone who needs to hear a special word or thought learned from you. Guide us today, Lord. In Jesus' name, we pray. Amen.

APRIL 21: DO YOU COUNT TO THREE IN YOUR MIND?

Sometimes you just want people to do their job. It can be tempting to think or say, "just do it" and throw your hands up in frustration. As an entrepreneur and leader, we can have trouble delegating. Many have started companies themselves and done almost every job there is to do in the company. Therefore, we can believe, right or wrong, that we know how to do the job. But knowing and reality are different, and when you add communication to the mix the whole issue of delegating can be jeopardized. Sometimes we just need to take a break and count to three? You know, like you have heard parents do with children. I am going to count to three Jimmy, and I expect you to be here with me by the end or else! But counting to three is not the way to build stronger relationships. It is a very authoritative way to operate.

We can often do better by using three concepts to further drive our delegation: sharing the why, what, and how. Why do we exist as a team? What is it that we do? How do we get it accomplished? If you cannot motivate an employee or team member by reminding them of the why, what, and how then it is probably time to find them another team or organization. Everyone is valuable but that does not mean that everyone can be a valuable enough resource to be on your team.

Our team members must be able to find a place where they might be able to contribute as a member. Where have you been short this last week as leader? Another way to ask is where have you counted to three? What would be the result if you went to extend the conversation and had it in the framework of why, what, and how? We can be accountable whether leading or following to remember all three. Would that be a good use of your investment in the people on your team?

In the Bible, Joshua, like Moses, as he prepared to leave this world, gathered the tribal leaders and addressed them to remind them to follow God. He had been told by Moses that the people would not follow and do what they were supposed to do. But Joshua did not count to three, he focused on the why, what, how. Where have we been short over the last week in our relationships that did not honor Christ? Have we been tempted to assume that everyone on our team knows or is remembering why our organization exists?

Team members should know what it is that we do to create value and their part in the processes in how we go about doing it. We can do this with our faith community, in our neighborhoods and in our homes with family. The challenge is that we are human, and we sin. We fall short and through Christ have the benefit of living with the grace of God. Jesus and the benefit of grace is a big part of our why. Where can you share the why, what, and how this week instead of the one, two, three? I think our families and faith communities will appreciate it when we set the example.

Let us pray.

Heavenly Father, we are thankful that you love us enough to have shared the why with us. We know that the way to you is through your son Jesus Christ. Help us to share the why with our brothers and sisters in Christ here on the earth and in the relationships that we have. Help us to share the why message with those that do not have a relationship with Christ yet. Make our words reflect your why instead of our excuses. Remove the excuses of why we have not achieved excellence and guide us to execution. When we fail to execute our why, we come to ask your forgiveness again. Thank you for not counting to three, Lord. In Jesus' name, we pray. Amen.

APRIL 22: GREAT STONES OR BAD BRICKS?

We make many choices daily in our finances, in our faith, in our relationships, and in our businesses. We also live with the results of the choices that we have made in the past. While the effects of the past choices still are with us, we will have more choices to face tomorrow. They just keep coming at us. It is like the choices build up a foundation for us. Each decision is like stone after stone being added to the foundation. When we make a decision which turns out to be a bad one, we need to address how it will affect the foundation. Do you leave the stone in the foundation as it is? Or maybe we need to give it some extra attention to make sure that we strengthen its part in the structure. We might add some mortar around it or change the stones that might sit atop of it on the foundation so that the foundation maintains its overall stability.

Sometimes we need to remove the decision entirely and work on that part to get it back to structural security again. As an entrepreneur or leader, where do you have any stones that need removed in your foundation? It is best to address them sooner rather than later. The longer you wait the more the foundation and the stones built upon it are going to settle. But the foundation will not be secure. The stability of the foundation is likely to falter under times of stress which could jeopardize the entire organization. In the next seven days, what is the first thing you can do to remove a stone and replace it with a secure decision?

As brothers and sisters following Christ, we make foundational decisions as well. We effect our relationship with Christ, our families, and our churches like stone after stone being added. The good news is that when we add a bad stone here, that Christ has died on the cross for that stone. We are forgiven, that is, if the cornerstone has been laid in our own lives. Jesus is willing to help personally repair us as we repair or replace stones in our foundation. In the Old Testament, Joshua closes his chapter of life by reminding the people of the stones laid by the decisions of God which have influenced their lives. He challenged the people to remember the foundation laid and stated boldly that, "But as for me and my house, we will serve the Lord."

That statement is a call and question to us today as well. As we make decisions today, how will they serve Jesus, and how will they build a strong foundation. What decision can you make today that will impact your foundation? Do you need to go into your foundation and address some stones? It is not too late to repair or replace. Do not wait as the foundation needs to be solid moving into the future. Where might you be able to come alongside someone that is asking for help with their foundation? Where are you making decisions in the next seven days that are foundational in nature? Are we asking Jesus if they are adding stability to the foundation that is in place?

Let us pray.

Jesus, thank you for the cross. You are the cornerstone of my life and my foundation. Assist me in placing the stones of my foundation in alignment with you. I want to choose my stones wisely to withstand the times of uncertainty of this world. Let the winds of time blow. Let the rain pound against it. Let the earth shake. Let others attack my foundation, but we can withstand it all because of you. On solid rock, we stand. In Jesus' name, we pray. Amen.

APRIL 23: YES, NO, MAYBE

How important is consistency? It is critical. When we understand that, there are certain things we can do to advance excellence in our lives as entrepreneurs. How do you start your day or your business's day? It either starts in an excellent manner or it does not. We might not give it any thought sometimes, but you set the tone for the balance of the day, every day when you do that. How do you close your day? It happens every day because you must rest personally even if your business is open 24 hours. You cannot avoid the close of your day. What do you do consistently to close your day? Consider where the weakest part of your business systems or delivery is. I would bet that if you ask your friends, employees, or customers that they would say it might be that the team is consistently there in that weakness. But in knowing that, you have the greatest opportunity to fix it.

What might be your weakness is someone else's or some other teams' strength. By adding to your team, you might find solutions to work past weaknesses. Just because you are an entrepreneur does not mean you have to be doing it by yourself. As leaders, will we choose to be consistently weak and fail to deliver maximum value, or would you rather not? To believe that the failure in the cycle of consistency will somehow be broken by wishful thinking is penny wise and pound foolish. Where have you or the team been consistently frustrated, non-performing, and weak? Who can you work with to address it in the next seven days? Where have you been consistently value driven? How can you do more of that in the next seven days? What is the first thing you can do about it?

Jesus led an amazing life and miraculous healings occurred all around him. He taught wherever he went as the disciples and the crowds followed. But the Bible shares a life with the consistency of Jesus' actions. I love what it says about his days in Jerusalem during Holy Week. In Luke 21:37-38, we read that every day he went to the temple to teach, and each evening he returned to the Mount of Olives. The crowds gathered at the temple early each morning to hear him.

Can you hear the consistency? Think big, boldly, and broadly about where you are not being consistent in your life. No one needs to tell you where it is. You are likely able to see it and know where it is happening. What might occur if we invite Christ to be able to join us in those moments to bring us his consistency? We can rely on Jesus to allow his methods to impact our methods. Sometimes all it takes is for us to stop and invite him to those moments. When we choose to collaborate with highly consistent people in our faith, we can trust that Jesus may set the bar at a different level of success. When we allow our consistency to be broken, we settle. I do not want to settle when it comes to my relationship with Jesus. What about you? What is the first thing that you can do in the next seven days?

Let us pray.

Jesus, you are always consistent. Your love never leaves us as you continue to share your love through your word and through your people. In our weakness, we leave you. Our inconsistency separates us from you, and often we feel loss and pain when that occurs. Help us to be more consistent in our lives so that like you, going to the temple and returning to the mount, we too can share in your love. Help us to enhance love by being in relationship with others, especially when they can bring their value to grow in you. In Jesus' name, we pray. Amen.

APRIL 24: HIDDEN TREASURES CAN BE FOUND

Unseen resources can be out of sight and out of mind. The air conditioning system at your place of business is out of sight, but you probably know when it is not working. You can sense when the climate you are operating in is not the right fit. But what about the resources that each of our team members have? Think about the experience, the trust, the education, and wisdom that they have. Those resources are unseen but might be the most important resources we have. The attitudes of our team members may just be the most important resource that they possess. They affect the creation and shaping of our products, services and the value we provide. They affect the delivery as well. Often there is nothing more destructive to the value we deliver to our customers than a bad attitude.

Could it be that there is nothing more valuable and important than a positive and encouraging attitude? Where might your customers be better served by checking on the attitudes of your team and self? Where have you restricted your value with your attitude to your team? The attitude of the leader sets the tone for the organization. What can you do in your organization in the next seven days about the unseen resources?

There is a radio station organization with the tagline "positive and encouraging." In Ephesians, the church is described as having the wisdom of God displayed by the unseen rulers and authorities. You can find that in chapter 3:10-11. We all possess unseen resources that might be used by God. All of us. Do you think of yourself in this manner? It is true, God has shared his wisdom. The people that we are in community with want to help us, and they need your help as well.

What unseen resource do you possess? It might not be that difficult to see the power when we think about the days that our attitudes have been lacking the positive effect we desire. What could you do to share an attitude in a way to honor Christ? Could the world be a better place if we ask Jesus this week to help us share our resources with one another? I think so. It might be the unseen attitude that can affect others the most.

Giving a gift out of anger, which is an attitude, will not be received like a gift given with respect, love, and appreciation. Unseen resources can be incredibly valuable, and we sometimes do not give them much credibility or importance. What unseen resources can you ask for, and which ones can you give in the next seven days?

Let us pray.

Jesus, God has made us in his image. We have attitudes and talents that are unseen and hidden. Help us to discover them and to help us bring you, the light of the world, to shine before us. Let each of us display the wisdom that you can send through us. In Jesus' name, we pray. Amen.

APRIL 25: LOOKING FOR CONTRAILS?

Do you remember seeing the water stream of vapor behind some airplanes or rockets? They do not last forever and in fact their existence is very short. They do not add to the flight or experience for the passengers or crew. I do not think that the staff at the terminal are concerned about them in the slightest. They are worthless to the airline company. But let us challenge that perspective of being worthless. I believe that the contrail is valuable to us on the ground as we look at them. We notice them when we are not traveling by plane. It is a reminder of when we traveled or when we might again. It is a reminder that people are moving, that technology helps us, and that the world is smaller than it used to be.

How often do you witness a plane flying in the air without a contrail? I think it is easier to notice a plane when it has left a contrail. It might be especially true if it is one that has been expanded by the drifting winds or breezes. How is your business leaving a contrail? If it is not leaving a trail behind it, then it might be missing the opportunity to have your message impact others with little effort. A bigger question is what personal contrail are you leaving behind for your employees and team members?

Employers and leaders that leave a contrail are more likely to be noticed. They can leave a better legacy or witness a better value. Where might your efforts and energies not be contributing to your contrail? Who can help you shape it if it is not the way you want it to look? What will you do about it in the next seven days?

As a follower of Jesus Christ, we can be asking ourselves today, "What contrail am I leaving behind me?" It might be that I am sharing the word of God. I might be bringing people to Christ. So, am I or am I not leaving a trail? Are you or are you not leaving a contrail? Jesus left us quite a contrail to follow.

> "Let your light shine before others, that they may see your good deeds and glorify your Father in heaven."
>
> MATTHEW 5:16

It is important to leave a contrail that glorifies the Father. It can start with a focus on a Sabbath day of rest and worship. Preparing our hearts and minds to connect with God sets the stage and starts a contrail that can last for the balance of the week. The start of that trail catches the eye and can keep Jesus at the top of our mind. When Jesus is at the top of our mind the opportunity to love even our enemies seems achievable. It can be just as transforming as the airplane engines are to the sky. With the plane we see a clear sky, then a plane, and then a contrail. With our focus on Christ, we can see hatred, then see ourselves obeying Christ, and then the effects of love will follow. Where might we work this week to improve how our activities glorify the Father? Is there anything more important than glorifying him?

Let us pray.

Heavenly Father, you are the pilot of the world. It is your creation, and we give thanks for our role in it. Help us we pray, to bring the attention to you, to glorify your love for us and those that follow Christ. May we this week pay attention to where we are headed and what our activities are. May the effects of our path bring others to you. Use our contrails for your love as we can be instruments in the world to reach others. In Jesus' name, we pray. Amen.

APRIL 26: OUR BIGGEST COMPETITOR IS OURSELVES

Businesses are always in competition. Sometimes the competition is internal between departments battling for parts of the budget. They can also be in competition in the marketplace with a product or service from another provider. But as owners, we face a different kind of competition as well. The competition of the needs of our families versus the needs of the business. These personal needs of the family can even be in direct conflict with one another from time to time. When that occurs, decisions will be made, and they are likely to occasionally lead to a feeling of guilt somewhere. The decisions that lead to a feeling of guilt might be the most difficult. Regardless of how beneficial the result might be, the guilt needs addressed. It needs to be reconciled.

We also need to be mindful that our customers and other businesses could be suffering through guilt as well. Guilt is a saboteur in many ways, but it certainly is to our mindset. As leaders, our ability to recognize guilt and to develop a process for reconciliation might change our family, team, and organization. If we reconcile any guilt quickly, our purpose can get back on track quicker for better results. Where might you be feeling some guilt because of your decisions of the past? What can you do in the next seven days to reconcile it? Our focus can be distracted when guilt is being a saboteur. What is the first step?

As brothers and sisters in Christ, we know the power of forgiveness. We also know the robbing power of guilt. It drains us of energy and love. It keeps us from being close with Jesus. It says in Proverbs,

---

"Fools make fun of guilt, but the godly acknowledge it and seek reconciliation."

PROVERBS 14: 9 NLT

Let us focus on acknowledging our own guilt and ask to be reconciled. When we have it, we can feel like it is a great chasm that we think we can ignore. Ignoring it does not make it go away. The judgment can stop when you are reconciled. So just how long will you wait for reconciliation? Where was the guilt in your last week?

Perhaps we can find some small starting point and get practiced at the process of reconciling. We would be wise to remember that our brains want to be right. Being guilty means that we were not right at some point. That is what allows our subconscious mind to ignore it, which tolerates it instead of reconciling it. It wants to forget we were wrong. The brain does not want to focus on the wrongs, it always wants to be right. Our neural pathways in the brain can change, though. Research has proven that. Are we willing to take the first step for ourselves to be reconciled? What is the first step you can take in the next seven days?

Let us pray.

Heavenly Father, we fall short constantly. We remove ourselves from you with our actions, thoughts, and words. We acknowledge that we fall short but affirm that you are always there. We come to you now. We are taking the first step to being reconciled with you. Help us each step of the way along this path. In Jesus' name, we pray. Amen.

APRIL 27: TICKETS AND BACKSTAGE PASSES

How many people are connected to your entrepreneurial team? It is an easy question, but it is more difficult than you think. Go ahead, take some time to think about your answer before you read on. Your count is probably too low. Did you remember to count the customer and his family? What about your business-to-business associates that support your value proposition, your vendors, accountant, bookkeeper, attorneys, and insurance people? We have internal and external team members regardless of whether you work with a for profit or not-for-profit enterprise. There is a lot going on backstage. We can look at the delivery of your product or service as being delivered on the front stage. The rest of the team is backstage or offstage and out of the building.

The basic concept of front stage and backstage is one that I learned from Strategic Coach. Does everyone who is backstage come out to deliver the performance? The answer is no, they probably do not. We might bring them out occasionally. Is there anyone on stage currently who does not need to be there? We might ask who we should bring on stage occasionally. Everyone likes to be appreciated somehow.

Is there any value in bringing people onto the stage? If not, then we are not maximizing the value for the clients when extras are there. On which stage do you maximize your value? Where are you spending most of your time, front, back, or off stage? What can you do about it over the next seven days?

In the book of Judges, we read about a prophet named Gideon. A favorite story from Gideon is something that relates to the resources we have and use. Gideon was sent to fight a king. At first, Gideon has a large force with him, God has him send back anyone scared, but that still leaves a bunch of people on the front stage for battle. He sends some more back by sorting the people by how they drink their water. As a result of the separation, he has a bunch of people backstage and just what is needed on the front stage.

God wanted the minimum on the stage so that he would be glorified, not Gideon. In our relationship and walk with Jesus, where are we on the stage when we should not be? I think in the early days of our relationship we might have been scared to take the stage when we needed to be there. But we need to remember who the Director is and how to glorify and honor Him.

Where might you be hanging back when you should not be? We need to watch and pay close attention to our calls to be on the stage as well. Both are important to honor Christ. What do you think an adjustment to front, back, and off-stage activity can change? Change the limit. What is the first thing you will do about it today?

Let us pray.

Jesus, you are the star of the show. You have asked us to be part of the cast. Help us to hear your call to come on stage as needed to honor you. Make our work on stage and off be so that we might become in relationship with the lost and bring them to you. In Jesus' name, we pray. Amen.

APRIL 28: WHAT'S NEW?

So, what is new in your business or on your team? You have had and added great thoughts, wonderful people, acquired resources, technologies, better tools, and systems in the past. But what is new so far, this year? If we are not adding something on a continual basis, we could be slowing or stopping our growth. Have you reviewed any of the new ideas from the start of the year? Doing that alone might create something new.

Keeping a continuous newness of thought process in place challenges us to stretch. It is especially valuable with those items that we are comfortable with. It is a great exercise. If you are not growing, you are decaying. Where have you seen those fresh green sprouts of spring in your business so far? If we do not stop and be accountable to measure and review, our minds will allow us to be comfortable and remain in a status quo state.

When the sprouts of spring show up, it is because they have received some water and experienced a temperature change. You must add water if you are going to grow a plant. As a leader, we need to be accountable to monitor for the new shoots on our teams, products, and services as well.

We add water or accountability to assist in the growing process. If you have seen some sprouts, what can you do to nourish and water their potential? If you have not seen any new areas, what can you do about that in the next seven days?

Jesus came on the scene as something new. He was inspirationally new daily to all those that had not encountered him. He continued his teaching daily and amazed the people that He encountered. His newness is so inspiring that He sprouted fresh green growth in you and me here some two thousand years after His death. Even after He left the earth, His focus on the "new" still changes people today in our world.

So, what about you? If we are to follow Jesus as his disciples, is it possible that we too can inspire others to something new? Where are you being a new person this year? Are you growing in your faith, in your love, in your relationship with Christ and the world? When pain or suffering have our attention, our growth might be stifled, but it does not have to be that way. Christ made a way for us to do something new.

> "Let this be written for a future generation, that a people not yet created may praise the Lord."
>
> PSALM 102:18 NIV

What do you want to become new in your life? Who can be in a new relationship with Christ because of you? The biggest obstacle to the new items in our lives, including our faith, is normally ourselves. Perhaps you need an accountability partner who will love you, not be judgmental, and provide you with some occasional accountability water. What are you going to do in the next seven days to find something new?

Let us pray.

Heavenly Father, we thank you for all things new. Make our eyes and hearts open to something new today. Make the winter of our hearts be filled with the freshness of the new of spring. Make the spring rains wash away the distance between ourselves and Jesus. Guide us to seek out the newness of the day. In Jesus' name, we pray. Amen.

APRIL 29: DEPUTIZE YOUR AUTHORITY

With ownership of a business enterprise comes authority. But that authority is irrelevant unless we put it to use or put it into action. If you are authorized to manufacture fishing poles, nothing happens until you get the plant and resources put together to do exactly that. Sometimes we need authority to be granted to keep people from harming others as well. But sometimes people use authority to keep people from doing good. Authority can develop a power complex in the ego of the one authorized. It can be a tough balance. But authority used for people to do good is the exponential use of authority. It is an exponential way of thinking.

Authority used to delegate and to empower others can be awesome. It helps others and helps society to grow exponentially and is the best use of authority. So, how are we choosing to use our authority? Where are we using our authority recklessly or in a hurtful or demeaning manner? Where are we not using our authority at all? Where are we using our authority to help others grow exponentially? I am curious, what is the first thing you can do this week to grant authority for someone else to grow exponentially?

As followers of Jesus Christ, we know where the ultimate authority comes from. But that authority has come to earth and has been distributed.

> "Jesus called his twelve disciples together and gave them authority to cast out evil spirits and to heal every kind of disease and illness."
>
> MATTHEW 10:1 NLT

It was not used for bad. It was not held and used to keep others useless or powerless. You have been granted authority to share the Savior Jesus. We have been given the word to share with others so that we might be in action and in a Christian loving relationship as His church.

What are you doing with your authority? Businesses grant different levels of authority throughout their organizations, and God has granted each of us some authority as well. What will you do with it this week? He did not give it to us to sit on the shelf and gather dust but grants it so that His love can grow exponentially. Where will you use the authority from Him, for Him, in the next seven days?

Let us pray.

The skies are clear, and the sun has risen. Once again, the day is new, and we awaken from the darkness and come into the light. Just as you sent Jesus into the world to be the light, you have sent the light of the day to us. We have read of the authority granted by you in the Word. We know your love and ask that you grant us confidence to use our attitudes, our abilities, and our love to use the authority you have granted us. We ask that you walk with us as we encourage each other to find the lost and to share your message. We do so under your loving authority. May we be able to be the exponential growth agents that you have authorized us to be. In Jesus' name, we pray. Amen.

APRIL 30: TAKE TWO, AND ACTION!

It is a pleasure to meet you. What do you do? It is a common question. It is one of the easier starter points in a conversation with someone new. If you have a specific job, a label of the job or career might be easily described. When you talk to a business owner, though, it can get complicated. Some business owners own a service of some kind which really provides just an income. They might choose to focus on income building instead of business building. Other entrepreneurs are more focused on building a transferable business. Either way, they are self-employed, so what do they do?

Entrepreneurs want to introduce themselves in an appropriate fashion, but they do so many tasks, the message can get polluted. How many times do you get the opportunity to reintroduce yourself? If you do not do a good job the first time, do you get another chance? If not, I ask why not? I think you can. I think that there is no barrier to doing another introduction except yourself. Our own ego can get in the way. We just need to be clear about what we want to have happen the next time we do it. If you need to take two, you should be able to ask for that.

What do we have to lose, if anything? The time used in the first meeting is past, it is done, and we cannot get it back. It is part of your past experiences. We can choose to be in relationship to meet again, though. Where would you like to have a "take two" moment from the last week? What is the first thing you can do in the next seven days to make it happen?

As Christians, God has granted us a "take two" moment by giving us forgiveness through Christ. But we can often miss the mark. We can miss the opportunity to do great by not doing a good thing. That seems like a really good use of a "take two" moment to me. What have you done this past week that you would replicate again, which would glorify God? What benefit could be had by you if you were to do it again? What benefit would someone else have if you did it again? Taking another "take two" allows one to improve something that did not go as well as it could have. What has not gone according to your plan this past week? Maybe a "take two" is an appropriate use of your time.

But if you do the same thing as a "take one" you will probably have the same experience. Let us prepare differently for the "take two." In Judges 13, we start to read the story of Samson. Samson was the first born of Manoah. An angel of God is reported to have told Manoah's wife of the birth of the special child. She hears all the information, but she wants Manoah to hear it right away, so she runs and tells what she can. Manoah though wants more information, so he prays for a "take two." God grants the request, and the angel appears again. This time, his wife runs to Manoah when the angel appears, and Manoah is part of the second appearance. We know that God is okay with this because that is what forgiveness is all about. What can you do to prepare for a "take two" in the next seven days?

Let us pray.

Heavenly Father, we are so thankful for your forgiveness. We know that we need you in our lives. We seldom do everything to the full glory of you. We seldom do it to the full expectations of even those we are in relationship with. Help each of us to improve ourselves when we do a "take two." The only behavior that we truly control is our own. Help us to better prepare our agenda for the next meeting. Influence our agenda to be acceptable in your sight. May others be able to interpret our messages with you receiving the honor. Come and assist us to put our ways aside as we shape our "take two" to do it your way. In Jesus' name, we pray. Amen.

MAY 1: BUILD DIFFERENT AREAS

As entrepreneurs and leaders, we can be extremely creative. It is what many of us do. But creativity is not necessarily valuable as it takes shape. Many times, creativity must be transformed into part of the value proposition. That is where our team can come into play. Ideas, systems, products, services, payment methods and marketing are all part of the entire process. Where have you been creative this past week? It might have been in any of those different aspects of the value delivery process. We are challenged sometimes to get others to help us in our creative process. If you have something creative that could add to your value proposition, who can you involve to help advance it? If we believe that all we have to do is be creative, we will likely stall.

When our attitude begins to draw us inward and only to our own contribution, we need to consider an adjustment. Is there something going on in your company or team that is creative that you have not participated in? Why? When we think about sharing our own creativity, our attitude toward others might be a barrier to accelerating it. What can you do to be supportive of creativity with the whole team? What can you do about it in the next seven days?

In our faith, sometimes we can grow because of others. Where are others doing something creative to overcome an obstacle? To grow ourselves, we might be able to adopt ideas of creativity from others as well. Those ideas could be our study of the Bible, it might be our prayer life, it might be something as simple as copying an encouraging attitude. Regardless of the action, tapping into someone's creativeness can bring us and our relationship with Christ better value.

In John 2:1 NLT, we read where Jesus' mother asks him to help with the wedding. This is the story where the water was turned into wine. Mary moves the celebration ahead through Jesus. She did not do anything but launch someone else. Where might you be moved forward by someone's idea? What are you doing that others might be able to benefit from? An attitude that we must keep things to ourselves for too long can restrict value. But in our faith, Christ has asked us to grow in a completely new way. Growing different attitudes takes work, but it can be done. How can we use others' creativity and share our own to glorify Jesus? What can you do about it in the next seven days?

Let us pray.

Jesus, you did many miracles, including turning water into wine. Today, I want to ask for a miracle in our own lives. Help us where we have not been willing to accept others' help. Move the Holy Spirit among us to advance our relationship with you. I want a stronger relationship, and I can do something about it by adopting a new attitude or a new behavior. Open us to be ready for that change. Help us to help others as they desire to advance with you as well. Shape and transform us like you changed the water into the wine. In Jesus' name, we pray. Amen.

MAY 2: WHEN DEW DROPS BECOME ROCKS

In business, we are faced with many ethical challenges. This seems more so in our business life than in our personal life because often we have employees. Those employees expand exponentially the opportunity to run into those situations. Many employers that I meet can speak of some non-negotiable standards but often they have not been clearly defined or communicated. If we have not defined our standards, then how can we expect our employees, our systems, and our customers to operate within them and thereby reduce the ethical challenges?

I like to call the company or organization's ten non-negotiables the core principles. These ten core principles are what our team operates around. There will be many activities that one will do without thought towards the core ten. But the more important the decision, the more important it is that it falls within the intent of the core. But staying within the core will not always happen. What then? Just because a violation of a non-negotiable occurs does not have to mean termination. It does mean that we have been compromised somehow.

Maybe it means ethically, profitably compromised. Maybe it means physically, mentally, or emotionally compromised. Where might you or someone on your team have violated what you believe is a non-negotiable in the past? It might be that the core ten were not communicated and known. What is the first thing you can do about identifying or communicating the core ten in the next seven days? The strength of our teams depends on it.

As Christians, we too have some non-negotiables. These could even be the basis for some, if not all, of our non-negotiables for our family, business, and relationships. These are not like dew drops that simply appear and disappear based on the conditions of the weather. We know that we might violate God's law this very hour, but we have God's grace that surrounds us. He gave two non-negotiables to us, His law and Jesus Christ. These are non-negotiable. Jesus is the non-negotiable for both me and you as believers. Once accepted, there is nothing you can do to remove Him as He will always take you back when you go astray. He is the rock, the cornerstone, steady and unchanging, but we are like the weather and storms which are constantly changing. We are the ones that move between the ways of the world and the way of Christ.

However, we can take the path towards becoming rock solid in our faith. Jesus liked rocks and stones as he charged Peter to be one in Matthew 16:18 NLT. Where can you transform your dew drops into solid rock in your faith in the next seven days? It will take a high intensity and focus to do so. The rewards are worth the energy and effort. All we need to do is to start with our thoughts and remember that we are seeking to practice, not expecting perfection. That perfection comes later when Jesus welcomes us to his rock collection.

Let us pray.

Jesus, you are the cornerstone. We want to be the stones of your wall and your way of life. We do not want to trust in the ways of the world as we know they will evaporate just as quickly as they appeared. Help us to transform our faith into action and words that glorify you. Turn the dew of our morning into the stones that construct a pathway to you. In Jesus' name, we pray. Amen.

MAY 3: MATH DIVISION VS DESTRUCTIVE DIVISION

Businesses require different talents and skills for their value delivery. Some need manufacturing plants, engineers, and salespeople. Others need lots of technological support, banking services, web page development, and support. What a business does not need is departments and divisions to operate in silos, working in their own manner without concern for the other departments. When a department goes rogue, doing what it needs without concern for the rest of the business, there is almost certainly going to be expense and distraction from value. When engineering overlooks small errors to meet an unachievable deadline, disaster looms. When accounting cannot balance, fraud and accusations are just around the corner.

When sales teams promise numbers which cannot be delivered, customer satisfaction and loyalty will suffer. The result can often be a company turning on itself. It is very tough to turn that ship around unless it is handled quickly. Strong leadership steps in and addresses the holes and cracks when they become seen. Leaders that wait too long will likely face more than cracks but breaks and chasms that might not be repairable. It can cost us the most important resource you have, which is one's team members. Where have you seen signs of the divisions of your company or team not working together? Where might there be some cracks or holes that can be repaired in a healthy manner because you have addressed it quickly? What can you do about it in the next seven days?

In the book of Judges, chapters 19-20, we read a lengthy story about a Levite and his concubine. He goes to a faraway city to retrieve her and has a layover on his return. A group of men from the layover city, which is part of the tribe of Benjamin, attempt to sexually assault the man. Instead of assaulting the man, they wind up assaulting and killing his concubine. Upon his final return, he notifies all the other tribes. A battle ensues, many lives are lost on both sides. The tribe of Benjamin is almost completely erased as only a few warriors escape with their lives.

Where are you divided against something in your faith? Do you have a difference of opinion with a family member or someone in your church? As we attempt to be in a loving relationship with Christ, we must fight our own perceptions. What we see is not the truth but our own opinion. Jesus has seen it all and knows the truth. Maybe we should attempt to at least think what His perspective might be. Where have you had a small difference that is separating you from another? It requires leadership on our part to take on a new perspective. Just because we have an opinion does not make it right. What can you do to close the gap quickly in the next seven days?

Let us pray.

Heavenly Father, you are the Creator, and we are the ones that separate and create the gaps in our relationships. Not only do we make gaps from Christ, but we make gaps with our relationships as well. Be with us as we attempt to repair those gaps. Help us to see them quicker, repair them with compassion, and move into the future repaired and restored. In Jesus' name, we pray. Amen.

MAY 4: SHARING A CUP OF TEA

Letting people go can be difficult. As an entrepreneur, it can be one of the most difficult things that we do. That can still be the case, even if we know it is the right thing to do. It might help us to make better decisions in this case, if we have a list of employee exit scenarios. Why will your employees or members of a team leave the company? Some scenarios could be that they might get disabled, retire, die, or find a better position suited to them somewhere else. But it is possible that the most difficult exit scenario is the one where the employees' actions are inconsistent with your companies why.

When they accomplish their results in an unacceptable way in your value proposal, it is probably time to let them move on. Have we done a great job leading our employees by establishing our why? Where does your lack of communication with your team leave you exposed? If we view our employees as investments instead of expenses, we should always know why we have them. If we view them as investments to be grown, we will ensure that they know why they are a good fit. Are your employees and team members investments or expenses? Where might you have used an expense perception in the last thirty days? What will you do about it in the next seven days?

In the book of Judges, chapter 21, we find a story where the results of the actions of Israel do not seem justified. They had killed off the tribe of Benjamin except for 400 warriors. They felt sorry that they had annihilated a tribe, one of the twelve tribes of the nation. Their next action was to kill the people from the territory of Jabesh-Gilead, except the virgins, so that they could allow the virgins to become wives to the 400. But there were not enough women, so they allowed the remaining single men of the 400 to kidnap their wives from Shiloh. This sounds messy, unloving, and unjustified. It does not show an attitude of love towards others. At that time, Israel did not have an earthly leader. They certainly were not following God's direction and law. The nation had forgotten their why.

God had chosen them to hold them in a covenant relationship. There could be places or events in your relationship with others where Christ might have said "Ouch, that hurt." If you cannot think of an example now, you can probably remember the opposite is likely. Where are you saying ouch because of the way others have had unloving actions toward you? Maybe the first step towards repentance and repair is to think about why the hurt exists. To think is to have a thought. I like that letter T. What is the first action you can do in the next seven days to add a "T" to the "ouch" which makes it a touch? Perhaps shaking hands or sharing a forgiving hug might be just the right touch that is needed.

Let us pray.

Heavenly Father, we thank you for your grace. But today we are going to ask for your touch to be in our lives. We have been the recipients of actions that have caused us pain. And Father, we have done things that have been harmful and hurtful to others as well. We ask now for your gentle touch, a touch of compassion, a touch of love, and an extra dose of forgiveness so that we might repair our relationships. In Jesus' name, we pray. Amen.

MAY 5: BALANCE AND ACCOUNTABILITY CHALLENGES

I remember a particular flight once that I was on that got delayed. No, it was not weather or a mechanical issue. What else could it be? Fuel was the issue but maybe not what you think. It was not that we had too little, nor was it that we had too much. It was that our fuel was out of balance. The culprit you see was the right wing was loaded almost full while the center tank and the left wing were not. The plane was not balanced. What is not in balance in your company, on your team, or in your family?

We waited while a technician pumped fuel from one wing to the other wing. Problem solved? Nope! The pilot then checked and found out that the main tank had too much. I guess it might have gotten overloaded moving from one side to the other. The balance still was not optimal, and he called in the pumper truck for that one also. If things get dicey in the air, it is too late to have any mental energy focused on getting the plane prepared for an issue. The pilot wants the craft at peak performance every time it takes off.

Where might your team be out of balance and not operating at peak performance? As a leader and team member, we can be in an accountability relationship to help one another come back to balance. I think of the playground when they had a seesaw. You needed a partner to make it work. Who can you ask to help you be accountable? What can you do about it in the next seven days?

In John, chapter 4, we read about Jesus meeting the Samaritan woman at the well. She was a woman who was thirsty for living water. She probably had not been operating at peak performance because Jesus tells us that she had been married five times. She was not married to the man she was currently with. We cannot know her circumstances completely, but it sure sounds like we might agree that her balance needed some adjustments. What does Christ do when He encounters her? He offers her the ultimate balancing. She claims that the Messiah is coming, and He clearly acknowledges that He is the Messiah with the "I am" statement. Her testimony to other Samaritans brings many others to a relationship with Christ.

Where are you out of balance today; in your faith walk, in your relationship with Christ, and in relationship to his church? Do you need to call for assistance like the pilot called in a technician or a pumper truck? We can choose to be accountable in our faith journey just as we can in any other part of our lives. We might bring others into a relationship with Christ as we get rebalanced and become accountable. Why not? There is nothing wrong with our accountability helping others to grow in Christ at the same time. What can you do about it in the next seven days?

Let us pray.

Jesus, you can always balance the scales. It does not matter which scales I put into a state of flux, you know what needs done. Send the Holy Spirit to guide us and the teams that are in my life. Send the tools so that we might deploy them. May it all be used to honor the Father and to bring others into a relationship with you. Send us loving, compassionate but strong accountability partners. In Jesus' name, we pray. Amen.

MAY 6: THE RIGHT TIME TO HANG UP

What do your two companies look like? What services and products and value propositions do they offer? That is an interesting question because many entrepreneurs will respond that they only have one company. All entrepreneurs have at least two companies. Those companies are present company and future company. Present company is focused on delivery today and on the past. It has developed a value proposition that might even provide a revenue stream into the future. But the future company is about the new and better value proposition. It is about not being a commodity or staying in the past. It is about being an industry leader, a shaper, having a why for your business.

Ask yourself who you would like to do business with when you go out to acquire a product or service. The choices are twofold. One might choose a company that only cares about their present and past relationships. One could also choose a company that cares about their present and their future relationship with you. Who would you choose? As a company, where might you have a stronger value proposition by having a two-company approach? How can you collaborate with others to grow the present and the future company? To do so will require your leadership and team members to collaborate in a new and different way. What is the first thing you can do to improve your approach in the next seven days? Could it be a focus session on the future of the company?

Do you remember the story of Ruth and Naomi from the Bible? We read in Ruth 1:1 NLT, how Naomi's husband and then her sons passed away. She had two daughters-in-law that her sons left behind, no grandchildren and no seemingly good prospects about the future. She did what she thought best and emphasized that the daughters-in-law should go on and lead a new life by going back to their biological families. But Ruth knew about the present and future company concepts.

She knew that the future with Naomi was bigger than the past and bigger than the present. She decided to go with the future company option. She did not gamble and throw the dice to make the decision. I do not think that she had the viewpoint that she was leaving anything to chance.

Where are you hung up and staying in the past? Perhaps there is someone else that you respect that might collaborate with you to move on. Ruth chose Naomi, and there are many other examples of people choosing a partner to move forward. Jesus sent the disciples out in pairs and their emphasis was totally on helping people have a bigger future by following the ways of Jesus. How can you collaborate with others to grow in the present and the future? Where is your concept of a bigger future lacking, weak, or not envisioned with clarity? What are you going to do about it in the next seven days?

Let us pray.

Jesus, I am ready to hang up on the past because I want to be in the present and the future. I pray that we might go ahead and hang up the receiver so that I do not hear the negative of the past. Help us to push the end button. We pray that you guide us to be ready to let you hold our hands and walk into the future with you. Lead our progress together. Guide us as we hold your hand instead of the telephone. That conversation which represents the past sometimes keeps me from holding your hand.

But not today, not right now, as your hand is all we need. In Jesus' name, we pray. Amen.

MAY 7: QUESTIONS, CURIOSITY, AND MIRACLES GIVE LIFE FLAVOR

What questions have you been asking your teams lately? I think questions give the ability to surprise and create discovery. Questions can lead to creativity and enhance a creative moment. Sometimes they can do it so well that it is seemingly miraculous. But who you ask those questions to makes a difference. Henry Ford is quoted as saying, "If I had asked the people what they wanted, they would have said a faster horse." The best questions sometimes are those that are asked of ourselves and of our teams. How often are we questioning ourselves in a manner directed specifically towards our next seven or ninety days? How often are we asking our teams to share their insights directed to the creativity of the next thirty days? If we are not asking the questions, I am almost certain that we will not receive any answers.

Questions that are genuine in curiosity relieve pressure, frustration, and stop or slow the release of cortisol in our brains. They create the opportunity for something to be discovered. That sounds like a treasure hunt possibility. If you have not found any treasure lately in your enterprise, it might be because of the lack of curiosity. Treasure does not go seeking a treasure hunter, it works the other way around. What is the first thing you can do in the next seven days to ask some powerful questions?

You might be familiar with the miracle of the five loaves and the two fish from the Bible. It can be found in the book of John. What you might not recall is that Jesus asked the disciple Philip a question first. The question was, "Where shall we buy bread for these people to eat?" Philips' response, as any response that the disciples gave to Jesus' questions, showed where they were at in their perceptions. Philips' answer was focused on how much it would cost just to buy a single bite of food for the crowd.

Andrew, however, answered, "Look, here is a small boy with five loaves and two fishes, but how far will that go?" The answer exposed an opportunity for a miracle. If Jesus did not ask the question, we might have simply missed the opportunity to learn and witness the miracle.

A curious question for me to ask you, the reader, is "Have you been asking any questions this week of yourself or just been going through the motions?" Some might ask, "I wonder what would make my worship experience be more moving this week?" Others might ask, "I wonder if I will invite the Holy Spirit to be with me during worship?" What question might you ask yourself before we settle in for worship this Sunday or for your Sabbath? When will you take the time in the next seven days to reflect on the questions that are sitting on your heart or mind?

Let us pray.

Heavenly Father, you are the Creator. We do not have to know everything, but we do want to be in relationship with you. Clear our mind's eye of the everyday routine and help us to explore questions that draw us closer to you. Guide us, Lord, and share your wisdom and direction for our path as we question ourselves. May the questions lead us to answers, gifts, and the miracle of your love. In Jesus' name, we pray. Amen.

MAY 8: GIVE IT UP, LAY IT DOWN, OR LEAVE IT BEHIND!

Does your company have a product or service that does not fit? The products and services of an enterprise need to be a right fit to provide maximum value to others. A right fit is a seemingly natural extension of your "why." They need to be something that fits your personnel as well. If they do not fit your personnel, then you wind up having people selling and supporting something of which the value proposition will be significantly underdeveloped. Think of a trained preschool teacher being lead administrator of a nuclear power plant. Or think of a trained veterinarian roaming the facility as the sanitation department worker. These trained people have a skill set that is valuable, but they are being deployed ineffectively. The nuclear power plant is not going to operate to its peak efficiency.

So, what do you do when you have something that is not a good fit? You cannot necessarily make it fit if it is not part of your value proposition. Maybe we start with the value proposition and make sure that it is a part of the big picture. Then we can move on to see what part it is and how we can use it. If it is not a right fit, consider letting it go as it is a better resource for someone else. Where do you believe you might have something that is not a right fit? Do you know there to be some other right fit products or services that you have not built the support system for yet? Think of an attitude that someone on your team has used that was not a right fit for your team and culture. We likely do not tolerate that bad attitude for long. Why would we tolerate a wrong fit product or service? What is the next thing you can do in the next seven days?

In 1 Samuel, chapter 4, we read where the Philistines captured the Ark of God. Nothing good came from having the Ark with them. They soon figured out that it was not a good thing to have in the home, the town hall, or in their temple for Dagon or the city, so they got rid of it. They just got rid of it. It was not sold at auction, and they did not put it on Craig's list. There was no concern about what it was worth. In fact, they went to great trouble to make sure that it was going to be gone for good, and they paid with time, energy and their gold to get rid of it.

Where are you keeping something in your life which is not a "right fit" for your relationship with Christ? If it is a significant issue, you might need to use a significant amount of time, energy, and gold to rid yourself of it. Sometimes we have developed habits that keep us at a certain capacity. I believe that this is true in our faith as well. Reading the Bible might be an example. For some, reading through the entire Bible seems like an unachievable goal. But to those that have read it year after year it might become a little stale. Adding some journaling, prayer, and even music to the habit can create a new experience. We can also cut out items when they no longer fit our future relationship, which makes room for something new. Is there a better use of your resources in the next seven days? What is the first resource you can use to reduce and rid yourself of something that is not a good fit?

Let us pray.

Jesus, I do not like the parts of my life that I continue to hold onto that are not a good fit for me. You, and my love for you, are a good fit because you have come to us as a gift, and we have accepted you willingly. But these unfit things have yet to be left abandoned for some of us. You never abandon us though. Thank you. This week, I am going to move away from at least one thing in my life that is not a good fit. Guide me, strengthen me, and embolden me as I use my energy, time, and resources to rid myself of it. Send brothers and sisters in Christ to assist me as you see fit. In Jesus' name, we pray. Amen.

MAY 9: MIXING BELIEFS OR FLOUR AND YEAST?

Belief in your value proposition might be the most important part of any business. Would you want to do business with a company if the owner did not carry with them a high level of confidence about their belief in their services? If the owner does not carry that belief, then the team will be challenged as well. If the opposite is true, where team members do not carry the belief, there will probably be conflict also. The team members will not be working together for the benefit of the long-term goals. Sure, they might be able to get along for a while, but the value proposition will suffer. When beliefs are different, we might expect that behaviors will also be different.

What can be really challenging is that beliefs can and will change over time. For many teams, the value of their product and service has changed over time. If the value has changed, the beliefs have changed also. The great variable in this paradox is people. What do you believe about your value proposition and your company? How does it match up to the rest of your team? What is the first thing you can do about it in the next seven days?

In the Bible, the sixth chapter of the book of John can be a very challenging area for readers. It shares Jesus' discussion about being the bread of life. John shares that many who were followers up to this point left the movement when this occurred. How can Jesus be the bread of life? Does he have yeast and flour in his pocket? How can we all eat a man, or is he going to feed us to keep us from starving? Obviously, some of the followers did not make the connections needed and did not carry the belief.

We might do well to examine where we are out of alignment with our own beliefs and what Christ taught. It might be that we have not spent enough time questioning, studying, or understanding an issue. What we believe might not be correct, but it is our perception for the moment. What can we do this week to challenge our own beliefs and perceptions? One belief we know is true, that Christ came to suffer on the cross to be in relationship with us.

For today, let us be intentional about focusing on what we believe and be curious about what others believe. No judgment is needed. If we catch ourselves comparing or being judgmental, may it be about the difference as to what Jesus might have believed. What is the first thing you can do to align your perceptions with Christ's values?

Let us pray.

Heavenly Father, you are all knowing, and we are limited by what our minds allow us to see. Help remove the fog in our minds' eye. Let us see the colors and shapes as they really are. Help us to move around to see different perceptions so that we might come to know the perception that Christ knows to be true. May the clarity that results be clarity that promotes the love and relationship that we have for Jesus. In Jesus' name, we pray. Amen.

MAY 10: EXPECTATION AND POSSIBILITY PERSPECTIVE

How well do you know your products and services that your business offers? That might seem like a unique question, but it relates to results. We give our time and energy as inputs to our value propositions. But often we do not know the full results. What we think the results are going to be often are not all the results that occur. This is illustrated in our world by the way that others take our products and services and improve and modify them. If we absolutely were assured of the "why" of our business, I think that we would probably be in relationship directly with those improvements.

The results of our business are exactly related to our "why." When was the last time you inventoried the results of your products or services? Not just an inventory of the ones you expected but what occurred? We can be assured that the others that receive the results of our products and services might be asking that question themselves. Why would we give up our valued-added results? If you are being generous because of it, then no effort will be needed. It is a wonderful gift. If you want to capture something for it, then it will require your leadership to reshape your possibilities. What is the first thing you can do to capture that value?

God expects results from us. He knows that our free will is going to result in some people being brought into a tighter relationship and some not. At the end of Samuel's life, the book of 1 Samuel tells us that the nation of Israel wanted a king to rule. No more prophets for them, as the neighboring countries had kings and that is what they wanted. They really had not thought about all the results. They were focused on something else which appeared to be the behavior of Samuel's sons. Their leadership desires were not focused on God.

As a brother and sister in the Christian movement, where are you focusing your leadership results? Are they Christ based results built on a relationship with him? Have you looked recently at the results and done your own inventory? No one else has the responsibility except you. If you were to take an inventory of the results you are experiencing, you will have the direct ability, with our Savior's help, to deploy new words, new actions, and new relationships that expand his kingdom. An inventory based on a possibility mindset is a leadership-based idea. What will you do about it in the next seven days?

Let us pray.

Heavenly Father, the week after Mother's Day is a week to celebrate relationships. Help us to inventory ourselves. Assist us with the process of truly seeing the opportunities that are in front of us. Our past does not control our future as it only shows us where we have been. We are thankful for those relationships, and the mothers that brought us into the world, but you define love and the opportunity for our future relationships. Guide us now as we seek to draw nearer to you and to have results that are focused on you first and our presence here secondly. In Jesus' name, we pray. Amen.

MAY 11: GIVE ME YOUR WALLET

Change can be a scary thing. It seems to be everywhere. But is it really? Change is a powerful agent because it can challenge us to look at ourselves, our teams, and our purpose. Just because a new technology exists, does not mean that you need to change. It can, maybe even it should, challenge us to revisit our purpose once again. But not many changes that occur really affect our purpose. Change is more likely to affect the what or the how of our value proposition. Are there significant changes occurring in your business right now? Are they challenging you to do something new? These types of changes might be easier to adapt to if we place our focus first on our purpose. People do not fear change. What people fear is loss.

If something new does not change or challenge your purpose, then there is really nothing to fear. A change to something other than purpose is just another way to have impact. There have been great inventions and applications of new ways to accomplish items. They do not have to bring fear with them. Think of communication systems and how they have changed. Speaking was modified by writing.

Writing was modified by a postal system. Postal systems were challenged by the telegraph and the telegraph by the telephone. Today the voice of mankind is challenged by the email or text of the written word! Perhaps we might consider changing our perception first with curiosity. What is the purpose that I will choose to lead today? What is the first thing you might do this week to lead the changes you are facing?

In the Bible, John 7 is riddled with change. Jesus' brothers showed their colors of doubt which we all might battle at times. The Jewish leaders were looking for Jesus and not for good. Some in the crowds were speaking questioningly of Him while others praised him. This all affected how He went about his day, but it did not change His purpose. It did not keep Him from going to the festival either. The changes of the day around Him affected what and how He moved but His purpose held true. At the end of the day, I suspect that my purpose and your purpose will not be changed at all. I also suspect that we will be challenged as to how or what we might do, and that is okay.

Let us greet that for what it is. It is simply a call to us to remember how to love others and what we can be doing to be in relationship with Jesus. Let us recall and take comfort in our purpose. Where might you have misplaced a high level of stress and anxiety on something that is not really about a change of your purpose? There are many messages that attempt to draw our attention and create fear in us. We might think of an image of Jesus taking our fears from us and tossing them into a pit where they are destroyed. We might give them to him and be done with them. The serenity prayer speaks about change. Nothing in the serenity prayer takes us off purpose but it brings us to Gods' purpose. What can you do about leaving anxiety of change behind in the next seven days?

Let us pray.

Father God, we pray for those today who do not know you. We know our purpose is to grow closer to Christ and to bring others to him through the Holy Spirit. Bring your comfort to us as we consider the changes of our world. Guide us in what we give attention to and how we address it. May your Holy name be glorified with our changes and our change of heart. In Jesus' name, we pray. Amen.

MAY 12: RETURNING EMPTY HANDED

As the leader of teams, we expect our team members to carry out their tasks and accomplish what we set out as goals to achieve our purpose. So how do you handle the situation when a team member comes back empty handed, unsuccessful, or the task is incomplete? There are many reasons that this could occur. It could be a lack of training. It might be that you have a great person doing the wrong thing.

Maybe something has happened to the team member rendering them temporarily or even permanently incapable? It could also be that it did not get completed because they ran into a situation that challenged them at their very core about the company's purpose. If your purpose gets lost, fractured or separated from a team member, then you can expect them to disrupt the value delivery system. The tasks our team members are asked to complete will probably be disrupted as well.

Where might anyone on your team be out of sync with your purpose? When one looks back briefly into the past, we all can find some moments where the purpose and people got fractured. When bones get fractured, we take great care to get medical attention and address the problem. Our teams and team members are the most important assets we have. It takes a courageous leader to be accountable for giving the fracture the attention it needs. What is the first thing you can do to address it in the next seven days?

Do you remember there was a festival occurring once when the Jewish leaders sent out guards to arrest Jesus? But the guards came back empty handed. It was not that they could not find him. They came back empty handed because they listened to the crowd and to Jesus and they were amazed by his teachings. They were challenged by Jesus' purpose and found his purpose to be a higher calling than their original purpose of arresting him. They made the decision to abandon their orders. All the investment made into them in the form of schooling, training, guard seminars, and leadership seminars were ineffective after they heard Jesus.

We read about this amazing event in the book of John 7:32 NLT. So, the question of the day is where are we training ourselves to our highest purpose? There is no concern with our training as compared with anyone else. We each have an individual connection and means to be of value and purpose in this world. I must ask myself though, where might God be asking me to serve in his purpose? If we are connected to Christ, then we are also called to grow in Christ. Growing means that I need to change. I should want to change, and it is okay.

It is all right to let others who can train me and lead me do so. If others have the right purpose in Christ, I will grow towards a stronger relationship with Christ by the training I receive. Where can you assist others with your attitude, talents, and skills? Where can others assist you with their unique attitudes, talents, and skills? As a leader in your faith, we can be accountable to promote and participate in this type of training and growth. What is the first thing that you can do in the next seven days to advance the kingdom by doing either?

Let us pray.

Heavenly Father, you are so good. Our challenging and pluralistic world distracts us from our purpose. Many people of our world have not connected to a definite purpose. We pray today that you might assist us where we might be short in working on our purpose. Help the distractions to dissolve before our very eyes like sugar dissolves in water when stirred. Help to shape us into your purpose, not into the purpose that leads us into more sin. Guide us, Jesus, we want our training and our lives to follow you. In Jesus' name, we pray. Amen.

MAY 13: WHAT ARE ACCEPTABLE EXCEPTIONS?

What are your expectations today? It might be that you will delegate with your team. You might have a date planned with a loved one. Maybe you have some appointments on your calendar or have some projects planned. But with those expectations of the day will come interruptions. What are you going to allow for exceptions to keep you from progressing today? What exceptions will you take to your team that will keep them from performing to the best of their best ability? Our exceptions or excuses can keep us from achieving elite performance. They keep us from fulfilling our promises.

Did you make any promises this week or this morning? If we do not make any promises, we certainly will not keep any. Living without making promises allows us to make exceptions and excuses more easily. Where did you miss the opportunity to make and keep a promise last week? Where could your team's performance have been enhanced by making and keeping a promise from you? What is the first thing you can do about it in the next seven days?

When Saul lost the kingdom, it was his lack of fulfilling God's expectation that caused it. Saul broke the covenantal relationship that was created. God, through Samuel the prophet, had sent him to war to eradicate a people, no exceptions. That makes it a level of a promise. But Saul gave in to the warriors, the people, and let them loot the country as well as keeping the king alive. These were exceptions that kept the level of fulfilling a promise from occurring.

Where can we, as brothers and sisters in Christ, make some promises this week? I think that our worship and our walk with Christ can be strengthened by making and keeping some promises to God and to ourselves. We do not have to make life shattering promises to honor Jesus. He will accept the small promise as well if we will just keep them. Our promises will help us live into the behaviors that draw us nearer to him. Making promises to one another in the church helps us to collaborate more effectively. What area of your faith can you make a promise in the next seven days?

Let us pray.

Heavenly Father, you gave us the promise of the rainbow as well as your son Jesus. Send your Holy Spirit this week so that we might strengthen our ability to make promises, to uphold them, and to draw nearer to you. Our promises to you are a way to honor you. Embolden and strengthen us through our intentionality and promises, to draw nearer to our families, to our church, to our brothers and sisters in Christ. In Jesus' name, we pray. Amen.

MAY 14: DO YOU DO DANGEROUS ANYMORE?

In what areas is your team or company not advancing in a dangerous way? Most might answer this question that our team does not do dangerous things. We do not risk failure, embarrassment, capital, or our security. We do what we know, and we do it how we know to do it. Is that your company right now? If nothing is being done that seems a little dangerous, then it seems that fear might have the upper hand right now. You see, the fear that surrounds us as leaders and entrepreneurs will tend to become higher when we have another level of success. It is easy to get comfortable in our comfort. In our comfort, we can begin to be less of a pioneer, leader, or innovator because of it.

The good news is that if you can leave personal judgment aside for a moment you can gain some clarity. The fog can clear. What if we could ask our clients and customers what they think or feel we are afraid of? What might our team members say we are afraid of? What would your family members say you might be afraid of in the family? It seems that anywhere we are afraid today could be the most profitable area to explore.

I doubt that our fear has just popped up suddenly, but it has probably been around for quite a while. If so, we have not been taking advantage of confronting it so those profits that might be available have been stacking up like inventory. It is either that or it might be that someone else has been offering and serving where we have not. Where are your biggest fears right now? What is the first thing you can do about it in the next seven days?

The history of King David throughout the Bible is filled with lessons that apply to our lives today. The main story that many remember about the king is when the boy David faces Goliath. As the nation of Israel and the Philistines face off against one another, they wind up spending more than a month listening to Goliath taunt King Saul and his troops. An entire month listening to the taunts. That is a great example of fear. Both sides were deeply comfortable in fear. Everyone was comfortable except the giant Goliath. Even the warriors on the Philistine side were afraid of death. Why should they risk their lives in battle if Goliath risked his? They could comfortably sit back and allow Goliath to handle the entire battle. They were comfortable and confident that Goliath had this. But when David approached, the tables were turned. The outsider came to the situation, and he was not trapped by fear.

You likely know the rest of the story. Where might fear have us trapped in our walk with Christ? What is it that you are most comfortable with in your faith and relationships with others in faith? Where are you not living a little dangerously? Remember, anything that your mind's eye believes is dangerous is something to fear. That perception is going to keep you right where you are and comfortable. Is it really that dangerous though?

No judgment against us personally, but what might God be able to handle for us in the situation? If you have not invited someone to pray with you, led a prayer for a small group, or attended a church, why not? If you do not invite others to church, why not? Those just might sound like dangerous places to us, and they just might be the places that God's love might profit the most. What can you do about it in the next seven days?

Let us pray.

Jesus, we do live in life with our comforts and our fears. Help us to develop a vision of a fearless life. Help us to move forward boldly for the Lord of our life. May our attitudes of fear be recast into the foundation by which we move forward. May the face of fear be transfigured by the love of God. It is time to do battle with our fears Lord, as the only fear justified is the fear of being without you. In Jesus' name, we pray. Amen.

MAY 15: COMING ABOARD STARTS WITH ATTITUDE

As entrepreneurs and leaders, we can get focused on our teams and that can be a good thing. But that can be a challenge as well. When we protect our team, we can be restrictive. It is that restrictive outlook that can keep us where we are as individuals and a team, instead of pushing us forward to what we want to become. Can you recall times that you missed opportunities to add great people to your team? What about times that you missed the opportunity to add a great resource that might increase your profitability? Why is it so easy to overlook them when they occur?

It is likely to happen because it is change, and we fear the loss of at least our planned path forward. Our minds do not want change, they want the status quo. We can get protective. What might be an incredible, life changing opportunity in front of you this week? Stop for a second and think about it. Where might you be this week that could expose you to new resources, new ideas, and new people?

Our attitudes going into the week are some factors that might help opportunities to be seen. Curiosity is an attitude that will help. If we point our nose to the grindstone our eyes will remain there. Taking at least a once-a-day pause to be curious and look around is a good activity challenge. I wonder, will you see an opportunity to meet someone new? Maybe we might even chat about how you have used this book. That might be an opportunity. Will you choose to keep your head down and your nose to the grindstone? What is the first thing you can do about it in the next seven days?

We have opportunities to live, love, and grow in our faith as well. We read, "But he said to them, 'It is I; do not be afraid.' Then they were willing to take him into the boat, and immediately the boat reached the shore where they were heading." John 6:20-21. This is the story where Jesus walked on the water to catch the disciples in the boat. "Hey fellas, it is me Jesus," is my paraphrase. The disciples were missing the opportunity to experience Jesus in a special way.

I can relate to that, can you? There are times during the day that I could be forgiving, more loving, be more inviting, and show more kindness. I am in that boat where my nose is to the grindstone and almost oblivious to all that is going on around me. Focus is a great tool that we certainly need. But the mind needs both certainty and variability. If I was just focused on experiencing Christ's still quiet voice, I might miss his message in the scriptures. What about you? Where might you be keeping your mind on rowing the boat and miss the opportunity to invite Christ to join you in it? Perhaps if we were being curious, Jesus might ask us to walk on the water with him. What will you do to get out of the boat this week? It could start with your attitude to be curious when and where it might happen.

Let us pray.

Heavenly Father, thank you for the blessings that you have granted us. Open our minds and hearts this week so that we might share your love and show it. Remove the storm clouds, fog, and forests that are keeping us from seeing those who are near us and need us. Make our eyesight clear, our hearts compelled, and our feet moving forward in relationship with you. In Jesus' name, we pray. Amen.

MAY 16: THANKS 10,000 TIMES!

As leaders and entrepreneurs, we have at least two separate units to make sure to honor. Those two units are our team members and those we serve. What do we do to honor our commitment to them on a daily or weekly basis? I can think of many things that we do for both units. For the team members, we arrange for financial pay, some get benefits on tier one while others have tier two benefits. We provide technology for them, great workspaces, give appropriate training and leadership.

For the customers, we deliver a front-stage experience with backstage support. Front-stage experience is connected to the customer client exchange, the physical environment, the product value proposition and to their feelings of satisfaction. The backstage experiences are the processes and people that make the front stage happen.

When we, as the leaders of the organization, keep our focus on these two units, we can appropriately appreciate and acknowledge their work in an honorable way. When we take the focus off these two units, we might expect the value proposition of our team to go down. Our value proposition as the leader might decrease as well, if even in just the subtlest of ways. We must be careful about what it is that we honor. Where have you missed the opportunity in the last thirty days to appreciate or acknowledge your team? Where might your value proposition be enhanced with your clients by honoring their contribution? What can you do about it in the next seven days?

King Saul was the first anointed King of Israel, chosen by God. Wow, chosen by God. That is just a humbling statement. What an honor. But do you remember what happened to Saul? Read about it in 1 Samuel 18:7 NLT. Down the slippery slope he goes, and eventually, David replaces him. As I read the story today, it was Saul's anger over the words that the crowds cheered that made me pause. Saul was upset because the crowd was chanting and raving about David's slaughter of 10,000's and only Saul's slaughter of 1,000's. It is not long after this before the spear is slung at David and the relationship goes downhill. So much for God being honored! So much for David being honored.

Where might we need to honor our other brothers and sisters in Christ? It just might be that your words of affirmation and acknowledgement could be the words that might move them closer to Christ. Maybe an encouraging word to them will let them move boldly towards a new practice in their faith. When we speak those words of affirmation, the Holy Spirit can move others. Will we treat those words like treasure to be kept for ourselves, or will we share that treasure? Who can you acknowledge and affirm in the next seven days? What focus can you place in your mind to make that happen?

Let us pray.

Heavenly Father, we acknowledge you. You are the Creator and the blessing. We want to draw near to your son Jesus Christ who sacrificed His all for us. We can honor you by following His example. We can honor you by sharing the love you have given us. Help us to leave behind our concern for our 1,000's and affirm the other 10,000's. We move away from your love when we draw the attention to us for honor. Help us to transform any honor for ourselves into value to others in ways that honor our relationship with Christ. May the glory and honor be yours. In Jesus' name, we pray. Amen.

MAY 17: WHO WILL SETTLE FOR AVERAGE?

A person once shared with me the following idea. Everyone can be average. Entrepreneurs and leaders will have the opportunities to do multiple above average things. Helping them to take advantage of the things that are above average opportunities was his advice to me. As a leader or business owner, where are your above average opportunities? I like the idea of seeing on a balance sheet a line item for AAO, above average opportunities. Do you have room on your balance sheet for that line? Are you actively engaged weekly, thinking about this idea and who helps you with them? If not, you might miss the listing of your biggest assets. Are you excited about sharing those ideas with your family and your teams? Where do you currently have that list of those opportunities?

Are you treating them like inventory, sitting on a shelf somewhere where they are gathering dust? Are they buried and forgotten at the bottom of your handbag, or folded up and hidden in your wallet? If so, you might miss the opportunity because it was not at the tip of your tongue or the top of your mind. There are only about forty-five days left before the first half of the year will be exhausted. Do you have a half-time activity planned to examine the opportunities you have missed or have captured? What is the first thing you can do this week to focus and plan to take advantage of an opportunity before that half-time event occurs? Your leadership might be determined by how well you prepare and experience half-time.

The Bible is full of people that had above average opportunities. Moses, King Saul, David, Joshua, The Disciples, John, every recipient of a miracle, the blind, crippled, and diseased had above average opportunities. If you made a list of those who were given opportunities in the Bible, who would you list? I challenge you to do that right now. Go ahead and write them here in the margins, list them on your phone, post them, text me, just make a list quickly.

Congratulations on making a list. Let us point to that list. If God gave these people, people like you and me, an opportunity, is it reasonable to think he is going to give you an opportunity as well? We can probably make a list of people in our lives that have had great opportunities. I believe that those in your sphere of influence, regardless of their station, could list you as someone that has had opportunities.

Our brothers and sisters in Christ, and the lost of the world, are counting on us to take advantage of the greatest opportunity that there is. Being a disciple, follower, and sharer of Jesus is the biggest opportunity for a Christian. When we decide to follow his way of living, we can see the world as an opportunity. How might you exhibit leadership in your faith by taking advantage of an opportunity? What are you going to do in the next seven days to take advantage of it?

Let us pray.

Heavenly Father, you gave us Christ to walk the earth and then brought him back after death through resurrection. What an opportunity! You sent the Holy Spirit back to be among us. What an opportunity! We are on this earth right now, with those who are lost and with those who you have found. Help us to take advantage of the opportunities that you place in our path. May we honor your capabilities by using our voices and hearts. May the words of our mouths bring people's hearts to you. In Jesus' name, we pray. Amen.

MAY 18: WHICH HIGHWAY?

Business owners direct a team of people on a path. On what path are you taking your team? I like to think that the first thing to know is why we have chosen the path that we are on. When you think about it, we have lots of paths. The easiest path is the one of least resistance because the limitations have been removed from it. So many paths are available that maybe it is possible to think that we can take any path. We are unrestricted in which path to take, but there are paths that are not established. I have been to places where a path does not exist. For whatever reason, the path is not there. It is probably because of the landscape, or the best use of the resource was not to have a path.

In our business world, we can expect that if the landscape does not have a path, then we are blazing that trail ourselves. That is a lot of work as there are going to be many hurdles to make that path. It is the transformational change of the path and the obstacles that can make big differences for our clients and team. A value proposition can be enhanced when we make clear the way for our clients. Where is your team currently blocked on its path? Where are you blocked on your path, and what can you do about it in the next seven days?

As a follower of Christ, we find ourselves on a very different path than those who do not. Our paths are crossing all the time. These cross points give us the opportunity for others to know us, to know our path and to know our Savior, Jesus. Our paths also will have occasional obstacles. There might be crashes of some kind that we wait to be cleared. Maybe a physical obstacle like a boulder or tree has fallen onto the path causing a delay or closing the path. Maybe we have not given much thought to our path which has us stuck in a traffic circle.

In Proverbs we read, "A lazy person's way is blocked with briers, but the path of the upright is an open highway." Where might you have briers on your path? Is it time to remove them completely, or will you just keep squeezing by them until you come up against them again? If we are stuck maybe it is our responsibility to become unstuck. Our limits are temporary, and our brothers and sisters are available to be of help as well. Clearing the limits for ourselves might clear the path for the future. What is the first brier that you would work on in the next seven days?

Let us pray.

Jesus, the road is full of opportunities and risks. There might be robbers and thieves along the side of the road just waiting in anticipation to take advantage of us. We seek the comfort of knowing that you will be with us through anything. Send your light of love to show us along the way so that our path is clear. We want clarity of our vision on the path to follow you. Make our hands and minds skilled and ready for the obstacles that appear on our path. Guide us to intersect with other paths to glorify you. In Jesus' name, we pray. Amen.

MAY 19: DO WHAT I SAY

As a leader of a team, providing value to others matters. It is easy sometimes to get caught up in the value proposition for the clients and customers and to fail to remember the value proposition we provide to our team members. We have two items for sure to deliver to our teams. They are doing and saying. You have probably heard the phrase, "Do what I say, not what I do." But here is a turn on that phrase, "Do what I do, in your own way!" That puts accountability on us as leaders in the form of our actions. As team leaders, our actions and behaviors are important. They set the tone of the relationship, and its tone will establish some limits to our success. The actions can be like musical chords that harmonize.

Others can be in tune and create a melody beyond our one single tone. When our actions are in opposition to our words then the relationships are probably going to weaken. We set the stage for people to be out of key in either the sharp or flat degrees. They might even change the keys. Weakened relationships eventually result in reduced value propositions. Where in the last thirty days have your actions been at a lower standard than you might want in the organization? Where have we as leaders fallen short of the example we want to display and lead with? Are we comfortable expecting our team to be doing what we do? If not, what is the first thing you can do about it in the next week?

In the Bible, we have several examples to study, understand, and hopefully pattern our doing after. King Saul showed us how to be paranoid and revengeful. It seems unless he was at war with another country, he was going to hunt for David and bring him to his doom. David, on the other hand, had a different attitude on doing. Do you remember when Saul went into the cave alone? Find it in 1 Samuel 24. David and his group were hiding in the back. It would have been easy to end this rivalry right then. But David chose to cut a piece of the cloth from Saul's robe. That action moved Saul emotionally. David's doing changed the expectation of his team and then transformed Saul when David shared the event with words.

When Jesus was walking around Solomon's porch, the Jewish leaders were following him. They listened intently to what he was saying. But Jesus was explaining to them that what he was doing was more important than the words. They could not even understand his words because they wanted the words to meet their perception. Our actions can speak louder and with more clarity than our words. Where can my actions this week set a better example in my walk with Christ? Will you share your change with others through words, action, or both? What is the first thing I can do about it in the next seven days?

Let us pray.

Heavenly Father, you have created us as a people who are constantly doing. You have asked us to follow, to worship, and to love among others. We pray today that you might come alongside us as we decide what to do. Help us to assist others to do as we do when we are loving, forgiving, and worshiping. Encourage others to teach us how to do what they do as well. In Jesus' name, we pray. Amen.

MAY 20: LET LOVE PUSH OR PULL

Anger is an intriguing emotion. I am not a trained mental health expert, but I think I know where anger comes from. Anger seems to come from a separation of our expectations with the reality of what is now. Many times, it is delivered to a person who serves as the messenger of that difference. I call that difference the spread. It seems like the bigger that spread or the longer that spread is, the more anger one can feel. Does it work that way with you? As leaders of teams, we might be well advised to remember that anger is not what is going to close the spread.

Two ways to close the spread are changing the perception or setting new and different expectations. When is the last time you felt some anger about your team, your financial affairs, driving on the roadway, or your personal relationships? Can you define or see the spread of the situation? What is the first thing you can do about it in the next seven days?

Brothers and sisters in Christ, here is a serious question. Did Christ get angry? Do you think of love when you ponder on the effects of anger? They do not seem to be words that belong in the same sentence or even paragraph. So, if Jesus stood so much for the concept of love, how could he get angry? But he did! He had anger in the temple with the money changers, in the garden when people would not stay awake, and in John 11:33. We read that a deep anger welled up in Jesus concerning the people's actions when Lazarus died. The spread occurred.

It appears to me that his expectations were not the reality of the moment. It might be that He wanted others to believe in Him, to trust in Him. Mary and Martha had seemingly restricted their belief that Jesus had to be present to save Lazarus. Jesus does not have to be present to miraculously change things. Our faith and trust in Him can do that. But the lack of meeting the expectations on Jesus' part did not keep Him from His why. He could dispense with His anger it seems, and He helped Lazarus rise from death. The last time you got angry, did it take you off track? Where might you have gotten angry in the last thirty days? What can you do in the next seven days to get on track and close the spread?

Let us pray.

Heavenly Father, you have shown us love and examples of anger. The Bible is riddled with anger in people. It speaks of your anger as well. Help us to close the spread of expectation and relieve the anger. May love act as the power from both ends of the spread to push anger out so that it does not exist for now. Thank you for your blessings, thank you for your sacrifice for us, and thank you for your love. Let love push this very moment, this very day. In Jesus' name, we pray. Amen.

MAY 21: THIRTEEN BROTHERS OR SISTERS?

As business owners and leaders, it is common to set up layers of supervision and management in companies. We learn to delegate authority to those layers, and we teach those with authority to supervise their workload and advise their teams. If we do not do this, we run the risk of teams operating for several different purposes or reasons. That will not serve a value proposition very well in the long run. But as entrepreneurs, who is on our supervision and advisory team? I like to believe that the more advisers we have, the more successful we might be. We might have an attorney for drafting legal documents and to handle legal matters. A bookkeeper will help to keep us on track to know the financial score, while the CPA will be able to offer tax preparation and advice on the projected results.

Who is helping us to overlook and advise over all that as a group? Who is helping us to monitor technology tools? Where might your team's supervision and advisory roles be lacking? Where are your team's supervisors and advisers doing a great job, and have you thanked them lately? But as an entrepreneur, where does your team of advisers need improvement? I do not think that there could be any more important adviser than the ones that help us! That is because we are the primary risk takers for the entity and our team. Just because you are an entrepreneur or team leader does not mean that you have to do it alone. What is the first thing you can do in the next seven days to improve it?

"Plans go wrong for a lack of advice; many advisers bring success."

PROVERBS 15:22 NLT

I think there is a lot of value in having people in our lives to help share their perceptions of the challenges and successes that we come across. Jesus had a team of at least twelve. Those twelve had even more that were close to them. Those twelve could support one another, love one another, and help each other through the good and bad times. As believers, our personal "whys" are connected. But we will be at different places on our paths in our walk with Christ. We can use different perceptions to draw us closer to God. Where do you want to strengthen your walk or pick up the pace?

Your adviser might be someone who is able to hold a flashlight for you if the path is too dark for your comfort level because your hands are full. Jesus had twelve, which made a team of thirteen brothers. How many do you have? I have heard the phrase, "Jesus is my copilot." But if Jesus is our copilot, who here on earth helps to be your navigator? Who is the first person you will add if they make the time and give the energy? What is the first thing that you might do in the next seven days to build your adviser team?

Let us pray.

Heavenly Father, you have shown us the way. But the path is narrow, treacherous at times, and sometimes dark and destructive. Help us to have a team that will walk with us, advise us, and love us. May our relationships be connected to each other through you. Guide us as we seek to strengthen our brothers and sisters. If thirteen brothers were good enough for Christ, it is good enough for me. Help us to grow each other in your love and draw us closer to you. In Jesus' name, we pray. Amen.

MAY 22: WHEN GOOD IS NOT GOOD ENOUGH

Supply and demand are two basic economic rules. Businesses of all types are involved in a value exchange of products and services, and they attempt to meet the demand of internal and external clients. But demand is not equal to long-term profits. This is especially true when the demand or the customers making the demand do not fit your company's "why." The demand and the customer must be a right fit, or our company probably is not the proper value proposition. This is true regardless of how amazing your company is. This is true regardless of how wonderful the customer is or how profitable the demand might be.

The human attitude of greed can weave its way into our transactions, and when it does, the value proposition gets polluted. Where have you met demand in the last ninety days that seems to be unprofitable or a wrong fit? A wrong fit is like a size ten shoe on a size six foot. The foot will go in but to run will be sloppy, clumsy, and probably result in someone falling on their face. What can you do to address any situation of a wrong fit? It might be that you need to stop the value proposition and allow others to meet the demand. It might mean that you could take a proper fitting shoe back to the clientele that was fitted incorrectly. What is the first thing you can do in the next seven days?

Sometimes a good fit is not a good fit at all. In 1 Samuel NLT we read about King Saul dying. He is in battle, and he loses. He, as well as his sons, are all lost in battle. But Saul's death is not a quick one. He is severely wounded but is left on the battlefield suffering. He asks someone to end it. In 2 Samuel 1:10 NLT, an Amalekite does him in and thinks that he has done a good thing, so he continues his good deed by taking the crown and the king's things and delivers them to David. David accepts them and hears the story about Saul. When David finds out that the Amalekite killed the king, he orders his men to kill the Amalekite after asking him why he thought he was the one to kill the anointed one of God.

King Saul had a demand and the Amalekite met it by supplying a quicker death. I think we can all think back to an event in our lives when we thought that we were doing something good which turned out a bit different. Our good does not have to turn disastrous to learn from it. It could be good turned into merely average or bad.

Are we as brothers and sisters focused on our supply of love and following Christ? We have been asked to follow Jesus, so do we choose to follow Christ? What is the first thing you can do about your supply in the next seven days?

Let us pray.

Jesus, it is hard to follow you at times. We are constantly barraged by demands. The faster pace of our economy, technology, and world seems to inundate us. Help us to slow down, to think about the energy of our love that we supply and demand of others. Stop and take away other influences that sometimes make inappropriate demands of us. Guide us on our paths, where we are, so that the demand that we meet is yours. May we follow you. In Jesus' name, we pray. Amen.

MAY 23: SAY NEVER AND MEAN IT

One aspect of being in business or being a leader is to deal with accepting rejection. Every business is in relationship with potential customers. Every leader has team members that follow them at some level. Some people say no. They are not ready to accept your value proposition. I can think of new managers or supervisors that come to a team that are rejected by those that they are to be leading. But those rejections are a point of view that is only good for right then and there. Our ability to share the possible results of that opinion or perception just might be what could convince them to work with us differently. When someone says that they will never participate one can use the focus of our imagination to find a potential example where someone would choose "never."

Where have you seen a person's "I'll never be a customer," change to an actual customer or even a raving fan? Where have you seen someone on your team turn from a "never attitude" to please may I? Where have you turned from a never? If we help our customer or team members turn from never, I think it makes sense that there are places that we should be turning from the never as well. Today, as we focus on the upcoming week, where do you anticipate a never might exist? Where is your never answer getting in the way of enhancing someone's life? What is the first thing to do about it in the next seven days?

As a brother or sister in Christ, what will you never do as a sin? We might want to be careful before we ever use that word never. It normally represents where we are right now as a point of view. Where might you be trapped in a never phrase? Do you say, "I will never forgive," so you will not love those you hold a grudge against? If Jesus were to ask us why we never forgave a person, is it possible to have an acceptable answer?

Have you ever said, "I will never support that?" Does that mean there is no circumstance that would cause us to stop withholding our support? Do we say, "I will never give." When we say that, we might have our focus on keeping something for ourselves. Jesus does not want us to hold Him for ourselves. We are to be sharing Him. Perhaps a more loving word than never is maybe, might, or possible. If we keep our focus on never, our issue, like Peter's feet, is likely to stay as is. But doing so is likely to keep something from blossoming that could honor God. What is the first thing you can do about your never in the next seven days?

Let us pray.

Jesus, I have had lots of nevers in my life. But living with never statements might be like living in the never land of the story of Peter Pan. I've felt like I would never turn away from you, but I have conveniently forgotten to forgive my brother and sister at times. Guide us to release any hate that might have hardened our hearts. We fall short of your call daily, but we come to you again and again. Guide us and thank you for accepting us. I pray that your light shines and never goes out. May that be the only never that exists. May it never be extinguished in our lives. In Jesus' name, we pray. Amen.

MAY 24: WHEN IS MORE THAN EIGHTY TOO MUCH?

Eighty percent, is that good enough? Sometimes it just might be the perfect piece. We work with teams. If a project is designed correctly, there are many suggestions that lead us to believe that we should only complete eighty percent of it ourselves. The other twenty percent should be done by others. That allows you to focus only on the part that you are best at doing. This is a place of unique gifts that go beyond trained skill and talent.

I find many times that when we go beyond the eighty percent level, we get in other people's way. We restrict the energy and results of our teams by doing this. If you do not have others that you collaborate with, then you might only be able to get eighty percent done. This is where your ability to be a leader requires us to assemble resources.

Resources may be internal to your team and enterprise, or they might be external resources that you collaborate with. Think about the software that people use on their computers. How many people write their own software for everyday usage? How are you coping while holding fast to eighty percent? Do you find yourself constantly encroaching on your teams' space? How is your team doing with the other twenty percent?

What can you do to assist them with their twenty? Do you simply need to get out of the way? What is the first thing to do in the next seven days to improve your results thinking about the eighty twenty rules? Our Monday debriefs might be a great place to start with our teams to find out how that ratio can be optimized.

King David was bringing the Ark of the Lord from Judah to the city of David when

Uzzah touched it and died. David was distraught and could not bring the Ark to the city because of this. He sent the Ark to Obed-Edom. We read this in 2 Samuel 6:1-10 NLT. It stayed there and blessed the people there until David could accept the presence of the Ark later. I like to think of this in relation to the eighty/twenty principle. Obed-Edom had it for twenty percent, and it did not go to David until he was ready for it. Then and only then was David able to maximize its use for the Kingdom. It was ready for the eighty at that point.

Sometimes we think that we must do it all. We become self-reliant instead of using the eighty/twenty concept. Where might you be able to share with others in your walk of faith, giving them the opportunity to share with you the twenty? Where are you able to bring the twenty and team up with others to do their eighty? Your eighty is someone else's twenty that they need. Where might we be keeping God from doing twenty because we are attempting to handle it all instead of what our part? Let us pray.

Heavenly Father, you have blessed us. Each of us is full of endless possibilities. Help us to have clarity of vision so that we might see where we can be the eighty. You do not expect perfection from us, just our best in a way that honors you. Help us to join with others to glorify the results. May you bless us most when we work collaboratively. Like a choir, Lord, blend and direct us so that the Holy Spirit might move. In Jesus' name, we pray. Amen.

MAY 25: LEAVING A LEGACY REQUIRES WORK

As leaders, regardless of what we lead, we will leave something behind when we are done leading. Are you leaving the what, the how, or the why? The most important aspect of one's legacy is the "why". Our "why" exposes our influence on faith, family, finances, fitness, and of your product or services professionally. If your legacy is restricted to your "what" it may be all about your product. As the marketplace modifies your product or service, the history of its development will become just that, something of the past. If your legacy is restricted to "how" you did it, then you can expect its impact to again be lost as others are able to modify the "how" for a better value proposition. My mind reflects today on people that knew their why. They influence me the most.

Who in your organization today has impacted you the most? Who has influenced your organization the most besides yourself? Today is a great day to think about how to honor and remember them. Those people influenced us, but they did so with a limit. It is up to us to define and make a bigger impact so that the limit of our influencers does not limit our legacy. What is the first thing you can do in the next seven days to do just that?

King David reflected upon his blessings. The book of 2 Samuel in the Bible shares this with us. He had physical blessings as well as spiritual blessings in his life. He thought to himself that he should use his physical blessings to honor God by building a temple for the Ark of the Lord. But God did not want him to do that. He told him no, that anything that was to be done would be done by a son, not David. David's legacy was going to be about his spiritual blessings.

What is your legacy going to be about? It might be centered on the physical blessings, the spiritual, or it could be both. Our legal systems will require our physical assets to be dealt with, but they will not require you to do anything about your spiritual blessings. I have many people who have acknowledged the limits of their physical presence on earth and therefore have sought legal advice to make an estate plan.

But do we have a limit in place that has kept us from defining the limit of our spiritual journey? As a follower of Jesus, we might be wise to recognize that an earthly estate plan deals with the things of this world. But a spiritual legacy plan deals with our faith and the influence it will have on others. What can you do in the next seven days to start your process of leaving a spiritual legacy?

Let us pray.

Heavenly Father, the people and things of this world are temporary. But you have offered us eternity through your son, Jesus Christ. Help us to shape a spiritual legacy for those that we lead. May we follow your guidance, like you guided King David. May our worldly transfers be reflective of what our spiritual legacy emphasizes. If we have only one legacy, then let it be representative of a life lived with you. In Jesus' name, we pray. Amen.

MAY 26: GARDEN GLOVES AND CLIPPERS

As an entrepreneur or leader, many of us are part of a team. With teams, there often comes a chain of command of department heads, managers, or supervisors. Those in the chain of command are normally those who are respected people. We respect their talents, skills, and capabilities and have given them responsibilities. Sometimes our actions can be inconsistent with our vision, and the chain of command are people that will likely witness it when it happens. This can be true even though we are the ones with the most to lose. Before acting inconsistently, it might be as easy as asking the chain of command their perspective on the moves that we are considering.

I suspect that not everyone's perspective might be needed, but there are those that we have a strong enough relationship with to trust and ask. In fact, just the thought of asking them about a situation might provide us with an answer. This may be especially true when we are operating outside of the scope of the established vision. Where might you be considering making a move that is inconsistent with your vision? If there is someone on your team with knowledge or valid insights to the move, you might ask yourself what they might think. Will you consider asking them in person, not by email, text, or phone? This provides a level of accountability that leaders sometimes ignore. What is the first thing you can do in the next seven days to bring clarity of vision to your move?

Jesus referred to himself as the vine, his followers the branches, and God the gardener. You can find that in John:15. As brothers and sisters in Christ, as branches in the vine, our branches need pruned occasionally. We grow best when we are focused on the right areas of growth. No extra shoots or suckers are needed to waste our energy, resources, or time. But often we are too close to see them as such. We can be in relationship with each other to see where God might desire us to be pruned. David needed pruning when he sinned towards Uriah and his wife, Bathsheba.

I would like to think that had David asked his general, Joab, about the action of moving Uriah to be positioned to be killed, Joab would have objected. Uriah is described as nothing less than a man with a strong character. Why did David not ask? I want to believe that he knew what he was doing was wrong, but he did it anyway. We often do not prune ourselves. I am not sure that we even can, but it is obvious to me that our understanding of someone else's perception might just be enough to help to prune us.

Do you have relationships you trust enough to ask their viewpoint? No judgment is to be cast onto them. Can they find a way to support your viewpoint and an opposing viewpoint as well? Who is the first person you would trust in their ability to share two viewpoints with you? Do you have an area where you would appreciate two viewpoints right now? What is the first thing you can do to get them in the next seven days?

Let us pray.

Heavenly Father, you have the ultimate viewpoint. You have cast a vision for us, and we continue to follow and to stray as well. You have also given us grace and provided forgiveness through Jesus Christ. As we grow in relationship with you, we know that we need pruning just as the plants need pruning for the best harvest. May our viewpoints be clear but not judgmental. May other viewpoints be shared in a loving manner and used by us in a way to honor you. May the pruned pieces be discarded and soon be forgotten in the sight of the Gardener. In Jesus' name, we pray. Amen.

MAY 27: THE LESSON OF FIVE SEVENS

Which time frame will we choose to be intentional about? Will it be seven minutes, seven days, seven weeks, seven months, or seven years? Sometimes when we get into an area where we need advice, it comes later rather than when we could have maximized it. Better late than never is a phrase you have probably heard. As leaders, we can challenge ourselves to think about the five sevens. Our decisions made in the next seven minutes can have a large impact on the other seven based time frames. If late is better than never, then leaders can be challenged to use faster alternatives and questioning. Knowing which one to use is an important tool. Seven months may be better than seven years, and seven days may be better than seven weeks and so on. But we might see that some decisions will have a positive impact over the entire spectrum.

Those are decisions to be made in the quickest fashion. What decision can you make that will lead you to act in the next seven minutes, which in turn will have a strong impact in seven years? What can you do about it in the next seven days?

In the book of 2 Samuel, Absalom's sister is sexually assaulted by his brother Amnon. Absalom kills Amnon out of revenge over two years later in a detailed plan laid out for us as readers. It is after the fact though when King David is faced with hearing the news. He is misinformed. Instead of hearing that Amnon is dead, he hears that all his sons are killed by Absalom. But Shimea advises the King to ignore the news because it seems he knew of Absalom's' anger and desire for revenge. Shimea did not interject himself into the situation prior to the act of violence.

Maybe he could have and maybe he should have, but the debate of today's devotion is not about should. Today's point is, we have the ability now, in the next seven minutes or seven days, to take action that will have an impact for Christ for seven years and even eternity. Will we show up with a decision or advice significantly after the fact or can we shape something now?

If we are struggling anywhere in our faith right now, it is now that we can decide to have an immediate impact. What keeps us from that decision, though? Oftentimes it is the lack of an accountability partner. Who can you collaborate with to be accountable in deepening your walk of faith? Regardless of where you are on a faith path, an accountability partner can help. What is the one thing you can do in the next seven days to help be a partner or find one?

Let us pray.

Father God, time is not relevant to you. A day to you is but a blink of an eye to us. We ask that as we blink, that we might see those actions and decisions that will affect our relationships with Christ for the long haul. Let us not put off eternity for seven years, seven months, or even seven weeks. Comfort us as we make those decisions which will bring you honor and glory. Let us decide how to share our story and collaborate to do so. In Jesus' name, we pray. Amen.

MAY 28: TWO LEADERS PUT TOGETHER

Just because you are a leader, an owner, or an entrepreneur, does not mean you have to do it alone. As leaders, we know the importance of leading our teams. But what about leading leaders? Today's thoughts make me wonder how many leaders I am leading in some way. I wonder how many leaders you might be leading. It could be that the more leaders you lead, the great the indication that you might be having more influence for exponential growth and exponential giving. It seems that the more one gives, the more one is available and open to receiving more as well. If true, then pouring into another's leadership abilities gives back to us as well and drives us to be better leaders also.

This does not have to be a direct result, but it sure seems to happen often. Where can you lead more leaders? Where might you be connected to a leader that has the potential to lead more leaders as well in your organization? When we think about others with the potential to lead, we might move courageously to have a conversation and provide affirmation for them. What is the first thing that you can do about it in the next seven days?

Joab was a general for King David. The books of Samuel talk about him quite a bit. Joab knew that King David loved his son Absalom even though Absalom had done some terrible things. Absalom worked against his father, his father's family, and against the nation as he did it. But Joab, as a leader in the military, was in a relationship with the king. He helped to move a wise woman to have a conversation with the king about the situation with Absalom. Her discussion opened the king's eyes to a different way of thinking. Eventually Absalom was invited back to the nation by David. Leaders, affecting leaders, who then are affecting more leaders.

Think about how Jesus Christ has influenced leaders that you admire. Where might you be able to be in a relationship with another leader where you are not doing so now? We just do not know how the Holy Spirit might move when we take a new perspective. But if we move leaders, our direct impact might just become exponential. Who is the first leader that comes to mind when you think of your sphere of influence? What is keeping you from collaborating with another leader to expand the kingdom?

Collaborating does not have to always add, but it certainly does find a way to multiply. If we are going to multiply anything on this planet, I suspect that multiplying the impact of Jesus and the kingdom of God here is a worthwhile effort. What is the first thing you can do in the next seven days with a leader that just might possibly lead to an exponential result?

Let us pray.

Heavenly Father, you are the Creator and have made the leaders. We pray for our leaders. We ask that you comfort them as we ask them to lead. They reflect, analyze, coordinate, and communicate. We humbly ask that you might send your Holy Spirit to guide them with love and compassion. Send it where needed and send strength and courage where it is needed as well. May we play the role that you might have us fill that brings you honor. Comfort us we pray as we reach out to those leaders in the next seven days. In Jesus' name, we pray. Amen.

MAY 29: OLD SOLUTIONS GET OLD RESULTS

When experience is not enough to address a problem, the impact just might become the most important focus. As leaders, we help to solve issues, challenges, risks, and dangers. It can be a quick fix to use an old solution. But often, old solutions are not a right fit. I might be tempted to believe it is a right fit but as the leader, we need to confirm that an issue is resolved. If not resolved, placing our focus on what impact we want our solutions to have is crucial. This can be a real challenge because of our attitude to assume, even believe, that we are right. Our brains want to believe we are right as it saves us energy. Thinking about the impact will allow us to address many alternatives to a problem.

Even asking if a solution is a right fit for all, some, or none of a problem helps to slow our perception and give us some time for critical thinking. Whatever the challenge, shaping what we want the result to look and feel like can show us the path to a faster resolution. It may eliminate many options as they will not be attuned to the impact we want. Starting a challenge resolution with an attitude that multiple solutions exist will help us to find the right fit for now. Where is your team not having the full impact you would like? Do you have an impact statement for the challenge? Where is the first place you would like to make an impact this week? What is the first thing you will do about it in the next seven days?

In the Bible, we read that Jesus is taken to Pilate at the request of the Jewish leaders. One place we are told is by the writer of the book of John. As Pilate listens to the complaint, he first tries to solve the challenge with an old solution. He offers to release Jesus in the old tradition, the tradition that one criminal is released every year. We do not know if Jesus' situation even qualified for this exemption. Pilate was not even convinced that he was a criminal, nor do we know if this was the right time of year to do such an action. We just know that it was an old solution. But it did not work. The Jewish leaders and crowd that were present demanded a different person to be released.

Pilate was still in the unenviable place of having to be in judgment. Where have you been stuck in the last thirty days about a decision? Like all brothers and sisters in Christ, maybe we should all have less judgment and address a different type of attitude, like curiosity, to find more impact. Will our impact be one of hate or compassion, of forgiveness or resentment, or be serving Christ or serving ourselves? What impact do you want to begin shaping this week? What is the first thing you can do about it in the next seven days?

Let us pray.

Jesus, we get stuck. Not just in the mud, but in our ways, in our hearts, and in our minds. Help us to leave behind the solutions of the past when they are not the right fit. The solutions of the past most likely will result in the same problems that we have today. Help us to know the impact we can have for you. A world with resolutions that have a larger impact for you is a world that we would desire. We ask for comfort as you move us into the unknown. Make our attitudes to be those that are influenced by you. In Jesus' name, we pray. Amen.

MAY 30: ADD THE "R"

As a leader, we face many challenges and coordinate many resources. But often the difference between bad to great can be a very small difference. Often it might be just one more resource. Where have you added one extra resource to a project that made the difference of success for you? For me, it has been a little more focus at times, while at others it has been just another person's words. At other times, it has been another person's talents or skills. At other times it has been someone else's life lesson that I have learned from.

What is it that is the most important project you are working on right now? If you were to add one more resource this week, what is the one extra resource you have or can acquire which just might be the resource to enhance the project? Perhaps our best focus is to find that one resource that would accelerate, enhance, or provide value that we are missing now. What is the first thing you can do about it in the next seven days?

As brothers and sisters in Christ, we have the opportunity to make a difference. That difference can be a catalyst for someone else's growth. It might be that we could be part of a healing process for another physically or mentally. As a possible resource, we can remember that we do not have to be something huge that makes a difference in someone's life. Even small things change things, like the letter "r" for example.

"Guide my steps by your word, so I will not be overcome by evil."

PSALMS 119:113

The Psalmist is saying that adding the "word" to our lives makes a difference. It is a resource. It is like adding to that which we already have. Consider how we can add the "r" to our life. Do you have something you would like to overcome? That might mean that something is in front of you as a project whether good or bad.

Focusing on the project and handling the project is adding the "r". We become an overcome " r" when we do this. Where might you need a resource this week? Where is it that you might be the resource for someone else this week? Go ahead, I dare you, be the "r" this week and contribute to help someone. Be an overcomer instead of overcome. Can you begin by being a focuser on the opportunity? What is the first thing you can do about it in the next seven days?

Let us pray.

Jesus, you are the great overcomer. You showed us how to overcome death and give us eternal life. You guide us along our path, but we often lack the resources we need in this world. Help us to look to you and to each other as the body of your church for the resources we need. May the talents and gifts that you have blessed us with be the resources others might use to draw nearer to you. May the honor and the glory of the Fathers name be known. May you send the Holy Spirit now to assist us as we become the resource you have called us to be this week. In Jesus' name, we pray. Amen.

MAY 31: IS BEING FIRST A MATTER OF BEING FIT?

I have two interesting questions to pose to you today. The first is, "When are you first?" and the other is "Why are you first?" As the leader of a team, we often strive to be the first. This can be especially true in business where competition may be prevalent. Our market share, first to market with our ideas, and profitability are often spoken about in a manner that focuses on us achieving some level of firstness. But that desire, treated as an objective, can come at a huge cost. Resources can be used up, misdirected, and work against our long-term vision of why we serve our customers.

Some might read this lesson and feel uncomfortable that I am even challenging being first. Is that you? I am absolutely okay with being first, but we need to understand why we want to be first.

Where have you been first, and it was not what you expected? Where are you striving right now to be first? Are you absolutely crystal clear with your team and customers and have their buy in as to why you are wanting to achieve that status? I believe that we might have a new term to use when being first is aligned with the when and why of being first. I will call it the condition of firstness. As a leader, what is the first thing you can do in the next seven days to confirm the state of firstness in your leadership and organization?

The race is on. Verse John 20:4 shares the story of Peter and another racing for the tomb. The other reaches the tomb first but does not go in. I wonder why he did not go in. Remember there is not anything wrong with being first but the why is important. The disciple might have wasted much energy in being first, he might have run by someone who was in need, or he might even have damaged his relationship with Peter. His reason might have been to prepare the way for Peter, to be a scout of some kind, or to be in prayer to honor God. I do not need to know his why, but I do need to know mine.

Do you know yours? Where in your walk with Christ might your activities not be aligned with Christ's first? If you are feeling that something is not in sync, or you are out of sorts, it might be a good exercise to check your why. You might ask why because it will draw us closer to Christ. Leaders, what is your why in your faith? What is the first thing you can do about it to gain clarity or share it in the next seven days?

Let us pray.

Heavenly Father, before anything there was you. You were and are first. Often when we run the race, we too seem to get focused on our vision of being first. As we refocus our efforts on the why of our first, we ask for your comfort. Identifying our why is likely to make us uncomfortable and reject changes. But if our first is not aligned with you, the joy in the Lord may be diminished. May our achievements with being first bring you the honor and the glory. In Jesus' name, we pray. Amen.

JUNE 1: THE VIEW IS SPECTACULAR

The view is different from any perspective you choose. As a leader or an owner of a business, the viewpoint of activities is different from those performing the duties. Each person's perception of the space around them is different. The mental environment is different, and they experience a different set of memories and neural pathways about them. But it is easy to buy into the belief that what we see individually is the truth. It is like my perception is the correct one. If mine are correct, I might find it easy to believe that other perceptions are likely to be wrong unless they are similar enough to be like mine. The fact is that they are just our perspectives.

We each individually give meaning to that which we see and experience. Where is your company or team you lead ready to exponentially grow but you seem to be stuck? Maybe a different viewpoint can bring a different explanation that may allow you to cross the tipping point.

Who is a person that you respect and are comfortable with? Perhaps their perception of our sticking point could remove some self-imposed limits that we have as an obstacle in our way. What is the first thing you can do in the next seven days to get a different perspective on your sticking point?

As people, we are filled with perspectives. They are not necessarily right or wrong, they are just perspectives. But where in our walk with Christ might our perspective be several degrees apart from Christ's perspective of what he wants for us, or even from us? In John 21, we read the story of Jesus appearing on the shore while the disciples are fishing. He asks Peter three times if he, Peter, loves Jesus. The third time he asked, Peter's feelings were hurt. Why did his feelings get hurt? Was it something Jesus said? The answer is no. It was not something Jesus said, but it was what Peter interpreted.

It is what he perceived. I am curious, where might you think that you have harmed someone else in the last seven days? Is that a correct perception? I ask with no judgment cast on you. What is the first thing you can do to bring the relationship into a better bond? Perhaps we might consider the perception of what Jesus would do or say. Could sharing a conversation with the other party about what Christ's perception might have been of the situation help? What can you do about it in the next seven days?

Let us pray.

Heavenly Father, your perception is all knowing. As humans in the world, we shape our own perceptions from our own points of view. Help us to align our behaviors with your love regardless of our limited perceptions. In Jesus' name, we pray. Amen.

JUNE 2: WHY DID CHARLIE BROWN KICK THAT BALL?

Stress! Ugh. Ever heard of Charles Schultz and the comic strip Snoopy? Do you remember how Charlie Brown used to attempt to kick the football and Lucy would always pull the ball away? Charlie Brown would land flat on his back again, again, and again. Where is something not working again and again in your business? You might have a situation where a system or person is constantly pulling the ball away. Can you change the system? Can you change the person and give them something else to do? Why are we kicking the ball at all? Maybe we can play a more productive game. What is the "again and again" you can recognize from the last six months? What is the first thing you can do about it in the next seven days?

In the book of Acts 1:3, we read about Christ being with the Apostles for forty days. Forty! Do you recognize that number from the other lessons of the Bible? It is a significant number. There were forty days and nights of flooding for Noah, forty days in the wilderness for Christ, forty days of lent and so on. So where might we be struggling and failing again and again and again, maybe even forty times in the last forty days?

Where do you want to make a clear and clean break with an old way that does not bring joy to your life? Where and what is bringing on stress? How about for the next forty days we do something about it? Just do it for forty days. Do not think beyond that time frame. All we need to do is think about changing the system, the person, or play a different game. Let us see what would happen if we did that in our own worlds. I can only imagine how my relationship with Christ might be improved. How about you? What is the first thing you can do about it in the next seven days? I cannot wait to hear from you about your successes.

Let us pray.

Heavenly Father, when the season of summer arrives in the northern hemisphere, it is a time that brings thoughts of swimming pools for some, harvest in the plains states, and school being out for others. But this summer, we pray that you comfort us as we look to change the complex to the simple. Guide us in our journey to change so that we might glorify you. Changes us so that we forgive and love each other more.

Change so that our relationships with Jesus become stronger. In Jesus' name, we pray. Amen.

JUNE 3: HOW STRONG IS YOUR CONFIDENCE?

Where does the confidence of your organization, your team, your family, or you come from? Does it matter? I like to believe that it does. Does confidence come from cash flow, people, or something else? Confidence is critical, but confidence with only one person will not necessarily move an organization. Confidence does not guarantee that people will work together. It might keep them from collaborating. Confidence of one person will not necessarily grow a family. As a leader of an organization, our value proposition is best served when we have confidence in why the organization works?

In your organization, where is confidence lacking or lagging? Lack of confidence might be your organization's biggest liability. It can even be an expense because when we lack confidence, there is likely to be a cost. The same can be said for cash flow confidence and the same for lack of confidence in our families. How can we as leaders collaborate with others to raise the confidence of one another? This exercise of enhancing confidence through collaboration transforms liabilities into assets and expense into income. What can you do about it in the next seven days?

In the early church, confidence was high. Acts 2:42-47 shares some of that growth and development of that confidence. But the passages that follow in Acts 5 share the story of Ananias and Sapphira and how quickly that confidence is taken aback. Where is your confidence strong and growing? Where is it weakening? A confidence booster for believers is to remember the power of the risen Lord. We remember that he came back again and died for our brokenness. For those that do not have a relationship with Jesus, they are missing the benefit of the confidence of our faith.

I am curious if we might be able to recognize when others are lacking confidence. It might be an opportunity to share why we have such confidence. Brothers and sisters, be strong and courageous as we know that our Savior lives. What is the first thing that you can do to transform a lack of confidence from a liability into an asset? Remember who your Savior is? It might be to transform your own confidence, or it might be to enhance other's confidence. When we help to build and provide confidence in others through Jesus, we are collaborating in a powerful way. What is the first thing that you can do about it in the next seven days?

Let us pray.

Heavenly Father, we have confidence in you. But our world strips and attacks it constantly. May the shield of faith be the best of armor against that attack. Send your Holy Spirit today to lift the shield for those believers who have lost the strength to hold onto it. Help us to use our shields to bring others and lift them up to your message. In Jesus' name, we pray. Amen.

JUNE 4: YOU WANT ME TO GET WET?

Organizations deliver products and services. They might deliver to other organizations, to individuals or both. Regardless of the model, they are concerned about customer service. We can ask what our customer service approach is. Do we have a wait and serve approach, or do we have a serve approach? Often, I find that as a customer, it is easy to notice the companies or even employees that have a serve approach. Those companies greet you. They meet you. They ask questions and they come to you. Coming to you does not have to be intrusive though. But often the concern of being intrusive is what begins to push back or suppress the efforts to serve. We do not want to scare them off so let us just allow them to tell us when they want us.

That is one thing that we might tell ourselves. It is the skills of the customer service people that know how and when to move forward with our clients. Where is your customer service team the best at serving? Where is your customer service team in need of training and improvement? Being in service requires training and intervention to overcome the basic human survival instincts to protect us individually. Serving others requires an intervention to get started. What is the first thing that you might be able to do about it in the next seven days?

In 2 Samuel 1:15-18, we read about King David's return after Absalom's death. These passages show some different ways that people might serve. The king is returning, and the passage is focused on him arriving at the river. Some had to be asked to assist the king with the crossing and bring him back. But they did not even reach out to acknowledge the king at first, let alone serve him. Some came to be ready to be in service and awaited the king to show up. But there were a few that ran into the river, inconvenienced themselves by getting wet to serve. It is humbling when someone loves us that much through Christ. It says that they crossed the shallows, helping him in every way that they could.

Brothers and sisters in Christ, are we getting wet? Are we getting in the water to help in every way that we can? I recall so many passages where Jesus gave the example to serve, to heal, and to feed. Yes, even when it is inconvenient. Our inconvenience is a gift of love regardless of the level of wetness. One might wash their hands, get sprinkled on, pull someone out of the bog, or wade into the waters. Where might you get "in the water" this week? Getting a little wet can bring relief from living in the dryness of the desert. What is the first thing you can do in the next seven days to get wet?

Let us pray.

Heavenly Father, thank you for the gifts and talents that we all have. Help us over the coming days, weeks, and months to be in service to you. May we get into the river deeper than we ever have before to honor you. Comfort us as the water might be uncomfortable but allow us to serve you. In Jesus' name, we pray. Amen.

JUNE 5: UNTIED INTO UNITED

When a team is united, much can be accomplished. The synergy of the team can help us to achieve and thrive together. It can even protect, overcome, and elevate the weakest component. This happens because it operates on a higher level. We are better together when we have united into an agreed purpose, value offer, or why. But when a team is not united, serving apart and unaligned in purpose, it operates at a lower level. The weakest component then is restrictive to the overarching results. The weakest link holds us back, slows the team down, and can cause the team to disintegrate at worst. Where might your team be falling short of its possible result? Could it be that it is not united? Did you see that if you get the "it" of united backwards, it spells untied? All it takes to get that word spelled is to have one letter out of place.

That is very similar to what can happen to our teams. The impact can be substantial and significant. It might be that someone on your team is not speaking up and saying what needs to be said. Some team members have been set aside, dismissed as unimportant, and devalued. A result can be that they will not put themselves out in front of others even if it would help the team. Self-preservation and limitation can occur. When that happens, a team is untied. Who might be untied in your organization? This is an attitude that leaders can address with their teams. When they do, they can raise the impact of the team in total. What is the first thing you can do about it in the next seven days?

In the book of Acts, 4:32 NLT, we read about how effective a united team can be. All the believers were united in heart and mind. They felt that what they owned was not their own, so they shared everything they had. As a follower of Christ, we awaken daily with a choice which is to be united with Christ or not. Our thoughts, actions and words will reflect if we are united or not. When we are weak, it is our united affiliation that can lift us from the depths of despair. It can lift us from our sense of failure. Where do you feel you are struggling to be united?

Do you have friends or family that do not seem to be united right now? As believers, we are the church, and we can be the ones to help others get tied into a stronger relationship with Jesus. Who is the first person that comes to mind as someone that seems to be untied? Just because it is your opinion that they are untied does not mean it is true. If our own attitude is one of being united, then we can seek to be united with those struggling as well. If we are united, then we can help others get tied to Jesus and the church. What is the first thing you can do about it in the next seven days?

Let us pray.

Father God, our hope is in your son Jesus. Strengthen our bond, give us courage, and unite us. Make the Holy Spirit rest on us and bind us. May we be united in a manner that glorifies you. If there is sin tied to us, then let your power be in us to untie it. Make our thoughts, actions, and words reflect our desire to be united in Christ. In Jesus' name, we pray. Amen.

JUNE 6: HOW NOISY ARE YOUR EXITS AND TRANSITIONS?

Transitions can be difficult. But they can be amazing as well. The difference between the two different outcomes often is communication. Thorough communication rarely comes easily to many people. Our own ideas, beliefs and doubts can pollute progress. This can be true for leaders who are balancing new ideas, launching, and shaping projects, and ensuring progress is being made. That is what is referred to as being in your business. But transitions or exits are more about working on your business. A leader who is an entrepreneur must spend time doing both tasks of working on and in the business.

Where might you or your team be restricted in a transition or exit area? When the restriction occurs, communication can be the primary tool to help. What is said and heard can deliver powerful results. Leaders can start the conversation in many ways, but curiosity can lead us to start faster. For this week, I challenge us to consider it "I wonder week." How many times could we start a tough conversation by sharing the phrase I wonder and then allow the conversation to move forward. What is the first thing you can do about it in the next seven days?

We read, "Solomon became king and sat on the throne of David his father, and his kingdom was firmly established." 1 Kings 2:12 NLT. Chapter 2 describes the transition conversation that King David made with his son Solomon. It seems obvious that there was a focus on communication. The king shared with him to be strong, to follow the commandments, and to confirm new leaders to serve him as advisors because king David's advisors had taken a different path. Where might you be ready for a transition? You might even be a part of a transition that you did not ask for.

Where is the communication lacking? Part of the growth journey of leaders includes some pruning. That might mean that not all the team, including past leaders, will come with you or your successors. Communication can be the most powerful tool for empowering those in a transition and can be the most powerful tool to destroy a transition as well. I wonder, where do you desire to communicate better this week? I wonder if we will see the transitions and be ready to speak and lean into them. What is the first thing you can do about it this week?

Let us pray.

Heavenly Father, we need you. Help us to be able to work on ourselves and on our communication. Sometimes we need others to help shape the conversation. Often though, we need to move the conversations out of our heads and into our hearts to shape them with you before we have them with others. Guide us and lead us Lord so that the generations may be communicating with each other. May our transitions be strong ones that honor and glorify you. In Jesus' name, we pray. Amen.

JUNE 7: NEW RESOURCES CAN MULTIPLY RESULTS

As the leader of a team or a company, we make decisions about resources. What resources are you in need of today? If you do not need any resources, you might not be stretching or have your eyes on growth. If you deploy what resources you have, one certainly can be successful. But unless you change the resources, you might expect to receive exactly what you are receiving today. We can expect that change will certainly come to us, and if we are not strategic, it will divide. If we monitor and focus now, the change we deploy through new resources might actually multiply results instead of adding to them.

What if we were to focus on our value proposition today and why we exist? Would that change our perception of our resources and multiply? What resources might we acquire to provide more value? What resource would you add to your team today? Do you lead multiple teams that need different resources? Which resources could the different teams use to make a large impact by the end of the year? Without one's leadership and energy being given to the evaluation of resources; new ones will likely go untouched. What is the first thing you can do in the next seven days to add those resources?

As Christians, we left our old selves behind when we accepted Christ. We were born again and given a chance to change. We get to lead a different life. Not a life of perfection but a life where we can grow in our faith and pursue a life that is a journey along a path with Christ. What resources do you need on your path today? King Solomon of the Old Testament needed resources when he became king.

> "Now, O LORD my God, you have made me king instead of my father, David, but I am like a little child who does not know his way around."
>
> 1 KINGS 3:7 NLT

Solomon asked for wisdom. The scriptures tell us that he was given great wisdom and he set up a team of great advisers who had roles in specific areas. Those advisers were resources.

What resources do you need on your path right now? Will you allow anything to keep you from acquiring them? Who is the first person that comes to your mind that might help you be able to acquire those resources? How many different advisors do you have that help you in your faith journey? I can think of at least four different characteristics of my faith which are my giving, doing, being, and attitude. In each of those, I can see at least four more subcategories. That makes sixteen different areas that I could deploy an advisor. How might you pray about new resources for the week? What is the first thing you can do about getting those resources in the next seven days?

Let us pray.

Jesus, we claim our walk with you on our path. We acknowledge that the path has twists and turns, hills and valleys. We know that you walk with us and that there are resources available to help us along our journey. We pray that our eyes are open and that our hearts might be moved when you place resources near us to help us. We know that mountains might be moved when we call out your name. Set aside our fear as we draw you near and as we seek the resources to live a life with you. In Jesus' name, we pray. Amen.

JUNE 8: UNIQUE IN MORE WAYS THAN WE KNOW

Teams are important for entrepreneurs. We lead them as well as being a part of them. There is a concept that focuses on developing teams around the people of the team contributing only their unique ability. The unique ability is a special talent or skill that they have. It is unique so much so that when they do it, it appears that they are energized when they do it. It might look natural for them, become easy to do, and they might even seem passionate about it. Who do you immediately think of as someone on your team who operates under their unique ability? Imagine if the leader could design a system for the team where that person spent most of their time doing that unique ability. Where do you operate on teams that are frustrated? It just might be that you are witnessing the wrong mix of unique abilities on the team.

As team leader, would it be an asset to know your unique ability as well as each team member you work with? Perhaps a more significant way of leading is achieved by spending more time in our unique ability. Choosing to be intentional about spending more and more time in our unique ability is a way to create positive and encouraging limits. Limits do not have to be viewed as negative. Do you want your brain surgeon staying up all night sanitizing the operating room and then operating on you? What are you spending most of your time on? What is the first thing you can do about your unique ability in the next seven days?

In the Bible, we can read examples of unique ability.

> "Therefore, please command that cedars from Lebanon be cut for me. Let my men work alongside yours, and I will pay your men whatever wages you ask. As you know, there is no one among us who can cut timber like you Sidonians!"
>
> 1 KINGS 5:6 NLT

As a brother or sister in Christ, where are your unique abilities? Are you a silent prayer warrior or maybe a great person to welcome people? Could you be an evangelist or maybe a cook in the kitchen? God has blessed us all with unique abilities. There are many scriptures that teach and speak about spiritual gifts. Each of us has them, but they can be like buried treasure.

Sometimes we have to seek them out and discover them. Where are you frustrated in your results? Could it be that we are not using our unique abilities when that happens? Maybe we have limits that have been put into place by our understanding, or by our education, or by our systems that we practice our faith through. God wants our best of the best so maybe we can focus on our unique abilities this week and see what happens. What is the first thing you can do about it in the next seven days?

Let us pray.

Heavenly Father, thank you for creating us. You have made us in your image and created unique abilities in each of us. Allow us the ability to remove our barriers and habits so that we might use our abilities more. May we honor your gifts to us by using them to glorify your name. Help us to keep from placing those gifts on a mantle to collect dust. Let us move ourselves to show your love and compassion and to follow Christ. Allow us to show our unique abilities like Christ showed his ability to love. In Jesus' name, we pray. Amen.

JUNE 9: DO YOU HAVE HISTORY AND HISTORY?

What about your past or your history makes your future bigger? As a leader of a team, we can benefit by knowing about the past. It holds lessons that we can use in the present to shape the future. I have heard of mistakes being called costly before. I think that those costs can be reclassified into investments when we use the knowledge to grow and make a bigger future. But knowing the past and living in it are two different issues. I do not think living in the past does much to help cast or obtain a bigger future.

Living there is restrictive, which is why people might use the words to hold onto the past. Where are you living in the past? Where might one of your team members be living in the past? Does it make sense that if team members are in those different places in their minds that it is going to be difficult to live out a bigger future? What is the first thing you can do to help move into the present and start building a bigger future in the next seven days?

The entire chapter 7 of the book of Acts tells the story of Stephen. He is being tried by the Jewish leaders. When asked if the charges against him are true, his response is to tell of the history of Israel. He shows us by his recalling of the history that he was an intelligent man. He could recall and share the story. If Stephen was talking about the past, his accusers were happy to listen. We might think that they were stuck in the past and wanted to keep it that way. That is not why he is being tried though. It is the addition of Christ to the story that brings his death.

Christ coming to redeem us for our sins is what changed this intelligent man's life. Where might you want to live a stronger life with Christ? We must be able to move from what we know of the past into the present before we can move to the future. Where are you stuck? I want to believe that we are as intelligent as Stephen was. He could move from the past to the present. What is the first thing you can do to move yourself in the next seven days?

Let us pray.

Heavenly Father, the past can be a record, or it can be a teacher. We pray today that your lessons taught to us through the Bible be brought to us in the present. May I apply them in my life to walk with you in the future. Put your commands on my heart and make our love to be lived out from it. In Jesus' name, we pray. Amen.

JUNE 10: IS A GRADUATION PERMISSION TO STOP LEARNING?

As entrepreneurs or team leaders, we are often the ones to hire or bring on new people to our team. Do you look for people that are highly educated, highly educable or both? If we want people on our teams who are lifetime learners, we might pay attention to the educable area. A team member who believes that they have learned all they need will be a limited resource. They might have stopped growing. Those who are highly educable can learn while working with our team. They will need team members around them that know how to share and help others grow. A team that is growing has a large potential for profitability and for value.

Where might your team or its members have stalled in their growth and learning? Where are you concentrating your growth and learning? Where might you be stalled? I am curious as to how your team members would respond if asked where they think that they have stalled. Would they be able to see the barriers that have caused it, or would their leader have an idea? Our ability to collaborate to help one another keep from getting stunted is powerful. What is the first thing you can do about it in the next seven days?

> "I pray that your love will overflow more and more, and that you will keep on growing in knowledge and understanding. For I want you to understand what really matters, so that you may live pure and blameless lives until the day of Christ's return."
>
> PHILIPPIANS 1:9-10 NLT

I think that we can sometimes get concentrated on our living, loving, and serving with Christ. But we are called to a lifetime of learning as well. Graduations are not just acknowledgements of your past accomplishments but may be catapults to another level of learning. For some, the learning stops. Formal education in a school district stops for members at some point. But where might you have stopped learning about Christ? What study could you take up for the next seven or forty days? Would it be a worthy objective to study Jesus more? Starting with a minimum level objective just might be the answer to a deeper connection. It could be a path to reacquaint ourselves with him. What is the first thing you can do in the next seven days?

Let us pray.

Jesus, we want to know you more. Walk with us not only in service, in love, but also in our quest to know and learn more about you. Draw us closer to you by strengthening our knowledge of you as well as strengthening our love for you and your church. Open my mind's eye to your lessons so that I may truly see and live. In Jesus' name, we pray. Amen.

JUNE 11: WHEN IS CARVING OR CUTTING STONE A SILENT ACTIVITY?

Our world is noisy. Even in the closed environments of offices, homes, and buildings the whirs of computers and air conditioning systems are constantly operating. I once was caught in a vehicle during a severe rainstorm when hail began to fall on our car. Each hail stone hitting the roof made me think that I was inside of a drum while a rock and roll song was playing above. Sometimes we need silence though. We can find value in silence. There are things that happen behind closed doors, in silence to those outside of those doors, that are most appropriately handled there.

Those activities are backstage or behind the scenes to us and often they should be. Where might your team be operating with too much noise? This can happen when our team might be sharing their voice or sounds at inappropriate places? I can think of times that words have been shared in the public's eye that were better addressed behind closed doors.

In the silence, though, some of the most valuable work can be done. As a team leader, are you finding some valuable moments in silence? These can be moments where you can wrestle with your thoughts of strategy, be creative, and find compassion or strength. We can be renewed in our silence as well. Inspiration has certainly been found in the silence. What might happen if you multiply the silence in your coming week? Where might you be able to use silence more effectively in the next seven days?

Shaping construction stones for a foundation or a building is a noisy process. Industrial hammers, heavy equipment, and transportation methods to haul them are all loud. When transported by truck, they are chained to the frames of flatbed trailers. I can hear the steel chains ringing and clinking as they are tossed around in my mind. Even in Biblical times, the hand tools to shape stones would have been noisy. But in our faith, we can find value for us in silence. In 1 Kings 6:7, we read that all the stones for the building of the temple were finished at the quarry.

No iron tools were heard at the temple construction site. How cool is that? Stones show up finished, fitted, and moved into place. Where are you working on your faith to be so prepared to be moved into place silently? It appears that there are appropriate places to chip away at our stones as well as having some silent safe havens. Where might you be chipping away at stones that you can identify a better place for the noise of chipping? What is the first thing you can do about it in the next seven days?

Let us pray.

Heavenly Father, we come to you in prayer. But often we do not take the time to come to the silent spot to connect with you. May we take the opportunity to find you in the silence. May we sing with zest and zeal in worship. May we speak to spread your word on love. May we use the clamor, song, and silence all to glorify you. In Jesus' name, we pray. Amen.

JUNE 12: ABANDON SHIP!

Leaders lead and they help us leave. Where have you as an entrepreneur, or as a leader, had to leave something to move forward? There are areas of our past that we have had to abandon to make room for improvement. What brought us here is not generally what will take us through our next step. Do you have examples of great leaps of success towards a goal? I would bet an evaluation of the circumstances would show you at least one thing that you had changed and left behind to achieve the new. Where might you have something that needs to be abandoned?

Choose wisely because leaving behind your core values is not likely to serve your future well. What issue is causing you frustration today? What might you do to be able to abandon the frustration? Sometimes our attitude to keep things can serve like an anchor. That attitude of keeping instead of giving can be both productive and restrictive. Where can you consider giving away and releasing something that could serve to launch you into something more valuable for yourself and for others? What is the first thing you can do in the next seven days to do that?

As brothers and sisters in Christ, we are called to support one another. We are joined together in the love of Jesus. We were born again and called to live a new life with him. We are asked to abandon some of our old lives. In 1 Kings 9:6, we see God's warning to Solomon and the people of Israel, not to abandon his laws. But we know that the people did abandon their call. They continued to worship other gods and idols. It will cost the nation of Israel considerably throughout their history because of their disobedience. But the good news is that God sent us Christ. Our call is to abandon hate and greed and seek the love and compassion of Christ.

Where might we have abandoned our connection with one another? Where do we need to make that connection again? Abandoning the right things is a power tool for us, and it can start with an attitude that it is acceptable to do so. Abandoning things might seem like it carries a negative connotation, but I believe it is the attitude that we carry that can make it be positive. Abandoning can even be encouraging. Where is it that we have taken on something that is drawing us away from Christ that would be purposeful to abandon? What is the first thing that you can do about it in the next seven days?

Let us pray.

Heavenly Father, send the light of the world into the dark places that we have created. Make your love and compassion help us to abandon the dark. May we find the light of your love where others might have hate. Encourage us as brothers and sisters to connect us in Christ and encourage us with abandoning the things that do not honor you. In Jesus' name, we pray. Amen.

JUNE 13: WHEN A STRATEGY FAILS

As entrepreneurs and leaders, sometimes the strategies that we decide to deploy do not work. Yep, we experience failure in our businesses. It happens. We suffer from failure on our teams as leaders. But what do you do when a strategy not only fails, but it turns out to be harmful and inappropriate? Do you gloss over it and press on to get to your goal another way? Do we address the inappropriateness before we move on and find a new strategy or roll out new tactics? If we do not address it, I think that it might weaken the team and momentum.

It can result in putting fissures in the foundation of our teams. If we weaken our team's foundation, we eventually weaken our result. The structure of our team can collapse when it is put under pressure or shaken. The effect to the foundation is a result just like the effects of an earthquake on builders near the epicenter. Where might you need to address something that turned out to be inappropriate? This question is one that can help us put an intense focus in a critical place. What is the first thing you can do about it in the next seven days?

There are many stories in the bible where people, their strategies, and their tactics failed. Adonijah failed to capture the crown from King David and the crown went to Solomon. But after the king was seated, Adonijah made another gaffe. He asked his mother to request a favor and get a woman for him from the king so that he could marry her (1 Kings 2:13). We never read of an apology to the king. The king had tolerated the first major insult of attempting to steal the crown until this request came. It was the straw that broke the camel's back. King Solomon ordered Adonijah's death.

Where are you in a relationship with someone and you need to request forgiveness? How long will you wait? It is possible that if a wound is left to fester the next action that the wounded might do could be of harm to you or the relationship in some way. There are moments in our relationships that our focus is important to be placed on forgiveness. That action of forgiveness is exemplified by the sacrifice on the cross. What is the first thing you can do about asking or giving that forgiveness that you are holding onto in the next seven days?

Let us pray.

Heavenly Father, we have sinned against you and one another. Help us to have the courage to strengthen our relationships by asking for forgiveness. When we are asked to forgive, may we be able to breathe, love, and eventually find compassion for our brothers and sisters in Christ. Make our hearts forgive with joy and love. We have your examples of Jesus to understand what forgiveness is. Empower us to follow it. In Jesus' name, we pray. Amen.

JUNE 14: DO WE HAVE WORTHY ADVISORS?

As entrepreneurs and leaders, we know the value of advisors. We have likely heard from others during all aspects of growing others, growing services, and distributing products. But when we use advisors, it is important to know why they do what they do. It is as important as knowing our own why. Can you think of an advisor that has been on your team in the past where you just did not seem to connect? Looking back on that relationship now, can you see where your purposes were not in sync? If we use advisors who are not working in coordination with our why, we are likely to run into conflict with the advice. What can you do to improve your advisor relationships? Where are you missing advisors? When we deploy our leadership skills the area of advisors is not to be ignored. What is the first thing to do about it in the next seven days?

> "But Rehoboam rejected the advice of the older men and instead asked the opinion of the young men who had grown up with him and were now his advisers."
>
> 1 KINGS 12:8 NLT

This passage speaks to let us know that advisors are worthy relationships. But as brothers and sisters in Christ, we must choose very wisely. When we agreed to accept Christ, and to follow him, we allowed him and the Holy Spirit to be advisors. Who else would you like on your team as advisors? Are we prepared to tell others why we want them as an advisor? Are you prepared to ask a future advisor why they believe that they fit as an advisor to you? I think it is reasonable to ask and know if we have advisors who are not followers of Jesus? If they are not, in the role as an advisor they need to know of the importance of our faith. What is the first thing you can do to change your advisory team in the next seven days? Changing the team does not mean we have to add or get rid of anyone. The Lord Jesus Christ and the Holy Spirit can change anyone if they are given the opportunity..

Let us pray.

Jesus, you are my strongest adviser. Send the Holy Spirit to move me and my team of advisors. Help me to build upon our team so as to serve you. Walk and ride with us today. In Jesus' name, we pray. Amen.

JUNE 15: THORNS FLOATING IN A RIVER

Leaders of multi-generational businesses may have hidden obstacles. It can be one of the most challenging areas for successors to overcome. That which we know are obstacles seem to draw our attention and our fear. We must prioritize, overcome our fears, help our teams to overcome their fears and lead. That seems daunting enough, let alone having possible lurking challenges waiting in the dark for our companies. If leaders from the past have left hidden obstacles, they can be like mines waiting to explode for the leaders of the present or future.

Those issues might have been issues that simply did not get completely resolved. If so, the people with those challenges may be waiting for others who have less knowledge, experience, or confidence to become the new leadership. When that happens, the obstacles might attack with a vengeance. Have you asked a previous leader this question, "What are the three dangers of the past that might come up again under someone else's leadership?" If you are thinking about that transition going forward, it might be a worthy conversation for your successor. What is the first thing you can do in the next seven days to address it?

King David of the Old Testament was a great warrior, combatant, leader, and man of God. His kingdom eventually was handed to Solomon. In 1 Kings 11:1-25 NLT, we read about where the kingdom begins to fall apart. Where did the enemies and uprising of the kingdom come from? You might have guessed it because of the notes before. They came from the enemies of King David. The victims of King David's conquests are the ones who return to help weaken Solomon's rule. That does not sound like forgiveness to me. I can relate to that. Sometimes I can hold a grudge or get wrapped up in it, thinking it has to be my way. I think I have said more than once, as a parent, "because I said so."

When I do that, I just might be creating an issue down the river. Upstream, I might have resolved the problem for now, but the current might just move that problem on down for someone else. The problem might even spread throughout the river polluting the entire ecosystem. It might be out of sight, but it was not resolved. Where might we have created an issue that we have simply floated on down the river where it is out of sight? Has it happened at your home, maybe at work, or even in your church? Wait a minute, it is not your church because it is Christ's church. He left no lingering issues. What can you do to address the limits of the obstacles you might be encountering or that we have placed and forgotten about? What is the first thing that you can do about it in the next seven days?

Let us pray.

Father God, you see it all and you know it all. Help us this week to see past our first impressions, past the challenges and conflicts of the day. Inspire our answers and bring us clarity to seek resolutions that solve issues to their core. May they be neutralized and dissolved where they are created. Help us to see where we have allowed issues to float and move past us. Allow us to send messages to those who are down river or send us ourselves downstream as needed to help with the cleanup. May we be humble and ask for forgiveness as we seek to repair and restore. May your name be honored and glorified as Christ walks with us on this journey. In Jesus' name, we pray. Amen.

JUNE 16: THE GOOD, THE BAD, AND THE USEFUL

Allocating resources is near the top of every leader and entrepreneur's priorities. But we are focused first on results and creating those results often takes us into an area of not using resources efficiently. Results and resources can battle one another. Think about a vehicle that is designed to travel at a very high speed. Now imagine the mechanic on your team has put a limit of only half power for operating the machine. The focus on the result will often discover where the ineffectiveness is occurring. Measurements help us to monitor the resources. What resources are not being used wisely? I do not want to think about using resources in terms of only good or bad means.

I ask us to think about using resources and how to use them to increase the manner of multiplying usefulness and helpfulness. Where do you think that resources are being used for the most help and usefulness at your company? If we intend to increase, then we can start by giving the current situation a score. Ask your team what score they might give the area you are willing to consider as a discovery area. I suspect that many on the team might have some ideas while others might not. Once a team can shape some ideas, an entire team can be accountable to make improvements. What is the first thing that you can do to improve it in the next seven days?

In Acts 10 NLT, we read that Peter had a vision that challenged his awareness of what was good and bad regarding the food the people were to eat. He declared in his vision that he had not eaten any of the unclean or bad foods. But the vision taught him to go and to be useful as God has a message for everyone. Next thing you know, he is having a conversation with a Roman centurion who was the captain of the Italian Regiment. I think that might have been unnerving and scary. The Roman government were the conquerors to whom the nation of Israel was living under. It turned out to be a very helpful and useful conversation, though.

Where might our understanding of good and bad be missing God's mark? Think about what seems to be bad and consider how at times it can serve God's purpose. Something that is bad in our mind's eye can cause us to be fearful. But on the other side of fear is freedom. Perhaps we might be able to be accountable to adopt a change of mindset faster. Are we willing to switch to a mindset of being helpful and useful? What is the first thing you can do about it yourself in the next seven days? Who will be your accountability partner?

Let us pray.

Heavenly Father, you have made the fish in the streams, the lakes, and the oceans, and they all have a purpose. Help us and our brothers and sisters in Christ to find where we can be useful to honor you. May our highest use be that which brings others into relationship with Christ. May you strengthen us today as we cast our words with care. In Jesus' name, we pray. Amen.

JUNE 17: HOW MANY DAILY CHOICES DO WE MAKE?

We make choices all the time. Every situation we encounter will present choices even if we do not recognize the opportunity as a choice. However, there are some that are more significant than others. Choosing salt or pepper is an easy decision and can be done at almost every meal. As a leader of a family, organization, or team, are you going to be value driven or profit driven? That may just be the biggest choice you can make. However, they are not mutually exclusive concepts. Salt has its own flavor compared to pepper, so they are mutually exclusive. But can they be put together?

You can be profitable even when your focus is geared towards giving value first. Where are you struggling with decisions right now? Are they value-based decisions which support the vision of your company? Are you struggling as a leader with a decision to give others value on a personal level? Perhaps the struggle is one of giving value to those that are not in a relationship with you now. Our teams might have an idea of who we are not giving value to. What is the one area that you might feel is in question today? What is the first thing you can do about it in the next seven days?

In 1 Kings 18, we read about a prophet named Elijah and the prophets of Baal. Elijah throws down the gauntlet and tells the people of Israel to decide if they are going with God or Baal. There cannot be two, or even three gods that you will worship and continue to have a relationship with the one true God. For those of today who live in our modern world we can ask ourselves the same thing. Where are we living with more than the one true God in our lives? When we do so, it is like we are attempting to empty the entire spice rack into our lives instead of being the salt of the earth where God is concerned.

What might be taking your eye off the God that resurrected our Savior Jesus Christ? When we allow idols to gain our attention, we distract ourselves from God. When we begin to worship those idols, it might be that we inflict insult and cause pain. It can be difficult though to identify what has become an idol to us. That is where our team, the members of God's church, might be able to collaborate with us. Who are the three people that you believe you can have a trusted conversation with about what could be on the path of idol status? If you are struggling, make a decision. If you are not struggling, how can you provide value to another by being curious and listening to others? What is the first thing that you can do about it in the next seven days?

Let us pray.

Heavenly Father, you are the one true God. You are the Master of the seas and the fishes. You are the true spice of life, and we ask you today to help us to remove our blinders that keep us from seeing how we might be worshipping other things. We want to worship you. Hold us in the palm of your hand today so that we might love one another as Jesus loved the disciples. Let your power and love be the flavor of life that we seek. In Jesus' name, we pray. Amen.

JUNE 18: WHEN DID YOU LAST YELL EUREKA?

Sometimes as leaders or as entrepreneurs we can discover things. Things that are new may be exciting, may add to your value proposition and energize your team. Our minds like stability and variability both. There is a balance that it seeks. Have you had any new discoveries in the last thirty days? Has your team been excited to share something new, or could it be that they are at work in a grinding repetitious fashion? Many times, people can get or slip into an old groove.

Once you get into a groove it can be difficult to get out. But a new perspective can challenge the groove. One way out of an undesirable groove is to fill the groove so as you move forward, you rise from it. How can you energize your team today to look for a new discovery? Think about a fishing analogy. If you fish in the same spot each time you fish, will you probably catch the same kind of fish? Who on the team can you inspire to seek a new discovery? Who could inspire you to find a new discovery? What is the first thing you can do about it in the next seven days?

Do you recall ever reading or hearing about Rhoda from the Bible? She made a huge discovery. You can read about her in the Book of Acts. Look for her in chapter 12.

Her discovery was so energizing that she had to run and tell the news. It was such a discovery that when others heard her, they dismissed her and made up excuses as to why she said what she said. They began to interpret her experience for her. But it was the interpreters that got it wrong. They were not ready or willing to look or listen for new discoveries. When have you been the discoverer in the last thirty days?

God's creation is at hand, and the Savior is ready to help others in his discovery. Maybe we can be energized like Rhoda this week. There is no more important discovery that we can help with than to help others discover our Savior Jesus Christ. Without people sharing the good news of Jesus, they may never make the discovery. When we know Christ as Savior, our discoveries do not need to stop. Our relationship can continue to grow by seeking even more new discoveries. What is the first thing that you might have to do to make way for a new discovery in the next seven days?

Let us pray.

Jesus, today we ask for your assistance. Help us remove our stressors and excess tension. May the blindness fall from our eyes so that we might see anew. May our discoveries of the day include your love in a new way. In Jesus' name, we pray. Amen.

JUNE 19: TABLES TURN AND SO DO ATTITUDES

As leaders, we love it when a plan of action comes together. The resources get aligned, teams move, and our value proposition is implemented so that results happen. But how do we react when the tables turn? Those might be times when all the planning is ineffective, resources are squandered, and energy and time is seemingly wasted. It might be due to an internal or external situation, but it does not matter because it just did not work. Then what do we do?

I think we might remind ourselves that we still have a value proposition, a great team, and the capability to work through it. The value is why we do what we do. Are we remembering to be of value even in the rough spots, when things are not working? Our attitudes will be challenged when the plan does not come together. How fast can we recognize the attitudes to keep us from finding the value quicker? What is not working right now? What is the first thing that you can do about it in the next seven days?

We have a great example in the Bible of a person that had a bad day and the tables turned. King Ahad of Israel is one of those examples. King Ben-hedad was on his way to conquer Ahad. Ahad was overwhelmed so he surrendered. That was a bad day. He was required to give away his wives, his children, and his treasure. When Ben-hedad wanted even more, God allowed Ahad a blessing to battle back. His troops routed Ben-hedad and things were looking up. But God had instructed Ahad to destroy the King and he did not. Things then went in the wrong direction for Ahad once again, and he was attacked by a lion and died. I think that would warrant an ouch in our minds when we read it. You can read the entire story in 1 Kings 20. When things turn on us it is easy to get down or even depressed. But do not let the lions scare you, for we have Christ.

We have our brothers and sisters in Christ, and we sometimes just need to call on them for help. I think when the tables turn, our first reaction might be to pray. But our second step just might be to seek help from the church. Where have the tables turned in the last 30 days for you? Who is the first person in the church that comes to mind as someone who might be able to provide insight? If time, geographic logistics were removed, and financial resources to you were unlimited for this purpose, who would you reach out to? Is your attitude in the way to reach out? What is the first thing you can do about it in the next seven days?

Let us pray.

Heavenly Father, guide us. Lead us where you might have us to go, to help one another, and to share the love of Christ. Guide our hearts to adopt attitudes that enable us to find you faster. In Jesus' name, we pray. Amen.

JUNE 20: HOW DO YOU START?

When we are in a group setting, how do you start a meeting? As entrepreneurs and leaders, it is often our role to start off a meeting. But how seriously have we thought about the start? It sets the stage for what will happen next. It can set the tone of the entire meeting. It will captivate and include others and draw them into its purpose if done well. If not done well, it might just be the tone setter for mediocrity. Where can you improve your starts? A great runner is at a serious disadvantage if they do not start well in a sprint.

When we operate among other great runners, that start is critical. Some organizations and some leaders can start consistently in a leveraged way because of their focus on the importance of the start. How might we sharpen our own focus to start better? What is the first thing you can do about it in the next seven days?

How do you start a group prayer? Many do not feel comfortable praying aloud as one of our largest fears is public speaking. But finding a comfortable way to start is an easy way to begin feeling a little more at ease.

> "So Paul stood, lifted his hand to quiet them, and started speaking. 'Men of Israel,' he said, 'and you God-fearing Gentiles, listen to me.'"
>
> ACTS OF THE APOSTLES 13: 16 NLT

Paul shares with us one way to start a meeting. He lifted his hand. We can lift our hands, fold them, and then announce a verbal countdown. Preparing our mind for prayer is important for ourselves as well as for groups. Sometimes people can have an experience that does not go well and therefore they will avoid it in the future. We can challenge that attitude by our ability to focus. Focus can be put on the beginning and often that can be all that is needed to move the movement towards God instead of ourselves. Where can you remember a start that you would do over? Perhaps we can have a stronger start with our focus being placed on it. God chose to make the end of Jesus' life be the beginning or start for us. What is the first thing you can do in the next seven days to make your next start even better?

Let us pray.

Jesus, you offer us a new start every day. We can leave our sins behind because of your gift and the grace offered to us through God. Shine your light on us as we start things new in our daily lives. Make our starts be respectful, honorable, and glorify you through the manner that we do them. In Jesus' name, we pray. Amen.

JUNE 21: ASKING AND ACTING

As leaders of families, companies, or organizations we must communicate. Two critical parts of our communication are asking and acting. How common is it to ask of others in your organization? It can be a challenge to always ask with respect when we get hurried or are stressed. The way in which we ask can affect the honesty of the answer we receive. We also might consider that every brain wants to be right when challenged with a question, but our answers are almost always, if not always, our opinion. Our answers reflect our perception of the question which often can be disconnected from what the questioner is really asking.

Value starts to come when we put the ask together in a way to have thorough communication. But value takes off when authentic communication is partnered with action. Where do you need to put together a stronger connection between the two items of communication and action? People wonder how some teams can achieve exponential progress so quickly. Imagine that a team you are on is not communicating at peak efficiency. If you can imagine that or see it happening on your teams now, you know that it impacts the value you deliver. When team members spend time and resources on inappropriate activities it impacts value as well. When the leader addresses both issues, it may become a multiplying effect on value for the team and the customer. What is the first thing you can do about addressing either issue in the next seven days?

"But the king replied sharply, 'How many times must I demand that you speak only the truth to me when you speak for the LORD?'"

1 KINGS 22:16 NLT

It is easy to see the conflict in the king's words here. He had asked the prophet many times, but he did not like the words the prophet shared with him. Those words required the king to change his ways. We know our sins and our sinful ways, and I believe that it is normal to want to keep those quiet and to ourselves. We do not ask others about them as we want to protect our ego and our public image. But acting on things that honor our relationship with Jesus is just that. It is honorable. What is something that you could get a trusted person's opinion about to result in better actions that you desire for yourself?

When the leader gets better, everyone gets better. Our own communication with others is a great place to start then. Who are the three people that you would trust to have a conversation with and what is keeping you from having that conversation? Sometimes the action in our heart and mind has to occur before the communication will take place in our head and with our tongues. What is the first thing you can do about it in the next seven days?

Let us pray.

Heavenly Father, you have given us a great gift in our Savior Jesus Christ. Guide us and comfort us as we ask others for help. May we as brothers and sisters in Christ, ask and answer respectfully. Make our minds be open to new ways that honor you when we act. Let us move away from our sins, one at a time, one day at a time. In Jesus' name, we pray. Amen.

JUNE 22: DO NOT THROW STONES

Leaders, words, and actions can be misinterpreted. Do you relate to that statement? Think back over the last year to where others might not have been on the same page as you with a project or task. When we do not make the correction to the perception immediately it may just get tougher and tougher to change it. This is very important when it comes to our value proposition. When other individuals' perceptions are different from the big picture we paint for them, frustration will likely occur. Profits and value delivery will be at risk and resources wasted. Like an artist painting oil on canvas, the leader has the brush to bring clarity.

When we do not achieve clarity in our vision for others, the tree we paint might be interpreted as a bush, a flowing plant and at worse a bouquet of dandelions. Looking back over the last six months, can you identify an event which was a conflict of clarity? Conflicts of clarity are conflicts that occurred when our team members were not working with the same vision. What are the top five objectives for the next quarter, and will your team have clarity about them? The limit of clarity often rests with the leader. What is the first thing that you can do about clarity in the next seven days?

> "When the crowd saw what Paul had done, they shouted in their local dialect, 'These men are gods in human form!' They decided that Barnabas was the Greek god Zeus, and that Paul was the god Hermes since he was the chief speaker."
>
> ACTS 14:11-12 NLT

Paul and Barnabas were misperceived. Eventually they wound up getting stoned as part of this story. As brothers and sisters in Christ, we live in a worldly environment. There are distractions and lots of people around. We constantly have a challenge of living according to the love and call of Christ. Our actions will be perceived by others and sometimes we may not do a very good job of creating clarity just by our actions.

Will we live boldly enough that we will use our hearts to find the right words to create clarity? Where could your actions currently be misperceived in your family, workplace, relationships, or church? Remember this, the strongest muscle of our physical body is the tongue. It alone has more power to influence and move others towards a relationship with Jesus. What is the first thing that you can do about it in the next seven days?

Let us pray.

Heavenly Father, your love and words are true. But our ability to see with clarity is often challenged. Help us to communicate clearly and lovingly to make sure that others receive your true message. Let grace abound today and be with us. Place your love and guidance in our lives today. In Jesus' name, we pray. Amen.

JUNE 23: WHO CHANGED THE RULES?

When rules change, I think that it is reasonable that the players might change as well. As entrepreneurs and leaders, both of those changes can be critical to our success. We get used to our rules, our circumstances, and our routine. But those rules also exclude some others as well. If your rules state that you must work on Monday, and someone has a conflict on Monday, you cannot very well expect them to apply to be a member of your team. But to change the rules and allow this team member to not work on Monday allows for a different team dynamic and result. When rules change, it takes leadership and conversation to occur for the members to understand and agree to stay with the new game.

It makes sense that if you cannot play by the new rules then you probably need to find a new game. No judgment on the people, but old rules provide old results. New rules provide a new result. It seems reasonable to me, and I believe it is a pattern proved throughout history. Where do you need a new set of rules for your organization, family, finances, or fitness plan? They might be as important for your organization as they are for you. What is the first thing that you can do about it in the next seven days?

In Acts 15:1-35, we read about the church going through some rule changes. For the Jews of the nation of Israel, God was their God. The Israelites were the chosen ones. Their set of laws were for them from God. So seemingly, if God was going to be for others in addition to them, certainly the old rules would apply, they thought. But they learned quickly that this was not to be the case. Jesus Christ was the establishment of a new set of rules. The old ones might still be around, but the new ones must be applied as well. Imagine if the game you were playing had rules changed during the game. You roll the dice which results in a rule change. You now collect a prize of $1000 for passing go in the game of Monopoly instead of $200. The $200 was the old rule.

That would change the game. Rents do not have to change, nor the prices for the properties, but there will be more blessings when you pass go. You might want to play by the new rules under that new blessing. But you could just stop playing the game or refuse to collect the excess, but the other players will be collecting the higher blessing. Jesus Christ is the biggest gift one can ever receive. Where are you fighting the new rules? Where are you playing by the old rules instead of the new ones? Perhaps it is time to be accountable to a new set of rules. What is the first thing you can do about it in the next seven days?

Let us pray.

Heavenly Father, thank you for your gift of Jesus Christ. Help us to open our eyes and hearts to your unending love and the new rules that we accepted when we accepted Christ as our Savior. Guide us and comfort us where we are resistant to the rule changes in our lives. Help us to work through the new rules that we might be dealing with and to focus on Christ as we do it. In Jesus' name, we pray. Amen.

JUNE 24: GRAB A BRANCH, PRUNER, AND SOME COMPASSION

As entrepreneurs, leaders, or team members, we might be seeing multiple team members on a regular basis. In our relationships with those team members, we are likely to know when they get downtrodden, get in a slump, or even get depressed. But being an observer who cares about results, we have the ability to offer a new perspective with compassion and sensitivity. We can offer a new means to raise them up. That will require us to do our own intervention. You must cut down the old chain of events we would choose and allow a new direction to have the opportunity to start. It can be like pruning a plant.

When pruning, one must take the tool of a pruner and apply it to the plant to remove the shoot that is not desired. Think of a plant where the blossom is past its glory and is shriveling up and decaying. It is time to prune that blossom so another may happen again. Where in your team is someone down for the moment? Helping others to have a better experience as part of our team is a piece of our collaborative work. What can you do in the next seven days about it?

We read in the Old Testament a great example of something being lifted that relates to helping people as well. Do you remember the story of the ax head?

> "'Where did it fall?' the man of God asked. When he showed him the place, Elisha cut a stick and threw it into the water at that spot. Then the ax head floated to the surface."
>
> 2 KINGS 6:6 NLT

The ax head could not be found until someone else helped. We are called to help one another as the body of the church. But no one can make you take action to do that but yourself. Where are these opportunities to share with someone, to lift them up? No judgment is needed, just your willingness to cut your own tree down and let it reach into another's situation to offer them a way up. We must be willing to prune ourselves and stop long enough to help others to achieve this. If we do not do the intervention, then our growth will continue, and they might suffer because of it. Doing so is not a handout but a hand up. What is the first thing you can do in the next seven days to make your change that will allow you to stretch out and help someone up?

Let us pray.

Jesus, you offered to help us up when you came down from the cross. It is your resurrection that gives us hope and inspires us to make changes in ourselves. Those changes might include changes to our own behaviors that are uncomfortable. Empower us to make an interruption to our normal patterns. Engage us to give us the ability to extend hope. In that hope, we might be able to bring others to you. Guide us this week as we interrupt to do exactly that. In Jesus' name, we pray. Amen.

JUNE 25: SOME, ALL, OR NONE

As entrepreneurs and leaders, we have the responsibility to direct our teams. Many leaders will struggle with the role of delegating. It is often the case that we are giving round tasks to people who have skills that are triangular. When the round task is larger but weaker than the triangular skills, we will damage the task by attempting to force it into the other space.

If the circle is strong, it will damage the triangle. When failure occurs with delegating to our team, we might be tempted to take back all of the parts of the project. This can be especially relevant if we have damaged the team when we delegated in the past.

Great leaders do not intentionally harm others or want to repeat doing so which makes it easier to take back the project. Some of the project might be our best fit though. The key word is often the word some.

A project does not have to be all or none on your role. Where might you have all of a project because you have not shared it with the right people yet? Where do you need to find new members to do part of a project? What is the first thing you can do about it in the next seven days?

"When they heard Paul speak about the resurrection of the dead, some laughed in contempt, but others said, 'We want to hear more about this later.'"

ACTS OF THE APOSTLES 17:32 NLT

The keyword that speaks to me today is "some." We have an all-knowing God. He is an all-forgiving God because of Jesus Christ. We can proceed in life, taking care of what it is that we can do. Let us focus on the parts that allow us to contribute and which glorify Christ. That is not everything. Nor is it all. It is some and that is one major benefit to having a church community to belong to. Let us be in relationship with our brothers and sisters in Christ, so that when you do your some and I do mine, we might give all to glorify Him. Where might an all or none attitude be keeping you from moving forward? How might we share and trust our brothers and sisters to help us? What is the first thing you can do about it in the next seven days?

Let us pray.

Heavenly Father, you are the All, the Alpha, and the Omega. We are your people, and we come to you through Christ. Help each of us, as a small part of the whole, to find a way to contribute. Guide us to let go of the areas where our attitudes of all or none are restricting our growth. May we see clearly what some looks like instead of only all or nothing. Make us have the strength and courage to act upon it. In Jesus' name, we pray. Amen.

JUNE 26: YOUTHFUL ATTITUDES

Look around. Go ahead, actually look around in your life the last week and see where you can find the youth. I think that it is wise as leaders of companies, organizations, and families to find the youth. If we do not find the youth and connect them with vision and clarity, they might begin to wander without purpose. We want to connect with them to bring them into a pattern of success with us because we will not have the attributes of youth for long. We can shape ourselves better by sharing our insights with those that have a different perspective. There may not be a better way to find a different perspective than to find someone a couple of generations behind you to discuss it with.

Where might your lack of connections with youth be hurting your advancement? Where has your connection served you well? Differences among the generations will certainly include differences in attitudes. Where do the youth have different attitudes that you are experiencing? We can recall when we were younger how we might have had attitudes that were different than the attitudes that we have later in life. What is the first thing that you can do to explore youth around you and their attitudes in the next seven days?

"Joash was seven years old when he became king."

2 KINGS 11:21 NLT

Can you imagine the political leader of your country being seven years old? That seems crazy to me in my culture. But the fact is that there is probably a future president of the United States or some other leadership position of another country that is seven years old right now. How are they being shaped and influenced? As brothers and sisters in Christ, we have a responsibility to the youth of the world. We can cast a vision of success which would include love and respect, or we can cast a different vision. Regardless of what vision is being cast, they are absorbing and watching. What vision are you casting? If our attitude is one that keeps vision for ourselves and does not include the youth, then we might have limited our potential together. What is the first thing that you can do about it in the next seven days?

Let us pray.

Heavenly Father, you have inspired us throughout the ages. We have been created so that we age and change as we grow and develop. Guide us as we influence the youth and the youth influence us. May we connect with each other in a means that grows our world that is honorable to you. Help us to take the opportunity to be in a relationship with our youth. In Jesus' name, we pray. Amen.

JUNE 27: WE HAVE MORE CAPACITY THAN WE KNOW

Leaders of companies and organizations deploy resources by combining their past experiences, their knowledge, technological tools, intellectual property, and human energy. We might often think that we have it figured out because we achieved a level of success. But no one person has everything needed for the benefit of others. We are limited by what it is that we can gather and deploy right now. We are able to expand upon our experiences when we invite others to join us. We can grow and deliver our value propositions better by building a team. Where is the most important area of your organization for you to add to? I am curious. Imagine if you had the ability to clone yourself three times.

Your clones would always act in unison and for your benefit while being capable of doing different tasks. They would be able to fulfill any role or responsibility including new ones you have not handled yet. What three things would you deploy your clones to do? If we place our focus on what our own clones would do, we can start to evaluate others who can fulfill the roles for us. Who might be the best person who would add to your team? What is the first thing that you can do to focus on your cloning capability in the next seven days?

Where are you confident in your faith? One can be tempted to stop growing when we find some confidence and competence in our faith. Confidence and competence do not have to cause complacency, but it requires focus to continue the growth. We can be teaching others who might be less confident. If we can teach others, even if it is the basics, then we are capable of learning as well. In the book of Acts, we read about Apollos.

> "He had been taught the way of the Lord, and he taught others about Jesus with an enthusiastic spirit and with accuracy. However, he knew only about John's baptism. When Priscilla and Aquila heard him preaching boldly in the synagogue, they took him aside and explained the way of God even more accurately."
>
> ACTS OF THE APOSTLES 18:25-26 NLT

We might learn from this that there are lessons that each of us can master. The journey to master an area brings us value and may result in us being of value to others like Priscilla and Aquila. Others might include those who have already shown a level of confidence or competence in their faith. Which way are you being called right now to place your focus? Will you share with another, or will you choose to learn from another? What is the first thing that you can do about it in the next seven days?

Let us pray.

Heavenly Father, you have wonderfully made us. We are never at our full capacity although we often think or act like we are. Help us to strip away every notion that I am full. Strip away my short sightedness of my areas of confidence. Bring your clarity where others might be able to help us to draw closer to you. In Jesus' name, we pray. Amen.

JUNE 28: ARE YOU YELLING, SELLING, OR BEING COMPELLING?

Do you use logic or your heart to make decisions? The answer is that we use both. But I think that what compels us as leaders is not the logic of a decision, but it is the heart. When we think about the combination of our why and our value proposition, we often find passion. Passion seems to be a matter of the heart to me. The logic of our value propositions is certainly important, but the logical thoughts and steps we take are not necessarily compelling until the heart is involved. When the heart is not involved with our team, we might find ourselves selling them. If frustration settles in an area where the heart is not involved, then yelling might occur. Where has your heart not been as involved with your world and decisions as you might have wished it to be in the last thirty days?

It could be that your logic has been getting in the way of your heart. Being a leader sometimes means that we must do an inventory of our heart. When we find that the inventory there is low or depleted, we need to address it. As leaders, we also can accept the responsibility to help others inventory their hearts. If it is in their heart then it is their issue to solve, not ours. But a leader of leaders helps others to fill up that space which can benefit on an exponential level. What is the first thing that you can do about it in the next seven days?

As brothers and sisters of Christ, we can be moved by our logic and by our hearts as well. But I think that God works mostly through the heart. Our hearts can be warmed with love by the Holy Spirit. Christ moved people, not through logic but by the heart. His parables teach us by allowing us to relate the thoughts of the parables through our own eyes which allow our hearts to influence us. Our decisions that we come to through the heart are compelling decisions. They move us. Whether they seem right or wrong, we move because of them. The Apostle Paul had the same thing happen to him.

> "Afterward Paul felt compelled by the Spirit to go over to Macedonia and Achaia before going to Jerusalem. 'And after that,' he said, 'I must go on to Rome!'"
>
> ACTS OF THE APOSTLES 1:21 NLT

Where is an area you are missing that has compelling momentum? Maybe it is that you are concentrating on logic instead of the heart. When we trust the Holy Spirit and ask for it to help us, we open our hearts to the encounter of God in our daily walk. Where can you open that area that might be a little bit closed this week? It will do your heart good to fill it up. What is the first thing that you can do about it in the next seven days?

Let us pray.

Heavenly Father, you are the Master of the heart. You have moved people through their hearts throughout the ages. We ask that you might remove the cloak of logic where it might be holding us from loving you more. Bring your love to wash us clean and remove the stickiness of our limited human logic. Move our hearts and minds to honor you. In Jesus' name, we pray. Amen.

JUNE 29: SEVEN COMPETED WITH JUST ONE

What areas are calling for your attention today? I would say that there are many. It could be accounts payable, accounts receivable, marketing, advertising, website, blog, pricing, legal, sales or service. It could be sons, daughters, aunts, uncles, mothers, fathers, grandsons, or granddaughters. How many items or messages are calling for your attention? Are you being pulled in many directions? If so, maybe for today we need to bring some focus and clarity, block by block, to make progress. Let us clear the clutter for ninety minutes at a time.

Let us give our focus on just one priority during that time. We can then celebrate a transition time in which we can give thanks for our progress before we move on to the next topic for ninety minutes. Placing some limits on ourselves can be a very productive task. Many times, we allow the perspectives of others' priorities or technology to dictate tasks for us. That may not always be the right priority for us to follow as the leader. Maybe a short break to transition to the next focus is in order. What is the first thing you can do in the next seven minutes that could impact the next seven days?

What do Succoth-Benoth, Nergal, Ashima, Nibhaz, Tartak, Adrammelech and Anammelech have in common with God? They were considered gods and worshiped by the foreigners who took over the territory of the Kingdom of Israel in the book of 2 Kings 17:30-31. Were those people distracted or what? They had the opportunity to worship the one true God, but there was much in the way. I can relate because there are many things in our modern culture that want our worship. The demands want our time, actions and behaviors, and we can approach the concept of idolatry if we are not careful. Where might you benefit by focusing on the next ninety minutes? What part of your life is more important than being in relationship with our Lord and Savior Jesus Christ?

It can be difficult to be a leader to your family, your marriage, your team, your enterprises and causes when we realize that they all have multiple demands. But Jesus asked us to follow him and to make him the cornerstone. If you cannot clear the next ninety minutes for him, maybe you can use the next seven minutes to find some time for the one true God. What is the first thing that you can do about it in the next seven minutes or seven days?

Let us pray.

Heavenly Father, the one true God, we come to you at this time, recognizing that we are distracted. We realize that there are many items that want our attention, but there are none more important than you. Let our vision be clear and may we make you our priority today and this week. In Jesus' name, we pray. Amen.

JUNE 30: HALF TO GIVE AND HALF TO RECEIVE

As leaders of families, companies, and organizations we give. Our value propositions are actually about giving to others. In our families, we give love. In our companies and organizations, we deliver goods and services. We receive love back from our families, and our companies receive money and resources in return for their giving. But where is our emphasis? Is it on the giving or the receiving? By placing our focus on our giving or delivering of value to others, we might be able to develop raving fans. I think that this might just be the best way to have a continuously improving value proposition.

We must stay open to receiving and be thankful for it, though. I am not suggesting that we only give. To give, you must have something to give, but we always have an inventory when we have a team. In companies, they receive gifts because someone believes that we have earned them. The ability to give and receive places a responsibility of being accountable to our team members. That accountability starts with us as the leader. Where can you put an emphasis on giving this week? What is the first thing you can do about it in the next seven days? Will you be accountable to that first action?

The apostle Paul carried a message to the world. He was giving and sharing the gospel. He writes about hard work and helping others. But how do you support when your focus is on sharing and giving to others? It might start with making sure that what we are giving fits the needs of the people we are sharing with. It may not be the best sharing to give someone a Bible written in English if they read Spanish. We can achieve a level of accountability in our sharing and giving by measuring the result of the impact. This is a challenge to us in our world today, just as it was for Paul's in his day.

> "And I have been a constant example of how you can help those in need by working hard. You should remember the words of the Lord Jesus: 'It is more blessed to give than to receive.'"
>
> ACTS OF THE APOSTLES 20:35 NLT

Where might you have a stronger focus on giving for the second half of the year? Have you realized that half of the year is gone? What can you do to put an emphasis on giving in the second half of the year? Will you allow yourself to be accountable for an intentional increase in your giving method that you determine is right for you. Remember, what you measure matters. That is why you measure it. What is the first thing that you can do about it in the next seven days?

Let us pray.

Lord Jesus, you gave your all. You taught us how to receive and how to give, but we allow distractions to remove our focus. May our emphasis be on giving for this second half of the year. Empower us to be accountable to you, and thank you for your grace and forgiveness when we fall short. Keep our hearts open to receiving and be thankful for the blessing that you and others send to us. In Jesus' name, we pray. Amen.

JULY 1: A FEATHER DUSTER

People do not plan to fail; they fail to plan. Someone has said that before, and leaders either live it out or not. The quality and impact of a leader may be a result of this one issue. Do you have a plan? I bet that many of you do. When we look at our plans, we might find that components could be missing. If your plan is missing components, then there will be missing results that we desire. Do your plans include a plan for growing your faith, growing your relationships with family and friends, and growing the people on your teams? Do your plans include serving your neighborhood, your community, state, or country? Where is your plan possibly absent from these areas of concern?

It is not too late to amend the plan for the year. Half the year is gone, so when was the last time you saw your plan? It is probably time to pull it out and look at it. Let us make the last half of the year the best six months of plan implementation ever, while at the same time having our value delivery system operate at the highest level as well. Who will you be able to recruit to help you carry out the revised plan? Collaborating with others can be difficult, but most of the valuable things in life do not come easily even though they are simple to see. What is the first thing that you can do about it in the next seven days?

As a brother and sister of faith, what is your plan to increase your faith and to draw closer to Christ this year? Without a plan we just might suffer more frustration than we need. The people of Israel and Judah knew this.

> "Hilkiah the high priest said to Shaphan the court secretary, 'I have found the Book of the Law in the LORD's Temple!' Then Hilkiah gave the scroll to Shaphan, and he read it."
>
> 2 KINGS 22:8 NLT

The people of God in the Bible had been led by many kings to do the wrong things. Most notably was their behavior of worshiping false gods. They had forgotten about the plan, the covenant that their ancestors had made with God. They even lost the scroll and misplaced it.

Where is your written plan and goals about your faith journey for the year? Is it lost like the nation of Israel? Maybe it is time to pull it out and review the first six months to experience more of the power of God in the second half of the year. What we measure matters even in our faith. We do not measure to earn our way to heaven. We measure and have goals because as a leader we want to influence the world for Christ's mission. We measure to assure that we love others more and seek to draw closer to God. If we are going to love others more, the first step might be to collaborate with others to increase the impact of that love. What is the first thing you can do about it in the next seven days?

Let us pray.

Jesus, join us as we think about our past. Comfort us as we review to refresh our point of view. We want to draw closer to you and ask that you inspire us to give, to be, to do, all with a humble attitude. Make our plans and progress follow your path. In Jesus' name, we pray. Amen.

JULY 2: READY, SET, TURN AROUND!

It is common for people to root for the underdog. Think of the underdog stories from past Olympic competitions. Turn arounds are amazing and can be redeeming. I mean one hundred and eighty degree turns in the other direction might be the most difficult thing to accomplish. I think this might be the truth for the perceptions with our teams when they are off and out of alignment. Just because you, as a leader, might believe that a turnaround is appropriate does not mean that your team believes it. Let us face it, as a leader we probably taught, trained, supported, and rewarded efforts and energies about the old way. We have probably supported the past direction and the result got off course somewhere. Variables take us off course regularly.

Can we really expect a turnaround with our team to be accomplished so easily? I think not. But if your move is from a product or commodity perspective to a value proposition, you just might have to do it. Another example of a great turnaround could be the challenge of beginning to support someone in your field who you used to oppose. But the difficulties of the examples might just show how rewarding it would be to accomplish just that, a complete turnaround. What is the most difficult and rewarding thing that you could turn around in the next six months? The rewards might include new relationships, new team members, and record quarterly revenues. What is the first thing you can do about it in the next seven days?

As brothers and sisters in Christ, I do not think that there is anything more blessed than when we feel close to Jesus through the Holy Spirit. It just melts the concerns, fears, and worries of the world away. But we make it difficult as we allow other things to distract us. We can allow our emotions and our thoughts to direct us instead of allowing our faith to lead us. Think of one of the great leaders of the early church, Paul. Here is part of his conversion conversation.

> "'But Lord,' I argued, 'they certainly know that in every synagogue I imprisoned and beat those who believed in you. And I was in complete agreement when your witness Stephen was killed. I stood by and kept the coats they took off when they stoned him.'"
>
> ACTS OF THE APOSTLES 22:1-20 NLT

What would you do if a person like Paul visited you today and had changed his perspective one hundred eighty degrees? Would you be ready to forgive him and be in a relationship with him? Do you think you could accept him in a leadership position at your local church or possibly at your children's Sunday school? I suspect that we all need to turn one hundred eighty degrees around with some issue in our lives.

Which one do you feel being led to change? I expect that there are several areas of our life that could use a turnaround. Do not be fooled to think that the turnaround is easy. They take determination, persistence, hard work, and commitment. With the help of the Holy Spirit, it is possible. Call upon the name of Jesus and start the work of the turnaround. The only thing keeping us from doing that complete turnaround is ourselves. What is the first thing you can do about it in the next seven days?

Let us pray.

Heavenly Father, we want to draw near to Jesus. We live in a world that is full of sin and distractions. We allow other things to get in the way. Guide us and support us as we find the courage to turn around like Paul did. Habit by habit, thought by thought and word by word, encourage us to help others as they turn around as well. In Jesus' name, we pray. Amen.

JULY 3: WHAT ARE YOU LEARNING?

As a leader, I suspect that one has to continually learn if we want to continue to grow our people. We study through course materials, presentations, explore at industry meetings, and be in relationship with our teams. When should one stop learning? The answer just might be never. Could that be one of the secrets to living a healthy and prosperous life? If so, then we probably want our entire team to be on a path of learning as well. What might be the most important area of learning to accomplish for the balance of the year? Being a lifetime learner is seemingly an attitude.

I am not sure that the idea of being a lifetime learner is one that permeates throughout every culture. If it is not in every culture, it is not likely to be present on every team. What can you do to promote learning for your team? One might find that their own attitude towards lifetime learning is restricted or that one is finished learning. What can you do to promote learning for your team? What is the first thing to do to put the experience of learning into action in the next seven days?

As a follower of Jesus Christ, we have an all-knowing God. But as brothers and sisters in Christ, we have a limited perspective. We have brains capable of many incredible things, but we allow ourselves to limit them. Our brains are the most powerful computers ever known, which are only limited by us. What can you do to learn more about Jesus Christ and yourself, which will help you to draw nearer to him?

"Intelligent people are always ready to learn. Their ears are open for knowledge."

PROVERBS 18:15 NLT

Maybe the text of the book quoted here is a strong place to start or to finish. Either way, be strong and courageous in your learning. As I think about the people who heard Jesus speak and teach, I wonder if they were continuing to learn, prior to meeting him. If they were not, maybe that is why his message was greeted by so many and done so with eagerness. Were their hearts and minds wanting to learn about a better way of life and of salvation? What is the first thing that you can do in the next seven days to further your experience of learning?

Let us pray.

Heavenly Father, we have the word, the Bible, as a book that ties us to you. Let us use our time wisely and make sure to incorporate learning into our activities. May the pleasure of entertainment and other worldly distractions be offset by our desire to know you. Comfort us as we seek to have new habits which bring us into a better relationship with Christ. In Jesus' name, we pray. Amen.

JULY 4: WHO TO QUESTION, LISTEN, OR TELL?

Three activities of leaders include listening, talking, and questioning. These are all valuable parts of our world, but the most valuable might come from listening.

Listening allows us to move into creative mode. It is a result that requires us to change our perspective. It causes us to think, evaluate, and decide where to move in action. Talking does not necessarily move us. Questioning on the other hand is impactful. It moves others to share information with us and themselves. Next to listening, the questioning skills that we use are powerful when they get in sync to our listening. Where is there much being spoken about in your week or day? Is there any listening going on there? I am sure that you are in relationships where either listening or questioning can bring some value to them.

How would your team react if you listened to them at a deeper level in the second half of the year? It can take courage to be curious and question others because we do not want to hear of our failures as leaders. Leaders can give themselves too much credit for the results that occur when sometimes it is the alignment of the team that is bringing value. To get aligned as a team will require all three of the listening, talking, and questioning skills. I think the order of importance is probably listening, questioning, and then talking.

I am going to deploy some of the listening skills in my relationships this week. Maybe you and your team might benefit if you deployed either of the concepts. We are blessed to be able to do both as leaders, to question and to listen. Which is your focus going to be more on this week? What is the first thing that you can do about it in the next seven days?

"'I'd like to hear the man myself,' Agrippa said. And Festus replied, 'You will—tomorrow!'"

ACTS OF THE APOSTLES 25:22 NLT

Festus had a problem, and his problem had a name. It was Paul. Yes, he had Paul imprisoned and did not know what to do about it. One lesson we can learn from Festus is he began sharing information to listen to others for some assistance and guidance. It is interesting that Agrippa's statement herein does not have a question mark at the end because it is an indirect question. As brothers and sisters in Christ, sometimes it is appropriate to be indirect, but often we need to be more direct. But direct does not mean judgmental. When we question, without judgment, we may allow ourselves to listen to what is being shared.

Through a shared life with others, we can spread the love of Christ. That is certainly a benefit of walking in life with Christ. Where have you been talking more than questioning or listening? How might we grow and help others to grow by being curious and listening to our brothers and sisters? Perhaps there will be a day of questioning in our future. That would be a day where every word uttered would be a question. Sounds like a difficult task to achieve. Maybe it could start with just one conversation, just one hour, or just one morning. What is the first thing that you can do about it in the next seven days?

Let us pray.

Heavenly Father, you are always listening. If you are talking all the time, I do not hear you, but I wonder if you do not question us through our consciousness. Help us to love others by questioning them for the purpose of listening, not judging. Help me to listen. Soften my heart so that I may hear the message that might move us into action. Let the Holy Spirit guide our questions to soften our hearts.

Make our questions grow our relationship with you. In Jesus' name, we pray. Amen.

JULY 5: YOU MAKE ME SMILE

Words. There might not be a better tool to use as a leader than words. For sure, you can use a look of dissatisfaction to communicate. You can use a stare or glare or a smile to communicate also. But our nonverbal communication is open to a lot of possible miscommunications. Words have a more direct call to action and most of all words can be encouraging. Try looking at a team member somehow and without words, communicate that you think they have done a great job over the last six months. It is our words as team leaders and as entrepreneurs that have a positive influential power for those in connection with us. Where have your words been positive and encouraging in the most influential ways in the past? Has it been more than a week, a month, a year since that activity? If so, why?

When you take the time to add up the resources you have, I wonder if you put the number of positive or encouraging dialogues on the balance sheet? Our words can also slide to the other side of the spectrum of positive and encouraging to the negative and demeaning. There seems to be enough of that occurring without any need to put an emphasis on it. The words are one of your most influential and powerful resources and they cost nothing to use! Who might you share some encouraging words with that will affect your team for the next week or month? What is the first thing that you can do about it in the next seven days?

What sermon did you hear last week? If you did not hear a sermon last week, perhaps you might recall a sermon from the past. It seems that we might hear some sermon topics about sin, about love or it might be a combo. But it seems that in society, we can get put in the spin cycle of bad news. It is like the spinning drum of the washing machine rinsing away the positives of life.

> "The tongue can bring death or life; those who love to talk will reap the consequences."
>
> PROVERBS 18:21 NLT

So as a brother and sister in Christ, I ask, what words do you want to hear this week? It seems that the messages we hear can certainly leave us wanting sometimes. What words might you be sharing? We might be able to classify words as giving life or death.

There is always that in between ground though. Are the words you are sharing giving of death, life or somewhere in between? Are you out of balance for the type of words that you are hearing and using? I think that my sphere of influence might be a little better off if I were to use even more encouraging words. Being a better leader can start with some of the simplest tasks, and this might be one of them. Remember, just because it is simple does not mean that it is easy. What can you do to change how you are using words in your world? What is the first thing that you can do about it in the next seven days?

Let us pray.

Jesus, you sacrificed for me. You sacrificed for the good of the world. Your message is about love and loving the Father. Help us to soften our words of death and strengthen them for love and encouragement. Make those that we meet this week to know that our words are not weapons of destruction but works of love. Guide us as we treat our tongues as part of your temple that you created us to be. In Jesus' name, we pray. Amen.

JULY 6: ONE LESS TOLERATION

As leaders of teams, it is not uncommon to see where tolerations occur. But the existence of toleration can happen in at least two ways. One way is tolerating on purpose and the other one is just being blind to something. We can rely on ourselves to prioritize our activities and actions. Why tolerate anything? I am just about convinced that the only reason that we tolerate anything is because our minds are occupied with other issues that are more important. As the number of members on our teams increases so can our tolerance. The number might even increase exponentially. Where does it stop? Maybe it should stop with us. What are you tolerating today about yourself?

What might be the top three tolerations to start addressing, and who would be the best person to lead the change? When the leader gets better, everyone on the team gets better. We can teach and share the ability to stop tolerating what degrades and destroys the culture on our teams. People do not fear change, they fear the unknown costs of change. When the leader can illustrate the cost of not changing and illustrate a better way, teams follow. What is the first thing you can do in the next seven days?

Brothers and sisters in Christ, we can expect to tolerate many situations as Jesus gave us His way of life, and we live in modern times. We were told as much by the predictions of the stories of the Bible.

> "After two years went by in this way, Felix was succeeded by Porcius Festus. And because Felix wanted to gain favor with the Jewish people, he left Paul in prison."
>
> ACTS OF THE APOSTLES 24:27 NLT

Paul was left in prison for two years, not processed, not tried, just floating in limbo. That is being put in a situation where Paul had to tolerate being in prison. Obviously, Felix had higher priorities to address. We do not control the behavior of others as much as we can praise and forgive those behaviors. But we can control our actions. What actions and behaviors are you tolerating of yourself? Go ahead and list a few out.

It might be liberating to see your own list. What is on your list that you would consider changing? Who is the first person you would ask to help you to change it? Keep in mind what you have tolerated in the past might have become a habit and the preferred method of dealing with it. If that is true, you may need a trusted coach to come alongside to help you break it.

We are the church together. Together we can break the limits that we have put in place for ourselves and potentially lead others through their limitations as well. What is the first thing you can do about it in the next seven days??

Let us pray.

Heavenly Father, you love us and through it tolerate much from this world. But today we are focused on loving you more and we can do that by bringing ourselves into a stronger union with you. Help us to gain clarity to connect and to remove those obstacles that we seem to hold near and dear to us. Comfort us as we look at our own tolerations. To those tolerations that we are empowered to change, we say no more tolerating. For me and my house, we pray to be strong and courageous enough to change one small step at a time. In Jesus' name, we pray. Amen.

JULY 7: TIME CLOCKS ARE NOT ENOUGH

What keeps you accountable? As a leader, many of us do not have a robust system for accountability. The challenge for ourselves can be that without accountability, we may proceed with our already established patterns. This is a biological fact. The neural patterns of habits in our brains are powerful and become instinctive. Instincts trump intentions. Many of the best leaders know that they need to create a system to capture some time where the rule is reversed. Reversal of the instinctive pattern can occur to a point where our intentions can overcome instincts. That is where accountability serves those who choose to deploy it.

Imagine if you were notified that you had only five years to operate your organization or team and then it would be done. The team would be disbanded, or the organization would have to close regardless of its past success. Would you do things differently? Then I might ask, why are you doing them the way you are now? Instinctive and habitual patterns of your brain are probably why you are doing what you do. Where are you frustrated? Turning frustration into fascination might be as easy as establishing an accountability system. What is the first thing you can do about it in the next seven days?

What would you do with a second chance? King Hezekiah got a second chance.

> "About that time Hezekiah became deathly ill...Set your affairs in order, for you are going to die. I will add fifteen years to your life, and I will rescue you and this city from the king of Assyria."
>
> 2 KINGS 20:1-6 NLT

If you were given an extension to your life, would you do things differently? Many would not because of their habits. They would simply live with the same frustrations as before and get to experience them for a longer period. Where is the joy in that? But we have been given an extension by being able to live as beings blessed by Christ. Are you ready to get rid of some frustrations and turn them into fascinations? Maybe all you need is a little accountability to make some small but positive changes. What is the first frustration that you would like to resolve? What is the first thing you can do about it in the next seven days?

Who is the person that you are going to talk about your change with so as to create an accountability system? An accountability system can start with adding someone to be accountable to. If you do not know who to reach out to, reach out to us and the authors of the book can share some resources that can help. Will you take that first step? We are not asking you to leap across the Grand Canyon. Everyone can cross the Grand Canyon by taking the hiking trail one small step at a time. Jesus offered his step of following him. That small step is life changing. Are you willing to be accountable to make another small step? Let us pray.

Heavenly Father, you know our frustrations. Some are self-caused and others by the world around us. But my actions are mine, and today we want to become more accountable. Help us to gain clarity of vision and be willing to make the small changes needed to rid ourselves of the frustrations that keep us from loving more. Make our path clear and obvious to find accountability partners that can share in our lives. Guide us and comfort us. In Jesus' name, we pray. Amen.

JULY 8: TREASURER OR TREASURE?

As entrepreneurs and leaders, we recognize that our value propositions are delivered by a team. It is common to have two categories of people on our teams. The short term and the long term could be those categories. Both are valuable and can help to improve our services and products when they act as partners in our delivery system. If they are not engaged in the value system, we might consider them as just a resource. It is like they hold a title or a position of some kind. But when our team members, short or long term, are engaged, they are like treasure. Who on your team would you call "treasure" right now? What do you do to protect your treasure, your people?

Do you protect their attitudes, their mindset, their skills, their growth, or their families? In the world of employment, we place limits on employee benefits that have a financial cost. This is true even though it is possible that our team should be viewed as investments, not costs. How do you view team members, as investments or costs or both? It changes the mindset of the entire team when we view each other as investments, and it enhances collaboration. Does a team you work with need a higher level of collaboration? It might just be that a different viewpoint would allow us to invest in them by appreciation, affirmation, and love. What is the first thing that you might want to do about it in the next seven days?

"The man who finds a wife finds a treasure, and he receives favor from the LORD."

PROVERBS 18:22 NLT

I firmly believe that we can have only twelve of the deepest human relationships at a time. We know Jesus had twelve even though he touched many. But when you search for a spouse, I think that we look for a partner for our lasting earthly life. I do not think that we look for that short-term value but the treasure of a long-term relationship. We search to find someone willing to be part of our life through the good and bad, sickness and health, the thick and thin times. If you find that, you have found treasure. The Bible just might be the best treasure map the world has ever known.

Do we use it that way? If you have found a spouse, what are you doing to ensure that you are treating them like the treasure that they are? If you have not found a spouse yet, then know that you are a treasure that is yet to be found. Have you done anything to mitigate losses to your treasure or to help it grow and be more valuable? Do you invest in it with your time, your words, and your resources? Are you using the greatest treasure map? What is the first thing you can do about it in the next seven days?

Let us pray.

Heavenly Father, your good word tells us about spouses. You have designed us to be in a relationship with others. Help us to invest in the treasure of our relationships, especially with our husbands and our wives. Send your Holy Spirit to move us today so that our treasure might know just how valuable they are to us. In Jesus' name, we pray. Amen.

JULY 9: STRONG ALLIES BRING VALUE

When was the last time you worked with another leader? Sometimes as entrepreneurs our teams need to work with other teams. At those times, it is common that leaders work with other leaders. At that time, we work to figure out how another's value proposition can work in coordination with our own. Are we choosing a company to serve with that knows its value proposition? It is a stronger relationship and better for all involved when we choose in this manner. But if one of the companies is value based while the other is product driven, there will likely be a delivery or service snag at some point. The likelihood of a long-term relationship is limited in different ways.

The long-term value certainly is limited. Where is your company limited because of a misalignment? We all get misaligned. There is nothing unusual about getting misaligned. The question is how long we will allow ourselves and our teams to operate that way. A symptom of misalignment is friction and frustration. Are you or your team members frustrated? Be inspired today to choose to be less frustrated. Make the choice and seek out what is misaligned. What is the first thing that you can do about it in the next seven days?

It has been said that if you are not growing you are dying. When I think about that in regard to my faith, it is fear that can grip my mind. I do not want my faith to shrink, to withdraw, or to die in any way. I want my connection to the trinity to get better and stronger all the time. As brothers and sisters in Christ, I think we need allies in our journey. We need people at similar stations of their faith to be walking with us. We also need allies who are stronger so that they can help us to grow as well. But if one constantly is with others who are not helping to strengthen us, it might be time for a new ally.

"But the commanding officer wanted to spare Paul, so he did not let them carry out their plan.... So everyone escaped safely to shore."

ACTS OF THE APOSTLES 27:43-44 NLT

We can learn here that even those with somewhat opposing roles can still work together if the focus is on value. The commander of the soldiers taking Paul to Caesar certainly saw value in Paul. Where are your relationships strong and when was the last time you shared your appreciation? Where might your allies not be as strong as you might need for this part of your faith walk? This is a great day to be inspired, to choose to add another ally in your faith. Let us pray.

Heavenly Father, the winds, streams, sun, and oceans all work together to bring refreshment to the earth in the form of rain. We ask that your light help us to see where we need strong connections. Encourage us to share your love and our appreciation for those that are walking with us. Make those we align with to be pushing or pulling us to know you more. Make our efforts today honor you. In Jesus' name, we pray. Amen.

JULY 10: CELEBRATING SAILS AND RUDDERS

Things can change quickly in business and in our personal lives. Events can occur that swing our momentum in different directions. Has that happened in your recent past? As you look back, can you notice that the tension builds, fear sets in, and for some, panic ensues? As leaders, we might recognize that controlling the growth from tension to panic can be all about mindset. In the boating world, as captain we can set the sails, but we do not control the wind. When the wind changes, it is us that needs to adjust. It is not often that we must abandon ship, our teams, our clients, or our value proposition. Where has the wind changed in your business recently? What might you do to make some course corrections? The captain can turn the sails, manipulate the rudder, and even change the course temporarily to achieve the vision that has been communicated to everyone on the team. Do we allow the uncontrollable wind and our reactions to it to dictate what the next move is? Maybe we can adopt the curious mindset and remind ourselves of the importance of our attitudes. What is the first thing that you can do about it in the next seven days?

As brothers and sisters in Christ, we are not immune to the tragedies, the changes, or the advancement of our society. We will experience many trials and tribulations. But it is up to us to decide how to react to them. Do you remember King David retrieving the Ark of the Lord after Saul had ignored it? "David and all Israel were celebrating before God with all their might, singing songs and playing all kinds of musical instruments—lyres, harps, tambourines, cymbals, and trumpets." 1 Chronicles 13:8. But Uzziah died when he touched the Ark. It seems that the symbolic wind changed, and it changed David's momentum.

> "David was now afraid of God, and he asked, 'How can I ever bring the Ark of God back into my care?'"
>
> 1 CHRONICLES 13:12 NLT

Where has the wind changed in your faith recently? As participants in a broken world, our faith will likely be challenged just as surely as the wind direction will change. But remember, God is still the same. Jesus is still the Savior who died on a cross for you and for me. So, what will you do to adjust your sails and not abandon our Savior and His message? What is the first thing you can do about it in the next seven days?

Let us pray.

Father God, we are easily distracted. Help us to look for your light in the darkness. Guide us towards your love and remind us of the beauty of your world where you are the great constant. May we adjust our navigation to stay the course and to draw closer to you. In Jesus' name, we pray. Amen.

JULY 11: FIGHTING OUR HEADS AND OUR HEARTS

As leaders and entrepreneurs, we are always selling something. It could be our reputation, our team, a project, a viewpoint, or our value proposition. That is a good thing because our services and goods have a purpose. That purpose is driven by our value proposition and our why. But it can take getting to know people to really be able to transfer your vision of value to them completely. Where have you lost a relationship because you did not connect about your value? Where did a relationship stop progressing when you did not get to stay focused on your value? I think that our strongest value exchanges are when our customers and clients are in rhythm with us.

Where might you be out of rhythm with your professional relationships? When we are out of rhythm it is difficult to stay focused. Recognizing the misalignment is difficult because it requires the leader to listen to different perspectives than our own. It is much easier to play two songs at the same time and see how they are not in rhythm together. When you play songs in this manner, it is not enjoyable, creates frustration and almost an immediate reaction that causes at least one song to stop being played. If you do not control the song being played then the listener will have a different reaction like plugging their ears, walking away, or maybe something drastic like turning off the energy. Today is a great day to focus and evaluate the rhythm of the teams you are serving with. What can you do about being out of rhythm in the next seven days?

> "The people of the island ... when they had waited a long time... they changed their minds and decided he was a god."
>
> ACTS OF THE APOSTLES 28:4-6 NLT

Our first impressions can be wrong. The people of Malta first saw Paul as a victim of a boat crash, then prisoner, then a god. How about that for a change of first impressions? We are people called to be in relationship with one another, to work and worship, side by side. That call is not one to separate us through our individualistic ideas but to bring us into a relationship with one another and our Lord. Where might a first impression in the past keep you from growing in a relationship? Where might your impression of a brother or sister in Christ need a little deeper look? When we are in rhythm, our performance is enhanced. We will play a better concert for the benefit of our team. Our relationship with Christ can grow deeper. Today is a great day to focus on our Lord and Savior's perspective. How many times today will you replace your own rhythm with His beat? We must listen to the small still voice and drum beat to hear it because our own desires easily get our attention. What is the first thing that you can do about it in the next seven days?

Let us pray.

Heavenly Father, you know our first impressions. Help us to move through them so that we can be in relationships that honor you. Guide us and shine your light so that we can see the potential of others in our lives. Help us to open our ears and hearts to hear your first impression. Make our hearts' first impression see past the first impressions of this world. In Jesus' name, we pray. Amen.

JULY 12: FOGHORN OR FOG LIGHTS?

Entrepreneurs and leaders have teams. I have not met a perfect team yet, have you? Although many are building a unique ability team, the teams are made up of imperfect people and imperfect technologies. Just think of the times you have thought or said that a software program could be improved by doing this or that. We do the same thing with the people on our teams because of our judgment filter. Our judgment filter often is skewing the facts. Our mind often does not want change. It wants the status quo. It wants no fight or flight decisions, but it is constantly looking and interpreting things as such. Our fears and emotions sometimes get in the way of value. They fog the facts, so they are not seen. On our journey together as a team, it just takes one person to have the fog set in and we might miss a road sign that said, "exit here" or "yield ahead."

Our journey will go off course fast when that happens. Where might you or someone on the team be fogged in right now? You may not be able to tell. Who might you be able to ask? Maybe they can see clearly in some areas where we cannot. Being the leader means we can help many when we work to clear the fog. Use your horn, your fan, or shine the light. Do what you can to get relief from the fog today and do what you can to keep it from setting in for the rest of the week. What is the first thing you can do about getting through the fog in the next seven days?

Have you ever seen a fog bank roll into a harbor or across a prairie? One side of the bank is clear, everything within sight is visible and navigable. But that foggy side can be scary. If we awaken to a fog, one can be overcome with fear, resentment, and it can turn our mindset towards a victim like attitude. When we get offended or wronged, we often might feel as if a fog has rolled over us. But we can choose what our answer will be as followers of Christ.

> "Make allowance for each other's faults, and forgive anyone who offends you. Remember, the Lord forgave you, so you must forgive others."
>
> COLOSSIANS 3:13 NLT

Where might we have allowed someone else's actions to be like a fog to us? Fogs that set in can make us think that we have no options but to wait it out, so that it clears out on its own. We can clear much of the fog, if not all of it ourselves. No judgment needed, just action, and most of it is up to us. We are the ones that have the power to forgive. Our Savior is ready, willing, and able to assist as well. What is the first thing you can do to remove some fog in the next seven days?

Let us pray.

Jesus, you came and taught us about the ultimate forgiveness. We still operate in a world of fear, though. Help us to balance our daily perceptions so that we might keep the fog banks away from our relationship with you and our relationships with others. Make us to be fog busters for others so that they might see you clearly so that they can navigate closer to you. Guide us with the lighthouse of your love. May you send the breath of the Holy Spirit to blow the fog away where love might blossom in its wake. In Jesus' name, we pray. Amen.

JULY 13: CALGON, TAKE IT AWAY

I once heard that great companies and great entrepreneurs look to take something away that makes their customers better. I can see some validity to that statement, can you? They take something away and get paid for doing it because it takes resources to haul it off. Some take away physical items like rubbish and refuse, others take emotions or obstacles, and others might take away old results. What is it that you would get rid of today? If there was no restriction on what you could remove, what would you remove? It might be frustration, fear, anxiety, pain, suffering, inefficiency, delays, or even complacency. What would it be worth to have any of these items taken away from you today?

When you identify one of these valuable items to be removed you have identified a limit. If it has a value if it were to be removed, then we could certainly consider hiring someone to do just that. What is it that your company takes away for your customers? Have you ever looked at it from that perspective? Maybe your team can come up with better services and products when looking through this lens. It is not the only lens to look through, but it just might be a powerful one. What is the first thing that you can do in the next seven days about taking something away to benefit others?

As brothers and sisters in Christ, we are in relationship with each other and our Lord. Each of us is taking a journey and hopefully making progress on our own path. But we stray from the path. We get distracted, we sin, and as we do, we begin to walk further from Christ. We can be of value to one another by helping one another keep our focus on Christ. What is it that you would stop doing to draw closer to God? Is there a loving believer that you could trust to help you take it away, to help hold you accountable and remove the limit? If you ask, they just might be willing to help. It is appropriate though that we challenge ourselves first, not focus on taking stuff from others. What we think others might need to have taken away just absolutely might not be in God's plan. Remember what King David thought he should do?

> "When David was settled in his palace, he summoned Nathan the prophet. 'Look,' David said, 'I am living in a beautiful cedar palace, but the Ark of the LORD's Covenant is out there under a tent!'"
>
> 1 CHRONICLES 17:1 NLT

Was he taking away something from God that God did not need? There might have been value there if that was the case. Did David think that God was homeless, that a tent was not a good enough home for the Ark, and it needed a home? It might have been that David was feeling guilty about all that he had been blessed with. I do not think we will ever know, but I am confident that I do not need to take away anything from God. God has it figured out, certainly in relation to me anyhow. God might just want us to take away whatever is keeping ourselves from him. Among the descriptors of our God, we could use trash collector. Let us trust the ultimate refuse service, God, and allow Him to assist us in taking away our barriers. What is keeping you from God this week? What is the first thing that you can do about it in the next seven days?

Let us pray.

Heavenly Father, thank you for so many blessings. We have so much and allow much of what we do have to get in the way of our relationship with one another. Help us to remove the clutter, both emotional and physical. May we begin to find you behind some clutter of the past as we take it away. May we help to bring others closer when they ask us for help in removing their clutter. Let us praise, worship, and be in joyful prayer when the clutter is removed. In Jesus' name, we pray. Amen.

JULY 14: VISITING THE SCENIC OVERLOOK

Being an entrepreneur and leader means sometimes taking risks. But just because they take risks does not mean that they are careless, clueless, or operate haphazardly. They also learn how to mitigate risks. This can be a power tool for the successful advancement of their organization. It is like a tourist who visits the Grand Canyon. He might jump the pole fence and run to the edge, standing there with his toes reaching over the edge perilously, looking at the great reward of the view and vistas. That is risky. Where is the risk mitigation occurring? That leader is IN the risk, there is not much for risk mitigation here. But some entrepreneurs will look around first. They find risk mitigation by finding the helicopter service, the camera on an extension stick, or get on the internet and search for a picture taken by someone else.

While some see it risky, these entrepreneurs see value. They can ride on or experience the edge without fear of falling or sometimes of failing. They can rise above the risks and focus completely on the vistas because they are over the fear. Are you at the edge anywhere in your life, with your team or business? Would an accountability partner be a valuable person for you to be able to overlook faster? They are valuable to me and many others. What can you do in the next seven days to overlook the risks without being blind to them?

Anger! It is a tough emotion for many people to deal with. I would say it is one that requires work and our energy to manage. It is an emotion that can be risky for sure. But there is a great Proverb that might help us.

"Sensible people control their temper; they earn respect by overlooking wrongs."

PROVERBS 1:11 NLT

It seems to me that when one is angry, they feel like they are in the action that has made them that way. Somehow, they have bought into some type of harm, injustice, or victim point of view at that moment. This Proverb speaks to me to rise above. It makes me think about being told not to look directly into the sun. Do not stay stuck in anger but get above it and overlook it. Maybe that is a way to mitigate the risks of being in relationships with each other. I hope I can overlook that which might make me angry today. I hope the same for you. Where might you need to change to be overlooking a recent event? We can be accountable to others when anger rears its face. We can change our perspective by taking an overlook type of perspective. What is the first thing you can do about it in the next seven days?

Let us pray.

Father God, thank you for overlooking my failures. We are a new people through your grace and gift of Jesus Christ. We pray that we might be able to overlook the fears, victimhood, and harm that has been caused in this world. Help us to reach out to you and not be glued IN the events and actions of anger. You are the great overseer which if we draw near to you, we too can learn to overlook. In Jesus' name, we pray. Amen.

JULY 15: YOU WANT ME TO TAKE WHAT?

Value is what great entrepreneurs and leaders bring to the table. It is what we are about. If we are not, our true worth is not going to be much. Our true worth is measured by more than financial riches. One can provide lots of cheap and inexpensive products or services and get financially wealthy in the process. That is not necessarily equivalent to value. Our value and delivery systems are best utilized when the customer and client are receptive to them. When they ask for products and services, we provide and give. But if the customer has not asked, then we are giving something that is not likely to be valued in the first place.

The customer will not find value themselves unless they take it. It is difficult, if not impossible, to lead someone that does not want to be led. Think about the organizations that your organization relates to. Where might your connection with a business that is in service to you be weak because you are not taking what they are offering? Where might you have a customer connection that is weak because they are not taking advantage of the level of your expertise? Collaborating to fix the disconnect might just be a strong move towards better connections, service, and profitability. What is the first thing that you can do about it in the next seven days?

As brothers and sisters in faith, we are blessed with many gifts. But during our faith journey, it is common that we might miss seeing some of our blessings. We have been given much. But what is it that we are actively seeking and taking?

> "Fathers can give their sons an inheritance of houses and wealth, but only the LORD can give an understanding wife."
>
> PROVERBS 1:14 NLT

It is beyond my reasoning that I think that I could give my children a spouse. I can count on the blessings that God provided to me as a spouse. I remember my vows which said, "I take." Yes, I did take. I agreed. I accepted responsibility. I asked her, my wife consented, countered with the official ceremony request, and I took her offer. Sometimes I think that we might be missing connections to our Lord by not stepping forward and taking. Where has God provided in the past, and you failed to take it? Maybe we can keep our eyes open for the opportunity to take. I believe that God gives us many chances to take but we miss seeing it. If we are not willing to take, we probably are not willing to keep our hearts and minds open to the possibility. I believe that God can use us to collaborate in his ministry and message on earth. Do you believe that? What is the first thing that you can do about being open to taking on something in your faith in the next seven days?

Let us pray.

Generous and gracious God, thank you for the blessings. You have given so many blessings that they are beyond counting. There have been so many blessings, we miss the opportunities to take advantage of them all. Help me to remove my blinders so that I might see what you offer, so that I might take your opportunities. Help me to prioritize your opportunities for me over what the world might suggest are opportunities. May the opportunities to love, to show compassion, to provide support and value to my brothers and sisters of faith be met with acceptance and the willingness to take them as Christ took up the cross for us. In Jesus' name, we pray. Amen.

JULY 16: YOU CAN'T TAKE IT WITH YOU

As the leader of a team, or an entrepreneurial team and possibly an entrepreneurial family, we have much to pass onto others. I like to think that there are four specific areas to be sure to cover. We all have some level of individual financial lessons and thoughts we might share. We also operate in some concept of a society or civic relationship. We also have our ideas about the mind and body connection known as faith and fitness. Entrepreneurs have an additional area of concern which is of business lessons and business-related topics. What have you done to leave a legacy and communicate the lessons of importance of your time on this earth? If you do not make the dedicated effort to capture it and transfer it, the probabilities are that it will not be picked up by others. There is a significant difference between having a baton and passing a baton. Imagine a relay race where the baton is just left in the middle of a leg of the race. Leaving the baton does not have the same impact as passing the baton in an intentional handoff. There are valuable items that are intellectual property that are lost if we are not intentional about the hand off. Most people do not have a planned handoff of assets, let alone intellectual property and lessons. What is the first thing that you can do about handing off your baton in the next seven days?

It just was not meant to be. King David was not to build the temple for his God. But he knew that there was a legacy to be transferred.

> "Now, my son, may the LORD be with you and give you success as you follow his directions in building the Temple of the LORD your God."
>
> 1 CHRONICLES 22:11 NLT

We read about the four things that he gathered and left for his son Solomon. Stone, wood, and metals were the materials collected, and labor was applied to them to prepare and finish the materials for the temple. I like to think that there are four areas of our faith that we can be working on to prepare our legacy for our next generations. How are we giving, being, doing, and with what attitude? When we focus on Christ and His sacrifice, we can look towards ourselves in these four areas to draw nearer to Him. There might not be any better way to help the next generation than to help ourselves to connect with Christ first and then share with them our path. Just displaying your path might not be enough. One might need to share, to document and to talk about these four areas. What area would you like to draw closer to Christ in, giving, being, doing, or your attitudes? If we can be inspired enough to work on the areas ourselves, we have something that might inspire growth in others. Our ability to inspire today might be the first step in creating something of an inspiring legacy for our family. What is the first thing that you can do about it in the next seven days?

Let us pray.

Heavenly Father, your legacy to us is documented in the Bible and lived out in the hearts of us as followers of Jesus Christ. But through the temptations of this world, we separate ourselves from your love. Guide us and send us your Holy Spirit to touch us.

May we help one another to give, to be, to do, with an attitude that draws us nearer to you. In Jesus' name, we pray. Amen.

JULY 17: MAKING PROGRESS AND PROFIT

As entrepreneurs or as a leader on an organizational team, we can choose to focus on value propositions or on offering commodities. Commodity types of businesses tend to be shorter term-based businesses. The transactions are quick and generally price sensitive. Competition is almost always present for them, and the importance of relationships is downplayed. But value proposition businesses result in relationships. They are focused on value first. It is expected that a result of the relationship can be a mutually beneficial profit to both parties. It does not have to be a profit at the expense of one or the other. Our world of commerce has both types of businesses. It might just be that you could improve your profits for the next two quarters by focusing on your relationships.

Our attitude towards team members can sometimes lean toward relationships or transactions as well. We can think about the people on a team that have been present only for a transaction. The attitude towards them as temporary can be restrictive in many ways. One way might result in a leader failing to invest in them at full capacity. Why should one give the same energy and resources to those that will not be here for a long return? Can you sense the restriction in that attitude? Who is the first person on your team you might think about experiencing this type of restriction? What is the first thing you can do about it in the next seven days?

As brothers and sisters in faith, we know and declare that we believe that Jesus died on the cross for us. We have been made right in God's sight by our faith in that belief. But if we are made right by this action, are we flawless, forgiven, redeemed, made new and worthy?

> "Therefore, since we have been made right in God's sight by faith, we have peace with God because of what Jesus Christ our Lord has done for us."
>
> ROMANS 5:1 NLT

If we are made right, then we have peace. Peace, it says. Where might you be carrying anxiety? Why do you and I carry it? Why do we allow ourselves to be trained and influenced by the world and the influences of media or other messages when we are right in God's sight? Maybe we can begin today to give in and accept by faith that God's got this. Let us focus on one small piece of anxiety and replace it with the perspective that God might tell us we are okay in his eyes without the worry. An attitude of peace is not a commodity. It is not a short-term concept as defined by God. Peace with God is about a relationship. This attitude of peace is worth our attention and effort to deploy. If there are bigger fish to fry, let us invite God to fry them. Sounds good to you? What is the first thing that you can do about it in the next seven days?

Let us pray.

Heavenly Father, you have the world in your hands. You have the breath of the Holy Spirit to move among us and shift our perspective. Let us release our anxieties, worries, and replace them with the confidence of your hands. Help us to release concerns when we catch them. May we trust in you, in only you, and may you be glorified through the process. In Jesus' name, we pray. Amen.

JULY 18: EMOTIONAL TANTRUMS

As an entrepreneur or team leader, one can face many of the same challenges that we see from organization to organization. One of the most rewarding and challenging resources of any team is, well, the people. Of the forty or so challenges that I have identified, most organizations will list challenges with their team somewhere in the top three when prioritized for importance. What is it that you are doing to lift your people to new heights? New heights of attitude, education, and skill to the benefit of the synergy of the team may just be the most exponential effort we can have. Our accounting systems record the pay and benefits to our teams as an expense. I think that they are better viewed as investments. Are you investing additional dollars to help grow the team?

We constantly must reinvest in our facilities and equipment because they wear out. Friction of wind and rain wear on the exterior of buildings. Internal parts of equipment grind on one another which require oil, grease, and adjustments to keep them going. Giving oil to moving machinery is like giving forgiveness to those we are in relationship with. It is a requirement to extend the relationship. Do you view your team as something to reinvest in as well? Is there a line item in your budget for that? It might be that one of the best returns on capital in a company could be accomplished by investing in its people. If there is no focus on a maintenance and investment system an organization will likely not have one that is effective. What is the first thing that you can do about it in the next seven days?

Forgiveness is one of the four subjects that I like to include under the area of giving. One difficult situation to forgive is when someone has a display of an emotional tantrum towards you. This type of tantrum, when directed at you, can be downright scary. It makes some cower, others start to boil themselves, while others might even react back. None of these reactions honor Christ but neither did the tantrum itself.

> "Hot-tempered people must pay the penalty. If you rescue them once, you will have to do it again."
>
> PROVERBS 1:1 NLT

This Proverb does not give much assistance to us at first glance, or does it? Maybe it is telling us that our focus should be on being in a relationship with people so that tantrums might be avoided entirely. When was the last time you had a tantrum directed towards God? I expect that many who read this will acknowledge that they have had an experience like this. Many, however, will not see it as a common event. I can imagine myself throwing a tantrum towards God and imagine lightning bolts coming from the skies. I do not generally risk those lightning bolts.

Even if we are just tempted towards a tantrum, the thought of the lightning bolts is enough to stop most. Forgiveness is at the core of our deepest personal relationships as it is with our relationship with God through Jesus Christ. Who might you need to forgive for a tantrum that you experienced? Who might you want to ask forgiveness from for the tantrum that you gave? If God can have a focus on grace, I suspect we might want to consider it as well and place a focus on forgiveness. What is the first thing that you can do about it in the next seven days?

Let us pray.

Heavenly Father, we are so thankful for forgiveness. The restorative power that you give us through forgiveness provides the opportunity for joy. It is like a generator to our relationships. Bring our hearts and minds to a place today that might allow us to seek and ask for forgiveness where our tantrums of the past are keeping our relationships from growing. Guide us, Lord, and hold us in the palm of your hand as you restore our hearts and draw us closer to you. In Jesus' name, we pray. Amen.

JULY 19: LIVING UP OR LIVING DOWN?

Entrepreneurs balance the opportunities and challenges of their companies, that includes their employees and their families. That balancing act certainly has its peaks and valleys, but often it is those valleys that provide the best opportunity to learn. Valleys provide experiences that are priceless, often cost us, and they develop endurance in us. Endurance. That word carries some weight with it. It means that I must get up, lift up, or even push through some type of struggle, exhaustion, or challenge. As entrepreneurs, our team members share the experience of developing endurance as well.

What are the areas that you have endured in the past? How might your current team members learn from your past lessons of endurance that they might not be aware of? Our teams do not have to personally experience all the challenges to benefit from your endurance. We can share our endurance. That can be part of our leadership journey if we make the choice. Sharing our endurance experiences can build confidence in our teams faster. If your team or a team member is experiencing a valley, what wisdom of endurance can you share with them to boost their confidence? What is the first thing that you can do about it in the next seven days?

You might have heard the expression that "bad things happen to good people." It has been a common subject for many studies in the faith world over the last twenty years, probably forever. Why? Because it is true and has been true throughout time. If it continues to be true today, then we might have two choices. One is to run and hide under the covers and ignore what is going on in the world or in our sphere of influence. The other choice might be to embrace that the amazing blessing of our eternal God is worth the risk to love, share and endure. We are called to be compassionate people as Christians, but even more so we are challenged to be people who endure. We are called to fight the good fight.

> "For you know that when your faith is tested, your endurance has a chance to grow. So let it grow, for when your endurance is fully developed, you will be perfect and complete, needing nothing."
>
> JAMES 1:3-4 NLT

I like to think that we sometimes choose to live down. Living down is living depressed, being held back by ourselves or others, and being moved away from loving relationships with each other. The other choice is to live up. Living up is finding joy and moving ourselves forward to always be growing. It is about being in a relationship, enduring and loving. Where might you see an opportunity to live up? What is the first thing that you can do about it in the next seven days?

Let us pray.

Heavenly Father, it is a beautiful day full of opportunities and challenges ahead of us. We ask for your guiding light to shine upon us as we endure. We know that the fog will clear, the sun will rise, and that your love for us will prevail. We are the people of the resurrection. Because Christ was lifted up, we choose to live up today as well. Be with those that might feel that they are caught in the spiral of living down. Help us to help each other to live up. In Jesus' name, we pray. Amen.

JULY 20: ARE WISDOM AND REBELLION LINKED?

Leading teams can be very difficult if you do not know what your vision is. We must have a purpose that the entire team can buy into, or they will not fully commit their energies and resources to the cause. Sure, they might sit on your board, they might be a member, or they might work at your company, but you will not get the best from them. A value proposition organization delivers to its consumers, but it is the entire organization that makes it happen. Your most restrictive part of your system is in fact the determining factor of your capacity. It is the restriction to your value proposition funnel. Where might you be able to strengthen your weakest part of your team and systems by concentrating on your vision? Opening the funnel can occur when you strengthen the walls to stretch the restrictive elements. What is the first thing you can do to spread your vision in the next seven days?

As brothers and sisters in Christ, we have a purpose. Our purpose is to follow Christ by living a life as a born-again people. But it is at those times when we forget to live according to Christ that we suffer the effects of sin. We can accomplish much and overcome immense hurdles when we follow the purpose. You might recall King Solomon. Remember how he was remembered for being so wise, wealthy, and the chosen temple builder for God and the Ark of the Covenant. That is a vision of clarity and purpose. But do you remember this?

> "'Your father (King Solomon) was a hard master,' they said. 'Lighten the harsh labor demands and heavy taxes that your father imposed on us. Then we will be your loyal subjects.'"
>
> 2 CHRONICLES 10:4 NLT

The people asking for relief had worked with Solomon and for Solomon. But when King Solomon died, a mutual purpose had ended (the temple was built), and they were not willing to be in the same relationship. The next King did not establish a new purpose, and it all went downhill from there. The people wanted relief from hard labor and heavy taxes. Where might you be falling short in connecting your activities with the right vision and purpose? This missing connection is a limit to any leader and in our faith. What is the first thing that you can do about it in the next seven days?

Let us pray.

Heavenly Father, we give you thanks for giving us a chance to live a purpose driven life. Help us when we fall away, get distracted, or move into the darkness. Guide our families and our cultures to know your purpose for us. Let us listen intently for your still small voice in the silence. In Jesus' name, we pray. Amen.

JULY 21: EYE CHARTS FOR MEASURING

Leading a team successfully often requires us to know when to use external resources. As entrepreneurial or team leaders, it is easy to spend most of our time with our team or our customers. But knowing when to use external resources is also important. We can get trapped into believing that our team has all the resources we need. But remember, our beliefs are somewhat reflective of our perceptions, and they are often limited, if not outright wrong. This is why magicians' tricks work because they are really just trappings of our perception. Where is your team the strongest and weakest? How might an external resource help to exponentially improve either? An accountability partner changes our outcomes because what gets measured matters. Often the process of measuring will itself change the outcome. What is the first thing that you can do about it in the next seven days?

King Asa's history as recorded in 2 Chronicles is interesting. He was one of the few Kings to do good during his reign. His focus was on God much of the time. But later in his life he tended to get distracted. When he trusted God in the early years, the Kingdom was blessed. When he did not, things tended to go against him.

> "In the thirty-ninth year of his reign, Asa developed a serious foot disease. Yet even with the severity of his disease, he did not seek the LORD's help but turned only to his physicians."
>
> 2 CHRONICLES 16:12 NLT

Where might we be distracted, turning our minds and activities from Christ's message and relationship? Could it be that distractions come from entertainment by the television, media, movies, or sites on the internet? Do you get a daily report on the world somehow? It might be in the form of a news broadcast, a newspaper, or CNBC.-com. I am curious as to how you are getting a daily report or connection with God, or do you only connect with him on Sunday at best? Maybe our world would operate a little more smoothly, lovingly, and compassionately if we did so more often. Let us think about an accountability partner for the next week and measure whether we are connecting with God daily. What we measure matters. What is the first thing that you can do about it in the next seven days?

Let us pray.

Father God, we thank you for your consistency. You are always there. We are humbled and sometimes ashamed when we think about how little of our time and resources are spent on you. Support us, we pray, as we support our brothers and sisters in relying on you. May we progress in some small way weekly. The distance from here to there is achieved by one small step, day by day and week by week. In Jesus' name, we pray. Amen.

JULY 22: IT WORKED SO WELL, WE STOPPED DOING IT

Great teams build successes upon successes and failures. As leaders of family, entrepreneurial and volunteer teams. we have probably experienced this. Reviewing and improving on failed systems gets our attention first. That could happen because our brains pay attention to pain. We do not normally seek to cause pain or experience it. We find it easy to address failures which certainly leads to enhancing value. But a review of those successes might pay dividends as well. What was so successful in the past that you stopped doing it? I suspect that many of the leaders that read this today are going to think, "I've done that!" We all probably have; I certainly claim it.

Will you allow me to collaborate with you at this moment? If so, let me guide you through a quick review. I challenge you to actually write some answers in the margins or grab something else for notes. Think back through the last three years, to what three team members and to what three clients did you provide the most value? What did you deliver to them? In your opinion, what tools or resources were important to the success of the value you delivered? Can you see some recurring tools and resources among these answers? Are you using those tools and resources with your current team and clients? What is the first thing that you can do about it in the next seven days?

We are all on a spiritual journey and we each have our individualized path. Sometimes it has extreme dips and valleys while at other times it has hills and even mountains. But the current situation grabs our attention. When you drive over a hill so fast and the bottom of your stomach disappears, you notice it and nothing else. But thankfully, the feeling quickly stops. As we drive forward, when the next hill comes in front of us, we will decide whether to go at a fast speed or we might slow down. In our faith, we have made connections with God in the past. What worked so well in your faith? Have you forgotten it and how much it helped you? King Asa of the Bible certainly forgot.

> "Do not you remember what happened to the Ethiopians and Libyans and their vast army, with all of their chariots and charioteers? At that time, you relied on the LORD, and he handed them over to you."
>
> 2 CHRONICLES 16:8 NLT

Think back through the last three years. What tools and resources were important to your successful connection to Christ? How have you used them in the last ninety days? How might you use those same tools and resources in the next ninety days? We can easily forget what tools, resources, and people have helped us to collaborate in our faith. Our next step of growth in our faith might include collaborating with those resources. What is the first thing that you can do about it in the next seven days?

Let us pray.

Heavenly Father, with you all things are possible. It is us that puts limits on you. We limit you and we collaborate with you. We pray that you might still our hearts and minds at those times when we have limited you. Guide us to not get in the way of your miracles. May you be glorified through the meditation of our hearts and minds. In Jesus' name, we pray. Amen.

JULY 23: A FIGHT TO FLOURISH, FORGIVE, OR BE FOOLISH

Is your company or team doing battle? Are you preparing for a fight? If so, it might be that the focus of your energy has turned away from its value proposition. A fight for an entrepreneurial team might be generally based on the past and present instead of the present and the future. I like to think that a "value approach" business is about the present and how to build a bigger future. Fighting can be expensive and might even be a symptom of a team in decline. But transforming a fighting mentality into a vision and value focus takes leadership and an intervention. Are there sectors in your industry or your company that seem to be on the edge of a fight? Maybe the most productive idea is that we can look around for the leader who might be able to transform it and find a value approach. When we think of inspirational leaders of the past, we often identify their battles.

Mother Theresa battled hunger, poverty, and lack of resources. President Ronald Reagan of the United States battled a wall that divided people. President Lincoln battled the concept of people owning people. But the inspiration comes from the value of winning the battle not in terms of money. The battles fought above were inspirational because they were battles that valued the love of others. They were all certainly engaged in the present time and looking to resolve an immediate threat. But the results of the battle would be love in the future. What is the first thing you can do about shaping the results of your battle in the next seven days?

I grew up with a brother and occasionally we got into fights. As children, we acted out our aggression and frustration by fighting. I am talking physical wrestling and throwing a punch. When we allowed our viewpoints to be firm, our stance was cemented, and our value to one another was gone. The fights were about getting for ourselves, and we both were willing to let the costs of the fight be very high. Physical harm and even death are a pretty high cost. But we read some great advice about fighting in the Bible.

"Avoiding a fight is a mark of honor; only fools insist on quarreling."

PROVERBS 20:3 NLT

I was a fool instead of being a brother. Have you ever done that? As brothers and sisters in Christ, where might our foolishness be filling the spots in our hearts where forgiveness can live? I do not know if both foolishness and forgiveness can live in a bedroom of the heart at the same time. If we allow them to exist in the heart in different rooms, I suspect that it might be that it causes our heart to be unhealthy. Let us be inspired to move forward in our faith by choosing forgiveness. What is the first thing you can do about it in the next seven days??

Let us pray.

Heavenly Father, you are the one and only God, the maker of heaven and of earth and of the one bedroom in our heart made for forgiveness. Let us push out the foolishness of fighting that might have taken up residence there. Make our forgiveness to one another flourish. In Jesus' name, we pray. Amen.

JULY 24: WHICH DISEASE BUG WOULD YOU CHOOSE?

Are you plagued with TB? No, not tuberculosis but by team building. Have you caught the powerful bug that allows you to fulfill a value proposition? As entrepreneurs, we can create an income for ourselves, or we can build a business that provides value to an eventual buyer, income for others, and an income for ourselves which supports our families. To which company model do you belong today? If you have the income only model, maybe catching the team building bug (Tbb) would accelerate your success and your value approach. If you have the Tbb approach in place, where have you expressed appreciation to the team in the last seven days? The Tb bug is a worthwhile bug to spread and is rewarding on many different levels. It may be the most powerful of all "bugs." As a leader, who are you going to lead?

Is it only yourself, or will it be others as well? The decision will impact our attitude because carrying an attitude of exclusive self-benefit while working to build a team will be counterproductive. When we are fully committed to building a successful team, we will make sacrifices that benefit the team. Benefiting the team can be an integral part of providing value to the customers of our organization. What is the first thing you are going to do about spreading your appreciation and bug in the next seven days?

Brothers and sisters, I love the words "broken together." I think that I am still falling short of God's expectations and desires for me. Yet, I know He loves me. He wants a relationship with me and for me to be in a relationship with you as well. Are you broken also? Do you think and feel that your brokenness is your problem, and it is up to you and only you to address it? Our brokenness is an opportunity to allow God to glue us together.

> "This is what you must do. When you priests and Levites come on duty on the Sabbath, a third of you will serve as gatekeepers."
>
> 2 CHRONICLES 23:4 NLT

The whole passage in Chapter 23 is about how the prophet helps the kingdom to be restored by building a team. Notice this part is directing only one third of the group to a task. The other two thirds also get a specific task to accomplish, and they all combine to restore and repair what was broken. Where might you feel something is broken, and how could you simplify the problem into three parts? Who do you already know that could help you with each part? Which one might be the biggest priority to start with? Most importantly, will you ask God, Jesus, and the Holy Spirit to join in the restoration? Imagine a team of you, other Christians, and the Trinity working together to restore what might be broken. Putting the team to work might need to start with our attitude confirming that we are stronger together instead of going it alone. What is the first thing you can do about it in the next seven days?

Let us pray.

Heavenly Father, we are broken but we thank you for being willing to reach out to us. Let us join with one another in our brokenness as followers of Jesus Christ. Send your Holy Spirit today to be our glue that binds us together in actions of love for one another and not hate. Open our minds as we remember the words of Jesus when we show compassion to one another. We give you the honor as we worship your Holy name and give you all the glory as we become broken together. In Jesus' name, we pray. Amen.

JULY 25: CALL OUT BATTLE STATIONS

Some leaders prepare for battle when they look at the competitive environment. It is an easy move for our brains to get defensive and then go on the offensive. But it is not quite as easy to do a check of our perception, although it just might be the most beneficial thing to do. Is your industry being threatened by technology or the internet? Will you lose employees, and will your clients suffer when seemingly the threat or enemy wins? If so, we might circle the wagons and bar the doors and windows so that we are ready for the fight. This might seem like a reasonable approach. Some leaders choose a different approach. They might ask themselves, is this our fight? Just because it appears that there might be a battle does not make it your battle.

Is our focus still on our value for others when we are thinking those are battle lines or commanding others to take your battle stations? Many times, I expect the best strategy is not to spend the energy and resources that others spend on battle prep and getting to battle stations. Maybe we can use those energies and resources to enhance our value proposition. Where is your industry or your company crying out for battle stations? What is the first thing you can do this week to shift your resources, personnel, and systems to the idea of value enhancement? What can you do about it in the next seven days?

Brothers and sisters in Christ, not every battle is ours. We might be tempted to think or even feel that they are because we are close to them. But sometimes we are tempted to join a battle when we do not need to be. There is a story in 2 Chronicles where the Israelites are supreme underdogs. You might remember a spirit takes over someone in the crowd and they are instructed to meet the opposition but not to fight. When the army approaches, a miracle happens.

> "At the very moment they began to sing and give praise, the LORD caused the armies of Ammon, Moab, and Mount Seir to start fighting among themselves."
>
> 2 CHRONICLES 20:22 NLT

Where are you being tempted right now and feel defensive like you need to get to your battle station? What would happen if you would agree to step back for a minute or two and allow Jesus to handle the battle? Maybe it might be beneficial for us to even pray and ask God if he would take the battle from us. If anyone can win a battle it is our God, the Lord and Savior Jesus Christ, and the Holy Spirit. If they can handle the battle for me, then I just might be able to find more energy and time to love and have compassion for the others who are wounded in their battles. What is the first thing that you can do to give over the battle you are about to engage in? Can you focus on it in the next seven days?

Let us pray.

Heavenly Father, you know the battles of the mind, of the heart, and of mankind. Take our fear away and our desires as we are tempted to go to battle, especially when you would happily accept the battle for us. You are the love and guidance that we need. Find us and bring us to your drop off center where battle concerns may be given to you. May we find rest in the comfort of the palm of your hand after we drop them off. In Jesus' name, we pray. Amen.

JULY 26: WOULD YOU BE MY PARTNER?

I am a proponent of building teams. I think and have often shared about leaders and entrepreneurs using external teams that can bring us value as well as using our own internal teams to deliver value. But choosing your external partners is a very important decision. That choice may be possibly bigger than what your current interpretation includes. The choice will affect your team members, your family, possibly your value proposition itself and even your other external partners. Imagine what would happen if your communications technology providers failed and shut down your services one day! Imagine no internet access, no cell phone or landlines are available today for your team. One day turns into two. Two turns into a week. Your technology partner has broken down.

Would your team, your other partners, and your customer relationships with you be affected? Some partnerships are not designed to be permanent, and some are. Where might you need to find a new partner? Some partners may be willing to grow and change with you as your value becomes greater while other partners may not. If you had a new partner connected to your team what is the most beneficial thing that they could do which would benefit your internal team, your clientele, and other vendors? Choose wisely as you may start to see the exponential effect of these choices. The choice itself can be a catalyst for value. Leading by being willing to explore, evaluate, and choose can result in executing. Where will you start, I wonder. What is the first thing that you can do about it in the next seven days?

As brothers and sisters in Christ, we have become a people gathered. But we are in a relationship that is purposed for growth. In the farming world, a landowner has their ground examined and tested for what specific areas need strengthening so specific crops can grow. Not every fertilizer would be appropriate to apply. This is just like each of us is not the right growth partner for everyone we encounter. We read,

---

> "Then Eliezer...prophesied against Jehoshaphat. He said, 'Because you have allied yourself with King Ahaziah, the LORD will destroy your work.' So, the ships met with disaster and never put out to sea."
>
> 2 CHRONICLES 20:37 NLT

Although our long-term connection with some of our partners might not be a right fit, we know that the Holy Spirit is. Where do you have a right fit connection with others of the faith? How might you show your appreciation and let them know how valuable they are to your growth and future? If you have unfit connections like Ahaziah in the reading, what is the first thing you can do to right your ship? It is simple to see and understand when you put the silverware utensils in the drawer, the forks fit well with the forks, not the spoons. Both spoons and forks are in the utensil tray though. As a leader, it can be intimidating to ask someone who has served as a fork to leave the spoon area where you found them. We remember that just because something is simple does not mean it is easy. Many times, the simplest things are those that can grow our relationships and connections with Jesus. What can you do about it in the next seven days?

Let us pray.

Heavenly Father, thank you for our partners on earth. We experience joy because of them, but there is no greater joy than the joy we find in you, in Christ, and the Holy Spirit. May we be intentional about our partners here on the earth and ask that you bless our connections. May we have the courage to find blessings where they might not exist now. Make our church stronger than the utensil tray and guide us to find our place. In Jesus' name, we pray. Amen.

JULY 27: LAYER ON LAYER AN ISSUE?

As entrepreneurs, many of us lead teams that are results oriented. We coordinate resources of many kinds to deliver value to our customers. But when we are IN those processes, we agree to dig in and even get muddy. We get dirty, worn down either physically, mentally, or both because we are getting the work done. So how do you or the team get a renewal every day? We can relate to the concept of renewal by thinking about the clothes that you wear. You pick out the clothes for the day. They are fresh, clean, and presentable as you desire. You then wear them throughout the day, and you eventually take them off as they get soiled. So tomorrow comes and you choose something new. Even if you do not have a replacement set of clothes, one will lay the articles to air out at a minimum.

Where is your business not getting renewal? It might be in some departments, divisions, or with some of your people? They might be getting muddy and even create caked on layers if we do not create a way to have renewal. When you get your clothes soiled, and your answer is to simply put on more clothes, what do you think will happen? Nothing gets renewed but merely covered up or layered over. If we do this our divisions, departments, or people would be like giant puffballs of clothes, and somewhere beneath those layers is our purest value proposition. I am not sure that the layers of clothes would be attractive to our customers or one another. It would affect how efficiently your team operates. It seems reasonable that layer on layer would begin to limit us. The soil is then unlikely to be removed and becomes hidden within the company. That is not a results-oriented approach which looks internally as well as externally. Where do you know some layering has occurred in your company? You might find it if you go looking for limits. What is the first thing you can do about it in the next seven days?

We live in a broken world. But as Christians, our hope is not in this world. But when we live in that world, we get soiled like our clothes do. When we fail to love one another, it is like getting splashed with mud, walking into a dust storm or your food dropping from your spoon and rolling down your shirt. You are soiled.

> "The night is almost gone; the day of salvation will soon be here. So, remove your dark deeds like dirty clothes, and put on the shining armor of right living."
>
> ROMANS 13:12 NLT

Where do you need to remove the clothes of yesterday and be renewed? Christ came to show us that God offers that cleansing every day. The choice is will we accept it and put on the new wardrobe today. Let us be intentional about getting rid of our soiled layers and renewing more often. What is the first layer you want to get rid of? Where are you going to seek to renew? What is the first thing you will do about it in the next seven days?

Let us pray.

Heavenly Father, we thank you for your never-ending offer of renewal. Your grace is enough, and we fall away every day from it, but you have given us the gift of renewal. Help us to remove the layers that we think are comforting but are just layers of soil upon soil. Help us to remove them and to draw closer to you through that process. Let me start each day with a fresh wardrobe provided by you. Bring your renewal upon us now, and may we participate to put on the fresh of a new day. In Jesus' name, we pray. Amen.

JULY 28: DO YOU THROW OR CATCH MORE?

Congratulations. As a team, family, or business leader you are guiding others on a path. We have shared a thought before about companies and teams knowing their purpose. I like to think of the path as the purpose itself, and your team is working while moving forward or backward on the path of purpose. But do you control every step they take, their breathing, or where their eyes look? It could be that the most important thing to understand and communicate is that they are on this specific path. If team members are not excited to be on the path or do not like the path, then they are not aligned properly. It is okay to not like the path, but it is not acceptable or in their best interest to be on it then. Your team should be comfortable being on this path, but they do not need to approve your steps, nor do we need to approve everyone of theirs.

It is up to you to decide the path and the direction that your team will travel. If we do not lead in this manner, then judgment and resentment have a chance to grow and value to clients and customers might decay. Where is your trail or path of purpose not clearly marked? A big part of the path of purpose is accountability. How do you talk with your team about whether you are on the path and going in the right direction? Communicating with the team is like playing catch. We share a message with others which is the ball, and the team receives it which is the catch. Will you be accountable to make the path of purpose have a higher level of clarity this week? What is the first thing you might do about making your path clear so that others do not trip in the next seven days?

As brothers and sisters in Christ, we are all on a journey. Our paths all lead to the same place, but each path will have its own twists and turns. We will see each other going in different directions almost every day. Some will be celebrating while others are mourning. Some will be strong in their faith when others have weakened.

"Yes, each of us will give a personal account to God. So let us stop condemning each other. Decide instead to live in such a way that you will not cause another believer to stumble and fall."

ROMANS 14:12-13 NLT

These can be tough words for who among us has not judged others? The direction is clear. Refrain from causing others to stumble. It makes me think that when I cross someone's path, I can be intentional. I do not want to harm their journey, cause a collision, or trip them. We could do that if they were in a difficult spot, and we make them look up or turn their head quickly which might cause them to lose their footing. Although on different paths, we can be accountable to be in relationship with them to support and question with love. The only behavior we control is our own. The path is set before us, so we should choose wisely. Where might you be stumbling or causing others to stumble? Who can you help to catch in a stumble to assist them to stand instead of pushing them down? Who helps to catch you when you stumble, and have you thanked them recently for their support? Which decision is more important on your path this week; to provide clarity, or catch someone with curiosity? Will you be accountable to do something this week?

Let us pray.

Heavenly Father, we give you thanks for the path you have given us to walk towards you. You will be the one to judge us. May we draw nearer to you by judging others less and lifting them up. Help us to guide ourselves and our families on a path towards you. When we cross paths with others, may our compassion and ability to catch one another be more important than pushing each other aside or pushing others down. Catch us, lift us and may you be honored and share all the glory when we come to the end of our path. In Jesus' name, we pray. Amen.

JULY 29: DO PIRATES SAY, "ARRR, I LIKE ME SCARS?"

As a leader of a team, we will experience failure. If we do not, we really are not risking much. Sometimes we really miss the mark though. It is like shooting an arrow at a bullseye-ringed target. Sometimes you get the bullseye, other times you are in the rings and sometimes you miss the target completely. What is the last thing that your team did that missed the target completely? We could have those on our team that might want to gloss over and excuse the miss. But learning from the miss is vital to our growth. No excuses are needed but causes may be seen when we look back briefly. One important step that can be beneficial to us is to acknowledge how the miss affected the rest of our value proposition. The opportunity cost of a miss gives us the opportunity to apologize where needed. It can start the learning process and value enhancement. We can enhance even further by our teams learning what we should not be doing. One of the largest opportunities of a miss is to collaborate with others. If your red arrows consistently miss the target, would you consider finding a collaborator to handle the red arrows with you? What can you do to enhance your value proposition because you failed in the last year? Where are your red arrows? What can you do about it in the next seven days?

Fellow followers of Christ, where have you been broken in the last 30 days? Was it your words from the powerful tongue? Was it an act of selfishness instead of showing compassion? Maybe it was an act of sinning that directly hurt another person. The good news today is that our brokenness can be healed. Our wounds can be bandaged and treated with love and eventually all we might have left is a scar. Have you ever realized that scars are good? They mean that you have overcome. There are examples of many bad people in the Bible. One about as bad as they come was King Manasseh and at the end of his journey, he renewed his relationship with God.

"But while in deep distress, Manasseh sought the LORD his God and sincerely humbled himself before the God of his ancestors."

2 CHRONICLES 33:12 NLT

I am sure that Manasseh carried with him the scars of his bad years. We all have been wounded, but are you ready to leave behind the wounds of the past and accept healing? How about moving from the health of the healing process into the wisdom of knowing and seeing your scars? Do you have wounds stuck in the wound phase? Jesus can use our scars to help us grow and provide peace. Who will you collaborate with to move your wounds to beautiful scars? What is the first thing that you might do about it in the next seven days?

Let us pray.

Heavenly Father, you are all the grace we need. You have given and shown us the power of your healing and the way to be in relationship with you. Help us to see the wounds of the past as the scars of wisdom of the present. Draw us near you as we move our scarred hands into action in honor of you. In Jesus' name, we pray. Amen.

JULY 30: SETTLING FOR LESS?

As a leader, we balance the use of resources. Our teams are assembled with our people, their thoughts, and energies. We provide them with systems and procedures. We might even have materials or technologies to mix in. But when our service or product is ready for delivery, what words do we choose to share? Do we focus on how inexpensively we assembled it? Or could it be we focus on something else like how valuable it will be for our customer? To focus on our costs is not acknowledging that a value proposition company wants to achieve a win-win solution. We can be profitable, and our clients can be significantly better off because we have been in a relationship together. Where have your communications been focused lately? Do your clients and customers know you want to deliver a win-win? If we are not in relationships that are win-win then the relationship will be at the expense of someone.

We would do well to remember that the people on our teams are also customers. They make the decision everyday as to whether they want to be aligned with the team or not. When we lose sight of them as customers, we begin to see them as costs. Team members are not costs for a value company approach. They are investments that we make to provide value for the other external customers. What are you doing to inspire your investments to perform in a more valuable way? I suspect that the team leader who finds a way to inspire the internal customers to a high win-win level will see exponential growth. What is the first thing you can do about it in the next seven days?

Do you haggle about prices? I know that I have before. And I must admit that I have lied before when haggling and felt justified when I did it to get a better price. The whole process can challenge your perspective in many ways but maybe only if we haggle with the wrong person. How would you haggle with God? What price do we think is acceptable for God's grace? Is the price to have eternal life and love something that we want to minimize the cost of in the first place? It certainly is not worth any lie to others because you cannot pay for his grace anyhow. It is priceless.

"The buyer haggles over the price, saying, 'It is worthless,' then brags about getting a bargain! Wise words are more valuable than much gold and many rubies."

PROVERBS 20:14-15 NLT

Maybe we can share some valuable words in the hearts and ears of one another instead of focusing on how much is in our pockets. Where are you being challenged about the change in your pocket and the words in your head? Our negotiating and haggling in this world might tend to create a habit of negotiating with God. That is a slippery slope. Perhaps it is better to determine the cost of the actions of our faith and make a measurable commitment for what we can afford at this moment. Where might you be tempted to haggle or negotiate this coming weekend? How about being inspired to do no negotiating, no settling, and no haggling with our faith? I hope that you make it to worship and fellowship without negotiating with other activities. What is the first thing you can do about it in the next seven days?

Let us pray.

Heavenly Father, your word is Holy. The words from your Holy Spirit speak directly to our hearts. Help us to heal from the words that we share in this broken world. Guard our tongues, shield our ears, and protect our hearts from the attacks of this world. Bring us together with words of love, words of compassion, and words of truth. In Jesus' name, we pray. Amen.

JULY 31: GREETINGS DAY!

I want to ask us to consider, as team leaders, how do you introduce members of your team? It can be awkward to be part of an originating conversation or gathering and not be introduced. I've been there and I bet that you have too. I believe that it is a serious part of who we can become as a team. I have met entrepreneurs who do a great job of introducing their teams, while I have met others who do not introduce their team members at all. If we do not introduce them, we might fail to tap into the full potential of our team's value. We could be wasting energy as our clients and customers do not know to whom they can reach out to on certain issues. Where might you be restricting your value because you have not introduced someone? An introduction is one way to provide value to our team members as it provides affirmation, which is one of the four ways in which we can reward one another. We do not know what connection we might have missed out on when we fail to introduce others. There are social, professional, family, faith, or even hobby connections that might be made with an introduction. What can you do in the next seven days to introduce more effectively?

This is my friend, my brother in Christ, my men's covenant group brother, a go-to laugh partner, my best resource in the field of all things associated with printing, John. Yes, that is his real name and those are the real descriptors that I could use when introducing him. It might just be in a world of political correctness that we have forgotten how to introduce people. Did you take a class in school about how to introduce someone? What about at church? Did you attend a seminar or Sunday school class on how to introduce a fellow brother or sister of the faith? If we do not have the training to introduce others, it might just be that we are not deploying the skill and not having the impact that we can have for Christ. This question might just hit many squarely and to the point. How do you introduce Christ?

"Greet Apelles, a good man whom Christ approves. And give my greetings to the believers from the household of Aristobulus."

ROMANS 16:10 NLT

The entire 16th chapter can challenge our perspective of introducing. Are you having an impact on others with the means that you introduce others? How might we confirm our introductions even when we depart as taught by the way the writer of Romans did it? Introducing others in a meaningful way is likely best done when we have the correct attitude. Placing importance on introducing others challenges us to be focused on others and their value. What is the first thing that you can do about it in the next seven days??

Let us pray.

Heavenly Father, thank you for your voice. You have created the world and given us hope in Christ. You are the provider of grace, joy, and love, and you have shared it by sending us Christ. Watch over us as we use our tongues to introduce our brothers and sisters in Christ to one another and to those who do not know Christ yet. Send your Holy Spirit to be among us when we introduce Christ to others. Make all of our introductions bring honor to you. In Jesus' name, we pray. Amen.

AUGUST 1: ARE WALLS KEEPING YOU SAFE?

There is a good read titled, "How the Mighty Fall" by Jim Collins. As leaders of families, companies, and teams we might expect some falling to occur. Instead of an accidental fall, maybe we can focus on what we can start making to fall on purpose. Our why is our most important value proposition.

What is consistently getting in between it and your team, your family, or your customers? Can we design a means of dismantling whatever walls are blocking or obstructing our purpose? If it is not a wall we want, we can break it down, or weaken it on purpose and allow it to fall.

We have some trees at our vineyard in which their trunks were cut or scored so that they would stop growing and fall. The scoring was a way to let them fall. Engineers have put dams on rivers in gorges around the world to create hydroelectric power. The river rises, then it falls, and does so on purpose as it creates power to provide light to the world.

As a leader, I think that we do get to choose which walls are going to be part of our organizations and systems. Some walls were started for protection but can eventually become restrictions to our path of future growth.

If our walls are not for us, then they are against us. What is the largest wall that needs to fall to further your progress? What is the first thing that you can do about it in the next seven days?

Brothers and sisters in Christ, we have a great opportunity to recognize our challenges. Do you remember King Nebuchadnezzar?

"Then his army burned the Temple of God, tore down the walls of Jerusalem, burned all the palaces, and completely destroyed everything of value."

2 CHRONICLES 36:19 NLT

The King of Babylon came and destroyed all of Israel and left the land desolate for seventy years. It might be very difficult for us to destroy our own walls, especially the walls of sin in our lives. But we have the power of the Holy Spirit with us that can destroy the walls of our sin that get built around us. We do not have to accept that our bad habits are just how we are. We may choose to tear down even the longest and strongest of the walls that we have lived with. It simply takes us to do a flip, to do an intervention on ourselves to decide to let those walls fall. Once that is decided, we can begin to take action to start pulling out a stone here, scraping away some mortar there, and allowing the power of the flood waters of God to push against those walls. The cleansing water of God is offered to us daily. What wall have you allowed to stand in your path of faith? Are you ready for it to come down? Who are the most important people that you can share your readiness to have the wall come down? Let us focus on the one step we can achieve whether it is a first chip at the mortar, the pulling of a stone, or the crushing blow of the wrecking ball. What is the first thing that you can do about it in the next seven days?

Let us pray.

Heavenly Father, walls are all around us. Some are visible and others are invisible. We have allowed them to have power over us. Today, Father, we ask that you guide us as we examine our walls. Some we thought were keeping something out and away from us, protecting us. Open our eyes to recognize that some walls have been keeping us from a deeper relationship with Christ. Send your cleansing power, send your water. Make the walls come tumbling down, and may you be glorified as we stand upon the rubble. In Jesus' name, we pray. Amen.

AUGUST 2: A LEMONADE STAND

Did you ever have a lemonade stand as a child? If you did not, or have not ever been to one, I suggest that you find one soon before the summer is over. As entrepreneurs and team leaders we can take some lessons from those young entrepreneurs. At the lemonade stand, the product is simple. It may not be the best quality, nor the best looking, and you certainly take your chances on the flavor as the sugar may still be at the bottom of the pitcher. Where has your product or service gotten complex? At the lemonade stand, the personnel are key. Their dress is not a suit and tie but appropriate for the conditions, their eyes show their value, and the value exchange is more about relationships than the product. Where has our focus on personnel become a lower priority? At the lemonade stand, the offer is for a limited time only.

The exact hours are going to change, and lunchtime and snack time are questionable times for service. School will also be starting which means the stand will probably be gone soon. In fact, when it comes back it may be the little brother or sister or neighbor child who runs it next time. Where is your company focusing on the past or future instead of now? Where has your business or team forgotten these values of personnel, consistency, and service? Maybe it is time for a quick audit? As a leader, we are responsible for the audit. The three characteristics of the lemonade stand are keep it simple, have engaging personnel, and keep the time element for limited time only. What is the first thing that you can do to audit your team for these characteristics in the next seven days?

Sisters and brothers in Christ, the world is a complex place with lots of messages. We are hit every minute, it seems, with some kind of message whether it is our phone, the computer, or a billboard. But today let us remember this message from Matthew. "

> Then he said, 'I tell you the truth, unless you turn from your sins and become like little children, you will never get into the Kingdom of Heaven. So anyone who becomes as humble as this little child is the greatest in the Kingdom of Heaven.'"
>
> MATTHEW 18:3-4 NLT

The lesson of simplicity of the lemonade stand is spoken here. Maybe we can bring the love and innocence of the lemonade stand type of service to our neighbor. We do not have to know everything or be everything. But what if we were to just bring Christ with us so that he might quench the thirst of those that are driving by on the path of faith. The lesson that personnel are key to any success reminds us that we are to be in a relationship with one another. We will love others and be hurt by others but must be resilient and know that God will always be there for us. There is no location where we can have a lemonade stand where He will not watch over us. The lesson of having a limited time offer reminds us that the lilies of the field are taken care of and so are we. Shall we spend another moment in worry, thinking about revenge, withholding forgiveness, or withholding ourselves from blessing others? We all only have so many hours on the earth before we can spend eternity in another way. While we are here, it is not about the taste of lemonade, it never has been and never will be. What is the first thing that you can do about it in the next seven days?

Let us pray.

Heavenly Father, the lemon trees, soil, water, and sun are all yours. Comfort us as we allow our minds to bend our perceptions of the complexity of this world. Bring us back to our path where we might find rest in simplicity, in relationship, and in our time with you. May we come to Christ today and find him at every lemonade stand we stop at. May we open our eyes to the opportunities in front of us so that we do not pass them by. In Jesus' name, we pray. Amen.

AUGUST 3: COUNT, COUNTED, AND ACCOUNTABLE

Being a leader of a family, an organization, or a company has many different characteristics. Two of them that might just be the most important are being intentional and accountable. Leaders set the why, the tone, and the course. The intentionality of these three components is going to be seen, felt, and heard by your team members and your clients. Once our intentions are clearly communicated, we want our team to follow, and we will take measures to hold them accountable. But the leadership will establish the pattern and purpose of accountability. We, as leaders, might be the most important people to be held accountable. It is our personal accountability that our team will look towards as an example. Our ability to get their buy-in to accountability starts with us. We set the standard of accountability. How do you lead by example with your accountability? What measures are you monitoring for your team and for yourself?

How do you share successes or lack of performance? Is it by weekly meetings, some technology, or a combination? If you asked an outsider to look at your accountability system, where might they say you are at your strongest and weakest? What is the first thing that you can do about it in the next seven days?

My tongue gets me in trouble sometimes, I know. I have been married to a wonderful woman for over 30 years. She can tell you the many ways I might have done that. But when I take my time and avoid being quick to speak, my tongue seems to get less poisonous. As a follower of Christ, I believe that I can cause less harm and show more love by being intentional with my words. Having a method to be accountable for them also helps. Making promises on a weekly basis is how I do it. How do you allow others to hold you accountable for your words?

> "Do not trap yourself by making a rash promise to God and only later counting the cost."
>
> PROVERBS 20:25 NLT

If we are a considerate people, our promises will be intentional and less rash as the Proverb warns us. A promise made can be a promise kept. Where might you be able to make more of a considerate promise in your faith? The wisdom of making an intentional promise is powerful. Promises made intentionally move us forward and can connect us to Jesus. When I promise to read the Bible every day for one week, I offer myself to be exposed to the Holy Spirit. When I promise to pray for others on every Tuesday during the season of Lent, we connect with God in our prayers. When I promise to fast on Mondays during the month of August, I connect with Jesus and his suffering from being in the wilderness for forty days. What is the first thing that you can do to make a well-constructed promise in the next seven days?

Let us pray.

Heavenly Father, your grace is enough. Your gifts to us are as countless as our sins. We want to draw nearer to your love and know that we come up short. But we know that we can direct our attention and be accountable to one another. Guide us as we help each other to grow in our relationships. Help us as we work to be less judgmental and more loving. May we step forward with our promises to one another, to live, to love and to follow Christ. In Jesus' name, we pray. Amen.

AUGUST 4: WHEN WE ARE DOING

As entrepreneurs and leaders, we can impact others by our attitudes. We might ask what attitude we can share to provide the most value to our organizations. The first attitude likely to be valuable is to be appreciative or thankful. Regardless of whether you are showing it, we all want to be appreciated. If you are showing appreciation, you will likely connect with your team and your customers. If we can do this, an attitude of appreciativeness can be a form of a gift. The cost of that gift is zero, but the value can be priceless. Another attitude that is valuable is your "bigger" attitude. Is your past bigger than your future, or is your future bigger than your past? Having an attitude that your past is bigger than your future means that you are probably in decay. Decay does not normally provide much value, growth does. If your attitude is that the future is bigger, then the present is likely brighter, and it certainly has movement in a growing pattern. Where can you develop your "bigger" attitudes that could add value to your team? How can you share those attitudes and who on your team could it help the most? What is the first thing that you can do about it in the next seven days?

As brothers and sisters in Christ, we can be sharing the do's and the do not's. Have you ever looked at the Ten Commandments that way? In our everyday lives, I expect that we are caught in a combination where we experience both attitudes. But which will add the most value to the church and your faith? I think that the do's bring the most value. They keep us in a relationship. The do's are gifts that we can give.

"Ears to hear and eyes to see— both are gifts from the LORD."

PROVERBS 20:12 NLT

What words and attitudes have you been sharing recently? Have the majority been the do's, those gifts to others, or might they have been something else? What would happen this week or even just today if we were to focus on the do? I think that it just might make today a gift. Consider this, what will your team members feel if you do something that helps them achieve? How could a team member move forward if you do a special recognition of thanks that is not normal? Who would surprise you the most if they shared with you today that they appreciate the way that you lead? When we think of a name, we can see the power of doing. You can imagine a feeling that my question evoked. But it would be the actual doing of the person that would potentially build the relationship. That builds community. That is what builds our church community as well. What is the first thing that you can do about it in the next seven days?

Let us pray.

Heavenly Father, you have created the world and everything in it and given it all to us to be stewards over. Let us show our appreciation today. Be with us as we thank you for such a wonderful gift of the day. Thank you for the gift of Jesus. Thank you for giving us the opportunity to love one another regardless of the circumstances. Help us to see a different perspective when all we feel is fear. Guide us as we move from the do not to the do. May the glory and honor all be yours. In Jesus' name, we pray. Amen.

AUGUST 5: THE CHICKEN OR THE SERVICE DEPARTMENT?

If you ask a poultry producer what the greatest question is, what might they say? It might be, which comes first, the chicken or the egg. As entrepreneurs, which comes first, sales, delivery, or support? We build many divisions and tasks to support our value systems for our clients. But any task or division that begins to focus on its value only tends to harm the overall value of the organization. The value any company delivers comes in a total package. There is likely to be marketing, research, sales, billing, accounting and so much more. Without it being connected all together, you miss the value of the enterprise. Where might your team be focusing into a division versus being focused with all divisions? Is your team's progress and value to your customers being held back by a single task or division? Who on your team has the capacity to assist in finding a higher level of collaboration? Are there teams outside of your company that can help improve your collaboration? If you know your why, lack of collaboration among your divisions could be your largest obstacle. What is the first thing that you can do about it in the next seven days?

As Christians, each of us are called to become born again. We are refreshed, renewed, and cleansed of an old life. We then become part of a new family, the family of followers of Jesus Christ, which we know as the church. But we move forward as individuals, connected through Christ, growing in the community of church. Being in service to the world as God has asked us, provides value to the lost and to each other. In your faith, where are you not working with others?

> "I planted the seed in your hearts, and Apollos watered it, but it was God who made it grow."
>
> 1 CORINTHIANS 3:6

We do not hear much about Apollos today, and that is okay. We all do not need or want to be front stage. But we all come as broken and sinful people. But if we are renewed and cleansed it makes us all acceptable to be with. How might you work with others differently in your faith? How might your efforts to work with others be holding your growth back and stunting your faith? Choosing wisely and intently who to collaborate with in our faith provides the opportunity for exponential growth. What is the first thing you can do about it in the next seven days?

Let us pray.

Heavenly Father, you have built us as a people. We can be your church. Help us to look around and decide how we can come together to connect, grow, and serve. You are first, we are second, but we can together be a community with no need for a placement. Our place is in your love. In Jesus' name, we pray. Amen.

AUGUST 6: THE HEART, HANDS, AND FEET OF THE MATTER

As team leaders or entrepreneurs, we have many moving parts deployed to deliver value. I like to think of it like it is a body. Each part: the hands, the feet, the head, and the heart, needs the others to fully function or it will be limited. So, what is the lifeblood of your business or team? Could it be your value that people, or businesses are willing to pay for? While that might be true for a commodity business, a value-based business likely has something else. I think that the lifeblood of your team is the purpose that moves that value. Your why or purpose is like the heart of the body. If that is true, then we could lose sight of your why. Different reactions could occur like your heart might skip a beat. Other body parts might harm the health of the heart or endanger it. Your blood pressure might drop. You might even have a heart attack and the entire body begins to shut down and die. When the heart stops completely, in the world of medicine, every other focus drops immediately. The medical team will solve the heart issue first. Where has your team skipped a beat recently? Our inability to recognize the limits of the different parts is important. Without the heart, there will be no long-term value provided. Maybe a look at your purpose can bring your team back into rhythm. What is the first thing you can do about it in the next seven days?

As a Christian, we are part of the church which is described in the Bible as being

Christ's body. The message of Christ, the "why" of our faith, is as critical to our faith as our heart is to our body. We read,

---

> "People may be right in their own eyes, but the LORD examines their heart."
>
> PROVERBS 21:2 NLT

While we allow for distractions to occur, it might be best then if we consider the heart when we make decisions. The next big decision might easily be tested by asking ourselves, "Will Christ approve or disapprove of the action or result?" That gets to the heart of the matter. Where have you been asking yourself why recently? Has it been to answer the question from a worldly perspective which is limited? We can ask that question of why and seek the perspective of Christ? We have eyes to see and ears to hear. We have hearts to pump and stomachs to digest. We have all kinds of body parts with limits. But there is no limit to what Christ can do in our lives if we allow him to guide our limits. Are you willing to go until God says no? His perspective is likely to bring love, grace, and peace but it might require us to examine our own hearts. What is the first thing you can do about it in the next seven days?

Let us pray.

Jesus, you came to the world and shared your love. It was not the righteousness of the world that you sought to be with but the broken. You came and healed, loved, and taught. You were resurrected from the dead which showed us God the Father. Send your Holy Spirit today to separate us from the brokenness and from the emptiness. Bring us together so that we can know the joy of life with our Savior. May that knowledge in our heart lead to the righteousness of our minds. We pray because we have been born again to live with you in us. In Jesus' name, we pray. Amen.

AUGUST 7: ARE YOU INSPIRED?

As a leader in your family, for your team or at your company, where are you inspiring? Inspiring others may come in many types of forms. Sometimes it might be by sharing your creativity, while at other times it might be just by being a great listener. A leader might inspire in an email, letter or by phone call. Inspiring does not have to be a charisma charged motivational meeting, but it might be. Where have you been inspiring in the last thirty days? Regardless of the means, form, or type, being inspirational delivers value. As leaders, that is what we are about, value. Value is action that you take that helps others move forward while continuing to overcome obstacles. It is action that allows us to grow with opportunities. Being inspirational just might be the most important role of all of your tasks as a leader. It can be a challenge mentally to see oneself as being inspirational for others.

Ask yourself who the three people in your life were that you might have inspired. What is it that you did to inspire? Maybe today is the day to consider sharing it again with your team. I wonder how those on your team have inspired you and others. When that thought just occurred, we can tell that it might be easier to recognize when we have been inspired than when we have provided it. Inspiration is important and it brings value. How can you bring some inspiration this coming week? What is the first thing that you can do about it in the next seven days?

As a brother and sister in Christ, we are in relationship with one another. I have been reflecting on moments where others have had a positive impact on my life. It seems as if these moments are where others have been able to inspire me. I did not necessarily recognize it at the time that it was inspirational, but it really was. Those moments have happened in many different forms. Some were in professional development forms, others in challenges of health, and others have helped with my walk of faith. Where have you been inspired in the last year? How was it helpful to your faith?

> "So the king asked me, 'Why are you looking so sad? You do not look sick to me. You must be deeply troubled.' Then I was terrified, but I replied, 'Long live the king! How can I not be sad? For the city where my ancestors are buried is in ruins, and the gates have been destroyed by fire.' The king asked, 'Well, how can I help you?'"
>
> NEHEMIAH 2:2-4 NLT

So out of sadness, the king delivered value by taking notice and asking how. The king helped and he inspired Nehemiah to move forward in action. Where might you be able to help someone else today to move forward by asking, "How can I help you?" What is the first thing that you can do about it in the next seven days??

Let us pray.

Heavenly Father, we all have the ability to help others in some shape. We know because we were formed in an image of you. Your compassion and love go ahead of us wherever we travel. Be with us and guide us as we relate to one another. Give us courage to help others when we see the opportunity. Help us to be strong in heart and word when we ask others how we can help them. In Jesus' name, we pray. Amen.

AUGUST 8: THEMS FIGHTIN' WORDS

When we lead teams, we are likely on occasion to see or to be part of a quarrel or an all-out fight. Those quarrels or fights generally come from a desire to have something that we want. It is normally about us or our team over some other team. The focus is an I win, and you lose proposition.

Sometimes I wonder just how much energy and resources are wasted on the win/lose proposition instead of being generally focused on value delivery. This battle can happen internally to a company just as easily as it can occur externally between companies.

Where have the quarrels been lately that you are involved in? Have they been internal or external? Where might you be able to change the perspective right away from win/lose to value driven? I am sure that resources can be better used if we do. This can especially be true if the fight is occurring internally. Where is your team focused on battling in a win/lose scenario? What is the first thing you can do about it in the next seven days?

The weekend has come and is quickly departing or has left. Did it start or end with any quarrels? How about the last month or year, were there any quarrels then? In our competitive society, a quarrel is an everyday occurrence.

We see quarrels and fights in our homes, our neighborhoods, and even in our leadership of the government. But our quarrel or fight always starts with us. A quarrel is about my perspective and my inward thinking.

"You want something, but you cannot get it. You kill and want what others have. But you cannot have what you want. You argue and fight. You do not have what you want, because you do not ask God."

JAMES 4:2 NIV

I normally do not find God in the fight. Have you ever wondered where God goes when we argue or fight? Maybe he does not go anywhere. Maybe it is us that goes somewhere, away mainly from his love, joy, and grace. Where have you quarreled and have not come back yet? Who were the participants and are they away as well? I have known others who have never left the fight of the past and carry it with them with the wounds of the past. We all have the possibility to carry the quarrel forward. Is it in our best interest to carry the fight or to find where God has brought peace? There is always peace available during the fight, but you must look for it. Perhaps that is the fight, the fight to find God's peace when we feel the least like pursuing it. What is the first thing that you can do about it in the next seven days?

Let us pray.

Heavenly Father, our quarrel is never about you, it is about us. We might get upset or outright angry with you, but we are the ones with the problem. You are beyond reproach. We find our challenges and disappointments in our perspectives. Guide us today to navigate through the peaks and valleys. Make the arguments and fights, even those as vicious as Cain and Abel's, be transformed into relationships based on your love. In Jesus' name, we pray. Amen.

AUGUST 9: MORE THAN ROMEO AND JULIET

As an entrepreneur and team leader we see what our team members do and how they do it. But if you could reduce what they do and how they do it, could you identify just two purposes? I want to challenge us as leaders to look for two not one. What are your two purposes? There are great pairs like salt and pepper, the heart and mind, hot and cold, as well as Romeo and Juliet. What are the two purposes of your organization? What are the two purposes of your accounting division? Their two purposes will be different from the sales department. But all the departments and their people will serve the organization and its clientele. As leader, can you identify the pairs that you might think are the two core purposes of your divisions? Do they match up with what your division leaders believe the purpose is?

If not, then there is misalignment. Knowing what the purpose of each division is gives the team the opportunity to be aligned. When we are not in alignment, our values will be challenged. Our teams could function like a three-wheeled cart to which the wheels are never in the same direction. This will likely cause friction and frustration. Leaders at any level can look for the two purposes and the alignment that they are likely to bring. Today I am challenging those who are in the position of leadership to address the alignment. Is love, respect, or value missing from your alignment? What is the first thing that you can do about it in the next seven days?

In our faith, we are connected as a people. That means that there are at least two pieces. There is me for example, an author, connected to you as the reader. What great pairs can you think of from the Bible? There are more than pairs of people because we can think of pairs of actions as well. Mary and Joseph are a pair, but we also think of trust and obey. What two purposes are you living out in your faith in the next quarter while you serve God?

> "But from then on, only half my men worked while the other half stood guard with spears, shields, bows, and coats of mail. The leaders stationed themselves behind the people of Judah."
>
> NEHEMIAH 4:16 NLT

It will not be long after this point in scripture that we find the builders wearing swords and laborers carrying spears while they assemble the wall. Can you focus on just two purposes for your activities before the holidays arrive? Yes, there are many activities that you will do. But what is the purpose of all that activity? I'll be connecting myself and others to Christ and growing in my faith. That is connecting and growing for me. When we choose what the two purposes are, we can lean in and be intentional to them. Which will you choose? What is the first thing that you can do about it in the next seven days?

Let us pray.

Heavenly Father, you have created a means to be in relationship with you during life and death. Thank you for the opportunity to wake up this day and to experience all the pairs of this world. Help us to clearly see the choices that will draw us closer to Christ. Make our path shine brightly so that we can follow your light. You have called our purposes to be those that bring honor and glory to you. We shall be strong and courageous about our purposes for the next quarter. Guide us seven days at a time. In Jesus' name, we pray. Amen.

AUGUST 10: YOUR STRONGEST MUSCLE

As a leader, what is your communication style? Are you a strong silent type or maybe a free-flowing river of words? Our tongues might be the strongest muscle of the body. I think that it is certainly the most dangerous as it can bring down and destroy people, communities, and even countries. Have you ever been the victim of someone's verbal attack? One can be attacked even if speaking in sign language. A vicious dialogue in sign language does not have the same power on a person with hearing because of the delivery of the language. But the words can attack. So do the words from the tongue. When our teams get off course, how do we get them back on track? Is it with a strong and powerful tongue of correction, accusations, or blame? I have heard the voice of the navy's Blue Angels flight team during a show. The voice is calm and respectful even though the planes are hurling through the air at jet aircraft speed. Where has your tongue been too strong and harmed others? Where have you used a calming voice to keep others from hurling towards a crash of some kind? Maybe this week we can stop a crash before it happens by controlling our tongue. Use the muscle well this week and give it the exercise that helps and heals without limits. What is the first thing you can do about it in the next seven days?

It is interesting how our past patterns of behavior affect us in the future. Our speech patterns are no exception. Our tone of voice and the way we were corrected by our parents or guardians is likely to affect the way we correct others. But we are cleansed as brothers and sisters in Christ.

"To slander no one, to be peaceable and considerate, and always to be gentle toward everyone."

TITUS 3:2 NIV

Where have our old patterns popped up that were established prior to being cleansed in Christ? Maybe the love and compassion that we have been extended can tame the wild beast of our tongue. I have an image in my head of being in a cage at the circus and the lion tamer is me. But the creature on the pedestal in the ring is a tongue, not a lion or tiger. I think that more people have been harmed by these powerful tongues than have been harmed by lions and tigers. Who in your sphere of influence would you appreciate a taming of the tongue? I know that those I love the most would appreciate it if I would consider taming my own when I am tempted to use its power in a harmful way. They are the ones near it the most often. Is putting a limit on the use of our tongues worth our attention this week? What is the first thing you can do to tame your tongue in the next seven days?

Let us pray.

Heavenly Father, we listen for your still small voice in the depths of our hearts and souls. How comforting it is for us to not suffer from your tongue. For nothing could withstand its power. Guide us as we tame our tongues. Wash away our tongues' harming power and place on the tip of our tongues compassion and love. In Jesus' name, we pray. Amen.

AUGUST 11: A DRIED UP POND

Are you a purpose driven leader, stuck in a company bogged down in what needs done? As entrepreneurs and leaders, we know that our systems and processes are run in exchange for revenue. But when the revenues become the primary focus, we restrict value. I do not have the ability to measure endorphins yet, but when we connect with our clients at the why level I would bet they go sky high. That flow of endorphins picks up and gives us a boost. I believe when the "why" connection happens, that revenue flowing is just a natural extension of the relationship as well. It is as natural of a flow as are the endorphins. Where are your teams restricted from the why? That is likely where the revenue and endorphin flows have been dammed up, diverted, or maybe even dried up going underground. Maybe you can open the flow again or get some repairs done while there is a dry channel. A focus on the "why" is likely to help you spot the opportunities. It might even open the clarity to see other partners and team members that can help.

When ponds dry up, the landowner performs maintenance. Many times, the pond will be modified and serve better because of the experiences those connected with the pond have had. Landowners reshape the boundary, extend the dam or raise it, and they might even add an island somewhere that has been too shallow. Maybe a new island of revenue and value is waiting for those that are willing to evaluate the purpose again. Will you be accountable to be the one to lead the evaluation process? A pond will not perform maintenance on itself. What is the first thing that you can do about it in the next seven days?

As Christians, we can be a very productive people. Our call to love and be in a relationship has little if any restrictions. Our call however, is not to be disengaged, to be lazy or unproductive. Our faith walk can include a desire to find a way to provide value to others. Often the ways to provide value are things that others need or should want to pay for. If you are a great vegetable farmer, then I'll bet that you could take your produce to the farmers market where others would give you money in exchange for your product. Work is good, but what if we were to transform our work into a different perspective?

> "Work willingly at whatever you do, as though you were working for the Lord rather than for people."
>
> COLOSSIANS 3:23 NLT

Can you show up for work today envisioning that it is God's company or service? That he is the owner? How might you go differently about your professional duties today? If a person would apply for a position, how would God handle the interview? How would the applicant answer questions if they were answering to God? The results of working for the ultimate Creator are rewards that are priceless and unmeasurable. This concept is in alignment with the idea of building a kingdom-based business or a kingdom-based team. Where can you improve your value proposition this week? Are you willing to be accountable to building your team in some shape or format mentioned above? What is the first thing that you can do about it in the next seven days?

Let us pray.

Boss, Father God, thank you for the opportunities of the past. Thank you for shaping the world and me. We are your people. Put us to work as you would have us to do. Inspire our employment to bring you honor. Connect our work, while at recreation and play, to glorify you as well. Reward the work in our relationships with your glorious sunrises, sunsets, and everything else that we might need from you. In Jesus' name, we pray. Amen.

AUGUST 12: PUT ME IN COACH

As an entrepreneur, where do you go for training? As a team leader, where do you go for training? We are supposed to be the one in charge and ready to do the task at hand. Is that correct? After all, you were chosen or took the reins yourself to be the responsible one. I think that it is easy and common to be judged as a leader. Those judgements are normally comparisons of the organization's progress from one point in the past to the present. But as leaders, are we really looking from where we are today, in the present, to where we need to progress to? If we are a bigger future type of people, we are looking forward and when doing so, we just might see many areas of the unknown.

We can have a better sense of clarity and confidence then by being with others. Being led by them and their insights in their fields just might be part of our training as leaders. We can think of Olympic or professional athletes to look at in their early stages of development. Without the intervention and insertion of trainers, coaches, even teammates and opponents, they would not be able to develop. Where might you and your organization need to look for a coach? The future just might depend on it. Collaborating at a higher level might require trusting the perceptions of an outside viewpoint. What is the first thing that you can do about it in the next seven days?

Brothers and sisters, how is your training going? In the great game of life, we have the words of the Bible to guide us. We also have a Savior that has already paid the cost for our failures. But if we want to draw as close to God as possible, we may need to trust ourselves to help us improve.

> "I discipline my body like an athlete, training it to do what it should. Otherwise, I fear that after preaching to others I myself might be disqualified."
>
> NLT 9:27 1 CORINTHIANS

If we are focused internally, it can be difficult sometimes to see a view that might help us grow further. Sometimes we cannot see the forest because of the trees. Which Olympic athletes do you think are not coached? Who can you reach out to assist you as a coach and begin to collaborate? Picking an area of improvement in our faith journey and getting a coach might be what one can do to grow in your faith. What is the first thing that you can do about it in the next seven days?

Let us pray.

Heavenly Father, thank you for your guidance. Insert people into our lives that might help us to draw closer to you. May we love one another and find clarity and confidence together. Help us to serve one another and to be served without the judgment of this world getting in the way. In Jesus' name, we pray. Amen.

AUGUST 13: DO YOU SPEAK OR LISTEN?

As an entrepreneur or leader, have you ever been right and being right wound up hurting your value proposition? I don't think that this is uncommon. Our egos want to be right, and our brains function under the premise that we are right.

There are many scientific experiments that prove this point. In the next three seconds, think about the year Abraham Lincoln died. I'll bet that your brain experienced a little stress. Some of you might have googled the answer to get it right.

There are a few that even know the answer to which I would ask, why do you know the answer.

Knowing when Abraham Lincoln died has nothing to do with the future success of your team. The only way that answer is relevant to your future is if it applies to your company or your team's why.

Let's observe today and highlight where it is that we might be focused on being right.

If we are going to observe this, then let us follow it up with thinking about why it is important. Generally, we get better results when we focus on the why. It seems to me that the most inspirational people knew why they were doing what they did. What is the first thing you can do about it in the next seven days?

As brothers and sisters in Christ we have likely experienced conversations and challenges in our society that are focused on people being right. We have seen challenges among churches about who is right. "That is the right way!" and "That is the wrong way!" are challenges that tend to divide people. But as leaders, the question we need to start with is our why, Jesus.

This is the power behind the question, "What would Jesus do?"

"Be careful, however, that the exercise of your rights does not become a stumbling block to the weak."

1 CORINTHIANS 8:9 NIV

A focus on rights is not a focus on love. When you look back over the last seven days, can you see frustrations or conflicts that were really based on someone being right?

It would provide value to ourselves and the world to be focused on a question first instead of thinking we have the answer. We can find conflict and frustration around those who always insist that they are right.

Value is inherent in questions among our relationships. Will we choose to inspire relationships with questions? Perhaps we still think being right is the most important issue. What is the first thing you can do about it in the next seven days?

Let us pray.

Heavenly Father, as Creator of everything there is, you are all knowing. You are the one who is right. Amplify our ability to listen instead of making statements. Make the hush of the whispered question be exponentially more powerful than the shouts of our rights. We ask this in Jesus' name, we pray. Amen.

AUGUST 14: IT STARTS WITH ATTITUDE

It is important as leaders and entrepreneurs to have relationships with mentors and others. We can consider their examples and learn in private as they can be confidants. When things work great, it is easy to find team members to celebrate with. But when there are challenges and losses, we need someone as a confidant as well. The sooner we can overcome the feelings that come with loss, like guilt, disappointment, or shame, the quicker we can learn our lessons and move forward. Who do you have that you may go to today if things are not going well? There is power in being able to have reflections of others with a different perspective to help us get back on track. If we have an attitude that we can do it by ourselves, we are missing the use of powerful assets.

Where might you be off track, and who is the confidant you can go to about it? What is the first thing you can do about it in the next seven days? Where might you be off track? Are you stuck and thinking that you are the only one who can get you unstuck? This is a mindset trap that can be easily slipped into. The saboteurs in our mind are likely to creep into our space to influence our attitude. Who are the three candidates to consider as a confidant to which you can go to about it? If you do not have one, then find one. If you cannot find one, feel free to reach out to us. What is the first thing you can do about it in the next seven days? I want to confess. How many times have you heard that in the last week, last month, or last year? Once, maybe twice? Our desire to be strong and be right goes deep within us. But just as we can help each other grow and celebrate in good times, we should be able to count on one another in the bad times as well.

> "Confess your sins to each other and pray for each other so that you may be healed. The earnest prayer of a righteous person has great power and produces wonderful results."
>
> JAMES 5:16 NLT

We need brothers and sisters in Christ to have as confidants with which to bring our troubles to. We all fall short of what God wants us to be. Except for Jesus, even the greatest examples of faithful living have fallen more than once. Do you have a couple of accountability partners for your faith journey? Are you a partner for someone else?

What a relief it would be to take a load off of our backs. Our confidants and partners just might be able to help us. It might start by considering an adoptive attitude that others are willing to help and not harm us. What is the first thing that you can do about it in the next seven days?

Let us pray.

Jesus, you are our confidant. You have sacrificed so much for us, but often we need a confidant that will look us in the eye. We need their love and understanding without judgement. Our accountability partners can allow us to bare our souls when we need to, which can lighten the load. This world gets heavy sometimes, and it is often our partners that can help to pick us up. Give us strength to lift and not judge. Help us as the body of Christ to lift each other up to you. In Jesus' name, we pray. Amen.

AUGUST 15: WHO WILL BE AT THE PARTY?

As entrepreneurs and team leaders, how do you celebrate? Hopefully there are celebrations to be had because you have some wins. Sometimes people think wins are big things like life and death moments and they certainly can be big.

But wins might also be small individual parts put together, assembled, and delivered for value to our customers and clientele. It really takes a win and win mindset to get to a big WIN.

When we assemble the small parts into a win, is the celebration just mine, or the assembler? Maybe it belongs to the team? Team members of the past might even have had a hand in it. When you celebrate, are you involving the entire team? If we do not give the opportunity to the entire team to celebrate then we might not be affirming them and their contribution. I am not sure that there is much value in a method that only one person celebrates as an accomplishment.

Where are you not including the team in your celebrations? Do your divisional staff celebrate with the other divisions? Do your staff from other locations celebrate with one another from city to city or state to state? When we narrow the focus inward to our own celebration, we have a party of one.

Assign a value to that approach. Now focus the celebration outwardly to include the entire team. Assign a value to that approach. Which approach do you think has the higher likelihood of impacting your clientele? What is the first thing that you can do about it in the next seven days?

We have a lot to celebrate as followers of Christ. But it is interesting how easy it is to find something to worry or fret about. Just watch the national news at the start of the evening and they will show you how to avoid celebration. We can celebrate though, as we have received the greatest gift possible.

So how are you celebrating? Are you sharing your celebration with just those that you can impress, those like yourself, or can you celebrate with even the lost? We read about a celebration at the beginning of the book of Esther.

> "When it was all over, the king gave a banquet for all the people, from the greatest to the least, who were in the fortress of Susa. It lasted for seven days and was held in the courtyard of the palace garden."
>
> ESTHER 1:5 NLT

I am sure that there is a celebration coming soon in everyone's life that reads this devotion. Who might you include in the next celebration that has never been to a celebration with you? You never know how it might affect your relationship until you try.

Will our focus for celebration be inward or outward in the last half of the year? What is the first thing that you can do about it in the next seven days?

Let us pray.

Heavenly Father, I want to celebrate right now. I want to celebrate your compassion, your love for us, and our love for the church. I want to have a party with you, God. It is a party for you before the birthday party for Jesus comes. Guide us and light the way like candles brighten a birthday cake. Give us smiles to share and words that show one another we care. Let us celebrate these gifts that you have delivered today and the ones that you will deliver tomorrow. In Jesus name, we pray. Amen.

AUGUST 16: DO WE RECOGNIZE THE BIG

Big moments occur for everyone, but do you recognize them when they happen? As a value driven leader, this might be one of the most important actions we can do. To see a big moment and really sense that an opportunity arises, causes a little uneasiness, uncertainty, or anxiety.

In these moments, we might find a little tension, trepidation, and fear along with potential, excitement, and purpose. You never know when a team member is in the right place at the right time to have an enormous impact from a big moment. But to capture value we must take it, get through it ,and not run from it. Sometimes it takes the leader to recognize it as one of those big moments.

We can then help them to see past the fear and to mitigate the risks. Where have you had some big moments that you might reflect on and say, "I was made for that?"

Where might one of those be occurring for your team or your clients? As leader, the start of our work week might get a big jump forward by looking for the big in your present and future. I am curious, what is the first thing that you can do about it in the next seven days?

Hey brother, hey sister, do you believe that you were made for something? I mean to question us if God might have a specific action that He intends to have us do?

We have free will, but I just wonder if the Holy Spirit is supposed to reach out and touch us occasionally. If for nothing else, it might give us a glimpse of what eternal life might be like and share in something good that does no harm. Mordecai believed so.

> "If you keep quiet at a time like this, deliverance and relief for the Jews will arise from some other place, but you and your relatives will die. Who knows if perhaps you were made queen for just such a time as this?"
>
> ESTHER 4:14 NLT

Have you felt this way yet, that you were made for something? The first step for recognizing those moments may be to recognize and believe that it is possible. I believe we are. Remember, anything is possible through our Savior Jesus Christ. What is the first thing you can do about it in the next seven days?

Let us pray.

Father God, thank you for big moments. Thank you for the relationships that you grant us to be in, and thank you for your still small voice. May we be quiet enough in our big moments to listen for it. When we hear it, may we be encouraged enough to have the confidence to take the needed action to bring you glory and to bring us just a little closer to heaven on earth. In Jesus' name, we pray. Amen.

AUGUST 17: HONORING OR NEGLECTING?

Here is a challenging question for entrepreneurs and team leaders. Which part of your team do you honor the most? While you ponder your answer, allow me to reflect on some possibilities. If I say that I honor sales, as it brings revenue to the company, the company's reputation will suffer if sales support and production are not effective. If I say that I honor the team that keeps track of where the numbers are, then I expect that our sales team and the numbers might not perform up to your standards. The answer to where do we honor the most might just be that the honor needs to be spread among the entire team. It is true that at times, it might need to spread in an unequal proportion. When a body becomes injured, we give a quick review of the entire body but quickly focus on the injury. We then honor it by giving it resources, treatment, and care. Where might your attention and honor have been neglectful recently? What part of your team seems to be in a regular or even constant state of injury? Instead of dealing with constant injury maybe the team needs some changes that would help it to be less prone to breaking. What is the first thing that you can do about it in the next seven days? As brothers and sisters in Christ, I want to remind you that you have value, regardless of how broken you might think you are. I do not know what your calling is, what your spiritual gifts are, or how you might love others, but you are a valuable part of the body of Christ. God has a place for each of us. Christ came and was resurrected for you and for me regardless of each of our unique talents, capabilities, and skills. He has asked each of us to do our part though.

> "In fact, some parts of the body that seem weakest and least important are actually the most necessary. This makes for harmony among the members, so that all the members care for each other."
>
> 1 CORINTHIANS 12:22, 25 NLT

Let us live fully, not in fear of anything but to love, honor, and obey. Where have you not been living up to the call of Christ? How might you be able to live and love deeper? Where might you be able to reach out and help someone else up? What is the first thing that you can do about it in the next seven days?

Let us pray.

Father God, your design is too grand for us to understand. We are as different and unique as we could be and yet we are called to be one, the body of Christ. Lead us and guide us to honor one another in love. May our words of our tongues and actions of our hands and feet glorify you. In Jesus' name, we pray. Amen.

AUGUST 18: WHEN THE TRUMPETS ARE OUT OF TUNE

As a leader of a team, we know that we have a value proposition. I liken that proposition to the melody of a beautiful piece of music. But as leader, you are the conductor. There are many instruments in your organization. Those instruments of your team: accounting, marketing, and the IT department are like the trumpet, the violin and the drum of the orchestra. You direct all the instruments and listen for anyone of them to be flat, sharp and with the beat. When they are off, it is our role to be in relationship with them to bring them back to the melody, be crystal clear, and on the beat. We want them to be clear of any barriers which keep them from being part of the beauty of the melody. Where do you the leader need to work with others to gain that clarity? Your melody is at risk when they go sharp or flat. Being accountable as the leader means we need to have those talks when others are out of tune. What is the first thing that you can do about it in the next seven days?

Christ offers us the most beautiful melody by which to lead our lives. But as we interact with this world and those that are lost, we need clarity. If your notes as part of Christ's melody are not clear, the message might not make it to the lost. Are you tuning your instrument, yourself, on a regular basis? Are you in worship, are you studying the word, and are you asking for and giving forgiveness in your daily walk? Going flat or sharp is certainly going to happen and that will move us from the melody.

> "Even lifeless instruments like the flute or the harp must play the notes clearly, or no one will recognize the melody."
>
> 1 CORINTHIANS 14:7 NLT

Our Savior has given us the ability to join the melody regardless of how out of tune we think we are. Where might you need to fix your tone whether sharp or flat? To be accountable to move the tuner is our role. Jesus wants you in the melody. What is the first thing that you can do about it in the next seven days?

Let us pray.

Heavenly Father, you make the whole earth your orchestra, and we thank you for that. May the birds sing today with all of nature. May we join your beautiful melody with our hearts and minds. And as we do, may we play our part in tune with you so that others may hear with clarity your call to life with you. Guide us Mighty Conductor, make us your vessels today. Encourage us as we hone ourselves to be part of the melody. In Jesus' name, we pray. Amen.

AUGUST 19: DRIPPING FAUCETS AND PLUGGED DRAINS

Leaders and entrepreneurs, where is the water? Wherever water is stored there is potential. That potential can protect as well as serve. Think of the water stored behind a dam. It keeps the rivers below from flooding every spring. But it also assures that there is a constant supply of water for irrigation among the fertile soils along the riverbanks. Where is the potential, the untapped momentum in your organization right now? Is it flowing in a manner that maximizes its power to help? Could it be that it is being held back by a plug, unnoticed for what it could do? Before you look at any team member that might control a plug, it might be beneficial to know where you are the plug. It could also be that you have lost all your momentum and need to build up some reserves. A plug will most likely still be in place unless someone comes along to collaborate and starts to move it. Who can you collaborate with to get some potential moving? What is the first thing that you can do about it in the next seven days?

The power of water and its meaning in our faith is widespread, almost overflowing. We are baptized with water. We are cleansed and refreshed, born again in Christ. These examples represent some type of symbolism of water. Moses floated on the water and separated the water as Israel escaped the Egyptians. Noah built and floated in the ark as the water rose. We know water as Christians. We are steeped in so much historical water that we should probably be sloshing around as we walk. But water is either only good or bad. There is no in between. You can either drink it or it is unsafe to drink. Is it fresh or bitter? So today as brothers and sisters, we can relate that water to our actions.

"Does a spring of water bubble out with both freshwater and bitter water?"

JAMES 3:11 NLT

For the balance of our day today, will we be a spring of bubbling, even sparkling good water? Maybe our disposition has been that of bitter water. I bet a prayer might just have the power to transform the bitterness into something more refreshing. Prayer can be inviting and even cleansing for us and others that we have contact with. Are you ready for some fresh water for the autumn? We all have faucets that we ourselves have the strength to turn on. But some faucets need the help of others to turn for us. How can you collaborate in your faith to tap some potential? What is the first thing that you can do about it in the next seven days?

Let us pray.

Heavenly Father, you have washed the entire world, and we thank you for that. As we act out our sin, we dirty ourselves, and your creation. Bring the freshness that we may receive through your Holy Spirit. Let us awaken to the freshness like the grass that awakens to the sunrise with dew upon its blades. Make us shine in the brightness of your love and draw nearer to you. In Jesus' name, we pray. Amen.

AUGUST 20: DELIBERATELY DELIGHTED

Entrepreneurs and leaders are in the people business. They lead the people that shape the teams that deliver value. Maybe the definition of a small employer should be that everyone feels that they are on just one team. It is easier in a big organization to feel like you have your own team in your division or department. This can happen when you have multiple locations in different cities as well. Regardless of how many teams you have, you are still in the people business first. How do you express appreciation to your teams? Is it a delight to be a leader of this team? Do the people you lead know it? I believe that a team that works together can accomplish more than a team of individuals only working for their effort. It can be delightful to work on a cohesive team. Many people can relate to an interaction with a company for which the team member failed to be appreciated. We experience their negativity, their failure, and their mistakes when this happens. But when a leader can transform mistakes into investments for the benefit of the team, we can approach delight.

Think of the best investment you have ever made in a gift for someone else, for a spouse or family member. The thought of that gift will likely bring some delight to your mindset right now. How do you show where you are delighted with the team? We all like to be appreciated so maybe it would be a positive influence to show your delight to others. Are you willing to be inspired to share the mindset of delight today? What is the first thing that you can do about it in the next seven days?

As a brother or sister of Christ, Jesus is delighted with us. He comes willingly to those who are broken or are in need and delighted to be in relationship with us. As the body of Christ, we are called to do the same. We cannot ignore the fact that we will often be challenged. But often our challenges are our largest opportunities in disguise. We read,

---

> "For the Lord delights in his people; he crowns the humble with victory."
>
> PSALMS 149:4 NLT

Where are you delighted with your brothers and sisters that you are in relationship with? How have you told them that recently? Maybe a handwritten note, a special text, a call or an email might just make someone else's day. If God takes delight in us, maybe we should be sharing delight with others as well. The concept does not require exorbitant resources, just an exuberant mindset. This is a Friday challenge. Are you willing to inspire someone else's day by sharing your delight with them? What is the first thing that you can do about it in the next seven days?

Let us pray.

Father God, join us we pray as we celebrate our brothers and sisters. Help us to take delight in the word, in worship, and in our relationships. May we share your love for us as we anticipate being delighted again and again. In Jesus' name, we pray. Amen.

AUGUST 21: ARE YOU BLUFFING?

Bluffing is a strategy for poker players, not entrepreneurs or leaders. What is the test to know that this is true? Could the test be to ask yourself, as a leader, where would bluffing provide value to the person you are bluffing? Would your employees appreciate you bluffing about a raise? What would you think about a politician who bluffed? We do so much more by focusing on providing value than by faking our way through a value delivery process. We think through processes, develop resources, and engage people to deliver it all. Where might you have some situations where you could be doing some bluffing? Using a bluff requires the right attitude to be effective. Rejecting the bluff as an unacceptable technique is also an attitude as well. Do you want any of your team to bluff you or your customers? What is the first thing you can do about it in the next seven days?

Brothers and sisters, there is no place in our faith for bluffing that I can think of. We are called to either have the confidence to act or to not act. There is no in between. God does not need us to say anything towards a bluff because he can see the love or lack of it in our hearts.

> "The wicked bluff their way through, but the virtuous think before they act."
>
> PROVERBS 21:29 NLT

We know the power of the bluff to harm others because we have seen examples of it in our lives and society. The bluff is so powerful because its purpose is to cause others to take action because of the misinformation. You can even be an inadvertent victim of a bluff. Maybe you miss getting a value because of what someone else does in a bluff.

Imagine a coworker who would bluff about their capabilities and is assigned a task you desired. That is sad if you are more qualified for the task. It is easy to take a victim mentality when we think about bluffs. But our challenge today is to recognize where we ourselves are bluffing. Where do you need to accomplish something important in your faith? What steps can you take to honor the goal? Make a thoughtful statement of action, make a promise, and follow through in these next ninety days. What is the first thing you can do about it in the next seven days?

Let us pray.

Jesus, prepare our hearts to know that there are important steps in our faith to take. Light up our path so that we might not stumble. Help us to lean on our brothers and sisters to keep from falling. We do not want to bluff anyone. Remind us with your Holy Spirit, if we start to bluff. Let us follow through so that we might honor the Father with our words and our actions. In the name of our Savior Jesus, we pray. Amen.

AUGUST 22: THE PRICE OF WORDS

As entrepreneurs and leaders, we direct many resources. We even assign values to those resources. It is not uncommon for an organization to have a balance sheet of those resources. But some of the most valuable resources we have are not tracked on the balance sheet. Today I would like to suggest that the use of our words belongs on the balance sheet. What value do we place on our words? There are few things, if any, that affect all other values more than our words. Words can enhance or harm all our other resources. If you want to enhance your values, how might your words be able to do just that? Can you think of examples where others have used words which have harmed your values? We need to think no further than how valuable our employees and team members are. How is their value reduced when others use demeaning words towards them? If one resource could multiply the value of all others we would certainly focus on its use. I believe words have that power. What words might you focus on to enhance your team members' value? What is the first thing you can do about it in the next seven days?

As Christians, we know the power of the tongue. We have many stories in the Bible that warned us about the dangers of our words. Today, I want to highlight the positive power of the tongue. Our words can enhance our lives together as brothers and sisters in Christ.

"Kind words are like honey— sweet to the soul and healthy for the body."

PROVERBS 16:24 NLT

That certainly makes our positive words sound valuable. Our good words create blessings for others, they can be healing, and they can be encouraging. Words can affirm others and acknowledge their gifts which remind us just how valuable we all are. Sure, we are all broken in some means, but our words just might be the glue that connect us and bring us together in Christ. Where do you believe that someone could use some good words in your sphere of influence? What is the first thing that you can do about it in the next seven days?

Let us pray.

Heavenly Father, so often you speak to us in our hearts, but we don't actually hear your words. Our words in this world have the power to harm or to heal. Thank you for sending Christ to us and allowing him to share words of life and love. Sharing words of hope, health, and healing can restore us. Move in our hearts to share the words of healing with others. When we ourselves are feeling broken, inspire us to change our perspective with words that cost us nothing but are priceless in value. In Jesus' name, we pray. Amen.

AUGUST 23: CONFIDENCE TRUMPS FEAR

As leaders and entrepreneurs, we lead teams forward, into the future. But in the future, we will experience both risks and opportunities. Sometimes they are one in the same, but they need to be addressed. This is where value can be found. If you are removing or mitigating risks, then you are providing value and giving confidence. You do not find confidence packaged and for sale, but many products or services are attempting to do just that. Take away risk and confidence fills some of the space that the risks formerly held, at least in our minds. Where does your team enhance confidence in each other and for your clients? I find it interesting that when you enhance confidence you just might be removing a risk. Is that the way your team looks at it? As a leader, when was the last time you spoke to your team about their confidence? If your team is not acting with confidence, then they are likely to be feeling the effects of fear and risk in their work or their life away from work. The role of leadership calls for us to play the trump card of confidence. The role of playing the confidence card might be a worthy objective today. What is the first thing you can do about it in the next seven days?

Brothers and sisters, the world is a heavy place. I think of the old pictures from my childhood where Atlas held the world on his back. When we lose our confidence, it seems that the weight of the world comes down on us. But our confidence in our Savior has offered to remove that weight. We do not have to accept those heavy burdens. Jesus has already lightened the load and will take it in the future as well. Why then do we live in such sin and cause those heavy events to happen? I think if we take measures to mitigate our dangers, the confidence of Christ will be ever closer to us.

> "A prudent person foresees danger and takes precautions. The simpleton goes blindly on and suffers the consequences."
>
> PROVERBS 22:3 NLT

Where are you not being or acting confident? Maybe all you need to do is mitigate some risk and step forward with action to have some precautions in place. Who do you know that may help you with taking some precautions? In how many areas of your faith walk would those precautions help you to have more confidence? There may not be anything more important than our confidence in Christ and having confidence in this world because of it. Lead today with confidence. What is the first thing that you can do about it in the next seven days?

Let us pray.

Heavenly Father, you hold the confidence of the world in the palm of your hands. As we move away from you our risks, danger, and fear increase. Let us gather among ourselves and support one another to mitigate the fear with your influence. Let your light shine into the dark crevices of fear. Let us walk confidently now where we walked in fear in the past and may you be glorified and honored in the process. Holy Spirit come. Church family come. Hold our hands to take away our fear. Encourage us to be in the Lord's presence. In the precious name of Jesus, we pray. Amen.

AUGUST 24: STOP, DROP, AND CALL ROLE

As an entrepreneur and team leader we are in a relationship with our team. We are on a great journey with the team and our clients. But that journey can find us with our team members mysteriously off the path. There are butterflies and distractions that capture our attention. The distractions create limits for us. We all are subject to those distractions, which when followed, can find us going in opposite directions. As team leader, our teams progress and our peace of mind or confidence is affected by those not going in the same direction. Where have you seen a team member going the wrong way before? Did you stop and send someone to go get them? Did you go check on them yourself? When we find them, it is really up to them whether they choose to come with us in the direction of our value proposition or if they want to go in another way. Allowing our team to choose another path is critical to our success as we need our confidence. Where do you need to have a confident conversation to remove some limits? What is the first thing that you can do about it in the next seven days?

Brothers in Christ, where in your relationships has someone fallen behind and possibly strayed from your path together? Sisters in Christ, where are your sisters? Is someone stuck in the past? Has someone gotten disoriented and cannot find you? Listen closely, is someone shouting out in the distance and needs you to come back to get them?

> "But I had no peace of mind because my dear brother Titus hadn't yet arrived with a report from you. So I said goodbye and went on to Macedonia to find him."
>
> 2 CORINTHIANS 2:13 NLT

You are not alone on your path. We all at some point are the one turned around, disoriented and lost. At other times, we are the ones who can stop what we are doing. We are the ones to roll back to get our brothers and sisters in Christ. Where might the Holy Spirit be moving among your relationships? When we hit a limit that stops us in our tracks we might ask if there is someone we can help. What is the first thing that you can do about it in the next seven days?

Let us pray.

Like the world's foremost superhero, Lord, you have rescued us. You have the power to move our hearts, to drop our fears, and to roll the fog from our eyes. Send the Holy Spirit to move us today, to go back for others. Help us to find our brothers and sisters to be in relationship with one another. Be with those whose voices are too weak to cry out for help. Make the Holy Spirit cry out for them. Let the shouts, let the voices, let the whispers be heard. Quicken our step to find one another. In the name of Jesus, we pray. Amen.

AUGUST 25: ACCOUNTABILITY BATTLES COMPLACENCY

As a leader of families and organizations, is our focus on value? We would be wise to remember in their natural state they will go through a lifecycle and decay. By adding value, we grow those resources. The most valuable item a leader has at their disposal is its people. Where are you adding value to your team members? Are you helping them to grow, to do things smarter, and to use their unique abilities? Keeping your team of resources in their original state is limiting. That is not a value focused approach. Where might you have limited your team? As leaders, we are the ones who prepare an accountability system to address value through the organization. Accountability starts with the leader, and it ends with every member of a value approached team.

The story and history of Moses is familiar to all those who have seen the Charlton Heston portrayed Moses in the movie, *The Ten Commandments*. He was a man of God, and victorious in moving the nation of Israel. But his actions were not enough for Gods intent for us today.

> "So if the old way, which has been replaced, was glorious, how much more glorious is the new, which remains forever!"
>
> 2 CORINTHIANS 3:11 NLT

Gods value to us through Moses was enhanced by Jesus. It is easy for us to get complacent when we have success. Complacency is not valuable. It is not part of a growing or valuable energy. As Christians, can we find an area or two in our own lives where we have been limited by our complacency? There is so much capacity to love others and the need for our love is all around us. Where are you not growing but keeping status quo? We just might find some of Christ if we dare to venture on that part of our faith journey. What is the first thing you can do about it in the next seven days?

Let us pray.

Heavenly Father, thank you for men like Moses and women like Mary. Nudge us to move from our complacency. Move us to leave the actions of sin and to engage one another in the ever-growing love of Christ. Bind our growth to be with you. In Jesus' name, we pray. Amen.

AUGUST 26: DO HEARTS TALK OR SING?

Entrepreneurs deliver products and services to clients. But value-based businesses want more than clients. We want raving fans. I think that our connection to "why" really goes to the heart of our business. The constant beat throughout our team's activities delivers the lifeblood which drives value. The beat of the message delivery can be a challenge to keep consistent. When did you have your last "why" conversation with your team? Is your team comfortable enough with the "why" to share it with your customers? When we allow the team to get off the beat, our collaboration is not as strong as it can be. How long will we allow ourselves and others to be off the beat? What is the first thing you can do about it in the next seven days?

As men and women of faith, we too have a "why." That "why" is Jesus Christ. We are called to be in relationship with Jesus, the church, and the world. But how are we to share our "why" with the world when we are sometimes far apart in our views?

> "Whoever loves a pure heart and gracious speech will have the king as a friend."
>
> PROVERBS 22:11 NLT

It might be that we are to show others our love. Yes, at times we all struggle to share love. We can get bitter, unforgiving, and selfish. Of course, we are broken people in a broken world. But our Savior Jesus Christ showed us and taught us. Let us go out this week with our hearts in loving mode and find a way to collaborate on the same beat. We do not all play the same note but when we keep the beat with Christ as conductor, we know that love can win. Those we encounter will surely appreciate it. What is the first thing you can do about it in the next seven days?

Let us pray.

Jesus, you spoke your lessons. We have the privilege to be able to read them today. May we accept the challenge to love purely, speak graciously, and may God receive all the glory. It is in the precious name of Jesus that we pray. Amen.

AUGUST 27: IS PRESSURE ON YOUR HOLIDAY GIFT LIST?

As leaders of families and organizations, the holiday season certainly can bring its rewards. But it also can bring pressure on you and your team. Schedules get enhanced and modified. Patterns of production can change. Travel, gifts, and parties demand your attention as well. How do we deal with the pressure and stress as they bear down on us? The answer might be that they come down on us as part of the "what" and "how" of our value. There are three parts. Those parts are the why, the what, and the how. Simply remembering "why" we do, what we do, might be the key to some relief. Have you ever done a project that you would question why did we do that? The best time to ask why is before you do it. Why is this holiday season going to be different for your team? I might suggest that if we do not ask ourselves the "why" now, it will not be different. Why is the fourth quarter going to be the best quarter of your year or life for that matter? If you want to be inspired or inspire your team, perhaps we should find that answer now. What is the first thing that you can do about it in the next seven days?

As brothers and sisters in Christ, we are not exempt from the pressures of the holiday season. Our focus on Christ, our why, just might be the answer to releasing the pressure. Can you really have a perfect gift for the holidays? Are you expecting others to meet some kind of expectation in your life other than to be relating to you in Christian love? That question includes your family members. We read,

---

"As pressure and stress bear down on me, I find joy in your commands."

PSALMS 119:143 NLT

The Psalmist finds joy in the commands from God. Should we as followers of Christ be able to find joy in Christ? What are we allowing to take our attention from the commands and from Christ? Maybe a look right now at the calendar for the last quarter of the year would be important. Let us set our expectations now for why we will participate in a manner which will honor God. We can let our society and others shape our future focus or be inspired to take control and establish Christ as the focus. What is the first thing that you can do about it in the next seven days?

Let us pray.

Heavenly Father, thank you for the ability to love ourselves and others. In this world, time seems to get away, and when it does you might get away from us as well. When that happens, the pressures and stress can bear down on us. You have not given us any pressure but have given us mercy and grace. Let us remember why we have that grace. Let us remember our relationship with Jesus Christ. May the pressure and stresses of this world be washed away like the sands on the shore are washed by the waves every day. Second by second, minute by minute, let your wave of grace wash over us. In the name of Jesus, we pray. Amen.

AUGUST 28: TOOLS IN ONE HAND OR BOTH?

Entrepreneurs and leaders have valuable tools that they use in their organizations. Think about your tools that are deployed: software, hardware, buildings, supplies and so on. When these tools are put in the hands of our most important resource, our team, the combination can become exponentially valuable. But sometimes tools might protect. Warriors have tools that are weapons. We probably do not have tools to harm but as leaders we are to be looking where people are using the tools. In the right hand they provide value, in the left they might protect. Where can your team members use the tools in your organization for better value? Where might a protective tool be used to provide other value? Some of the most valuable tools that any team has is their core attitudes. Do your team members know of all the tools and have access to them? Tools that are not being used have limited value. Maybe the best quarter ever can happen if the tools are used differently. What is the first thing you can do about it in the next seven days?

As people of faith, we have tools at our disposal as well. Tools can help us to stay in relationship with Jesus Christ. The Bible, the church, and prayer are some of our tools. There are also attitudes that help us as tools to stay connected to Jesus. Attitudes of forgiveness and being kind are just two. How are we using the tools at our disposal? Are they being used to bring others to Christ or being used for our comfort? Are we reading the Bible to deepen our relationship with others or to defend a judgment we have made about others?

> "We faithfully preach the truth. God's power is working in us. We use the weapons of righteousness in the right hand for attack and the left hand for defense."
>
> 2 CORINTHIANS 6:7 NLT

Maybe some time spent inventorying the tools we have used for the last thirty days could teach us something. But a focus on using our attitude tools might connect us with others and with Christ. What is the first thing that we can do about it in the next seven days?

Let us pray.

Heavenly Father, you have made us in your image. Yet, we fall short of our potential because of our sins. Thank you for the gift of Jesus. Make the constant pounding of our reading of the Word shape our views like the blacksmith's hammer shapes the shield and spear. Allow our prayers to draw us closer to you, like the pliers draw the bolt and the nut together. Guide our minds towards those that love others. In the name of Jesus, we pray. Amen.

AUGUST 29: DO RIVALRIES RESTRICT OR ENHANCE VISION?

As leaders and entrepreneurs, we work with internal and external resources and teams. Have you ever thought about how many people your relationships affect? Your reach goes far, and it even includes those that maybe you do not desire to be in a relationship with. But a value-based organization focuses on results in a positive manner. Maybe our viewpoint can be focused on whether people are serving as part of our value proposition. We live in a big society, a big world, and a big marketplace. It seems unreasonable to me to think that one company or organization will serve everyone successfully. There are only so many spots on a team at any given time. Where do you need to fill some spots? Where might you look in a place that you have never looked before for some new team members? How might we adjust our thought processes about those that are not on our team now so that we might add them? Today the challenge is to focus on our team's reach and who we might be able to add to extend it. What is the first thing that you can do about it in the next seven days?

In sports, it is not uncommon to see fans and teams create or be involved in rivalries. I would bet that many engaged in rivalries do not know how the rivalry got started. A good question is where we might be living in rivalry in our own lives. What part of a rivalry, or the behaviors that we exhibit when engaged with rivalries, honors God?

"Work at living in peace with everyone, and work at living a holy life, for those who are not holy will not see the Lord."

HEBREWS 12:14 NLT

It seems to be easy to cheer for the home team, our family, our church. But it is God's church, and there is one Christ. We are all children of God. Where is the rivalry in that, and what does that say for our behaviors today? Maybe we can be teammates first before we begin any competition. We can think of where we are putting our focus when we are engaged in rivalries. The general attitude towards a rival is to beat them at whatever competition or game it is. Many times, rivals will do many unacceptable actions to get the win. Those actions would not be loving towards another. Rivalries generally will not help us to connect, to grow, or to serve. Rivalries restrict our actions. How might you change the focus of any rivalry so that love replaces its actions? What is the first thing that you can do about it in the next seven days?

Let us pray.

Heavenly Father, we thank you for the gifts that you have placed in our lives. We thank you for all relationships. But we also know that some of those relationships that we are living with are not strong and positive ones. Let us begin to reconcile ourselves first to your love. Open our eyes to all the children of God. May we do no harm to one another for we do not want to separate ourselves, or them, from the love of Christ. In the precious name of Jesus, we pray. Amen.

AUGUST 30: WHAT MIX OF WATER DO YOU USE?

Entrepreneurs and leaders drive value and therefore change. We would be wise to remember that we really do not multitask effectively as our brain handles one thing at a time. We cannot affirm our team at the same time as we correct them. Our brain uses two different parts for these actions. Our affirmations of our teams, families, and clients enhance value when we do it correctly. Doing corrections and affirmations in the same conversation can mix the signal and dissolve the purpose. It might be like trying to boil water while ladling out the hot and adding cold. We can look very busy in our processes, but the results are not going to be very effective. I wonder where your management team thinks that cold water is being poured? As leader, can we ask without judgment being cast on the person. As a leader, do you need to ladle out the hot or add in the cold? Doing both will not likely work in most instances. What is the first thing that you can do about it in the next seven days? In our faith, we cannot be thankful and worried at the same time either. I believe that science has proved it in our brain patterns. Where might you be concerned or worried? Do you see that you might have a choice to occupy the space and replace it with praise?

"His presence was a joy, but so was the news he brought of the encouragement he received from you. When he told us how much you long to see me, and how sorry you are for what happened, and how loyal you are to me, I was filled with joy!"

2 CORINTHIANS 7:7 NLT

Joy, I like that. If joy is missing, maybe it is because we have not been allowing thankfulness to occupy our mental space. If we want to be bubbling like boiling water for Christ, we cannot be adding cold water and expect the bubbling to last. We lead in our faith journey by finding space to trust God. We do not have to avoid real fears, but fears should not rule our lives. We have an abundant supply of love and capability. That abundance is challenged by the mindfulness of the fears of this world. Where can you lead in your faith to embrace the abundance and joy that God desires for us? What is the first thing that you can do about it in the next seven days?

Let us pray.

Heavenly Father, we are thankful for your creation, for the sunrise and the sunset. We celebrate and are full of joy when we think of our Savior Jesus Christ. Shine your light and joy into the dark places of our hearts and minds where worry resides. May we share your light with others who are seemingly stuck in the shadows. Encourage us through the Holy Spirit to keep out the worry. In Jesus' name, we pray. Amen.

AUGUST 31: WHEN PROMISES ARE SPOKEN LIMITS ARE BROKEN

Being a successful entrepreneur or leader takes time. We assemble a team, gather resources, and determine what we and our market believe to be valuable. Often it might seem that things move too slow at the beginning. Yet when our teams are really in the groove and ramped up, things might seem that they are moving too fast. But a great regulator is the promise. A promise to complete something in seven days obligates us. When things are slow, we have the capacity for many promises. When things are ramped up, fewer promises might be appropriate. But making promises seems to be a tool that we can overlook. When was the last time you wrote a promise down and shared it with someone? A written promise might be the most powerful tool for your team to use in the next seven days. If progress is too slow or too fast, consider making a set of promises to regulate your time. What is the first thing you can do about it in the next seven days?

As Christians, we are called to have one focus and that is Jesus Christ. But we often find ourselves caught in this world and its desires that it casts upon us. We must balance between the matters of God and the matters of the world. The power of the promise is often the great equalizer. We can always count on the promises of God.

> "Do not make rash promises, and do not be hasty in bringing matters before God. After all, God is in heaven, and you are here on earth. So, let your words be few… When you make a promise to God, do not delay in following through, for God takes no pleasure in fools. Keep all the promises you make to him."
>
> ECCLESIASTES 5:2, 4 NLT

Among your relationships, is there a promise that you would like to make to someone? A promise steps up our commitment to deliver. Where might you be able to make a promise this week? There is no better time than now to make a promise. What is the first thing you can do about it in the next seven days?

Let us pray.

Heavenly Father, you are the Master of the universe. Your promises are the promises that we count on. The sun will rise and the sun will set every day as your word does not fail. Pour out your confidence on us today and encourage our words to be those of a promise. Bless our relationships and make the powerful words we speak as promises guide our actions. In the name Jesus, Amen.

SEPTEMBER 1: WITH WISDOM COMES ACCOUNTABILITY

Entrepreneurs and leaders of teams are constantly moving people and projects. But what makes you and your team stronger than other leaders and other teams? Is it your attention to detail? Could it be your unique process? Maybe it is your attention to hiring great talent. I believe that the strongest leaders may be those who know why they do what they do. If you know your why and you lead your team with it, I believe that it puts you on track to be wise. This does not mean that other leaders are bad or that they cannot provide value. It just puts you at a very elite level of service and of strength. Where might you communicate your message of why you do what you do a little better this quarter? When a leader chooses to be accountable to live into their purpose the team will take notice. Are you willing as a leader to be accountable for such a task? The slightest improvements in strong teams make exponential differences. Maybe all your team needs for exponential growth is some accountability of the top, not accountability from the top. What is the first thing that you can do about it in the next seven days?

In our faith, I like to think that we all take a faith journey. We go down our own path and hopefully grow closer to God through Jesus. Along that path there will be many challenges, struggles, and opportunities. But remembering our why leads us to have more wisdom.

> "One wise person is stronger than ten leading citizens of a town!"
>
> ECCLESIASTES 7:19 NLT

When we are tempted, I think that our strength to resist might lay mostly with our understanding of our personal why with Christ. Where might you be able to strengthen your faith by asking yourself why? Imagine Christ asking you "My friend, why would you do this to our relationship?" This is choosing to live a highly accountable life. What is the first thing you are going to do about being wiser in the next seven days?

Let us pray.

Jesus, you came and sacrificed your all for the Father, for me, and for us. We come to the Father through you, through this relationship. I pray that we build our relationship to know you in our hearts and learn to share the power of our love. Why, because we are moving either with or without you and we choose with. In Jesus' name, we pray. Amen.

SEPTEMBER 2: CAN OUR COMPASSION MAKE A COMPLETION?

As leaders of families, organizations, and companies we are leading our teams in a direction. I will call your desired direction your true north. As we lead, there will be others leading as well. Some will be going in the same true north direction and others will not. It is reasonable to expect that an industry might be headed in the same direction as your team. That is where we might find some competition. But a bigger challenge than competing is to lead the industry. Can your team set the service standard or be the innovator in research and development, maybe both? What about your team collaborating to set the standard for the industry in establishing its why? Often, we can find ourselves competing, when the profits just might be found in leading. Where is your company leading the industry or where might you set your sights in that direction? What is the first thing you can do about it in the next seven days?

We practice our faith in our lives. But those lives happen in a broken world. We find ourselves disconnected from Christ when we sin. When others sin against us, we can feel resentment or possibly take on a victim-like attitude.

> "Do not seek revenge or bear a grudge against a fellow Israelite but love your neighbor as yourself. I am the LORD."
>
> LEVITICUS 19:18 NLT

Christ taught us to overcome the challenges and to be resurrected. Where are the brothers and sisters hurting that you might know? How can we be there in a manner like we ourselves would want comfort and compassion? Our ability to collaborate can help us to have compassion for others. Sometimes we do not need to compete but complete. Often, we do not need to provide the answers, we just need to be connected in love. What is the first thing that you can do about it in the next seven days?

Let us pray.

Heavenly Father, when we are broken, the days are long and sometimes the nights seem longer. But we thank you for the church and your love. Send us the compassion of the resurrection to complete us today. Send us the comfort and healing of another brother or sister in Christ. May our spirits and hearts be lifted together as we come again to you. In Jesus' name, we pray. Amen.

SEPTEMBER 3: OVEREMPHASIZED OR UNDERRECOGNIZED?

In your area of providing value to others, as a leader, what has worked well this year? When we are focused on value, I would like to think that we can be successful. But we need to be careful to see what we are to be credited for and what we are not to be credited for. There are always some unknowns that have contributed to our successes. There are also likely to be some places that we are being active that are not all that valuable. Our teams are a piece of the bigger value picture as well. If we can really focus on what we have been doing well, we can improve our value to others. Look closely, are you taking too much credit where the team is contributing? Is there a place where the team is getting credit where individuals have stepped up their game? A team's synergy is limited by the weakest member. How can you increase the value by looking at the team and extending their value? When you look closely, you may find your value proposition has also been undervalued in some way or by some people. The last quarter of the year is quickly approaching. Are we willing to be inspired enough to take the challenge to examine who needs to be acknowledged? What is the first thing that you can do about it in the next seven days?

As followers of Christ, we have been cleansed. We have been washed anew and lead a new life. So, what did you do to earn it, to work it off and to repay your debt?

The answer of course is nothing. All you did was to ask Jesus Christ to be your Savior and to believe in him. So, what credit do we get for that? The same nothing, I think, is the answer.

> "We will not boast about things done outside our area of authority. We will boast only about what has happened within the boundaries of the work God has given us, which includes our working with you...Nor do we boast and claim credit for the work someone else has done. Instead, we hope that your faith will grow so that the boundaries of our work among you will be extended."
>
> 2 CORINTHIANS 10:13, 15

Notice how this passage reminds us of our value here and the call to extend it. We can move forward with the love of Christ and take his message into the world. How are you doing with that task? What is holding you back from sharing this gift, this experience, and the most wonderful relationship we have been given the opportunity to live with? Overtime in a game is about a tie score but extending in our faith is about love. Perhaps we can think now of what impact our faith can have on others for the last quarter. The people of the world not only need love, but they also want love. What is the first thing that you can do about it in the next seven days?

Let us pray.

Heavenly Father, thank you for the gift of the day. Guide us today to be extenders, to be reaching out where we may not be comfortable. There is no greater value than spreading your word and love. Embolden us not to keep you a secret. Raise our voices, let us shout it from the mountain top and whisper it in the quietness of the meadows. May your love be extended and may you receive the honor. In Jesus' name, we pray. Amen.

SEPTEMBER 4: EXPECTATION OR POSSIBILITY?

As a leader, there is a value proposition that you lead your team in. Your purpose, which sets the stage for value, could be your strongest expectation filter. When customers know your purpose, they begin to set their mindset towards expectations of being in a relationship. They begin to expect and receive results. When the results achieved are above expectations, extreme value is received. When results can only be delivered to what you give in return for money, the transaction is more of a commodity. Those expectation filters can be pretty low. Low expectation filters provide the lowest value, if any. These expectation filters are therefore important. Where are your customer and client expectations best served? Where do you have expectation filters for your team and where are they set? When our attitudes about the minimum expectations are aligned, the value is protected for clients. If our attitudes are not aligned with expectations, we will be sure to find interruptions of service. Where are expectations not being met for you, your team or your clients? Like the air filter on any type of machine, our expectations filters need an occasional check and maybe even a replacement. Maybe your team is ready to change the attitude of expectation for an attitude of possibility. What is the first thing that you can do about it in the next seven days?

Brothers and sisters, what expectation filters might we have placed in our way to connect to Jesus? Are our filters based on some rule or law? The two words that are connected in my mind are expectations and possibility. Can you imagine what God wants you to discover, the level of love, compassion and relationships that are possible?

> "What more could I have done for my vineyard that I have not already done? When I expected sweet grapes, why did my vineyard give me bitter grapes?"
>
> ISAIAH 5:4 NLT

It might be possible that our expectation levels have restricted ourselves from the discoveries that God wants to share with us. Have we set our expectations merely on grapes instead of wine or the blood and sacrifice of Christ? Where have you set your expectations? These restricted attitudes of expectation are real limits. Are they safe, ordinary and low? Maybe today, we can look at raising our expectations to the level of discovery that God wants us to experience. Who might help you do an attitude reset? How might you raise the expectations? What is the first thing that you can do about it in the next seven days?

Let us pray.

Heavenly Father, your expectations are clear, and we come to you through Christ. We allow ourselves to be distracted. Life gets in the way of love. Entertainment gets in the way of the everlasting. Competition gets in the way of compassion. Today, we pray for a reset. Send the Holy Spirit to us now, in this place, and may our expectations take us directly to a new level of discovery with you. In Jesus' name we pray. Amen.

SEPTEMBER 5: WINDMILLS STAND STRONG

As a leader of a family, a team or a company, our resolve is meaningful. Resolve conveys strength to the entire team, and when we do not have resolve, it is our weakness that is conveyed. Does resolve matter? I believe it does. When our team's resolve is strong, synergy grows and power to deliver results increases. There are many forces that help to move a company. The forces are like the blades of a windmill. Each blade takes on some of the energy as the wind rushes by, and together they turn the spindle, gears and pump. As leaders, if we are not focused, lacking resolve, we can be like the gear being broken on the windmill. When our team lacks focus and resolve, it is like a blade being removed from the windmill's grouping of blades that catch the wind. We need to know why we provide value and have the focus to deliver it. Windmills provide water to the stock tank to keep the herd alive. That is valuable. What is your team's why? The rancher has firmly resolved himself that the wind will blow even though he does not know the time or the place. This develops the courage and conviction to put the herd in the pasture. How is your team delivering their purpose? Where do you need to share your resolve with the team members whose resolve might have been worn out by the wear and tear of the world? As leaders, our focus on others is what keeps the team providing value. What is the first thing you can do about it in the next seven days?

As a people of faith, the winds of this world blow upon us. The activities of this world and being a productive person is a call. We react and sometimes are moved by the call of the wind. But our faith is our strongest shield.

> "Israel is no stronger than its capital, Samaria, and Samaria is no stronger than its king, Pekah son of Remaliah. Unless your faith is firm, I cannot make you stand firm."
>
> ISAIAH 7: NLT

It seems to me that this passage is telling us that God wants us to stand strong. It does not say that the winds of change will not blow, that the thunderstorms will not come, or that destruction is guaranteed to avoid us. No, like the base of the windmill, which is anchored into the ground, we too are to stand firm in our faith. As we are anchored with Christ, we can count on God to strengthen that base through our study of the word, through living with our brothers and sisters of the church, and by being in relationship with Christ. Where might you want to check on the anchors of your base? Who are you in relationship with that you might be able to assist in strengthening their base? When was the last time that you focused on the foundation? What is the first thing that you can do about it in the next seven days?

Let us pray.

Heavenly Father, we are forever close to the comfort of the palm of your hands. Thank you for our relationships and your words. Even though the winds blow, and changes come daily, you do not change. We get scared and live in fear on occasion, but our faith is a shield. May we be inspired to be firmly planted in faith. We want to be anchored with you. In Jesus' name, we pray. Amen.

SEPTEMBER 6: A BROKEN BLINK

Where does one find the value proposition when disaster strikes? When teams focus on value, the financial ramifications during a disaster may become a matter of love, respect, and courtesy. It is not about the money. In a blink, things change. Can you imagine your eye getting stuck in a blink? I ask this because you might begin to feel discomfort with the thought of it. When natural disasters strike, our first concern is for the people. We become concerned about our family, our team, and our clients. Sure, there will be concerns about how our resources will require adjustments. But maintaining our focus will help to relieve the fear and help us lead. Where have you or are you experiencing fear? Maybe the first step towards removing fear is to move our attention to our value proposition immediately. Even in a disaster, you can still have value. Who would be the first twenty-five people you would want to talk to after a disaster? These people might be representative of who you value. For the few, disaster might even serve as a launching pad for building and enhancing value. Leadership is needed when disaster strikes. What is the first thing that you can do about it in the next seven days?

Brothers and sisters, we live in a world where the environment and climate of the world is ever changing. Sometimes it does so without regard to human life or property destruction.

> "In the blink of an eye wealth disappears, for it will sprout wings and fly away like an eagle."
>
> PROVERBS 23:5 NLT

But where do we find our biggest value proposition? I am sure it is in Christ. When we are a victim of a disaster, we experience loss. But Christ is never lost. He is always present, but it is us who become lost, even if for just a blink. Where might you be stuck in a blink? When that happens, it is going to be uncomfortable. Who can help you complete the blink and reconnect with Christ? Being a leader might just mean we help so that we get stuck less in those broken blinks. What is the first thing that you can do about it in the next seven days?

Let us pray.

Heavenly Father, thank you for our families, for our teams and our relationships. We are blessed by the people in our lives so much. May our relationship with Christ help us to maintain those relationships and to strengthen all of them through him. Guide us when we are caught in a blink. May our eyes see Christ first before we view anything else. In Jesus's name, we pray. Amen.

SEPTEMBER 7: A QUENCHING SYSTEM OR JUST A BOTTLE

I do not know who said different strokes for different folks. But as leaders of a team, entrepreneurs who know their purpose deliver value. How the team delivers their purpose is likely to look a little different to each team member and to each client. Delivery of a bottle of water to a thirsty eight-year-old soccer player will be different than to a plane-wrecked survivor at his rescue. Same product, same purpose and different value. I do not believe there is anything inherently wrong with the same product delivering different value. In fact, it might serve as proof that you are focused on delivering value instead of a commodity. It can also help us to see where we can deliver more value and create byproducts. A water bottle delivered to someone in the desert could have a reflective wrapper on it. If taken on the original expedition, it might become a distress signal if the traveler gets stranded in the desert. Where has your team found byproducts in your value proposition? When was the last time you looked for byproducts? What would your company do with the profitability that a byproduct could deliver? As a leader, we can look past the limits in our mind to find byproducts. What is the first thing you can do about it in the next seven days?

As a people of faith, we are in relationship with Jesus. Every area of our lives has the opportunity to change.

> "Out of the stump of David's family will grow a shoot— yes, a new Branch bearing fruit from the old root."
>
> ISAIAH 11:1 NLT

New fruit, did you see that? Something new has arrived because of Jesus. It does not matter when Jesus shows up to have new fruit. We wake up daily and have the opportunity to start with something new if we start with Christ. Where are we limiting ourselves to the old where new might occur? Do we welcome Jesus into our lives just on Easter and Christmas or do we welcome him on every Sunday? Why just on Sunday, why not every hour? What is the purpose of just getting something new occasionally when we just might be in stronger relationships if we welcome Jesus anytime we are in relationship with others? What might be the byproduct of that in your life? Could it be forgiveness, possibly a spouse, a new friend or compassion and love? I think those are worthy reasons to consider it. What is the first thing you can do about it in the next seven days?

Let us pray.

Heavenly Father, in you and through you, we can have all things new. Let us recognize the opportunities for the new fruit regularly. Help us to see the reflection of the message from the past to quench our thirst and see the new of today. Bring us into relationship with new eyes and hearts. In Jesus' name, we pray. Amen.

SEPTEMBER 8: TAKE A SEAT OR TAKE A STAND

Leaders, what are we standing for? That is an important question for us to answer. It drives us right to purpose. It gets past our temptation to tell what we do or how we do it. A plumber that knows what they stand for has a value approach that places them in an elite circle. If entrepreneurs cannot tell others our purpose, it might be that we are not going to build very strong teams. Where do you stand today? Does all of your team know your stand, and do they know their role? Does everyone have a stand on your team? When people do not have a stand, it is difficult to be accountable. If everyone is able to have a stand, as a leader, you should know it. As a team we have a higher level of opportunity available to us when we choose to be accountable to our purpose. What is the first thing you can do about it in the next seven days?

Brothers and sisters, what is your stand today? Are you uncommitted in your stand? It seems to me that we want to have our feet on a strong foundation and be able to communicate our stand. I expect that there might be a day of reckoning where someone will want to know where you stand. If you are not locked in and ready to state your stand then know that God is ready for you to shape it. He knows where he is in his stand, for he sent his son to save the world. That is his stand.

"For we cannot oppose the truth, but must always stand for the truth."

2 CORINTHIANS 13:8 NLT

This statement challenges us every day to choose to acknowledge it. Will you be accountable to accept the challenge or to embrace the day with a stand? It might be that one can be more comfortable closing their eyes to what is happening around them. That can lead to one sitting to avoid any attention. I choose to stand, with Christ, with you my brothers and sisters in Christ. I stand on the rock with you, to be lifted up by you and to lift you up when either of us slips and falls. What is your stand today? What is the first thing that you can do about it in the next seven days?

Let us pray.

Heavenly Father, here we stand, ready to cry out your name. We choose today to cry out your name in celebration and in pain. We ask for the Holy Spirit to speak clearly to us today. Move us in action. Bring us to rest and always to stand on the rock, our cornerstone Jesus Christ. Let the winds and waves move but make our foundation and footings solid. May we lean on each other as the motions tempt us. Make the firm foundation of your love connect us. In Jesus' name, we pray. Amen.

SEPTEMBER 9: YOU CANNOT STUMP ME

Leaders of families, organizations and companies need connections. Our teams are connected to other teams and resources like a grapevine. The base of our vine is our purpose, and every action should support the purpose. The roots bring water, and the leaves process the sunlight. The vine may reach more than ten times the length of the base. It will expand and go in a manner that we might not have imagined, and it will meet other vines as well. But if another vine's purpose does not coexist with our purpose, we need to change direction. Destructive or obstructive vines do not support our purpose. Is your purpose destructive in any manner? Looking inward at our purpose and pruning it for destructive shoots might be a valuable use of your time. Are you confident that your pruners are sharp? Allowing our pruners to help us collaborate with our team is critical to making our vines grow and be productive. What is the first thing you can do about it in the next seven days?

As a people of faith, we can be growing or decaying. Our growth may even spread like a vine. I am not sure that there is really any middle ground. Our prayer life can sprout, our time in the word can get intentional and our connection in worship might even bring us to tears of joy. But where are you not growing? Where are you stunted or allowing something to get in your way?

> "Even before you begin your attack, while your plans are ripening like grapes, the LORD will cut off your new growth with pruning shears. He will snip off and discard your spreading branches."
>
> ISAIAH 18:5 NLT

This verse tells me that my destructive actions, which stunt me, need pruning. Where has my vine wandered off to and found infertile soil and a harsh environment? We are called to be in relationship and grow so how can you grow with any obstacle that seems to stop us? That is where our relationship with Christ allows growth. That is where our collaboration with the church body can be like fertilizer for our vine. A stump blocking space and growth in the garden becomes the centerpiece that catches all of creation's eye when the morning glory vines grow on it. What can you do to overcome your obstacles and where can you prune your vine from the harsh environment that is not honoring Christ? Who do you trust to collaborate with to have a pruning conversation? What is the first thing that you can do about it in the next seven days?

Let us pray.

Heavenly Father, your love is so full of grace. Your pruning guides us. May we see our own actions that keep us from you and make the snips. Keep our minds sharp and our pruners sharper. In Jesus' name, we pray. Amen.

SEPTEMBER 10: NO SHIRT AND NO SHOES MAY BE A CHOICE

Are you a leader? I believe that strong leaders have an answer to the following question. If one were to be stripped of everything you have, what are the first three things you would want back? The answers of course would vary by leader, but they will be indicative of where those leaders place value in their lives. If we took everything away from your company, would you still be able to give value? At the core level of our business are our relationships. If you had lost everything, I would bet that the most valuable thing to gain back is your relationships. Many people, when asked the question, will not even think that relationships apply as something that they can lose! But we can lose relationships. Where might you have some of your relationships at risk right now? Which ones might need some energy and resources applied to them to keep them strong? Maybe our businesses are only as valuable as our emphasis that we place on those relationships. Which relationship are you inspired to grow deeper with? Think of them as plants, if the roots are not strong, if it is not fertilized and watered regularly, the plant or relation will weaken or die. The likely result of being inspired to grow with it will be more fruit from the relationship. What is the first thing that you can do about it in the next seven days?

As followers of Christ, we claim to have a relationship with him. Not only do we claim Christ, but we are called to be in relationship with the church. As we lose the things of this world, we are challenged to remember that our emphasis is on relationships not things. I might enjoy a game of golf with my friends, but if I have to choose golf clubs themselves or my friends, I choose my friends.

> "The LORD told Isaiah son of Amoz, 'Take off the burlap you have been wearing, and remove your sandals.' Isaiah did as he was told and walked around naked and barefoot."
>
> ISAIAH 20:2 NLT

Okay, so that is a great challenge for us today. We learn here that Isaiah was naked and barefoot for quite a time. He lost some things for sure, probably gained a suntan while he was at it. But it was to honor his relationship with God. I do not think that I have been asked to lose quite that much, but would I be willing to lose that for Jesus? Would you lose the shirt off your back and the shoes from your feet for Christ? Remember, regardless of what you lose, no one, no event, no tragedy or disaster can ever force you to lose your relationship with Christ. Where are you feeling called to get rid of something that might be in the way of your relationship? Do you have the courage to invest in the relationship by losing that something? Friday is our day to be inspired. Pick a relationship today and be courageous to grow it by making a choice. What is the first thing to do about it in the next seven days?

Let us pray.

Heavenly Father, your relationship is crucial and the most valuable thing that we have. Let us put our emphasis on it and the other relationships of your church and its mission. Make our focus be on family, not on golf clubs or frisbee's. Make the focus be on our brothers and sisters in Christ instead of brokenness and sin. May we always have value in you. In Jesus' name, we pray. Amen.

SEPTEMBER 11: WHAT ATTITUDE IS ESSENTIAL TO YOU TODAY?

As a leader, we can recognize that different teams have different values. They deliver them differently and they have different attitudes as well. For many, figuring out the real value is difficult. Part of the challenge of figuring it out is the attitudes we hold. For some, when they find the path of value, it can be lost. The value can get lost when others we are working with are holding different ideas about value or working with different attitudes. Some will depart from their value proposition to meet another's wants or needs. We are leaders who can be accountable to hold the attitudes that support our value. We do not have to give in when it comes to delivering our value. It is okay to say, "No thanks, we will pass this time." When we get distracted, our clients will not likely be served as we wish. Maybe if our focus is on full value delivery, our attitudes will be promoted and protected. Let us keep searching and let us continue to deliver value. Where does your team need to do some searching? What is the first thing you can do about it in the next seven days?

In our faith, the attitudes we keep can be promoted and protected as well.

> "But we refused to give in to them for a single moment. We wanted to preserve the truth of the gospel message for you."
>
> GALATIANS 2:5 NLT

There are issues of our faith that are essential, and there are others that might not be essential. For the nation of Israel, they had the law, and it was certainly essential to them. But we believe that God had a different vision and sent Christ. That is essential to us as Christians, but it may not be essential to the Jew. Have you ever had a conversation with others about what they believe is essential? Maybe being able to have a conversation without being judgmental about what others believe in is essential to grow in our faith. Being curious and leaving judgment behind is an attitude that promotes love. What is essential for you this week in your faith? Are you in the Bible, doing a devotion, actively praying or maybe attending worship occasionally? A focus on what is essential to you just might be the means to drawing closer to Christ today. Our attitude can be changed in an instant. What attitude can you make essential for that drawing nearer to happen? What is the first thing that you can do about it in the next seven days?

Let us pray.

Father God, we want to draw near to you today. Empower our hearts and ears to be open to the Holy Spirit so that you can access us. Make our actions honor you as we connect and serve in your love. Whisper with your still soft voice that which you desire to be essential today. In Jesus' name, we pray. Amen.

SEPTEMBER 12: HOW MANY LOVES DO LEADERS EMBRACE?

Leaders are lovers. I do not mean the romantic type although they can certainly be that as well. I mean that leaders will generally embrace the concept of love in one of two ways. There is the self-promoting leader. This leader looks to take credit for everything the team or members accomplish. The purpose of the team is to advance the career of the leader or to achieve a greater reward for the leader. There are several byproducts to this type of leadership. They may include higher levels of achievement, sales, and profitability. This type of leadership also has some high costs associated with it as well. I suspect that you know what those are if you have been around this type of leader. But the other type of leader and love associated with them is the lover of another. This type of leader has their focus on the customer, the team delivering value, and then themselves.

This leader has a focus on others first although they still must have some love of self. To work with others at a deeper level we need some love for ourselves. It is difficult for others to share their agape love of us when we do not have a level of love for ourselves. We just need to focus on the right recipe. Where does your recipe need some adjustment this week? Perhaps you do not think that your recipe needs any adjustment. If so, are you willing to ask those that you are leading how they would rank your leadership love. Let us place our focus on love in our leadership this week. Someone will appreciate it and it might be you. What is the first thing that you can do about it this week?

As a follower of Jesus, Christians have received a new life. We hold to the belief that we have wronged others and sinned. We also believe that Jesus has paid the sacrifice for our sins. We get reborn in heart and mind to lead our lives a different way. We still have the challenges to overcome the demands and desires of the world. We are asked by our selfish interests to succeed and to meet our culture's expectation of success as well.

> "Now I am coming to you for the third time, and I will not be a burden to you. I don't want what you have—I want you. After all, children don't provide for their parents. Rather, parents provide for their children. I will gladly spend myself and all I have for you, even though it seems that the more I love you, the less you love me."
>
> 2 CORINTHIANS 12:14-15 NLT

Paul shares in this passage that his actions are based on his love for others. He wants others, specifically to know that Jesus has sacrificed himself for them and that a different way of life is possible. The lens of love magnifies different objects. One lens will magnify ourselves while the lens of Jesus will magnify others and our relationship with them. As a leader who follows Christ, where can you put your focus on love of others at another level this week? It just takes one step to change the level. Which one will be the step for you?

Let us pray.

Heavenly Father, we come to you in love today. Guide our hearts and minds to recognize the need for love. Make our actions be those that are focused more on loving others than succeeding. Succeeding at the cost of love is no success at all. Draw us closer to you this week by encouraging our ability to lead with love. In Jesus' name we pray. Amen.

SEPTEMBER 13: HAVE YOU EVER GONE DIGGING WORMS?

I remember my grandparents taking me fishing as a youth. One of the first things we did was to grab a shovel and head to the garden to dig for worms. The soil was fertile there and worms were generally always found. The pond would be the next stop and as a general rule we almost always caught fish. What tools are your teams using to deliver your value proposition? You probably have a client relationship management system, a financial software or system, and maybe you even have an enterprise reporting program. But like the fisherman, if you do not use the right tool, the right resources, and use them in the right places, your results will not likely be what you desired. Fishing poles are not a very reasonable digging tool to find worms.

Hooks are not very good needles, although both are best when sharp. If your trip to the pond does not include hooks, then your trip with worms might not be very successful. Is your team using a project management tool as a client relationship management tool? It is likely that profits are not as deep as they could be if we were using the right tools for the right job or if the right people were doing the right things. The soil is fertile, and the pond is full of fish. As a leader, where might you need some new tools to reap better results to benefit your team and your clients? What is the first thing you can do about it in the next seven days?

As a people of faith, we have the opportunity to grow. Have we considered recently the tools, our people, and our places that help us?

> "A heavy sledge is never used to thresh black cumin; rather, it is beaten with a light stick. A threshing wheel is never rolled on cumin; instead, it is beaten lightly with a flail."
>
> ISAIAH 28:27 NLT

Do you have the right people in your faith, helping you to grow? Who are your accountability partners and who are you worshiping with? Who are you working with to connect people to Christ and what project management system are you using? The soil is fertile, and the pond is full, so are you ready? Our walk with Christ is rich and fertile as well, and there are many that do not claim him yet. A piece of our faith is the call to leadership and sharing the invitation for others to get to know Christ. The Holy Spirit will confirm a relationship, but you just might be the tool that God can use to bring someone to know Jesus. Is a relationship with Jesus the tool that you have been missing that might just restore a broken life? What is the first thing that you can do about it in the next seven days?

Let us pray.

Father God, it is a new day and we come to you in thanks and praising your name. Be a light unto our path today and expose the areas that we might grow in. Help us to find those that we can grow with and those that we might help grow. Make our minds dig deep into the Bible like shovels into the earth. Guide us as we fish for men, women, and their families. May your catch be plentiful. We know that each is a trophy to you as all are worthy, regardless of their brokenness. In Jesus' name we pray. Amen.

SEPTEMBER 14: DO YOU MARCH IN CONFIDENCE WITH BATTLE ARMOR?

So, you are the leader of a family, a team, or a business. Maybe you lead all of these, but where are you leading with confidence? Confidence is important to our value delivery to our teams and customers. But confidence is just as much about knowing what we can and should do as opposed to what we do not and should not do. Can you remember places where you or your team had confidence to do, when in reality they or you, were just not the right fit? I believe that the more we know what we should not do, the more it influences our confidence in what to do. It could be that the more you abandon the wrong fits, the capacity we have for the right fit increases. When that happens, confidence accelerates, maybe exponentially, and just as importantly, it does it appropriately. There is value in appropriate confidence. What is the first thing you can do about it in the next seven days?

Brothers and sisters in Christ, where are you wearing the armor of God confidently? If we are not fully dressed in it, where have we thrown off our confidence?

> "So do not throw away this confident trust in the Lord. Remember the great reward it brings you!"
>
> HEBREWS 10:35 NLT

Did we leave some of the armor behind like I have left my hat or umbrella at the church? Go back and get it. Did you have an experience and allowed someone else to take the armor from you? It is time for forgiveness and to take the armor back. It does not matter if they apologize. Your forgiveness is like purchasing a piece of armor. You are closer to being dressed. Have you misplaced your armor or gotten distracted like when I set my eyeglasses down and do not recall where I left them? Let us stop what we are doing and find our armor. Our confidence will receive a boost today, and we just might happen to contact someone whose life might be changed because of it. What is the first thing that you can do about it in the next seven days?

Let us pray.

Heavenly Father, you have given us armor to protect us from all that would attack our relationship with Christ. Today, we pray that our confidence be restored where it is weak. Empower us to pick up our helmets, locate our shields, put on the coat of mail, and carry our spears. Listen as we march with confidence today so as to find those that are lost. In Jesus' name, we pray. Amen.

SEPTEMBER 15: ARE YOU SHARP?

Leaders, are you part of a commodity or product team? I like to think of the alternative to this as a value delivery team. As a leader of a product team, concerns of sharpness, effectiveness, and efficiency can be important. But on a value delivery team, items that are concerned with why are the most important. When you are about value, the team delivers, and there is power in that team. The effectiveness of a single tool or person is not the critical decision like it might be on the commodity team. If you lead a commodity team, where are your tools in need of improvement? Who might need more training and attention? Many will recognize the equipment of a brush cutter, machete or lawn mower.

These tools must have a sharp blade, or the results will suffer. The tools on teams sometimes need sharpening. If you are a leader of a value team, how might you enhance and empower others? These concepts might make you ask yourself, "Do I have the right people on my team?" You might also want to ask, "Am I on the right team?" Leaders can build systems of accountability which help the blades that need to be sharp to stay sharp. Where do you need a higher level of accountability? What is the first thing you can do about it in the next seven days?

As fellow believers, we ought to be working as a team for Christ. But sometimes our words or actions get in the way. When we allow ourselves to get sharpened for the wrong purpose, we can injure others. Our sharpness can get turned on us quickly.

> "But God himself will shoot them with his arrows, suddenly striking them down."
>
> PSALMS 64:7 NLT

The passages before were talking about warriors sharpening their arrows to attack. We sometimes sharpen but need to be careful. We learn here that arrows might be returned in kind. I know that God can sharpen much better than any man or tool can. There is nothing more accurate in sharpening than God. We can choose to be accountable to be sharpened in our faith by those we are growing with. Perhaps you have the edge you need to make a difference in someone's life right now. Where can we be of use to Christ right now in the shape we are in? No sharpening required today, just serve. What can you do about it in the next seven days?

Let us pray.

Father God, we are being molded into what you want us to be. We pray that we obey your direction and listen for the small still voice. Put us to your use today just in who we are. Make our path take us where you want us to go. In Jesus' name, we pray. Amen.

SEPTEMBER 16: STOP THE CLOCK

As leaders, what time frame are you using today? Some leaders might have an important meeting planned. They might be acting in reference to that meeting. Others may have a project going on and are thinking about the end of their project. I like to think of time references as being in the present (the next seven days) and being in a bigger future. When somebody has a time reference of a bigger future, they know what they want to accomplish. They know who they want to be in relationship with. They know how they themselves want to be physically and mentally. They know the value of their bigger future and can even visualize some aspects of it with clarity. Are you taking the time to create a bigger future? Are the teams of your organization helping you to shape a bigger future? I think that one's future might be limited if we have not given our team the same clarity that we ask leaders to seek. How might you collaborate to build a bigger future? What is the first thing you can do about it in the next seven days?

Our time perception is important for us as a people of faith as well.

> "Go back to Hezekiah and tell him, 'This is what the LORD, the God of your ancestor David, says: I have heard your prayer and seen your tears. I will add fifteen years to your life.'"
>
> ISAIAH 38:5 NLT

I can and have imagined how my life would be changed if I were granted an extension. Can you? I challenge you to work with this process. What if your days on earth ended ninety days from now, what would you do differently? Would you live and love more, or would you spend your time doing exactly what you are doing now? I would think that if we really valued our relationships in this manner our activities might tend to look different. How might you change your professional activities to be of the most value? How would your relationship with your family change? How would your relationship with the Bible, the church and Jesus Christ change? Can you imagine, will you imagine? A bigger future with God just might be in the balance. There is no place like the present to begin collaborating with Jesus. What is the first thing to do about it in the next seven days?

Let us pray.

Heavenly Father, you have the perfect clock. It is made up of the arms of Christ. We cannot even know of your measure as our seconds may be millions of our years to you. Let us have a relationship with Christ that is not limited to minutes or hours. Guide us to be in relationship with one another, to be a valuable loving brother and sister. Let us join you, in your time, when we experience love. In Jesus' name, we pray. Amen.

SEPTEMBER 17: CAN MY LOSS BE MY GAIN?

As a leader, what is your attitude when your team suffers a loss? Losses might be a team member leaving, contracts lost, bids not awarded, relationships destroyed, or even losses to your reputation. So, what is your attitude like at this critical time? As leaders, our attitudes can have exponential effects on our team. If we show panic or fear, would you expect the same from your team? If you show inappropriate thankfulness and celebration, it might warn your team about their performance as well thinking, "I wonder if they will be happy to see me leave?" I think that the best attitude we might have is to be curious. With each loss, we can ask what will it require of me and the team in the next ninety days? With this loss, should we consider a different tactic or strategy? What are the three things we could do to mitigate the costs of this type of loss? Where is your biggest risk for a loss in the next ninety days? How might you mitigate the loss and create a questioning attitude right now before it happens? What is the first thing you can do about it in the next seven days?

As brothers and sisters of the cross, we know the loss that was suffered for us. But that suffering does not mean to imply that we ourselves will not suffer losses. Surely, we will have losses, but what attitude do we carry to the world at those times to the people that are lost? Our example is being watched.

> "'The time is coming when everything in your palace—all the treasures stored up by your ancestors until now—will be carried off to Babylon. Nothing will be left,' says the LORD."
>
> ISAIAH 39:6 NLT

If you lost everything today, what would you be prepared to say to God? It might be a real challenge for us especially if we are getting upset over the minor or even trivial losses that we suffer on a weekly basis. It just might be that in losing something today we make room for Jesus in our lives tomorrow. We take Christ with us when we go in service to anyone, including those being struck by a natural disaster? Where have you lost something in the last ninety days? What attitude do you want to share with your family and teams about it? What is the first thing that you can do about it in the next seven days?

Let us pray.

Jesus, we thank you for taking up the cross for us. Your loss is our gain. Be a light unto our path today to find you whenever we have a loss. May our suffering only be as long as our attention span takes to get refocused on you. May we flip our attention to you, faster than we can suffer losses. In the name of Jesus', we pray. Amen.

SEPTEMBER 18: TUMBLING OR TIPPING?

A leader of a family, organization or company is the one who guides the team. The work is like the captain of a ship, the outfitter in the wilderness, and the trail boss for the wagon train. Leaders lead the value proposition. They watch out and avoid dangerous environments like cliffs as well as to capture opportunities like water flowing at natural springs. Where might your team members be in unfamiliar territory? Do they have the tools needed to mitigate the risks? Do they have tools and the mindset to capture opportunities? If one of the highest investments we can make is in people, then providing them with adequate tools for the job at hand might be the tipping point to exponential returns. It could be that when we allow the lack of investment in people or the lack of use of tools, it becomes a tumbling point. One of our most critical tools are the attitudes our teams believe are the ones we connect with. What is the first thing you can do about it in the next seven days?

As we walk ourselves down our path of faith, we take some twists and turns. The trail is full of holes to trip and stumble from. There are edges of cliffs we can fall off of. But there are some sections that are loaded with wonderful fruits to partake of as well, if we can reach them. Our attitudes might keep us comfortable and unable to reach for help. But the Holy Spirit can assist us in our walk.

> "He chases them away and goes on safely, though he is walking over unfamiliar ground."
>
> ISAIAH 41:3 NLT

It is a true joy to know that we are walking along our path with others. And it is invaluable to know that we have tools to assist us along the way. The walking stick and the Bible give us something to lean on and provide stability. Our church and trail markers can help to point out the dangerous edges. The Holy Spirit might be the breeze to refresh us while our relationship with our friends are the ladders along the path that help us reach the fruit. Where might you show appreciation for those relationships today? Appreciation can be a core attitude. What tools could you be using to keep from getting tripped up? What is the first thing you will do about it in the next seven days?

Let us pray.

Heavenly Father, you know our path. You have given us free will as we walk upon it. We can see many holes when we are looking, but often, we are not looking in the right place. May we use the tools at our fingertips to avoid the tumbling points. We celebrate our relationships today for the fruit that they are. We ask that you bless them and allow them to be tipping points bringing us closer to Christ. In Jesus' name, we pray. Amen.

SEPTEMBER 19: SWITCHES AND GAUGES ARE NEEDED

As a leader, I like to think that there are some switches that we get to turn from off to on. When new team members decide to join us, it is a switch. The day we started a family is a switch. The day we started our business was a switch. But as important as the switches are we also have gauges. To truly deliver value, we need to have gauges that are monitored. Have you ever had a vehicle that had a non-working gas gauge? The simple task of trusting your vehicle to take you someplace is no longer simple. Your attention is drawn on a regular basis. Is there enough fuel in the vehicle to get you to your destination? Some might even begin to track their mileage. What gauges do you have in place for your team? Do you have any gauges for yourself? How are you measuring your excellence, your success, your finances, your team? I think that we can find it more valuable by having some appropriate gauges. When you do not have proper gauges or they are not working, your value delivery system will most likely run out of fuel. What is the first thing you can do about it in the next seven days?

As brothers and sisters in Christ, we all have flipped a switch. That was our declaration to follow Christ. But after you have thrown the switch, it is time to have some gauges. Where have you set gauges for yourself in regard to your faith? How would your compassion gauge, your love gauge, your forgiveness gauge, read today? How would your being in the word, your honesty, your trusting, your listening gauges read? How would your attitude of sabbath, sin, devotions, and prayer gauges read?

> "And may you have the power to understand, as all God's people should, how wide, how long, how high, and how deep his love is."
>
> EPHESIANS 3:18 NLT

Do you see how many times the word how is used here? If we want to know how much, it means that a gauge might be able to be used. As followers of Christ, I think that the gas and tire gauge for our vehicles should be less important than the gauges for our faith. What gauges might you put in place to have a deeper walk with Christ? Which of the gauges above might grip you today? What is the first thing you can do about it in the next seven days?

Let us pray.

Heavenly Father, you have created it all. You have thrown the switch. Let us take seriously our decision, our switch, to follow you. Help us to create gauges for ourselves. May the reading of those gauges draw us closer to a full tank with you. In Jesus' name, we pray. Amen.

SEPTEMBER 20: PURPOSE OR REPURPOSE

As a leader of a family or organization, we lead teams and direct resources. If we know our purpose, we are more likely to get the right people with the right resources. A recycling center takes what one believes to be worthless and gives it a new purpose. Your trash is their treasure. But how can that be? It is all focused on the purpose. Imagine if the recycling center though, had as team members pyromaniacs. This may not be the best example of the right people in the right place. What if the center used its capital to have flamethrowers and garden hoses instead of bins and conveyor belts? Wrong resources with the right people will not serve a distinct purpose very well either. But get the right people with the right resources and we will find value. It is like the recycling center which takes car and truck loads of other's trash and repurposes it where others are willing to pay for it. Your trash is truly priceless. Where in your team do you need a right fit person? If the right person walked in front of you, do you have a purpose statement ready to share? As a leader, one of our leadership roles is to put the purpose and the people together. Both could be priceless. What is the first thing you can do about it in the next seven days?

As followers of Christ, we all bring our special gifts. Sometimes in our own minds, our gifts do not seem valuable. I think that some people do not know their special gifts. When that happens, growth is restricted, it is stunted, and it holds the entire team back. We read,

---

> "He makes the whole body fit together perfectly. As each part does its own special work, it helps the other parts grow, so that the whole body is healthy and growing and full of love."
>
> EPHESIANS 4:16 NLT

Do you see the effect of having a gift and of being a part of the team? It resulted in growing with love. If we do not know and use our special gifts, we are restricting our experience of the fullness of love. What are your special gifts? If I were to ask you to gauge your use of your special gifts this year, how would you be doing? If you look into the future, the next thirty days, how will you be using your special gifts? It might be that the most beneficial thing to do, to experience Christ's love, would be to use these gifts. What is the first thing you can do about it in the next seven days?

Let us pray.

Heavenly Father, you have created each of us so uniquely. We give you thanks for these blessings and these gifts. We acknowledge that you bestow them upon us with love. We pray that you will help those that do not know their gifts, to be in a state of discovery. Help us to take what has been ignored or even discarded and repurpose it. Send the Holy Spirit to us now to gather us to grow as your people and to honor you with our words and deeds. In Jesus' name, we pray. Amen.

SEPTEMBER 21: VALUING THE ENTIRE BODY OF CHRIST

I have worked with persons with physical and mental challenges for most of my adult life. You probably have too. They are all around us—in the grocery store, at the daycare center, waiting on us in our favorite restaurant, checking us out at the convenience store, cleaning our homes, cutting our hair, attending to us in the hospital.

> "...members of the body that seem to be weaker are indispensable, and those members of the body that we think less honorable we clothe with greater honor, and our less respectable members are treated with greater respect...But God has so arranged the body, giving the greater honor to the inferior member..."
>
> 1 CORINTHIANS 12: 22-24

Our society does not always have the same reverence for those with physical and mental challenges.

As a leader, we have the power and the mandate to include all of God's body in the workings of our society. We have the power and mandate to value more than a person's ability to contribute to the bottom line. We can learn and teach others to value **all** of the people in God's body. We can learn the names of those that are indispensable. We can have a relationship with those that are indispensable. We can observe why some of the body of Christ are working two jobs or double shifts to make a living wage. We can make sure the indispensable are included, not just accommodated. We can employ ones with physical and mental challenges. We can treat the indispensable as visible, not invisible. Without them, our body of Christ is not complete.

Let us pray.

Gather us in, that we may remember the ties that bind us together in your love. Write your law upon our hearts, that others may find us to be generous and loving friends. Strengthen us by your Spirit, that we may live in love, a love that transforms our lives, even as we help transform the lives of others. And all of God's people said, Amen.

Rev. Brenda Davids
Great Plains United Methodists

SEPTEMBER 22: SPIRALS AND SPHERES

Who is on your team today and in your sphere of influence? I like to think of a team as a drawing. Imagine you put your pen on a piece of paper. Then a drawing expands as you draw a small dot and then begin to drag your pen around and around making a spiral. Our teams might be like the spiral. The spiral starts small and grows over time. It grows with different people being added and a larger sphere of influence is created as it begins to include external members of your team as well. How can you provide better value by adding some members to your internal teams? It may be that a great place to look is to your external team members. They have a perception different from yours which could be extremely valuable if they were brought internally to your team. If you could add an extra external team member today why would you add them? Whether it is internal or external, maybe your largest boost to profitability is contingent upon that addition. The entire team can be accountable to be on the lookout for new team members. Do you have an accountability system to add them? What is the first thing you can do about it in the next seven days?

As brothers and sisters in Christ, we are connected. We are connected to the church and our families, to Christ and our purpose. But who are we bringing along with us?

> "For the Sovereign LORD, who brings back the outcasts of Israel, says: I will bring others, too, besides my people Israel."
>
> ISAIAH 56:8 NLT

I was one of those outcasts, were you? I was invited into this team. Perhaps you might be the next one to come onto the team. Maybe you are the one that is accountable to invite someone else to the team. God invited us to a relationship through Jesus Christ even though we were outcasts. I am in that sphere and spiral now. We now have the responsibility, not just the capability, but responsibility to invite others. In your sphere of influence, like a pond, are you casting out into it to see if you can bring someone to Christ. Who might you be able to connect with that would help you on your path? Those that might help you might not be connected to Christ. But they might become connected by you. Some might build fishing poles, while others make stringers, string or provide transportation to a pond to fish. But they are part of the team casting. I believe that is the situation we are sometimes involved in. Let us look to external resources this week that might help us to connect with others. What is the first thing that you can do about it in the next seven days?

Let us pray.

Jesus, you are our connection. Our path might be like a cone, winding in such a circular pattern. But we want you on our spiral, moving up in a closer relationship with you. Send the Holy Spirit today to allow us to connect with others. Make our time together precious and priceless. May we connect, grow and serve because our time is precious. Draw us near you Lord, take us up the spiral of excellence. In Jesus' name, we pray. Amen.

SEPTEMBER 23: PROMISES AND PROGRESS

As leaders, we help set the stage for progress. We even create measurements to evaluate if we are declining, advancing or just maintaining. If we are part of a value delivery process, we want to advance. We need our goals to reflect those objectives and then put processes in place to achieve them. Some choose to see this as adding pressure. But another way to achieve this success might be by adding commitment. Where is your team committed to your goals? Where are you committed to achieve? One of the best ways to ensure we are committed is by making a promise to a minimum level objective and committing ourselves to a penalty of some kind for failure. As leaders, we can set those promises and commitments only for ourselves, but we can share them with the team. I like to believe that the highest achieving teams are committed to one another and make promises to one another. Where is your team committed? A highly committed team can collaborate by communicating their promises. What is the first thing you can do about it in the next seven days?

As brothers and sisters in Christ, we have been given promises to us by God. So where are we making promises in our walk of faith?

> "If you fail under pressure, your strength is too small."
>
> PROVERBS 24:10 NLT

I find strength in the promises of God. Do you? If our strength is too small, we might be too weak for the task. It seems reasonable to keep from failure, we should seek to be stronger, so that we can make more promises. Let us imagine that you made a promise every week of the year. You started with a promise that was small and was achievable so that you met your obligation weekly. Would you believe that this path would make you stronger? Would there be power in our promises to God and each other? Collaboration in our faith by using promises increases our trust in one another. We can certainly find power in the promises from God. What is the first thing that you can do about it in the next seven days?

Let us pray.

Heavenly Father, like the song says, we can stand on the promises of God. Guide us as we consider the power of our words and our promises. May our commitments be supported by our promises. Let us proceed with them hand in hand as we want to walk with Jesus, hand in hand. In Jesus' name, we pray. Together, Amen.

SEPTEMBER 24: IT IS PURPOSE, NOT PORPOISE

Do you have a purpose statement? Leaders need to know the purpose for their teams to operate most appropriately. If you can speak your customer's language but do not have purpose, where is the value? If you could tell the future, had industry secrets, or gave all your services away for free but did not have purpose, where would be the value? I think I will run a little test this week. Maybe you would consider joining me? Instead of asking what people do professionally, let us ask them why they do what they do professionally or at work. Work with the phrase a little before you use it. Start by asking yourself. Another great place to start would be to ask your team. One should probably not ask that question unless they have answered it themselves or else you might get caught off guard. Why do you do what you do? Why does your team do what they do? What is the first thing you can do about it in the next seven days?

As brothers and sisters in faith, what is your purpose? One might think that our purpose gets redirected regularly. A redirection might take one from filling the vehicle with gas, to grocery shopping, to what to prepare for lunch or dinner. We can redirect what we are doing all the time, but that does not mean your purpose has changed.

> "If I could speak all the languages of earth and of angels, but didn't love others, I would only be a noisy gong or a clanging cymbal. If I had the gift of prophecy, and if I understood all of God's secret plans and possessed all knowledge, and if I had such faith that I could move mountains, but didn't love others, I would be nothing."
>
> 1 CORINTHIANS 13:1-2. NLT

There was a purpose here being promoted. It is love. If we are going to grow with Christ, we might want to start with our purpose. For then we can make our measurement of aligning ourselves with God. What is the first thing you can do about it in the next seven days?

Let us pray.

Heavenly Father, you have created it all. You have made it good, and you have given us free will. But sometimes we get lost with our purpose. We see distractions that take our minds and occupy them. Once we know you, we know our purpose is to stay close. We can stay closest to you by living with love, by sharing the love, and by letting people know of your love. May the words of our mouth be words of love today. In Jesus' name, we pray. Amen.

SEPTEMBER 25: ABUNDANCE OR SCARCITY MINDSET?

Leaders, to which side has your team been leaning? Has it been towards abundance or scarcity in their attitudes? I think it might be that in a value proposition business we can find abundance. Our markets are larger, clearer, and our message is understandable and conveyable. We can find more "right fit" team members, both internally and externally. We have more confidence. Our profitability and generosity can blossom and grow best in abundance. But scarcity is also an approach that leaders can battle. Our brain's neural networks are wired this way. Scarcity is not about growth; it is about price and cost. Scarcity is about the battle of competition instead of being an industry leader. Scarcity is about fear and not about value. Scarcity is about the past and present, not the present and the future. Where are you in a scarcity mindset? Where can you and your team focus on transforming scarcity into abundance and fear into confidence? Value is waiting for us there. The natural instinct is towards scarcity. That means that to have an abundance attitude requires us to do an intervention of our instincts. What is the area that your team is struggling with a scarcity mindset? What is the first thing you can do about it in the next seven days?

When Jesus walked the earth, I think that he exhibited an abundance mindset. In abundance, we find love.

> "Love is patient, love is kind...Love never fails."
>
> 1 CORINTHIANS 13:4-8 NIV

I shortened this famous and well-known chapter. I like it because it has so many explanations of what love is not and what love is. The passage shows that love is extremely abundant when we allow it to be. We are called to love, and in my words, to be an abundant people of Christ. Who might help you transform where you are feeling fear and scarcity and turn towards abundance? Would that be a great mindset for the week ahead? What is the first thing you can do about it in the next seven days? If you are not willing to answer the question you might be stuck in a scarcity attitude at this moment.

Let us pray.

Jesus, we want you to be in our lives abundantly. Yet we find that we react so many times out of fear. We think things are scarce. We think that there might not be enough, that we have to compete, or we might somehow be a victim or lacking. All we really do is remove us from the incredible abundance of God's love. Take away our fears today even if just for a minute or hour. In Jesus' name, we pray. Amen.

SEPTEMBER 26: BARRIERS AND BORDERS NEED ATTENTION

As leaders, where do we set barriers? Do we even need them? I think that we do but barriers are always a two-sided coin. A barrier can keep something out, but they also keep things in. Barriers can establish an expectation to stay within, but then it can also restrict creativity. When we are producing a product with machinery, being within the limits of measurement to make the parts work together as designed is critical. But when working with our team, those barriers are more difficult to deploy. Measurements might actually help our teams to function if we can find the right measurements to use. Some have even attributed the lack of measurements in a job role to a significant part of job misery. Can you think of three barriers that your team knows about? Where do you have barriers in place but do not have measurements to back them up? Perhaps this week we might focus on our borders. Maybe they need to be stretched a little or maybe they need to be redrawn completely. Regardless of how we change the borders the measurements will need to change to promote the borders effectiveness. What is the first thing you can do about it in the next seven days?

As brothers and sisters in Christ, we face the temptations of this world. Our new life in Christ removed many barriers. It placed in our life the measurement of love. How can we measure love though? We read,

---

> "'Should you not fear me?" declares the Lord. 'Should you not tremble in my presence? I made the sand a boundary for the sea, an everlasting barrier it cannot cross. The waves may roll, but they cannot prevail; they may roar, but they cannot cross it.'"
>
> JEREMIAH 5:22 NIV

We know the measure to which Christ loves us. It was so much that he gave his life. God has placed the ultimate barriers of death to the side. Where might we have barriers in our lives that are not loving? Are we inviting an uninvitable personality to church? Are we loving people unlike us, especially if they seem unlovable? Much like two countries that have border controls, we place barriers in our lives. Are we being as loving as our loving God calls us to be when we place barriers to love? How might we focus on moving the borders of our faith to love others? What can you do about it in the next seven days?

Let us pray.

Jesus, you have removed the barrier of death. Walk with us and guide us as we work on the barriers we live with. Remove the barriers to loving relationships in our families, cities, and countries. Make our boundaries do more to spread love than to restrict it. May those that help us to grow our boundaries be blessed. In Jesus' name, we pray. Amen.

SEPTEMBER 27: COWBOY HATS OR BASEBALL CAPS?

As a leader, what do you wear as part of your uniform? Is it a baseball cap, a cowboy hat or maybe a fedora? Our uniforms make a difference, but the most important part of our uniform might be a helmet. Helmets serve a purpose; they are not just for appearance. They protect our heads, our minds and our ability to lead. Because of this,

I like to think of that protection of a helmet as confidence for a team leader. When we wear our helmets of confidence there are few tasks we cannot handle. Without that confidence, there is not much we can do. We can be trapped in mundane circumstances, be void of creativity, and be less productive. We certainly are less valuable to our teams and our purpose. Where have you as leader been wearing your helmet of confidence lately? Where have you or your team been missing theirs? Part of being a great leader is helping our team members to find their confidence and to wear it. What is the first thing you can do to put the helmet of confidence on anyone on your team?

As a person of faith, when was the last time you were in church? I want you to think back to what the people were wearing. Although the people were dressed differently, sweaters, suits, tee shirts and so on, they wore many of the same things.

"But let us who live in the light be clear headed, protected by the armor of faith and love, and wearing as our helmet the confidence of our salvation."

1 THESSALONIANS 5:8 NLT

The creatures of this world will attack us daily. Those attacks can result in our minds and hearts being ripped, torn, or broken. But it is our faith in Christ that we truly should be wearing. We can take our clothes to the seamstress when they need to be mended. As a result of that mending, we will have to pay a cost. But Christ has already paid the cost for our true brokenness and repair. There are no rips or tears in our armor of faith and love that Christ cannot repair. Where are you feeling broken today? Maybe it is time to put on your helmet of confidence. What is the first thing you can do about it in the next seven days?

Let us pray.

Heavenly Father, you are the tailor of the universe. You sent Christ to pay the price for all the brokenness of those that want to be mended. We come to you, the disheveled, ripped, torn and are showing the attacks of this world. Strengthen our confidence now as we know that Christ has paid the cost. In Jesus' name, we pray. Amen.

SEPTEMBER 28: WHY WAIT FOR RAIN?

Do leaders suffer from droughts? Droughts happen in many ways. They happen when a lack of rain harms plant life and crops. We can have business droughts and relationship droughts as well. These are times when we are missing a significant part of our purpose, of our value delivery system. The farmer and rancher that suffers from a drought have to seek their water. They haul water to their livestock and farmers must irrigate. But when you as a leader suffer from drought, do you seek more or do we go into some kind of wait and see mode. As a leader, much like the rancher, we are called to seek the water. We do not need to wait for the drought to stop as our teams need us more than ever at these times. When relationships are in a drought, they need us to bring energy and communication. Where might you be in a drought in one of these areas? What can you do to haul some water like the rancher, to end a drought? We are called as a leader to challenge the limits of the droughts in our lives. What is the first thing you can do about it in the next seven days?

As a people of faith, we can experience times when we feel alone. Times where we are not close to Christ. We suffer from a drought in our faith. Often, it is our decisions and actions that lead to these droughts.

> "They are like trees planted along a riverbank, with roots that reach deep into the water. Such trees are not bothered by the heat or worried by long months of drought. Their leaves stay green, and they never stop producing fruit."
>
> JEREMIAH 17:8 NLT

Where have you suffered a drought in your faith in the past? As you reflect upon it, do you see some choices that lead up to the drought? The key is that a "choice" is almost always ours to make. When will we forgive and realize that we can haul water? When will we repent, so as to come to the river and be refreshed? The sooner the better. Let us reject the droughts when we can see that Christ can make it rain. Jesus granted us permission to have those choices and he is called the living water. Where might you be needing some water today because you might be in a drought in your faith? What is the first choice you can make in the next seven days?

Let us pray.

Jesus, you are the living water. We pray today that our choices will allow us to drink from that water. Quench our thirst. Quench our droughts. Let our anxiety be drowned by your water of peace. Let rains of joy soak us to the bones. May we stand in front of you, dripping with drops of love, making a pool reflecting the glory and honor to you. In Jesus' name, we pray. Amen.

SEPTEMBER 29: LET GO AND STAND FIRM

As a leader, what are you holding onto? Is it profitability, maybe a new project, or even a new relationship? If someone were to attempt to take away something you are holding onto, you will most likely lose it if you do not have a firm stance. Your value you deliver, your why, is your stance as a leader. If it is weak, then one's ability to maintain balance is compromised and whatever you are gripping is easily torn away. It is easy to get caught up in gripping even tighter when something is pulled away. Often the correct thing to do as a leader is to be caught standing firm. A firm stance provides power to a grip. Does your team know your stance? How strong do you feel in your stance right now? Maybe today's focus should be on loosening our grips and being accountable to standing strong. What is the first thing you can do about it in the next seven days?

As a people of faith, we can be challenged by our cultures. Because we live in them, they can place a grip on us. But we also have a grip. What is it that we are holding onto?

> "With all these things in mind, dear brothers and sisters, stand firm and keep a strong grip on the teaching we passed on to you both in person and by letter."
>
> 2 THESSALONIANS 2:15 NLT

Having a grip is certainly natural. We need a grip but notice in this verse we are instructed to first stand firm. If we do not have a firm stance, that which we grip onto can be torn away. Where might your stance with Jesus not be as strong as you want? We can work out and exercise our bodies and muscles to strengthen them. Would it be reasonable to only focus on the grip of your hands? We often need to let go of our pain, grudges or even hate and that which distances us from others. Our stand with Christ is focused on love. How might you shift your grip this week? Are you willing to be accountable to someone else if you are willing to make a shift? What is the first thing you can do about it in the next seven days?

Let us pray.

Heavenly Father, we ask that you hold us in the palm of your hand. May a gentle pressure of us resting in your palms be enough of a grip that we never separate from you. Help us to see where we are gripping things that do not honor you. Send us a gentle reminder to improve our stance. Let the winds blow but let us stand firm with you. In Jesus' name, we pray. Amen.

SEPTEMBER 30: SETTING EXPECTATIONS AND POSSIBILITIES

As leaders, we set expectations and even have some rules. Without expectations, the energy of our teams would lack the direction needed to deliver value. We know in baseball that after a hit, the batter will run to first base. If the fielders catch the ball or advance it to the base before the batter gets there, he'll be out. Do you see the set of expectations here? The offense knows them, and the defense knows them. The coaches know them, as do the crowd and even the television spectators. What are the ten most important expectations for your team? What about for yourself or your family? Are they clearly communicated or do you or the team waffle at the thought of them, bending them as you need? In order to collaborate effectively we need some basic expectations. As a leader, we also have the responsibility to assure that possibilities are also maintained. Teams need both expectations and possibilities. Imagine how your team might be able to collaborate at a higher level if possibilities and expectations were clearly defined and encouraged. What is the first thing that you can do about it in the next seven days?

People of faith, what are your expectations for yourself? Are we living as a people for the short-term benefits and satisfaction? Do you recall Esau's limited time frame and expectation for satisfaction? We read,

---

> "Afterward, as you know, when he wanted to inherit this blessing, he was rejected. Even though he sought the blessing with tears, he could not change what he had done."
>
> HEBREWS 12:17 NIV

As a people of faith, we have so many stories and parables that teach us to hold on for the long term. We have stories that encourage us to not give in to the nearsightedness that tempts us. Where have your aspirations been too short? Where might you think out one, three, or even five years into the future? Can you identify ten top rules for your own progress with Christ? We can make some significant progress with just such a vision. With Jesus' assistance, we can change lives and bring Christ to the forefront. It is not time for tears of regret. Let us plan for some tears of joy. If we can choose tears of joy or tears of regret, which will we choose? Who in your community can you encourage to seek some possibilities and extend to them some joy? Each of us has the ability to collaborate and bring either type of tear to ourselves as well as others. What is the first thing that you can do about it in the next seven days?

Let us pray.

Heavenly Father, like a flock of ducks rising from a lake, let us make a joyful sound. May the joy of expectations that are centered on you command our attention. May tears of joy compel us to honor you. May we move closer to those tears and away from tears of pain and suffering. In Jesus' name, we pray. Amen.

OCTOBER 1: WHEN DO ANGELS SPEAK?

As a leader, are you focused on value? I think a focus on value is a great place to start. It begs the question; can we deliver more to others than we can get in return? If we do this, I think that we are more likely to have better team members, better teamwork and raving fans for customers. When was the last time you encountered someone giving you an extreme value? Recall the entire transaction for a second. What was the environment like, clean, organized and presentable or run down, dirty and disheveled? How were the people including the other customers? Was everyone edgy, angry and temperamental or were they pleasant and even energetic? What would you expect to happen to your team's profitability if it becomes value driven? It is all too common to meet people delivering their efforts and energies with mediocrity. How is your team positioned for the remainder of the year? This final quarter could be one of the most valuable of your life or it could very well be the most mediocre one of the recent past. The choice just might start with you. How about asking your team members which one they might prefer? I think I know which one your customers would choose. Will you be inspired to have a mediocre finish to the year, or will you be inspired to reject mediocrity?

As a people of faith, we just might be walking among angels.

> "Do not forget to show hospitality to strangers, for by doing so some people have shown hospitality to angels without knowing it."
>
> HEBREWS 13:2 NIV

How many angels have you met? I think that is an interesting proposition. I think a better question is how many angels would you like to meet in the future? I would like to meet a lot, especially if I can meet them here on earth. If you are like me, this passage holds a lot of potential for us then. What is holding you back from being hospitable in even the smallest of ways? Can you spare a piece of gum or an extra ten minutes to help change a flat tire? You just never know who you might meet and the next angel in your path might like a piece of juicy fruit, cinnamon, or spearmint gum. And remember, you do not have to be in the hospital to be hospitable. But to be hospitable is one of the ways God may find us valuable. What is the first thing that you can do about it in the next seven days?

Let us pray.

Heavenly Father, we are fortunate to live with your grace. Let us pray, move forward today, and be hosts for you. May we be in relationship with those both deserving and undeserving, and with those lovable and those that seem unlovable. May you set aside our fears so that we might meet the angels that you might place in our lives. In Jesus' name, we pray. Amen.

OCTOBER 2: DANGER! HIGH WINDS!

What is shaking? That is a slang phrase that I have heard as a greeting before. But what is shaking or shaky when we think about our teams and businesses? As leaders, we know that the winds will shake. That effect applies to our teams as well, as we expect that the winds will blow against our people. But are they anchored to your team's purpose like a tree is anchored by its roots to the ground? Generally, the only trees that I have ever experienced being uprooted did so because when the wind came, the soil's grip on the roots had been weakened by saturating rains. Is your purpose and its value you deliver, able to withstand the downpours over time? Do your team members know it? How might you strengthen the soil by planting more ground cover around your purpose? Could it be that you might have more training? If the attitudes and winds of the culture and society are constantly blowing, it can weaken our teams. As leaders, we can strengthen our teams by thinking about the attitudes that bind our connections. Ready or not, the rains will come. Our choices now will determine whether our team's purpose is buried deep within them. Our work to promote the attitudes that buffer the winds and saturating rains need our cultivation. What is the first thing that you can do today to impact the connection?

As a people of faith, we are not exempt from trauma, drama, or significant challenges. But the very essence of our faith is hope granted to us through Jesus Christ.

> "Therefore, since we are receiving a kingdom that cannot be shaken, let us pray, be thankful, and so worship God acceptably with reverence and awe."
>
> HEBREWS 12:28 NIV

This passage feels so empowering. It makes me imagine a person standing firm on a cliff facing the storm. The person's hair is blowing backwards while the rain blasts onto their face. Where have we been running away? As surely as the sun rises, we know the storms will come. But our faith allows our roots to be firmly planted deep with God and the people of the church. Let us join together and strengthen one another around the base of the tree to affirm one another. Perhaps we need to be encouraging each other to dig deeper into the soil. Let the world shake the pinecones from the trees, let it rattle the treetops, and let the waves of wind roll throughout the world. But for us, for our families and our teams, let us lean into the storm with our rock. What attitude is allowing our faith to be weakened? Perhaps we need to turn and face the storm instead of running with it. Maybe all anyone needs to face the storm is a person to encourage one another. If our roots are cultivated with others of faith, I suspect that the tree can stand strong. If our foundation is solid with one another and Christ, then let the winds blow. Is our attitude of rugged individualism and self-preservation keeping us from strengthening our foundation? What is the first thing you can do about it today?

Let us pray.

Heavenly Father, thank you for your blessings of the people that surround us. May we stand strong for each other. Help us to be fertile soil that digs deep into our relationships with our Lord, Jesus Christ. Our arms may flail, our hats may be buffeted in the wind, but you can always warm our hearts with your love. In Jesus' name, we pray. Amen.

OCTOBER 3: WHICH IS YOUR FOCUS?

As a leader, some might think that our worlds get more complicated by things getting added to our plates. But if our focus is on growing our people, I think our math is more likely to be based on multiplication not addition. Where is your team looking to add instead of multiplying? Is your team possibly settling for adding ten more clients when they could be thinking ten times the number of clients and satisfied customers? Would they like to reduce their problems and challenges by one or two or would they like to reduce their problems by ten times? I think value-based entrepreneurs are focused more on multiplication. When you look at your team do you think that they are adding or multiplying? Your team might be reflecting what you are doing yourself. Are you adding or multiplying? It can be difficult to change our focus from adding to multiplying, but the future of our team and the value we provide will be restricted by just adding. As leader, imagine what happens to a mathematical formula if you begin to interchange the math symbols of addition and multiplication. The result changes immediately. How can you multiply this week? What is the first step you can take to put your focus on multiplication?

As brothers and sisters in the faith, we can get trapped into manners of simple addition as well. But we remember we are to forgive seventy times seven, not seven plus seven.

> "Marry and have children. Then find spouses for them so that you may have many grandchildren. Multiply! Do not dwindle away!"
>
> JEREMIAH 29:6 NLT

The Israelites were not supposed to just add to their population but multiply. How much might you multiply the times you forgive this week? Will you read a single word in the Bible, or can you multiply the words and sentences? Will you love once this week or how about taking the opportunity to love a multiple number of times? It is a complex world, and God likes multiplication. Are you going to decide to add or multiply? Relationships are important to us. Which math subject do you think will grow your faith? Will we divide the impact that Christ can have on us or others? Perhaps we could be subtracting and removing those that disagree with us or maybe we should be loving them. Choosing to add is a choice. Why not choose to multiply? Our focus on the relationship with Christ is best served by our focus of multiplying His love in our lives. What is the first thing you can do about it in the next seven days?

Let us pray.

Heavenly Father, the world is yours and we enjoy the ability to live in it. Guide us this week as we reflect upon our ability to add. Help us to multiply instead of adding. We want your healing touch to multiply among all that are hurting. Multiply among us the opportunities to love and forgive. Help us to multiply the numbers of people that will come to a relationship with Christ. In Jesus' name, we pray. Amen.

OCTOBER 4: THE MLB DOES NOT PLAY NFL

As leaders, we build teams. Our teams are built with internal and external partners. As an example, the entertainment industry includes professional baseball. Those associated with the Kansas City Royals represent an internal team. But the New York Yankees are a part of the team as well. This is true because both are members of the Major League Baseball organization. If the Royals did not have other teams to play, there would be no entertainment. The teams have their own way of approaching challenges and capturing opportunities. Because of their competitive nature, they will not likely help one another out on the field. A leadership team from one industry might be able to approach a leadership team from another industry though. Could leaders from the National Football League help those teams in baseball?

When disputes arise in your organization, do you have an external team that you trust to come to your aid? It might be that we tend to focus on our competitive and independent nature. The stronger our value proposition is the more we rely on both resources, internal and external, to handle our internal challenges. Where does the same challenge continue to show its face for your team or clientele? Maybe it is time to consider finding a trusted external resource to help. Leadership on your team has different levels. On some teams, there is a focus to increase everyone's ability to lead. Do you need more leadership levels, more internal leaders or possibly some external leadership assistance? What is the first thing that you can do about it in the next seven days?

As a brother or sister of Christ, we are not going to be exempt from holding different opinions about things. That is true whether it is the color of carpeting being chosen, the interpretation of scripture, or of one's actions.

> "And I ask you, my true partner, to help these two women, for they worked hard with me in telling others the Good News. They worked along with Clement and the rest of my co-workers, whose names are written in the Book of Life."
>
> PHILIPPIANS 4:3 NLT

Even those whose names are written in the Book of Life have disagreements. But we have a true partner to help us. Have we invited that partner to help us or are we still relying on ourselves and our own perceptions to find a resolution? Where do we continue to find a challenge in our own lives? Maybe that is the first place to look and invite our true partner to help us. That just might be the grand slam. Metaphorically speaking, if anyone can hit a grand slam or throw a Hail Mary pass for a touchdown, it is Jesus. What is the first thing you can do to get an external viewpoint about your challenge in the next seven days?

Let us pray.

Heavenly Father, you are the great Creator of every partner that we come into touch with. You provided us Jesus Christ as the example of the greatest partner there is. You send us the Holy Spirit to be our partner in this world. Open our hearts to our internal partners and open our eyes to see when external partners are needed. As we walk this earth today, we ask you to place partners before us. Build our relationships with our partners upon our relationship with Christ. In Jesus' name, we pray. Amen.

OCTOBER 5: NO SABOTEURS ALLOWED

One of the many challenges of being a leader is the battle with ourselves. I suspect that each of us has had thousands of human interactions that have shaped us in some way. I like to think that those interactions can create characters in us. In our minds, we can cheer on the underdog, and we can be the underdog. We can be heroes and we can be villains. We can have a persona where we can encourage others, and we can have the persona of the saboteur that tells us that we are not good enough and that we cannot achieve. But one of the personas is the captain of them all. It is this persona that represents the best of us. The captain is the leader, and it helps me to remember that I can replace any of those personas in myself at any time. I believe that you can do that as well.

As the captain, we lead our teams, but it might help us to remember that our team members have the same issue of having multiple personas. That means that a member comes to work on the team and one of those personas can be engaged at any moment. As a leader, how do we collaborate with members and multiple personas? It might help to remember that everyone has a captain in themselves. Everyone can be a better leader when they spend more time being the best of who they can be. How are you collaborating in a way to encourage yourself and others to be the best of who they can be? Why will we allow the captain of ourselves to be limited any longer? What is the first thing that you can do about it in the next seven days?

As followers of Jesus Christ, we use the phrase being born again. I think that phrase changes how our captain will function in our lives.

> "Let the message about Christ, in all its richness, fill your lives. Teach and counsel each other with all the wisdom he gives. Sing psalms and hymns and spiritual songs to God with thankful hearts."
>
> COLOSSIANS 3:16 NLT

How awesome would it be for the message of love and grace to fill each of our personas? If our lives were filled with Christ, the personas that keep us scared and afraid of the hurts of the past would melt away. Our captain persona would gain strength and be more present. Our generous persona would show up more often. Our actions would change as well. Our minds would spend less time thinking and worrying and be occupied with the actions of doing. Do you have a saboteur persona that is holding back your faith journey? Perhaps the saboteur is focused on building treasure on earth instead of heaven. Maybe your saboteur is keeping you from attending worship with others because of their hypocrisy or the harm that someone of the church caused you. We all have likely had those moments where the saboteur creeps in and influences us. I believe that we can remove the limits of the personas. Where can we encourage one another to speak as captain to captain? What is the first thing that you can do about it in the next seven days?

Let us pray.

Heavenly Father, we come to you broken in a broken world. Guide us to use the power of love to be in relationship with one another. Encourage each of us to be more of the person that you have designed each of us to be. In Jesus' name we pray. Amen.

OCTOBER 6: READY! BREAK!

Do you belong to a team? Some who read this might be in a low spot and think that they do not belong. Regardless of your initial thought, give some attention to just how many teams you might belong to. Consider your family, the people of your company or division, your city, state, or nation. I think that there are many teams that we might belong to. Our teams are important because we are tied together, at least mentally, bound to one another for a purpose. How has your teams' spirit been doing lately? Is everyone on the same team moving in the same direction? Or might it be that a team member or two might not be carrying the load they have been asked to perform? As the leader of the team, maybe it is time for a huddle, a time out or even a halftime break.

In the world of professional sports, it is common to see a player huddle up when a player has something to celebrate. It would be interesting to see a study done to compare how often the team or players huddle up when there is a failure. My intuition leads me to believe that it is easier to huddle to celebrate rather than after a failure. We like to avoid pain and even avoid experiencing others' pain. When the pass is dropped or misplayed on your team, do you huddle up and encourage one another? Who needs some attention from your team? How about you? Leaders find a way to huddle regardless of the circumstances. They find a way to be accountable for the huddle. What is the first thing that you can do about it in the next seven days?

As brothers and sisters in faith, we are definitely different. We act differently, we are built differently, and we even communicate differently. But even so, we claim to be on the same page when it comes to Jesus Christ. We belong to him. But where might your connection with others be broken?

> "Long ago you broke off your yoke and tore off your bonds; you said, 'I will not serve you!'..."
>
> JEREMIAH 2:20 NIV

Many times, our brokenness has been our choice. Not good or not bad necessarily, but a choice. If you have broken a bond, or are separated from a team, you might be missing something very valuable. Think about your teams that support your walk with Christ. Do you have more than one? If not, why not? Why would we as followers of Jesus only have one team and yet participate on so many worldly teams? I will bet there are some other followers that would team up with you so as to walk closer to Christ. We read in the New Testament about the team that Jesus assembled. He recruited twelve disciples to join him. He formed a team in a way that we can copy. His team changed over time and so will ours. Even after Jesus left the earth, the team still continued on. The team expanded and even brought in some new members that used to be avoided, like Paul. How might you be accountable to expand your team before the new year? What is the first thing that you can do about it in the next seven days?

Let us pray.

Father God, thank you for creating such teams that we have in our lives. Empower us to do good works, spread your love, and have great words with one another. Make our team successes honor you and all the glory be given to you. In Jesus' name, we pray. Amen.

OCTOBER 7: PIGGY BANKS ARE NO JOKE

As a leader, we make decisions that are about the future. Those decisions sometimes are not ones that immediately help or enhance the present. Leaders hold the vision of what could be, not just of what is or what was. To have shade or fruit in the future you have to plant the tree now. As leaders, we must use some of the resources of today to be ready for the vision that has been cast of the future as well. There are several examples of the resources that are used today to achieve the vision. Leaders must use some of the precious time of the present to make the plans. Many people pay present dollars for insurance to protect against damage or harm coming in the future. If you want to build a building for your future team you have to acquire some land before you can build.

Capital, time, and thought are resources that leaders allocate for the purpose of an effective vision. Where can your team put some resources to use for the future and specifically for what you want to happen? Who on your team helps to share and cast that vision? Perhaps bringing in someone from your external network to collaborate with you could challenge you to shape a bigger vision. What is the first thing that you can do about it in the next seven days?

It is easy for some to get overwhelmed with concern for what damage can happen in the future. Every political cycle seems to bring angst about what will happen if this person or that person is elected. In our faith, we could also allow ourselves to be overwhelmed by the abundance available through God. As a people who have accepted Jesus, we have the ability to put forth efforts today specifically for our future reward. We can pray for tomorrow. We can set expectations for our worship for today and the week to come. Thinking only about what is on your schedule for the week could be shortsighted if we ignore how our faith and relationships might be strengthened.

> "For this is what the LORD of Heaven's Armies, the God of Israel, says: 'Someday people will again own property here in this land and will buy and sell houses and vineyards and fields.'"
>
> JEREMIAH 32:15 NLT

Jeremiah was just completing a purchase of land in a country that was about to be conquered and he knew it. The victors would soon own the land he bought. But he was investing his silver in the future that only God could see. Where can you invest your energy, love and forgiveness in a place that others would not expect? Maybe our benefits can be enhanced by allowing God to control our rewards instead of our focus being on what the world will return for us. That would be the biggest example of collaboration I think we could use. Where can you invest your energy this week so that Jesus can deliver the benefits? What is the first thing you can do about it in the next seven days?

Let us pray.

Heavenly Father, you can see the future. We give you thanks for the blessings of yesterday and today. Help us to invest our love, our energy and ourselves in a future with you and not just of this world. May the blessings of the past be multiplied to the blessings of the future. In Jesus' name, we pray. Amen.

OCTOBER 8: QUENCHING CURRENTS OF LIVING WATER

As a leader, our teams work to provide a product or service to others. But part of the delivery system is that we also need to take care of our team. Our ability to serve, just by ourselves, is limited. It is like we are but a drop of water. We are valuable when we contribute, but one drop will not quench a thirst. One drop of water may get a seed to sprout but it will not sustain growth for very long. It will likely shrivel and die without more drops. One drop in the swimming pool will not be very valuable to the swimmers or the divers. The lifeguards' job will be pretty easy though. But put several drops together and life-threatening thirsts can be satisfied. I believe that we all have a thirst to be part of something bigger than ourselves. Sometimes that instinct is suppressed but it is still there.

People join groups that do bad and evil things, but people still join. When we join teams, our lives get connected, become fuller, and provide the potential to increase impact. Get enough drops together and a current may form which can move things. How are you taking care of the drops that are parts of your team? Are you acting like water and oil which are not mixing well, or are you forming a powerful current to benefit others by moving them with value? Perhaps today we might be inspired to increase the power of our current by joining with others. What is the first thing that you can do about it in the next seven days?

As brothers and sisters, our faith may be our connection to our biggest team. Part of being a piece of Christ's church is taking care of one another.

"But those who will not care for their relatives, especially those in their own household, have denied the true faith. Such people are worse than unbelievers."

1 TIMOTHY 5:8 NLT

By ourselves, we are just a drop of water unable to even quench our own thirst. But working together with the people of Christ's church we are a movable force. We can change the world for the better. And it is Christ that makes that force become living water for us and others. Where might you be acting like oil and not mixing with others? Who do you know that can help you be a part of the unstoppable current and become an integral part of the current of living water? If Christ can change water into wine, then surely, he can take our oil and let it become water. Let it be so and may we be inspired to take the first step in the transformation. What is the first thing you can do about it in the next seven days?

Let us pray.

Heavenly Father, you have provided us with your living water. You have given us Jesus Christ. You have given us a family of believers and taken care of us. Let us now set our differences aside and figure out how to honor you by working together. Whether we drop gently or splash with great joy into your river, we will trust in you. Send a ripple of compassion to others and our families. May you form us into a movable current of love. Shape the banks of this current so that we might impact the world for you. In Jesus' name, we pray. Amen.

OCTOBER 9: WATCHING FOR BILLBOARDS AND ROAD SIGNS

Are you moving along a path of some kind? We might recognize that everyone is moving on a path of some kind. As leaders, we are moving forward on some kind of path with a team. The team that we lead is hopefully paying attention as we move. There are landmarks, signs and natural markers that help us to see the route we are taking. The landmarks can blend in as part of nature but must be given meaning by us as the leader for our team to be able to use them correctly. That process will help everyone to stay on track. But these landmarks are also good for a return trip. If our team can repeat a process, our own signs and landmarks would be important to repeat the trip we want to experience again and again. Sometimes teams are so busy on the path that it does not get marked well, and when that happens it is easier to get lost.

One critical component about recognizing and using signs is our attitude. Are we curious so as to look for the markers? If not, we can forget that we have been somewhere before on a path. We can lose confidence and get lost along the way. Where might your team be better able to serve with some road signs? What attitudes are getting in the way of being curious? If you have some, they might be blocking our ability to recognize the signs. A set of binoculars to see into the distance is only valuable if your curiosity will allow you to pick them up and look through them. What is the first thing that you can do about it in the next seven days?

As a people of faith, we are on a journey of faith as well. We travel on a path which Christ said was narrow. But the good news is that we have forgiveness and God's grace when we wind up getting off of the path.

> "Set up road signs; put up guideposts. Mark well the path by which you came. Come back again, my virgin Israel; return to your towns here."
>
> JEREMIAH 31:21 NLT

Where might you have gotten off the path recently? Have you strayed from reading the word? Have you made your entertainment your priority over loving others? Have you come to God in prayer already today? There are so many calls for our attention, and Satan knows that anything that gets your attention away from our loving God is a win for him. If we are keeping an attitude of curiosity, we can be looking for the signs of God in our lives. If our attitudes are keeping love for others at the top of our mind, we can find new ways to be in relationships. Where might God be shining the light to bring you back to his path? Do you have a pair of binoculars to look at and recognize the signs today? What is the first thing that you can do about it in the next seven days?

Let us pray.

Heavenly Father, thank you for your grace. We stray from you, we hurt others, and act selfishly at times. We make our own gods and idols, still today, like those people of the Old Testament. But we have Jesus and a relationship with him that reminds us that nothing is more important than you. Shine your light on our path to bring us back from the wilderness where we have gotten lost. Make the beacon in the sky draw us near and keep strengthening our curiosity and love to know you more. In Jesus' name, we pray. Amen.

OCTOBER 10: PASS THE PLIERS, PLEASE

As leaders, we work with both new and our tenured team members. As we add new team members, it is important to learn about their talents, capabilities, and their attitudes. Many leaders have tools accessible to help identify what people are capable of and how they work in their capacities. In baseball, a radar gun will show the speeds of pitches and a computer database will show batting averages. If a pitcher in a baseball game is not capable of hitting a curveball as a batter, then he is best suited to play in a league with a designated hitter rule. What tools are you using to help your team function at a higher level? Have you added a tool lately or went back to one used in the past? It might make sense that using the same tools gets us the same results. What if you are wanting a bigger future or a different future though? Maybe we should be looking to add tools for the benefit of our teams. But remember that a tool sitting in our toolbox that is not used does not contribute to our value. How might you focus this week on your tools? Perhaps one could do an audit of the toolbox. One could ask their team what tools they are using. You could even ask your external network what tools have worked well for them. What is the first thing that you can do about it this week?

We have been handed many things to us on our faith journeys. For many, the experiences with our families and friends, who are brothers and sisters with us in Christ, are important. They establish a foundation which challenges and changes our relationships.

> "I remember your genuine faith, for you share the faith that first filled your grandmother Lois and your mother, Eunice. And I know that same faith continues strong in you."
>
> 2 TIMOTHY 1:5 NLT

When we accept Christ, we are no longer just father and son, mother and daughter, but become brothers and sisters in Christ. But this change is a significant one that those not living in faith might struggle to understand. We are transformed and cleansed through Christ, and we need to adjust our actions and attitudes. Sometimes we need tools to assist us with those adjustments. Two tools that we might have access to which help us adjust are the Bible and the people of the church. Do you have to go to church to believe in Christ? If you do not have access to the people of the church, your toolbox is probably lacking. What might you do to improve the use of your tools? If we put no focus on using the tools, then we are most likely going to fail to use them. Using the tools helps us to draw close to God, build our relationships and experience more love. What is the first thing you can do about using the tools of our faith in the next seven days?

Let us pray.

Heavenly Father, thank you for the Bible and the ability to read. Thank you for the people that we connect with that help us to grow nearer to you. We ask that you continue to bless us and our growing relationships. May we find you in our actions together. Draw us closer to you through the people of faith that we experience. Move us like a nut is tightened to the top of a bolt. We want to become tight with you Lord. In Jesus' name, we pray. Amen.

OCTOBER 11: ARE YOU RUNNING TO AND FRO?

As a leader, what are you moving towards? Sometimes leading our team towards something also means leading them away from others. That means sometimes we need to say no. We need to avoid those distractions that do not support why we serve. We attempt to avoid places that we could serve without value. Can you think of examples in the past where your relationships just did not click? As you look at it now, was there really a great value exchange? Picking the low hanging fruit from a tree is easy. It can happen without planning, and it does not take much energy. Innocent people passing by can pick it. People that are lost and who wind up in the orchard will pick it. When we allow our team to have low value exchanges, we are not being the best of who we can be. It might be easier to talk about avoiding low value situations than it is to do it in practicality. I believe we want to give value. Sometimes we want it so badly that we try to deliver it in places that are just inappropriate. Where might your team be engaged in a misaligned value proposition? Leaders help the team get realigned. As a leader, who can help you to realign yourself? What is the first thing that you can do about it this week?

As brothers and sisters in Christ, knowing when to run from and when to run to, might be the most difficult things we decide. When we see evil in action, our fears might control us more than love. But Christ asked us to love. He asked us to turn the other cheek which is an action of love and not fear. It is hard sometimes to turn your cheek though.

> "But you, Timothy, are a man of God; so, run from all these evil things. Pursue righteousness and a godly life, along with faith, love, perseverance, and gentleness."
>
> 1 TIMOTHY 6:11 NLT

Maybe the best thing we can do is to run from evil and to do it while we are running towards something positive. We can make the decision to overcome our fears and insert a decision to run to that which honors God. Where might you be running from something without a conscious decision of running towards God? Every decision to run from evil can be a decision that takes us into an intentional direction. For some, knowing what direction we need to run before we get interrupted by fear or evil is the best tactic. As the leader of your faith journey, where do you want to run to in the next ninety days? What is the first thing you can do about it in the next seven days?

Let us pray.

Heavenly Father, you have given us the ability to decide. We thank you for your grace when we make the wrong decisions. Guide us today and gently push us in the direction that you might have us move towards. Help us to share compassion and love with one another to push away fears. In the name of Jesus, we pray. Amen.

OCTOBER 12: ECLIPSED OR SEPARATED

As a leader of a company or family, our connections to one another are important. It is the foundation of our relationships. When we are not connected, separation occurs. Too much separation can put cracks in the foundation which could lead to a break or collapse. What do you do to prevent excessive separation from happening? Some separation is okay, but as leaders we need to be able to bring ourselves and our team members back. If we as leaders are not able to do this well, we are likely to lose our members occasionally. As leaders, that is a cost we can mitigate. The eclipse of the sun and moon is a special event. The coming together of the two space objects is noticed by the entire planet. But the sun and the moon will always separate after the eclipse passes by. We need to be able to recognize the separations of our team and limit them. Limits can serve a purpose when they are intentional. What is the first thing that you can do about it in the next seven days?

As brothers and sisters in faith we are connected. When sin rears its head our connections to one another weaken. Look around your world and watch for hatred, anger, greed, envy, and jealousy. When you see them, I believe that you will find some separation and even brokenness.

"No power in the sky above or in the earth below—indeed, nothing in all creation will ever be able to separate us from the love of God that is revealed in Christ Jesus our Lord."

ROMANS 8:39 NLT

That is good news for us. All we have to do is read or watch the news to see the brokenness of this world. God revealed, through Jesus, that his foundation with us is strong. If nothing can separate us from God, then our relationship with the Creator is indeed unbreakable. Our trust in that foundation can help us to draw near to one another when we are separated. Where do you feel or believe that there is excessive separation in your relationships? For many separations, the only thing that keeps the separation open is us. When we choose to keep the doors open to our hearts, we allow our love to escape and love to come in from others. Are we willing to look for the limits? Will we seek them and allow Jesus to fill them where needed and to remove them when they restrict us? What is the first thing that you can do about it in the next seven days?

Let us pray.

Heavenly Father, thank you for your closeness and your bond. We pray for your guidance when we feel that an eclipse has occurred that separates us. Empower and strengthen us to remove the barriers to draw nearer to you. Open our eyes to the barriers that we ourselves create. Draw us together where sin would separate us. In Jesus' name, we pray. Amen.

OCTOBER 13: WHO LET THE PROMISES OUT?

As leaders, our words are important. They teach and inform, but they also can be formed to create an oath that strengthens. A strong team knows the power of communication. It is tough to be strong if you do not have a good communication channel. When we break our word, that channel becomes broken. Breaking your promise might be like breaking a pane of glass. Trying to pick up the shards of glass and to reassemble them is almost impossible. For some team members, a broken promise can do the same thing. What I find particularly interesting is that an individual makes a promise from their own conscious commitment. A promise made under duress is not a promise but coercion. Promises have different psychological powers that many people do not understand. Your promise is your oath, delivered by you, not under duress and it has uncommon power.

Use that power wisely by being quick to listen and slow to speak. Where has your team communication been broken by a broken oath? Maybe it is time to lead by repairing the channel of communication. One of the ways to start in the repairing process is to make some promises to yourself as the leader. Think about your words from last week. How many times have you actually verbally used the words I promise? We can tend to avoid making promises because we know that they hurt others when we break them. It might be obvious that leaders do not make promises that they are not willing to pay the costs to keep. We must be accountable as the leader to pay those costs. What is the first thing that you can do in the next seven days?

In our faith, your promise is a powerful tool in your arsenal to combat evil in this world. Your promise can show your commitment and your love for others. The promises of our heart are delivered by the strongest muscle that we have. That muscle is our tongue. This muscle can use its power to harm or to heal.

> "But now you have shrugged off your oath and defiled my name by taking back the men and women you had freed, forcing them to be slaves once again."
>
> JEREMIAH 34:16 NLT

I will bet as you read this, that you can think of times when people have given you a promise and did not deliver on it. That hurts. They broke their word. I bet that you might still have some feelings about a situation like that from your past. The fact is that others get that same feeling if we break our promises as well. Think about your current relationships, do you have any promises that you are close to breaking right now? Recall the importance of your oath and how powerful it is. If you want it to have the same power in the future, you must take care of it now. If we want to build our relationships in our faith, our promise can be the first step to doing just that. Do you have an area to be accountable for this week? If so, what promise is worthy for you this week?

Let us pray.

Heavenly Father, there is no more powerful word than yours. Guide us so that our words and oaths might become powerful in your eyes. May we honor you by honoring the oaths that we choose to make. Help us to build our relationships with our brothers and sisters in Christ by the promises of our lips. Help us to take our promises seriously. May our promises of today warm our hearts with you tomorrow. In Jesus' name, we pray. Amen.

OCTOBER 14: PLANT AND REPLANT PURPOSEFULLY

As leaders, our teams change over time as new members are added. Additions might occur to bring another member on in a new role, or they might come to take the place of a former team member's position. We sometimes transplant new people onto the team. The new team member has already been planted and grown in other areas of their life. They have served with other teams in some manner whether in their home, at their work, or in their faith. We have either made a hole for them on our team or let them fill a spot that has become vacant. But as a leader, that new transplant needs some special care for a while. Both my sons have worked on some landscaping crews and taught me to water the hole heavily and to use root stimulant for a successful transplant. They have taught me to choose your spot for the new plant wisely. Make sure that the plant will get the right amount of sun to nourish it. It seems that this is not too different from the treatment our new members to our team will need when they join us. I

f you are like me, I would think that you have seen someone who has not transplanted very wisely at some time in the past. I have certainly planted unwisely before. Our people are the most valuable resources and worth the attention needed to plant them in the proper way. As a leader, our ability to collaborate to have a proper transplant is critical to team growth. Where does your team need some special attention this week, and what root stimulator will you use to do it? Jesus just might be the greatest transplanter ever.

> "For they are transplanted to the LORD's own house. They flourish in the courts of our God."
>
> PSALMS 92:13 NLT

When we find Christ, we come broken. Our roots are tattered from the environment we have been living in. We might have insects that have been eating away at us or have a disease that affects our fruit or leaves, and our stalks might be suffering from lack of water. But Christ will take us as we are, and He cleanses us. We are new plants transplanted in a world of grace. Sure, we might see those pesky insects again, but our Gardener will be there to tend to us. We can collaborate with the Gardner, His resources, and His tools to grow and produce a fruitful life. His team, the church, will help to prune and cultivate us if we ask and become engaged. He will remind us that His gardening tool, the Bible, is right there within our own reach. Where are you feeling a little broken right now? Could you use some special attention, or maybe some root stimulator today? Why not pick up the Bible? Do you need some living water today? Then how about carving out time for some thoughtful prayer? What is the first thing you can do about it in the next seven days?

Let us pray.

Heavenly Father, we thank you for being the best planter ever. You seek to grow us and guide us to become closer to you. You sent your son Jesus to us to allow us to have your special attention. We are not farmed like row crops, but each of us is transplanted into a loving relationship with you. May we grow as we bask in your Son. May our roots grow deep as we seek your living water. Make us influence the environment around us as we grow to honor you. Hold us in the palm of your hand as the soil holds the roots. In Jesus' name, we pray. Amen.

OCTOBER 15: GRAPES DO NOT MAKE GOOD PUMPKINS

What value are you to your team? As leaders, your value and the value of the team need to be aligned for a chance at long-term success. It is perfectly okay not to be aligned with everyone. We are not going to align with everyone in the world. We are all created so uniquely and experience things so uniquely that it is just statistically correct to think misalignment will happen. But if your value does not line up with another, then the relationship is not likely going to be long -term based. There is stress, friction, and frustration that occurs when misalignment happens, and we will instinctively avoid it. Think of a vineyard for a moment. If your value is about grapes and making them into wine, then selling pumpkins probably is not of much value. But if you are a winemaker, the leader needs skills and knowledge concerning grapes. The team needs workers who will harvest. The team needs someone who designs the fermenting process. Members will also need to deliver the bottles and cases through distribution to be sold at retailers. Where might some on your team be distracted from the team's value? How might you bring the focus back to your grape or your value?

As a follower of Christ, what is the fruit that you bear? Have you ever thought of yourself as being a vine that delivers fruit for God? Maybe you deliver a lot of compassion? Maybe you are a teacher or maybe you work in missions. These might be your fruits. I think when we sin, our ability to deliver our fruits for God is hampered.

> "You people of Sibmah, rich in vineyards, I will weep for you even more than I did for Jazer. Your spreading vines once reached as far as the Dead Sea, but the destroyer has stripped you bare! He has harvested your grapes and summer fruits."
>
> JEREMIAH 48:32 NLT

Our sin seems to mess up our vine and its branches. Sin might plant the wrong seeds in the vineyard as well. When that happens, other fruits might begin to show up as if we grew them on purpose. Grapes showing up on pumpkin vines do not seem logical or helpful. Imagine a pumpkin, a tomato, a shoe, or a telephone growing from your vine. They are all fine if that is the fruit God has given you to be fruitful with. But what are you producing? Are you doing it with love and compassion while growing in faith? Or could it be that your pumpkin vine has been crosspollinated by sin? Where is your vine sprouting results that are not fruitful in the way that Jesus has asked you to be? What is the first thing that you can do about it in the next seven days?

Let us pray.

Heavenly Father, thank you for the blessings of this day. Guide us as we grow in our walk with you. May our hearts and minds take actions that glorify you. Move us as we take steps forward in our journey with one another and be fruitful. In Jesus' name, we pray. Amen.

OCTOBER 16: SO YOU THINK IT IS RANDOM

As leaders, we need team members. For employers, attracting and retaining quality employees is one of the most important aspects of leading a team. How is your team expanding this year? Some leaders have the same system that they have had for the last fifty years. No modifications might have occurred. Others might not have any system at all, and the process is completely random. When a new team member is needed, some type of search occurs, and a position is filled. Hiring at random will probably deliver random results. I do not think that random and value are found in the same sentence too often. Where is your process for attracting and keeping employees strongest? Why is it strongest, and why is your weakest area so weak? Maybe our attention or perspective needs an adjustment. If our attitude is that our system is good already then it is limited. Until we are turning quality applications away, our attitude might be about continuous improvement. Maybe all it takes is a ten-minute perspective review to see how you might improve it. Who can you talk to about it in the next seven days?

As a person of faith, what are you leaving to randomness? We are called to be intentional people. To love intentionally might just summarize much of the New Testament. That includes having compassion and support for one another. We live lives that are full of possibilities through Jesus.

> "An employer who hires a fool or a bystander is like an archer who shoots at random."
>
> PROVERBS 26:10 NLT

Where are you shooting at random? Is that how we want to be loved? Maybe we can find a deeper relationship by knowing that we will spend time in the Word, not just hearing it occasionally when we make it to worship. Maybe our relationship will grow deeper when our worship is not on a random schedule but the standard for the worship day. Maybe it is us that need to be less random when we realize that our God is always the constant. When our attitude of randomness and consistency ratio improve, we might find God in both. What is the first thing you can do about it in the next seven days?

Let us pray.

Heavenly Father, you have created the earth and the heavens. Only you can organize the randomness of the universe into love. Guide us out of our complacency so that we might leave randomness to find you more often. In Jesus' name, we pray. Amen.

OCTOBER 17: I AM TIED UP RIGHT NOW!

Leaders create and guide the process of value delivery. The team that is put together is guided and so are the customers or clients they serve. We assemble what today I will call a rope. We take "strands" and weave them together to create a billing process. Strands are woven to purchase machines, computers, and materials to manufacture. We weave labor, marketing, and management into the mix. But this rope that comes together is the rope of value. What does your rope do? What value does it provide?

Maybe it is used to attach others to teams like the rope on a lifeboat, or maybe it is a rope of rubber that surrounds and protects something. But our rope can also be used to tie and entangle others when it is not used appropriately. If that occurs, it might even tie up our own systems and value delivery. Ropes can be of various strengths. If your rope is weak and not doing a very good job of creating value, then it needs some focus. If your rope is strong but it is entangled in knots, it needs some focus. Where is your organization seemingly knotted up? Are you willing to put some focus this week on the rope of value with your team? What is the first step you can take today?

As Christians, we can act like weavers. Our actions are like the strands of a rope that we create.

> "He wove my sins into ropes to hitch me to a yoke of captivity. The Lord sapped my strength and turned me over to my enemies; I am helpless in their hands."
>
> LAMENTATIONS 1:14 NLT

We are to be following God's weaving. How are you weaving together love, compassion, and forgiveness? Another segment of your rope might be your sin, hatred, and selfishness. There is a section of our rope that deals with the relationships of our family, God, and our community. Are we using our relationship with Christ as the core that we weave around? Is Jesus the strength that everything else will adhere to, or have we made something else be at the core of the rope? Are your core beliefs concerned about your wealth, your comfort, or your happiness, as is so prevalent in this world? What might you do to improve your weaving and who do you know that can help? We will create the type of rope we want when we bring attention and focus to why we are doing it. Imagine building a rope with hundreds of different fibers available to you. Some fibers work for your life while others do not. Some would strengthen your faith, and some might weaken it. Some fibers might grow the rope while others might require shortening it. What focus will you put on building the rope that God is asking you to build to be the best you? What is the first thing you can do about it in the next seven days?

Let us pray.

Heavenly Father, you are the weaver and Creator. You have made each of us a strand of your world. You have encouraged us to weave and given us the tools to do that. Remove our actions that can put us in knots and entangle us. Thank you for sending us Christ so that our rope is one that will bind us together in love. In Jesus' name, we pray. Amen.

OCTOBER 18: FLINT FOUNDATIONS FAIL

As a leader or an entrepreneur, you become a type of builder. We build something but it starts with a foundation. If a business has setbacks, it is as if what we are building is brought down or disassembled somehow. If things fall apart in an organization, it ultimately will fall back to its foundation. The building that can be created can only be as large and strong as the foundation it is built upon. So, what is your organization's foundation? Does it have a good footing of concrete under it? What about rebar? Is your concrete reinforced with rebar? Or could it be that your business foundation was built on flint? One that builds a foundation with flint will eventually find out that the flint will fall apart. It ruptures and crumbles as heat and change finds the fissures and cracks in the stone.

Are you sure there are no blocks of flint in your foundation? It might be that if you are having trouble in building, you could be building on a flawed part of your foundation. As a leader, we have the responsibility to inspect the foundation. If we are building the team from nothing, we must place the cornerstone. If you are leading a team that was built by others, you might want to audit the foundation and look for the flint. Foundations can be repaired but they will not be if you do not do an inspection. Leaders do not get the privilege to not know if the foundation is faulty. Is there flint in your organizational foundation? What is the first step that you can do about it?

As followers of Jesus Christ, we have the opportunity to have our foundation rebuilt without cost. The flaws of our foundation, our sins, and our weaknesses, are repaired from his sacrifice.

"You will be desolate forever. Even your stones will never again be used for building. You will be completely wiped out," says the LORD."

JEREMIAH 51:26 NLT

This Old Testament reading shows the effects of living only under the law. But the law will always result in failure to comply. That is why we need a better foundation. We have a foundation that cannot crack, rupture, or crumble. That foundation is Jesus. When we commit our lives to that foundation it never needs to be rebuilt. We can begin a journey to build upon that foundation with our faith. We put up pillars of love, of compassion, and connect them through rafters of relationships. The failures and sins of this world, nor our sins or failures can ever destroy that foundation. Maybe the most important thing we can do today is to think about how strong our foundation is. Where are you feeling weak? A leader has the ability to change their perspective. Why not focus on your foundation? What is the first thing you want to do about your foundation hat in the next seven days?

Let us pray.

Heavenly Father, thank you for a foundation upon which to build our lives. You have paid for that foundation. The price was extreme, but you gave it to us for free. Guide us as we build our lives and relationships upon that foundation. Give us confidence as we place our trust on the foundation. Guide us to build upon it and comfort us when we are brought down by this world. Build us so that we never abandon our foundation. In the name of Jesus Christ. Amen.

OCTOBER 19: LESS LIMITS IN JUST ONE WEEK

As leaders of a family, company, or organization we all have the same twenty-four hours. Much of our time seems that it is already spoken for though. It does for me sometimes, and I suspect it does for you. But beyond our sleep and nourishing our bodies with food and water, our time is completely in our control. It is in our ability to take control of the time and spend it as wisely as we can. Our instincts are a challenge to us as leaders because we are human. We are driven by a big message receptor called a brain. The brain is always scanning for signals and messages that might indicate a perceived danger. Did you catch that perceived danger phrase? All dangers that the brain sees are not necessarily immediate dangers or even real.

When you are hungry your brain sends danger signals. You better eat or else I might starve. Are you really food insecure at that moment or just do not happen to be eating at the moment? If you would eat at that moment, would it make the stomach and brain happy? What do you see as the largest waste of your time in the coming week? Can you really afford to spend that time doing it or would your team or family appreciate you using the time in another fashion? Change the limits of your time by accepting the responsibility to be more intentional with one thing this week. What is the first thing that you can do about it in the next seven days?

As brothers and sisters in Christ, our time is precious as well. We have the challenge of the world demanding our attention competing with our desire to have time with our Lord and Creator. Where are you spending time being frustrated or worried? It might be possible that the next week would be more productive if it were spent with less frustrations or worries.

> "Do not waste time arguing over godless ideas and old wives' tales. Instead, train yourself to be godly. Physical training is good, but training for godliness is much better, promising benefits in this life and in the life to come."
>
> 1 TIMOTHY 4:7-8 NLT

Being frustrated might be a mental argument between what is wanted or desired and what is believed to be the obstacle to obtaining it. Why do we make time for those mental arguments? If we fill our time intentionally, we will have less time for those arguments. The lower importance arguments might simply be crowded out which might leave more space for love and godliness. Where are you struggling with arguments, frustration, and worries? Do you have time for it this coming week, or will you decide to be more intentional with your time? Will you accept the challenge this week to limit your frustration and worries? What is the first thing that you can do about it in the next seven days?

Let us pray.

Heavenly Father, our days are shaped by the rising of the sun and the coming of the night. Empower us to look at the presence of daylight to put you first. Comfort us as we remove what we have filled our time with as we have deemed appropriate. There is nothing more appropriate to spend our time with than you. Thank you for your forgiveness because we know that there are times that we have not been with you and that we have not listened when you have spoken. Aid us in making the time for you. May our stopwatches be reset, our alarm clocks cleared, and our calendars opened. In Jesus' name, we pray. Amen.

OCTOBER 20: WHAT IS A LISTENING PLAN

Leaders and entrepreneurs have some similar characteristics. One that is intriguing to me is that they are listeners. Sure, we all fail to listen to what others are really saying sometimes. But entrepreneurs must listen to customer demand, for without demand a product or service is worthless. I can think of many products or services where listening did not occur, and customers went away because of it. Have you seen it in your business or on your teams? Have you stopped offering a product because the customers abandoned the product? Think about the newspaper industry of the United States where the employed journalist numbers are down by one fifth. The local newspaper in our community does not publish every day of the week. But when we listen to our customers and team, we can find opportunities. In China, newspapers are growing and US newspaper companies that have transitioned to web-based delivery of news have a new revenue stream.

But we must really listen to our team and customers. The value of what we deliver can be enhanced when we listen to the words, emotions, and even the body language of those involved in our processes. The value comes when we transform what we have heard into what we can deliver. It is not about what you, the listener, want or need. For leaders, the best value exchange is always about others. Then we can be accountable for what we may provide and how we do it. If we step up our listening this week, we just might find the easiest path to more value. How will you be accountable to listening more?

As brothers and sisters in Christ, we know the following message well. Christ has died, Christ is risen, Christ will come again. It is a great and powerful message to those that believe. But do we listen with our ears and let the message soak into our hearts? Our hearts are where we listen to the message with our being and soul.

> "We must pay the most careful attention, therefore, to what we have heard, so that we do not drift."
>
> HEBREWS 2:1 NLT

The world has another message for us. It wants us to drift. It teaches us survival of the fittest, of comfort, and it all competes with the message that we received about Christ. So which message are we listening to? If we are not listening to God's message, then I would bet that we are probably hearing another message, or we are being focused on ourselves instead of Christ. When we are angry with someone, I believe that we are listening to ourselves instead of listening to "Christ will come again." It is easy and convenient to listen to ourselves and the messages of the world. They seem to yell and scream their messages. No wonder that the Holy Spirit is referred to as the still small voice. Maybe the next time something seems to really be demanding our attention and screaming at us, we should just pause to hear the still small voice. Will we be accountable in some manner to stop and listen more than we speak? What is the first thing that you can do about it in the next seven days?

Let us pray.

Heavenly Father, you are the Creator of the universe and everything great and small. Your voice can be as loud as thunder or as quiet as the mountain meadow at sunrise. Comfort us as we shield ourselves and withdraw from the screaming messages of this world. Protect our hearing so that the small still voice is heard clearly. Calm us as we listen with our hearts and minds. You have given us one mouth and two ears. Make us wise enough to use them in the ratio that you built us with. In Jesus' name, we pray. Amen.

OCTOBER 21: SOMEONE YELLS CUT

As a leader, is it ever appropriate to call a do-over? It might be important to do just that when our value delivery gets interrupted. When communicating with our team, we want our attitudes and hearts to be in the right place. If they are not in the right place, I suspect that our conversation will not wind up with the right result. At times it can then be appropriate to call a do-over. If our team is about delivering a blue product, then putting a red product in the client's hand will lead to disappointment. It is appropriate to call a do-over at those times. It is important to recognize that our brain always wants us to be right. But being right does not recognize the power of the do-over. Living life as a leader helps both yourself and your team avoid allowing regret to spend much time in our hearts or minds. If we can accelerate the do-over, then regret does not have much of a chance to live in the environment of our team. Have you ever been in an environment where regret seeps into the work environment? People can avoid rooms, people, and projects because regret lives there. Where might you want to consider a do-over for this week? Watch for it this week and see if you can collaborate with others to do it faster. What is the first thing you can do about it in the next seven days?

As followers of Jesus Christ, we understand the do-over. Our lives are to be modeled after it. When we accepted Christ, we chose to be born again. A life following Jesus is the ultimate do-over. If God gave us the ultimate do-over, I think it is a method that we can adopt in our lives as well.

"But the jar he was making did not turn out as he had hoped, so he crushed it into a lump of clay again and started over."

JEREMIAH 18:4 NLT

This verse from the prophet Jeremiah to the people of Israel speaks of God's desire for Israel to be reformed. We have the opportunity to wake up every day anew. The pains and suffering of yesterday are behind us. The joy of life with the gift of Jesus and the presence of the Holy Spirit are not limited. We are the ones who limit our ability to do over. Where might you use the do-over this week? Do you have a person on your team, in your family, or in your community that need to experience a do-over with you? Do you have a do-over that you need to complete in your faith journey? We all need a do-over every once in a while. Some of us want one daily. What is the first thing you can do about it in the next seven days?

Let us pray.

Heavenly Father, you are the Creator of the universe and the Master of the do-over. Your creation is born anew daily. You have given us the ability to experience it over again every day. Each day is a new sunrise full of potential. Empower us to leave the pain and suffering of yesterday behind. Deliver us your love in the relationships that we acknowledge today. Comfort those that are mourning and make our do-overs an eternity with you. In Jesus' name, we pray. Amen.

OCTOBER 22: ENCOURAGEMENT AND DISCOURAGEMENT RATIO

As leaders, we sometimes use measurements to determine if our team is being productive. Ratios are common tools to evaluate if a deployed strategy is working. If you see that your customers have five positive ones compared to one negative, you might be more concerned than when they were five to three. But what ratios affect our team? Are you aware that our brains are wired and built with five times the number of neurons dedicated to the negative compared to the positive? Our brains are wired to act like Teflon to the positive and Velcro to the negative. What words are we using with our team? This ratio exhibits why people want to be appreciated and just how often they need to hear it. Your team members may not get positive reinforcement anywhere else in their lives, so we might be well advised to change that ratio.

If our team is associated with the higher ratio, it makes sense that our members would feel more attached. Do you want your team to experience the lowest positive effect of any area of their lives with you? We likely want our members to have a positive effect on other areas as well as to have a positive effect by working with our team. Perhaps being a member of your team is what creates the positive and encouragement that drives all the rest. What do you want your team to create in you? Do you want to be negatively impacted, brought down, and discouraged? If being on your team does not have an impact on the positive and encouraging side of the spectrum, then maybe some shifts and adjustments could be considered.

As brothers and sisters in Christ, we live in a broken world. We all fall short sometimes, but our brains do not need something to be broken to find something negative to absorb our focus. Those negative neurons are always busy. But thankfully, we have the most positive gift ever received to live with. That gift is Jesus Christ.

> "Always be joyful. Never stop praying. Be thankful in all circumstances, for this is God's will for you who belong to Christ Jesus."
>
> 1 THESSALONIANS 5:16-18 NLT

Look at the power that has been given to us. The Bible is teaching us how important these thoughts are, but modern research is supporting it as well. We are being asked to concentrate and pay attention to the positive. Consider how much joy our own thoughts keep us from when we focus on survival and the negative. Where can you insert into your daily routine a place for the positive? It might be that you create a positive focus session at the end of your day. Maybe you could start your day with one. These are certainly worth our consideration, and the faster we implement for our faith, home, and teams the better. We are what we think, so why not think positive? What is the first thing that you can do about it in the next seven days?

Let us pray.

Heavenly Father, you are the Master of all the math and ratios that we ever might uncover. Awaken our minds to the best ratio of all, one Savior for all time. Strengthen our resolve to move from negative thought ratios to a positive thought ratio. In Jesus' name, we pray. Amen.

OCTOBER 23: ARE YOU A RECYCLER OR A REFUSER?

As a leader, one balances the use of resources. But some leaders have access to many resources and can acquire whatever they might need by making an ask for it. But other leaders must give more attention to resources because they are limited. If resources are limited, we might be more engaged to maximize every drop of value from them. This condition of limits can morph into the attitude and mindset of the leader and team. As a leader, do you try to remove every drop of energy from your resources? If you do that to your team, it certainly could create issues? Think about the people on your team. Do you want them to transition to their personal life without any level of energy for those that they love? Do you want the transition to be lacking energy with any relationship away from your team? Think about your physical resources? Is your time best spent by getting the last penny from your waste? If that is true, no one would pay a recycler to do their service. Do your clients want you or your staff to be concerned with cutting up wastepaper into notepads? Or might they want your focus on them and their issues of value? Where might your team need to give less attention to getting the very last drop? Where can your team insert a little more effort to provide what just might be of significant value?

As Christians, we have a relationship with our Savior Jesus Christ. Christ is the ultimate recycler. He takes every one of our sins and renews us. They are wiped away, and we are made new.

> "But Nebuzaradan allowed some of the poorest people to stay behind to care for the vineyards and fields."
>
> JEREMIAH 52:16 NLT

The captain of the guard recognized the value left behind in the destruction. The vines had value still. He knew if he cared for them, they would produce fruit. But our Savior Jesus, can produce the most valuable fruit possible. He transforms the eternally lost into residents of heaven. Where might you and I be spending energy in a manner that is not focused on our Savior? Even the captain saw the opportunity to save the fruit of the vine. All he had to do was ask some folks to tend to it. Surely, we can be in some relationship with others so that our Savior can share his fruit. Where is our attitude, dismissing others as not being worthy of being saved? Where are you overlooking the opportunity to share the best fruits we know of? When we continue to allow that attitude to reside in our hearts and minds, we might be allowing the heart to remain hardened and the mind to be polluted. What is the first thing that you can do about it in the next seven days?

Let us pray.

Jesus, thank you for restoring each of us. We know that sometimes we act in ways that are self-serving and unloving. We know that you have paid the price for those actions, but we want to draw near to you in our relationships. We want to taste the flavors of your fruits. We want our love to explode with living water, like an apple fresh from the orchard. We want the segments of our lives to grow like the segments of an orange or grapefruit. May it all be based around the center and core of you. We want the Holy Spirit in our lives. Peel back the layers of sin like we peel the banana.

Take whatever keeps us from you and remove it now. May we be the fresh fruit, the first fruits with you today. In Jesus' name, we pray. Amen.

OCTOBER 24: THE THREE S'S

As a leader, sometimes our team members become entangled with one another. They may get territorial and aggressive towards one another as they compete. They can become siloed, only paying attention to themselves, and value can be harmed. Team members can get entangled when their attention gets distracted because of their home life, personal relationships that are imploding, and situational frustrations. But who are they competing with? Many times, it is for the leader's attention, for resources for themselves, and it just might be for affirmation. If we are to bring the value our teams bring to others, then we must pay attention to the value that our team provides to one another. How do you help your team to be valuable to one another? Scolding, sarcasm, and shame can be powerful tools, but they leave behind a bitter taste that is not about value. We can give these three tools a name. I want to call them the three S's.

Can you recall when one of the three S's were used on you? Did they leave a bitter feeling in your heart? This method of communicating creates a neural network in our brain that can make a team member avoid the situation and sometimes avoid the leader. Do we want team members avoiding the leader? Let us think this week about the other tools that might help our team. Consider making your focus this week to be on affirmation, appreciation, and curiosity. Perhaps we can put an emphasis on doing them privately until we master their use. Using a tool publicly with a team member may not have the same effect that it does privately. Where, when, and with which team member might you start? Could it be yourself?

Brothers and sisters in Christ, how gentle are we being in our corrections and in our words of rebuke?

> "Opponents must be gently instructed, in the hope that God will grant them repentance leading them to a knowledge of the truth."
>
> 2 TIMOTHY 2:25 NIV

We need to have compassion for our opponents. I was cutting some trees the other day with my chainsaw. When I am running it, I must be very thoughtful as to the cut. Once I place a single cut, the tree cannot be repaired. It will never be the same again. When I cut a tree down, it is done. It will not grow back. The shade and wind break it provided is not easily replaced. In fact, it takes years for a replacement to grow back in. I suppose if one had unlimited resources, you could replace it with a great big tree, but that takes a lot of resources. Sarcasm, scolding, and shaming can be like those cuts into a tree. They can create a situation that can be difficult, if not impossible, to repair. Where have the three S's kept you from Jesus? The tools that we use in our faith that love others are likely to copy Christ. Which tool of love will you use this week? Let us focus on affirmation this week and make it our go-to tool. If you think appreciation or curiosity fit your week better, then make them your focus. What is the first thing you can do about it in the next seven days?

Let us pray, Jesus, from you there is only love. Even your discipline is done from love. Comfort us today to let our hearts be full of joy. When we are hurting let our compassion compel us. Help us to keep the scars from causing us to create sarcasm, scolding and shaming. Enhance our ability this week to connect, care, and have compassion. In Jesus' name, we pray. Amen.

OCTOBER 25: TWO PRIORITY ALIGNMENTS

Leaders and followers alike have a multitude of activities to pursue. I hear many people speak of their desire to be more organized, wanting to have an increased ability to manage their time. This desire might be driven to a positive result by focusing on the priority. Notice that I did not say priorities. If your responsibilities as a person were restricted so that you could only do five things, what would they be? Oftentimes when I work with clients, we will do an inventory of all the things that occur during their work or personal time. Even the mundane and habitual activities are listed. Checking email, opening mail, answering the phone, managing people, creating, or reading reports are just a few options. I am sure that your list goes beyond this. It can be difficult for the leader to identify what the top five activities of importance might be. What if it were only three? What if it were only one?

Perhaps this week our priorities might be examined. What is the one activity that if you do it to the best of your ability it could impact the people you come into contact with the most? When the leader knows their most important priorities, they can begin to have a multiplying effect on their team. Does your team know their most important activities? What would happen if you would begin to build a team that was full of members who just did their three most important duties every day? It would likely force you to build your team and it would take you to higher heights. If you can do it, so can your team. What is the first step you can take this week as the leader?

As believers, we are taught by Jesus that we cannot serve two masters.

> "No one can serve two masters. For you will hate one and love the other; you will be devoted to one and despise the other. You cannot serve God and be enslaved to money."
>
> MATTHEW 6:24 NLT

He speaks about money and God, but the lesson speaks to the concept of any two items. Our brain wants to survive and therefore seeks to avoid pain while finding comfort. We are wise to remember that our brain is something of this world, but it is not our soul. If we want God with all our heart and soul, then we need to put our priority in the right place. Today we can celebrate the resurrection of Jesus. It does not have to be the Easter holiday to celebrate it. Will we make it a one-hour affair or perhaps even shorter? Perhaps we can accelerate our focus this week on THE priority. How might you lead today to start the day and end it with the most important priority. I am sure that the elements and demands of the world are going to attempt to get in the way. But we are the masters of all that we do whether we are consciously making the choice or not. As the leader of you, will you make the priority list to include Christ today, this morning, or this afternoon? We have the power of choice and there is always a choice. What will today look like to you if you make the priority of sharing the love of Jesus with yourself and others? As a leader, you have the choice before you. What is the first thing you can do about it today?

Let us pray, Heavenly Father, You are the priority that we seek. Help us to claim Jesus when the things of this world ask us to claim them instead. Let our thoughts, words, and actions proclaim you. In Jesus' name, we pray. Amen.

OCTOBER 26: DO YOU MAKE COPIES?

As an entrepreneur or leader, we might be about value, and then again, we might not. If we are not focused on value our vision is restricted. We might only see the limits of products or services. We might copy and not create. We might be merely thinking about improving instead of innovating. We can ignore instead of imagining. Just think about the photography industry and the company Kodak. I remember as a child my mother driving by a little booth in a parking lot. She would fill out a form, drop in her roll of film, and hand it to a clerk. She would then go back weeks later to pick up the photographs. The business model was concerned with the best location and marketed a second copy at the same price. Notice the limits being recognized here.

The business was focused on the best location which is a limit. The marketing was about competition instead of value and copies were not creative at all. The model thought about different finishes on the photograph and looked inward at themselves instead of imagining. Today you would struggle to find a free-standing film drop off building. Is your team on the path of limits? What is your value? Do you see any creativity, innovation, or imagination in your team? These might just be a great place to put some energy this week to advance value for your teams and clientele.

As believers in Christ, I would like to ponder what Christ copied. What example of love did He follow and replicate? I think that instead of copying, He created. He made things new and showed us how we can do things new as well. In fact, He is all about new. New life is in Him and provides eternal hope.

> "And you will know that I am the LORD. For you have refused to obey my decrees and regulations; instead, you have copied the standards of the nations around you."
>
> EZEKIEL 11:12 NLT

As Jesus' followers, where are we being like the little photo developing booth business and thinking that copying is the way to move forward? Are we copying our neighbors, the world in pursuit of ungodly things, or of acquiring material possessions? Perhaps we are copying actions of the world that hurt and harm others and feel justified while doing it. Maybe our focus of copying anything should be on copying our Lord. If we are being like Kodak and just copying, we might have the same fate as them. If we copy Christ, we are more likely to live a true life of abundance and love. Breaking the limits of how we copy is a way to increase the abundance in our lives. Consider the things that you are copying in your relationships, your faith, in your health and profession. How might you copy Christ and bring that into any of these realms? What is the first thing that you can do about it in the next seven days?

Let us pray, Heavenly Father, we have new eyes to see and new ears to hear. Give us discernment so that we might know what we are copying. Make our efforts to copy be focused on copying Christ and not the sins of this world. May we copy his example of love and forgiveness as we walk and develop relationships in this world. In Jesus' name, we pray. Amen.

OCTOBER 27: THE IMPORTANCE OF OUR STAND

As leaders, we have many roles and activities we take on. Small or large, they all can be important. None may be more important than the ability to take a stand that represents the value of our organization. Without a basic set of ground rules, chaos is likely. When we have taken our role as leader seriously and developed our ground rules, we can find a space where we can take a stand. Think of your stand like an observation deck built over your life's activities. As you climb on top of the stand you notice that it is about a five yard or meter square landing. Once you have taken a stand, you can move in a direction left and right. You can move forward or backwards. You can move in any direction from the stand and stay aligned. Because the stand can be seen by you and the team, all are more likely to stay aligned.

Often, we might find ourselves without value when we have abandoned our stand. Our stand never leaves us even when we are moving left and right or up and down. It might seem counter intuitive that your stand is still present even when we are in motion on the ground. But the stand is always erect and ready for us to take an observation from. Once you make a stand it is us who move away from it. When our stand is no longer solidly under our feet, we can be attracted to other stands thinking that they might be more useful or valuable. But other stands are just that, someone's and not yours. As a leader we are accountable to create the stand. We may certainly use our team to help shape and build it, but we must be willing to stand on it one hundred percent. If one of the legs of the stand is built by someone else without your full confidence and endorsement, how high would you be willing to climb up it? Where can you improve your stand this week?

Brothers and sisters in Christ, are you sitting down? We are called to take the news standing up, with our feet planted firmly on our stand. I have heard many times in movies, and in real conversation people using the phrase, "You better sit down for this." But on Christ's sacrifice we stand. It is when we stand with Christ that we transform hate, violence, and evil. When we sit with our feet hanging from a chair, our knees to our hips form our laps. But our laps disappear and no longer exist when we stand. Transformation happens just that simply. But just because it is simple does not mean that it is easy to stand sometimes. The weight of the world seems to press us down and even hold us down, but that is when our minds are no longer on Christ. Paul tells the Colossians to watch out for our ability to drift. The drift is subtle and seemingly harmless as it comes across you in your life. But the drift cannot move those that take a stand.

"Jesus said to the man with the deformed hand, 'Come and stand in front of everyone.'"

MARK 3:3 NLT

The winds can howl, the earth can shake, and people can come and go. But we remember that Christ can calm the storm. He can relieve the pain and heal the hand. Perhaps this week we can begin the day by starting with the focus on our stand. Are you willing to be accountable to take the stand? What is the first step you can take?

Let us pray, Heavenly Father, your strength is unmeasurable. When we stand with you, we get the assurance of leaning with you. Our shoulders lean in and lean on your strength. Guide us today and allow us to feel your strength within us. Be with those that are missing their strength and do not know you. Send your Holy Spirit to be with those who are ready to take a stand with you for the first time. In Jesus' name we pray. Amen.

OCTOBER 28: CUBS, LISTEN UP!

As leaders of families, companies, and organizations we have a duty to continue to grow ourselves. We lead our teams towards a value proposition of some kind. We connect the team to that proposition and then we grow them in knowledge and processes. This pattern helps the team to know what to do and how to do it. But how are you, as a leader, continuing your growth? The team's value might be restricted by how much you are willing to grow. We can look to the world of nature and animals for a metaphor. A mother bear trains her cubs to hunt, graze, find shelter, and avoid danger. But that is about it. So, the cubs become good at hunting, grazing, finding shelter and avoiding danger. That is it. That may be enough for the bears of the world.

The limit here is the trainer, not necessarily the trainee. How are you doing as the lead bear? Are you in discussion with other leaders to grow in knowledge or have you placed a limit on yourself and went into hibernation? If we are going to grow as the leader, and everyone is a leader, then we need others to collaborate with us to grow. Will you do a study of some kind to grow? If so, you need someone to provide the materials to study. Will you choose to get a mentor or join a study group? Perhaps you have some people to ask to enter a new and special relationship with. Thanksgiving is in November and might just be the best time to reflect about our growth. Will you choose to hibernate or continue to grow?

As followers of Jesus, we are cleansed from our old selves and called to a new way of life. But that call is not about simply believing because if you believe, life changes. This life following Jesus is to be shared. Even the mother bear teaches her cubs some basics.

> "You have been believers so long now that you ought to be teaching others. Instead, you need someone to teach you again the basic things about God's word."
>
> HEBREWS 5:12 NLT

Is it true that if a mother bear does not teach the cubs their lives are in jeopardy? I think that answer is yes. We may not be too different as eternal life is in jeopardy for those we are in relationship with. Where are we planning to grow and to help others learn as well? As a bear teaches hunting, grazing, finding shelter and avoiding danger, we can be practicing love, teaching the Bible, doing worship, and praying. If we need to grow and help others grow, then we need to collaborate. How many direct ways can you see that you are collaborating? Do you collaborate to worship, study the Bible, or discuss the challenges of the world from a faith point of view? If we are being intentional about our growth, we can witness the specific ways to collaborate. If we are not growing well, we might see that we do not have the collaborators we need in our lives. Maybe you are the answer to others who need to collaborate as well. What is the first thing you can do about it in the next seven days?

Let us pray, Heavenly Father, you have blessed us with so much. You gave us the law and then taught us through Christ that our love is what you want from us. Train us in your ways to hear your still small voice. Help us to teach one another to draw close to you. Open our eyes to see how others can help us to grow. Open our hearts to know when we can be in someone's sphere of influence to enhance their growth. In Jesus' name, we pray. Amen.

OCTOBER 29: THE ROUTE TO OUR ROOTS

As an entrepreneur or a leader of a family, we are called to grow. We can think about either the family or the business, as a tree. Our team might grow like a tree. How does that happen? A seed or a transplanted root is put in soil. It is cared for by fertilizing, watering, and pruning. But if the roots do not develop, the plant will not survive. If we do not have a strong why, like our roots, our families and businesses could be stunted or fail. As the tree grows with its root system, it begins to take shape and transform season by season, bearing fruits, seeds, or pollen. These actions are like the what of our business. What products and services do you offer? If your roots cannot support the tree, it will likely fail.

The tree's growth might be enhanced when we think about how to harvest, how people might enjoy the shade, and how they might rest or nest in the tree. Leaders of families show concern by how others will be able to eat and have shelter by providing for them. But without a strong root system the tree will not prosper. What will you spend the remainder of your year working on? Some might choose to rake leaves as they fall from the tree. Others might think that the tree is going dormant and needs no work or attention. While this might be true, if your roots are not as healthy as they can be it is time to work on improving them.

As you look forward, do you see anytime to be spent working on your roots? Perhaps you can add an irrigation system to them. Maybe you can find a root stimulator. Whatever you do to improve the roots, know that the tree will be affected. What is the first step you can take in the next seven days to improve your roots?

As brothers and sisters in Christ, we too, are growing like a tree. But in our faith, we need to keep a healthy perspective on the why, what, and how. Our faith is based on our root system, our relationship with Jesus Christ.

> "It took root there and grew into a low, spreading vine. Its branches turned up toward the eagle, and its roots grew down into the ground. It produced strong branches and put out shoots."
>
> EZEKIEL 17:6 NLT

It all starts with the roots. Are we focused on getting ourselves deep with Christ? Are we soaking our roots in the living water? Are we reading the words of Jesus in the Bible to hold us close to him like the soil grips the roots? I want the comfort of Christ holding me firmly in this world like roots are held in the soil. How are you doing with your roots this week? Do you need a little water or have some pockets of air where soil could be? What is keeping your roots from being healthier and stronger? Sin, complacency, and even people can restrict our roots from growing. If we want the roots of our faith to be healthier, we must make the decision to remove the unhealthy influences. The difficult thing about removing restrictions is that it is some of the most mentally taxing work we can do. The question is, are your roots worth it? What is the first thing you can do about it in the next seven days?

Let us pray.

Father God, you have made the waters deep and the soil abundant. Thank you for such blessings. May you send your Holy Spirit this day so that we might draw near to you. Plant us deeply with Christ and enrich our lives. May we grow and bear fruit so that we might honor you. In Jesus' name, we pray. Amen.

OCTOBER 30: YOUR HONOR, I MAKE AN OATH

As an entrepreneur or leader, we cannot help but to be disappointed occasionally. Our value proposition systems and people are going to have failures. When that happens, disappointment is likely to appear. But when it does, our leadership might make a difference. When things fail with a product, one might make excuses, find fault, and focus on just mitigating the risk of the transaction. But leaders of value propositions want more. They start with why and that why lives as an oath. Where have you made an oath? Is your value proposition so strong that you meet it as if it were an oath? Making an oath is a matter of honor! One does what he or she can to protect their honor. Keeping an oath has a cost. We are willing to bypass shortcuts that might save money.

We will forego activities and opportunities because we have made an oath. It can be costly, but it has been said that there is never a wrong time to do the right thing. It is always right to keep your oath and protect your honor. When you think of the people, teams or companies that have made an oath to you as a customer, how do you feel when they meet it? Oaths that are kept and met continuously develop value, loyalty, and long-term profits. Do you have an attitude that allows you to make an oath or is your attitude one that pushes them away? Where have your team and you made an oath recently? If you have not made one, today might just be the best day to do so.

You do not have to be a Christian to know of Jesus. I ask, do you think that Jesus was an honorable man? As a follower, this is an important decision. As his disciples, we are to live our lives like he did.

> "Even so, he saved them— to defend the honor of his name and to demonstrate his mighty power."
>
> PSALMS 106:8 NLT

I have heard some people say that they like Jesus Christ but do not care for His Christians. I think that is because we sin and fall short. But making an oath, giving our word, and making a promise that is kept honors Jesus. What oaths have you made this year? I like to think that an oath is a promise made to another. But when I make an oath to another it is Jesus who serves as my witness and accountability partner. Our word, which is our oath, is a promise we make and make every effort to not break. People can be and often are afraid to make an oath. It hurts when others break a promise that was made to you. For that reason, we tend to avoid making an oath to not cause pain to others. What oaths, if any, did you make this year to start it? What work do you need to do to finish them? What is the first thing you can do about it in the next seven days?

Let us pray.

Heavenly Father, we come to you as a people who have received a promise. You have given us the promise of Jesus Christ. When we come to meet you, the most honorable judge, Jesus will be at your right hand. We want to claim Him and have Him claim us. Guide us today to make oaths that honor Him. May the honors of this world always be secondary to the honor we give you. In Jesus' name, we pray. Amen.

OCTOBER 31: IS THERE FUEL IN THE TEMPLE?

Leadership starts with us, all of us, that includes you and me. Every person is a potential leader, so if it starts with us, it might be that our leadership will be based on our physical and mental capabilities. Our leadership might be limited if our minds are cloudy or if our bodies are full of baggage and disease. You do not have to be a Mensa member to have a clear mind. A clear mind enhances your ability to reflect, reason, and appreciate your value proposition. You do not have to be a professional athlete to get your body fit. All you must do is start by recognizing it as a part of being a leader. Is your mind as clear and your body as ready to lead as your team would like them to be? It might be that either of these two issues are a limiting factor for the team's advancement. It certainly will affect your long-term value proposition for your clientele. It is difficult to serve if you are hurting, suffering from disease or not at your peak physically. Do you need to put some focus this week on your physical condition? What about your mindset? The physical fitness business has a great hit in January when people are making resolutions. As a leader, what do you need to do to focus on finishing what you started?

As Christians, I believe that we have been taught to treat our bodies as if they were Gods' temple.

> "And so, dear brothers and sisters, I plead with you to give your bodies to God because of all he has done for you. Let them be a living and holy sacrifice—the kind he will find acceptable. This is truly the way to worship him."
>
> ROMANS 12:1 NLT

If you have ever worked with a coach or trainer, you know that they push your limits. The stopwatch, the drills and the stretching are all part of the development of your perfectly built biometrically balanced "machine." It takes energy, resources, and maintenance to keep it so. Just like our faith requires stretching, we should be stretching physically. Our faith deserves attendance in worship and our bodies deserve action and movement which takes energy. Is your body the temple that God wants it to be? I think that the punishment of a crucifixion on our Lord's body shows the level of sacrifice God made for us. Where are you not giving the energy and effort to maintain the "machine" that God created for us to use? Perhaps the way forward is to focus on a single day that you can start something and make it happen. I do not expect that it is reasonable that someone goes from being physically inactive to being physically active every day at a high level. The ripple effect of change is a great big wave if we attempt it that way. Perhaps a smaller ripple of one day a week would allow us to ride the ripple instead of being overcome by a wave. What is the first thing that you can do about it in the next seven days?

Let us pray.

Heavenly Father, thank you for the gift of Jesus. When we think about the crucifixion, we can think about horror and then love. We cannot fully understand the pain and suffering inflicted on the body of Jesus. But we do know our own bodies, Father. Guide us so that we do not inflict pain and suffering on others or onto ourselves. Place those around us that might help us to keep our bodies the temples you would like them to be. Inspire us to fuel our bodies with good energy? Fuel our minds with wisdom from the Bible and discernment from the Holy Spirit. Fuel our hearts with love. In Jesus' name, we pray. Amen.

NOVEMBER 1: LIVING IN THE TREETOPS

As an entrepreneur or leader, how are you doing? If we are a value driven organization, we have a why, a what and a how. Today, I want to look at how we are doing. How are you providing value, as a team or as an individual? Are you better as part of a team or not? Just how often are you providing incredible value? To know the answer means that you are measuring your successes. There is a book that shares that a miserable job is one that does not have measurements. If we, as the leader, do not have measurements for our team, they are likely going to have moments of misery. Some leaders might not think that they have time to have measurables for team members. They might think that they know what to do. Team members have talents, skills, capabilities and have been trained.

Why would we have measurables then? Anytime we measure successes, we are likely to find failures as well. Are we serving with compassion and focus so that we know when to say no? If we know our team's measurables, we know where they will not perform well. That provides confidence. Knowing what your value proposition is means you will have the courage to say, "We will not serve. This situation is not a right fit." Is there is a better value for you somewhere else? Once we are comfortable with our "why" we can move with courage into "how" we do it. Effective leaders must measure and be accountable to help other team members measure as well. Where might you want to adjust your how's this month?

Brothers and sisters in Christ, how are you doing? This question, stated as I have done here, is deeper than the "how are you doing," by a passerby. We should be looking after one another and "how" we are doing. Jesus taught us to do the "how." He taught us to do it with love.

> "It took root there and grew into a low, spreading vine. Its branches turned up toward the eagle, and its roots grew down into the ground. It produced strong branches and put out shoots."
>
> EZEKIEL 17:6 NLT

In the branches and treetop of our faith we find the how. In the top of the tree, we find the blossoms and the fruit that are safe from the ground rodents that might reach up and snatch something away. We might find comfort by resting on a branch as well. Sometimes we might need to eat the leaves because of our hunger. We might even need to build a nest and stay awhile. As the leader, how are you serving at the top of your tree? Jesus is helping us by building a great root system and calls us to grow the treetops. Are you willing to live up there this week? Going up in the branches might allow you to draw closer to God. If the leader is willing to go there, then the team just might come along. What is the first thing that you can do about it in the next seven days?

Let us pray.

Heavenly Father, thank you for the gift of Jesus and giving us a way to know you on this earth. Help us to grow with Christ so that we might develop a relationship so strong that we can blossom. Let us pray, grow up, and spread like the trees of the forest. May we be in service so that others may come to know you. Help us to care for the sick and needy. Let us pray, bring food to those that are hungry, and water to those that are thirsty. May we in our service, share the living water, our Lord and Savior Jesus Christ. In Jesus' name, we pray. Amen.

NOVEMBER 2: IT IS MAGIC!

As a leader, whether in an organization or a family, it is important to find the positive aspects of our journey. What is it that positive thinking does to our bodies and outlooks? It might be the cortisol in our brains, or it may be the joy in our hearts, but something helps us to convert the energy into something productive. Negativity does not do much for me to make me productive. How about you? If someone says your task is not being completed satisfactorily, does it motivate you or does it make you feel judged? Does it bring forth frustration? Frustration tends to be limiting to me. It makes me think that I do not have time for other things. It limits me to think that I cannot go on until I solve this problem. It tries to tell me that I am stuck and will not be able to move forward. I think we can seek fascination instead. Fascination leads us towards the positive. Switching to being fascinated only requires us to authentically engage curiosity. I am curious as they said the door was locked. I wonder how I might get out. How might you be able to find something fascinating today which would transform the frustrations? Bust your limits today.

As brothers and sisters in Christ, we are not promised life without problems. Our path is not straight, and it is not always well lit. We will have dark times, dangerous times, and other times that are foggy at best.

"The godly will see these things and be glad, while the wicked are struck silent."

PSALMS 107:42 NLT

How might we be able to turn our frustrations into fascination in these dark times? When we read Christ's examples in the Bible you can certainly find fascination. Christ was able to transform so many situations. Examples include turning water into wine, blind people being made to see, and do not forget the telling of the women at the well who heard all about her past. I know that if I had witnessed any of these I would have been fascinated. Maybe our focus this week can be on doing the same. But we get to choose. Will we be frustrated, or will we be fascinated? I think a path of fascination is the more Christ-like life. What is the first thing you can do about it in the next seven days?

Let us pray.

Heavenly Father, you have given us a glorious day. Help us to find joy in the wonder of the sunrise and sunset. Help me to find the splendor of the fall leaves as they change from green to rust, to orange and to brown. May we find the fascination that you have shaped for us instead of the frustrations of this world. In Jesus' name, we pray. Amen.

NOVEMBER 3: STACKING OR SMOLDERING?

Leaders know that intentions are not enough. It is the results that matter because our intentions do not deliver value, our team's actions do. It might help to think of your team being responsible for providing warmth. In the spring, they set up camp in the wilderness. They gather and cut wood. You point out great logs and trees to burn. You choose hard woods that burn hot and for a long time. They stack and split the wood. They even cover it for the winter, allowing it to dry. But eventually, when warmth is needed, when the fire is needed, a match must be put under the tinder. The tinder must light, and then the flame begins to rise, catching the larger wood above. Throwing a match at the fire will not necessarily get it started. No fire, no warmth. Lighting the match and only using it to light a lantern will not heat the entire camp.

Dropping a lit match into the lake will not start the fire either. You can have great people in camp as well, but that will not light the fire. I am sure that your team has great people, but who is going to light the fire? You can have great resources available for your team. They may have great firewood, fire rings, and awesome matches. They can even have great expectations and intentions and think, "This fire is going to be so glorious and warming to everyone around it." But what will seal the deal is someone lighting the match. You can also find a spark or ember and set the tinder smoldering. Where have you allowed your intentions to be enough? That is like having stacked firewood. It does not warm anyone. The leader is accountable for the lighting of the fire. What might you do to light it today?

As brothers and sisters in Christ, we have accepted a new life. But the living water of Jesus is miraculous. We are called to be passionate in our faith, to live it and to love it. That is action. Our intentions are not enough.

"But instead, those sacrifices actually reminded them of their sins year after year."

HEBREWS 10:3 NLT

In the Old Testament, the blood sacrifices were apologetic and showed intentions. And over time, they were weak at best. But they had to be done over and over because the action to change did not occur. When we accept Christ, and truly accept that we want Him in our lives, we begin a relationship. When that happens, our hearts will want the warmth of His fire. Where have you been satisfied this year with intentions? Maybe it is time to stop stacking wood and get revived for Christ. No more just piling or gathering tinder. No more being satisfied with gathering flint to make a spark. Let us ask God to blow on the smoldering tinder and allow the love of Christ to create warmth. Be the one who is accountable to start the fire. What is the first thing that you can do about it in the next seven days?

Let us pray.

Heavenly Father, you have provided us with so much. You have given us Christ, the wisdom of the Bible, and a church to support us. Comfort us today as we prepare our hearts and minds to be in action for you. Let our hearts be warmed through your love for us. Allow us to transform the smoldering opportunities of this world into a fire of revived people. In Jesus' name, we pray. Amen.

NOVEMBER 4: THE FINE LINE OF TARGETS AND LIMITS

As leaders, I find that many times we help our team set targets or goals for achievement. But how do we know when our goals have become limits? I have seen many examples where a team has set minimum expectations for the future. Interestingly, those minimum expectations have been what was ten years ago a wild and crazy dream for others. So, where might we have created a ceiling where one does not need to exist? When we find a way to collaborate with others the possibilities can multiply. They can also subtract or divide if we collaborate with the wrong people. To have a system, process, and way to engage others sets the table.

When done, we can discern who can provide value when we collaborate and allow for exponential multiplication. Adding the wrong people can be like bringing a virus, germ, or cancer into what is otherwise a healthy organization. How do you know the difference in your organization? Are you lacking people in your organization to the extent that you are willing to allow a cancer or virus to join you? It is easier and more efficient to identify the cancers before they enter than it is to eradicate them once they infect and overcome what was healthy. Who on your team do you think has a ceiling or cancer keeping them from collaborating and what can you do about it?

As Christians, our faith has a history from the Bible. We read of how the ancestors of Christ, the family of King David, had expectations. The tent and the temple that were built for worship had their special rooms and special rules. Things changed when Jesus arrived though.

> "And so, dear brothers and sisters, we can boldly enter heaven's Most Holy Place because of the blood of Jesus."
>
> HEBREWS 10:19 NLT

The rules of the Old Testament did not allow the people into the Most Holy Place of the tent or temple. There were limits. With Christ, those limits were removed. We still today battle the limits that we place on ourselves and on others. Where are limits keeping you from growing with Christ? What limits are keeping someone you know from knowing him? One of our most powerful tools to grow is to collaborate with others. We have been blessed by generations before us to have created the church. Members of Christ's church grow together even while being different in many ways. Jesus can help us collaborate when we allow our hearts and minds to do so. How might you collaborate with someone in your faith in the next seven days?

Let us pray.

Heavenly Father, there are limits that help us to grow and limits that keep us from growing. Help us to see the ones that are keeping us from a stronger relationship with you so that we can remove them. Guide us and empower us to do just that. Send us those that help us to collaborate in our faith. In Jesus' name, we pray. Amen.

NOVEMBER 5: BROKEN CAN BE LOUD

How long has it been since there was a communication breakdown for you? It happens at home, on the field, and in an organization as well. As a leader, are we being active to fix those breakdowns? If we are not in action to repair communication, then we are part of the breakdown. If we will not step up or step in to fix them, they are likely to remain broken. Broken channels of communication will not deliver our message nor our purpose. Think about the energy supplied by the energy power grid. You likely have a physical line that connects to it, and you use the energy as it comes across those lines. If the line breaks, what would you do to fix it? I would think that you would inform the power company or call an electrician that might be able to fix the break.

If no one gives the notification, then the lack of power will continue, and people will be stuck without power. Our communication lines are more difficult to see when they are broken than are power lines. There are often symptoms of broken communication lines. Frustration, overlapping work, and attitudinal outbursts are only a few. When we see them, we might want to do an audit of our communication and fix the channels. Do you recognize any of these symptoms in you, your team, or family right now? Are you willing to risk the costs associated with being out of energy that communication provides? What is the first thing that you can do about it this week?

As Christians, we certainly have our language which might be confusing to others. The narthex, the altar, the baptismal font, the blood of Christ. Not only can we confuse people with our words, but sometimes it is how we say it.

> "If anyone loudly blesses their neighbor early in the morning, it will be taken as a curse."
>
> PROVERBS 27:14 NIV

Have you been confused, even offended, by how loudly someone has said "Amen" before? Can giving someone else directions around your church be difficult? I find that it is better to show someone where the washroom is rather than give directions. We might want to watch our use of acronyms and abbreviations, as they can be confusing. Perhaps we should only use them when they are used when working with a group of mature believers. That might be a good idea. Where have you caused confusion and miscommunication with your church language? What five words might you be able to use this week to avoid confusion? I think that we might consider some five-word expressions. We could use, "how would you say it?" and "explain it to me please" to increase communication. Which of the two could inspire a higher level of communication in your faith? What is the first thing you can do about it in the next seven days?

Let us pray.

Heavenly Father, thank you for the language of love that you shared with us in Jesus. Bless our thoughts and minds when we communicate with others. Help us to be self-aware when using language so that it does not hurt or offend others. May our words, thoughts, and actions all honor you. In Jesus' name, we pray. Amen.

NOVEMBER 6: I HAVE TOO MUCH

As leaders of families or organizations, we have a balancing act to do with our teams. It is possible that some of our responsibilities are to assign and delegate tasks to our family or team members. It is like the rain falling on the farmer's field, the crops need it to grow and provide a harvest. The pieces of the process should fit together and provide their own part of the value proposition. Good seeds, moisture, sunlight, and soil nutrients all need to work together to create a crop for harvest. But too much rain is not good for the crops. In fact, too much at the wrong time can wash away the seeds planted in the fields which waste resources. Too much rain can create runoff and even turn waterways into transportation routes for soil. If too much is given to a team member, the same result can happen. The former efficient processes might become waterways carrying our value away from where we want it to be.

Where might there be a disconnect from too much in your organization right now? It could be an expectation issue, or it might be a delivery time misunderstanding, or it might be an attitude issue. An excess of an inappropriate attitude on your team is like that excessive rain. It can flood those on the team that may tend to be downcast in their personality. It can soak others and weigh them down like a wet blanket. Where can you make some adjustments to change the attitudes of your team? Imagine what it would be worth if you could control when and where it rains. We cannot control the weather but as a leader you can impact the attitude of your team. What is the first thing that you can do about it this week?

As the holidays approach, it is a good time to be mindful of such runoffs. Where are we living in excess? Loving someone is not always shown by acting the same way every time. I know that some of my loving behaviors have been interpreted by others as being enabling. I was not trying to achieve that when I thought I was just being loving. Where might we be pressing too much which could result in us stunting our growth as well as others being stunted?

"A ruler who oppresses the poor is like a driving rain that leaves no crops."

PROVERBS 28:3 NIV

Too much rain can cause floods. Property can be destroyed, growth destroyed, and productivity halted. In our relationships, too much can transform loving intentions into resentment. It can dissolve trust and grow isolating behaviors. Where might we be working on our own too much when our brothers and sisters in Christ can help? If our attitude is focused on ourselves, we likely have too much rain. If our attitude believes that we have to do it all, we are likely in a flood zone. Maybe we can work together like the irrigation systems work for the farmer, where every distribution point for water delivers part of the load. Maybe that is the best way for us to deliver the news of Jesus Christ who is the living water. What is the first thing that you can do about it in the next seven days?

Let us pray.

Jesus, you are the living water. Guide us today to be open to the attitude of loving others. Help us to be understood in a loving way. Soften our attitudes where they have been hardened against loving you. Guide us so that we might follow your example. In Jesus' name, we pray. Amen.

NOVEMBER 7: STITCHES? YES, PLEASE!

"How are you?" That is a phrase that gets thrown around like a leaf tossed in the wind. But our leaders need to know the real answer. Just how is the state of your team? If they have suffered a rupture of some kind, they likely will be focused on pain and suffering instead of value delivery. Our state of mind is easily distracted when pain of any kind is in our arena. The relief of the pain will not necessarily fix any rupture or problem. Addressing the problem is a totally different set of activities. Think about stitches for a cut. The pain of the cut is just a reaction letting you know something needs fixing. But the stitches are to close the wound so that the skin and muscles may begin to heal with less threat of infection. Knowing the state of ourselves and our team means we must look for both the cause and the symptoms. As leaders, our pains might be affecting our outlook. They can also challenge our ability to see the ruptures and cuts that our team members have suffered. Value delivery might be at stake. Who might benefit by checking on their state of mind this week? Are you willing to put some focus on finding the leaks, the ruptures, or cuts? Your team might have pain that could begin to be mitigated if you can provide some stitches. No focus means there might not be any stitches. What is the first thing that you can do about it this week?

As Christians, we have been washed and cleansed through Christ's suffering on the cross. But that does not exempt us from pain and suffering. We are probably going to suffer from events during our lives but that does not mean we must do it alone.

"Know the state of your flocks, and put your heart into caring for your herds."

PROVERBS 27:23 NLT

What flock do you belong to? I am asking, what groups are you a part of? That is your flock. What is the state of your flock? I believe that we are being called to care for them through our hearts. Let us give them love, compassion, and support. But we can do more than just give to those suffering. We can support finding the solutions to the causes of their pain. That is a deeper level of compassion that goes beyond just words. It goes into action, like the doctor stitches up the cut, the healing begins. Who on your team might be showing some symptoms? Where are the cuts that have not been stitched? What is the first thing you can do about it in the next seven days?

Let us pray.

Heavenly Father, you know the state of us, your flock. We follow the Good Shepherd and as we do, we encounter the problems and pain of this world. Hold us firmly in your embrace when we are suffering in pain. But help us to keep clarity of mind so that we might know the state of our brothers and sisters. Empower us to act with compassion from our hearts to draw all the flock nearer to you. May our compassion be obvious, and our actions be a gift of love, not judgment. In Jesus' name, we pray. Amen.

NOVEMBER 8: MIRROR, MIRROR OF MY HEART

Do you have any mirrors around your organization or home? A mirror is a very interesting tool. You might not have thought of a mirror as a tool, but it is something that leaders should consider. You can take a quick glance in a mirror to check to see if your hair is neat and that your appearance is not disheveled. But you can also get serious and examine yourself in the mirror. When you look closely, you might see a thread hanging from a button. The freshness of your complexion might show and so might the wrinkles that show your years. You can also look at the expression of anxiety or joy that might be worn on your face. As a leader, how deeply are we looking at our team and family members? Are we glancing at them just to see if they look tidy or are we examining them?

If we are about a value proposition, we value our team members, and they deserve our focus. How might we mitigate their worries or their wrinkles? How might we refresh their activities like the moisturizer refreshes the complexion? If you are not using your ability to reflect upon your team and organization, then it is likely that we are missing those dangling threads that you can see in the mirror. If those threads get caught on something, it is possible that it will all come unraveled. Where might you want to look into the mirror of your business? It might be time for the leader to do some measurement and reflection.

As I remember, there are stories in the Old Testament where people were not able to look into the faces of Angels. Moses could not look at the burning bush. But as brothers and sisters in Christ, we are to be in relationship with one another. We are to love one another and have compassion for one another. But how can we do that if we will not even look at one another.

"For if you listen to the word and do not obey, it is like glancing at your face in a mirror. You see yourself, walk away, and forget what you look like."

JAMES 1:23-24 NLT

How do we love ourselves, as God loves us, if we will not look at ourselves? The mirror is a powerful tool for us. We might be glancing at it, or we can be looking deeply at our reflections. Are we looking just at our complexion, or can we look at how we are in action or not in action for God? Maybe we can find more compassion and be in more discussions with one another by starting with looking in the mirror at ourselves. We might not like what we see when we look deeply, but we can take comfort in the fact that Christ accepts us. We are refreshed by Christ, our living water, not some temporary face cream. We do not need to fear the reflection. Are you ready to find your mirror and be the leader in your faith journey? What is the first thing that you can do about it in the next seven days?

Let us pray.

Heavenly Father, you can see us both on the inside and the outside. But we get caught up in the activities of this world. We know that we fall short of your expectations to love because you have sent us Jesus Christ. May we reflect in the mirror and in our minds, as to where we might be in a stronger relationship with you. Guide us by your path and hold us in the comfort of the palm of your hand when we are hurting. May we have the courage to look deeply into the mirror of our hearts so that we might draw close to you. Might the reflection of our hearts honor you and glorify your Holy name. In Jesus' name, we pray. Amen.

NOVEMBER 9: GIVE A GUESS OR YOUR BEST?

Leaders of families, organizations and companies need different tools. Those tools have unique abilities. The claw hammer can pull out a bent nail so that something can be attached correctly. It can be easy to grab a substitute tool. I have grabbed a crescent wrench and used it as a hammer before. It does not work as well and mostly is just a waste of time and energy. It might even damage the inappropriately used tool. Our team members are great tools as well. They have unique abilities. Some pull insights and make decisions from financial data like the hammer pulls nails. Other team members might be able to tighten processes like the socket wrench tightens the bolt. Even the seemingly weakest tool has a unique ability. Where could you, as leader, use your tools more effectively? For many people, we want to hold on to the tasks that we have been doing regardless of how effective they are. This also gets in the way of us developing our unique abilities more often. That desire to hold onto those tasks is a limit. Will we do our very best instead of saying I guess what I am doing is okay? If we want to grow our results exponentially, we might want to get the team functioning in more of their unique abilities and remove those limits. What is the first thing that you can do about it this week?

As brothers and sisters in Christ, we make up the church. The church is the people. So, as a part of Christ's church, you are important regardless of what you do well or have done badly in the past.

> "They quenched the flames of fire, and escaped death by the edge of the sword. Their weakness was turned to strength. They became strong in battle and put whole armies to flight."
>
> HEBREWS 11:34 NLT

Christ's call is to do our best. That is not your guess and not just doing something so-so. Consider that maybe a great way to draw close to Christ is to do that which you are good or even great at. Are we confident enough to let our weaknesses be handled by the church and our team of believers? Can we find enough trust and faith in Christ to answer that call? Where are you willing to be bold enough to declare that you are weak in an area of your faith and allow others to help you? In many cultures it is not acceptable to show your weakness. It can even be dangerous to show a weakness. But those realities have limited applications. Are we willing to allow God to address those situations? We might be called by God to be the answer of strength to someone's danger if that were the case. Where are your unique strengths that you can use for Christ? If you can use the strengths of others to enrich your faith, then it is up to you to make that declaration. What is the first thing you can do about it in the next seven days?

Let us pray.

Heavenly Father, thank you for so many blessings in our lives. Thank you for making each and every one of us so unique and designed in your image. Together we come to be your church. One body, that when assembled through your strength, is the mightiest toolbox to address the challenges of this world. Build and assemble us through your love and guide us to offer ourselves as a tool to honor you. In Jesus' name, we pray. Amen.

NOVEMBER 10: BUT HE TEMPTED ME

As a leader, how many people receive the blame when there are errors? It is interesting how large the number can be. We can think about sports for a great analogy. Imagine it is the final game of the World Series and it is in the bottom of the ninth inning. There are two outs, bases loaded, and a full count on the batter. If the next pitch is a ball, the home team wins. Here comes the throw and the batter walks, the home team wins. Do you blame the pitcher? As leaders, our accumulative efforts are what delivers results. We all contribute to the successes and failures of our teams. When it comes to responsibility for results, we all are accountable. Where is your team lacking accountability? Do you have a formal and measurable form of accountability, or will we just settle and blame the pitcher? Why did the home team not have five or ten extra runs so that the loss did not occur? How did the bases get loaded? Why is that pitcher still pitching and what made the batter refuse to swing at the four balls?

As a follower of Christ, do we claim our faults, our problems, and shortcomings? Or do we too easily look for someone or something to blame?

> "When tempted, no one should say, 'God is tempting me.' For God cannot be tempted by evil, nor does he tempt anyone."
>
> JAMES 1:13 NIV

Have you ever heard someone blame God, or even question God? It is so much easier to cast questions or blame someone other than ourselves. I have come to ask myself the phrase, "Without judgment, what do you think?" That phrase helps me to change my perspective. Often that perspective change finds my lack of action or error. But before that question was asked, I was ready to cast blame or question others. Are we questioning God with that question or ourselves with, "What would Jesus do?" Can the question challenge ourselves and those that we are in relationship with? Where are you being accountable to others? How might you be able to be accountable to yourself? Having an accountability system is one of the steps of being accountable at a higher level. We can identify days or time periods to address priorities, figure out our role and responsibility to it, and then commit to making it happen. We can even add a promise or consequence for failure. When was the last time you made a promise and kept it? Consider that you might be more accountable if you did it weekly, or even daily. What is the first thing that you can do about it in the next seven days?

Let us pray.

Heavenly Father, we thank you for your grace. We thank you for your love that has said we need Christ, not judgment from others. Help us to see our shortcomings, sins, and blame. We ask you to help us to remove the log from our own eyes. We are on a journey in our faith. Open our eyes so that we might see how we can show your love by being accountable at a higher level. In Jesus' name, we pray. Amen.

NOVEMBER 11: NO LIMIT TO HOLD THEM

Leadership is not just managing people and processes. Leadership is about much more. In fact, I am not sure that leadership has a lowest achievement limit. It certainly has no limit for the largest result. I have seen the no-limit poker tournament games on television. There is always a limit to get into the hand. If all any player ever does is pay or meet the lowest limit, they do not win the tournament. Rarely do they ever even win the hand. It is the players that believe they can play the best game and take the necessary risks that have the best chance to win the tournament. Momentum enters in as a factor after the risk and reward does. The team at the table is a factor. Everyone at the table is making decisions about how to achieve no limit to their success. Deciding when to give up everything is when they have the best chance to succeed.

They learn the other players' habits, tells, and tendencies around them. What are your families, companies, or organizations values? Could it be that your team has too much attention being paid to the small limits of daily repetition instead of the big limitless results that are possible with value? Who in your organization tends to get stuck on the low limit and how can you work better together? Our ability to collaborate with them will break their limits. The leader can change the game. It can be like the leader gets to walk around the table and the opponents show their hands to help guide the team. Will you get up and walk around the table this week?

Brothers and sisters, what limits do you have in place from your previous life before accepting Christ as your Lord and Savior? The limits of our society are not the limits of God. We might expect these lower limits of society to be the minimums. Like in poker, we do not get the rewards without the no-limit approach of God.

> "Now all glory to God, who is able, through his mighty power at work within us, to accomplish infinitely more than we might ask or think."
>
> EPHESIANS 3:20 NLT

Are we trusting in the limits of the rules and regulations that society sets for us, or should we focus on the bigger results with God's unlimited boundaries? Knowing the limits of both is critical to share and show love. Where are you stuck with the lower limits? When we recognize that we are using the lower limits it becomes time for us to change the game. Who in your sphere of influence could you collaborate with to immediately change the game in your faith? If you want to play a better game in any type of card game, get someone who can shuffle, consider a coach, and play with others often. Who in your church might be that person with expertise? What is the first thing you can do about it in the next seven days?

Let us pray.

Heavenly Father, you are the Alpha and Omega. You have provided us a limitless life with all that matters because of Christ. Take away our self-imposed limits with regards to our love and compassion for others as well as for ourselves. Bring others into our lives that can help us to grow and share you with a broken world. Let us draw infinitely closer to you without limit. In Jesus' name, we pray. Amen.

NOVEMBER 12: ARE YOU IN THE CREDIT BUSINESS

Here is a question for all leaders and their teams to consider. What are the three most inspirational successes you have seen this year? You might ask why, as a leader, we should answer this question. The reason I think leaders should answer that question is because the answer affirms. We need to acknowledge and affirm our team members and that which we see is good. I believe that affirmation feeds our very souls. It tends to displace negative energy. It releases positive chemicals in our brains, and it prepares us to be moved. How often are we looking for that inspiration? I believe that all we have to do is to take a second look. Because when we look a second time, we will see something different.

Different chemical reactions will begin to take place the second time. Inspiration is all around us because of this. How often are you looking for inspiration and affirming it? Who has been inspirational to you in the last seven days? When we fail to affirm others, we open the door to allow someone else to do it. When that happens, we open the door for competitors and other teams to provide value. The more value our team gets from outside the organization the less they value yours. Perhaps it is time for us to give credit where credit is due. What will you do to affirm someone today?

Brothers and sisters in Christ, you amaze me. There are those of you that are fighting through tremendous pain. But you take comfort in the simple thought of resting in the palms of God's hands. You adjust your schedules and your activities so that you might join to praise God's holy name in worship.

> "I will praise you, LORD, with all my heart; I will tell of all the marvelous things you have done."
>
> PSALMS 9:1 NLT

Let us pray that we won't forget that we are made in God's image. We like to be acknowledged and affirmed. This has been studied and proven about us as humans. If we are made in God's image and we like to be affirmed, then our God wants to be affirmed as well. How often are we truly appreciating God? How often do we appreciate one another? Maybe our lack of appreciating one another might be reflective of our appreciation for our God. The polarization and isolation of thought and the way it should be in our mindset does not heighten affirmation or appreciation for others. It pulls us apart and away from one another. When we are pulled so far apart, we cannot even hear one another speak; we cannot affirm one another. Where are you separated and removed from others? Perhaps it is time to draw a little closer by sharing some affirming thoughts and words. What is the first thing you can do about it in seven days?

Let us pray.

Heavenly Father, you are amazing. Your creation is before us as your sunsets and your sunrises change the day. You remove the dark with the light. And with you, the pain and suffering turns into joy. Your holy name brings us joy. Thank you for the joy and thank you for warming our hearts. Lord, join us every third minute, on the hour throughout the daylight today. In Jesus' name, we pray. Amen.

NOVEMBER 13: STRUGGLE WITH SHAKING KNEES?

As leaders, are we ready to be shaken? There will be people and events that will challenge us and our teams. Our reactions at these shaking times are important. I think that if we can focus on our value proposition our reactions will lead us through successfully. Our attitude about the shaken moments can be influenced right now. We can prepare our hearts, minds, and team for them as we know they will come. When events shake our team and our clientele it is the value proposition that gives us direction. Without it, it might be that fear will give direction. Consider fire as an example. If the building is on fire and our team is in it, our focus should be on our team, clientele and any visitors that might be in the structure. Getting them to safety right away is the priority.

It is our value proposition which would have already addressed the backup contingencies. We would have already thought about those supposedly irreplaceable items. Running with value has purpose but running with fear has panic. Choosing purpose over panic every time is valuable but that requires leadership. Where might you need to be thinking about your attitudes during a crisis? How might your value proposition provide safety, purpose, and avoid panic?

Brothers and sisters, stand up. Stand tall with your feet solidly planted on the rock. With knees slightly bent and our heads held high we can stand and sway as this world shakes.

> "Since we are receiving a Kingdom that is unshakable, let us pray, be thankful and please God by worshiping him with holy fear and awe."
>
> HEBREWS 12:28 NLT

We are not called to bow to fear but to bow to God the Father and Jesus Christ who sits at his right hand. Let us stand firmly together against the world's attacks. Jesus will be there to pick us up if we fall. Let the earthquake and the buildings shake, but we will only bend our knees in a bow to the Father. The fear and panic of this world are replaced by the love and purpose of the cross. We have many attitudes, and they will be challenged. As we leave the world's concerns to the world we can change and take on the attitudes that Christ taught us. Where do you want to replace the shaking and fear with love and purpose in your life? What is the one attitude that is in the way of love? What is the first thing that you can do about it in the seven days?

Let us pray.

Heavenly Father, you are unshakable. We realize that to be shaken you must be in reference to something. It is our prayer today that our shaking be in reference to you. If you choose to shake us, give us the confidence so that we might dance nimbly on your dance floor. Let our feet be light and fearless. May our bent knees always bow towards you. In Jesus' name, we pray. Amen.

NOVEMBER 14: THREE, TWO, ONE, LAUNCH

Leaders, what are you doing to set expectations? Our brains have neural networks which are built as we learn. Those networks will automatically set some level of expectation which is relative to the past, not the future. If we want our teams to have the success we want for the future, then we must set new expectations. It is easy to do, just discuss why you want a result. Then you can establish what that result is to accomplish. Once we have the "what" figured out, we can set up how we will measure it. Great leaders might just need to set new expectations. New expectations lead to a bigger future, but the neural networks will only take us to the old. How can we get past those neural networks? Maybe it is just a countdown to set the expectations.

Three, two, one, launch. If you do not expect to land on the moon, the spacecraft will most likely not arrive there. It requires the leader to create a focus on the expectation. When we launch our teams, they will know where to go and how to do it. Where are your expectations too low or holding back yourself and your team? Where is your team living with low expectations? It is possible that a bigger future awaits and the only things holding you back are a set of low expectations. What is the first thing that you can do about it in the next seven days? I expect that you can set at least one new measurement.

As a person of faith, have you established new expectations? We learned from sin and lived with the result of it prior to coming to know Christ. But those neural networks are not what shape us now. Our expectation of our old selves has been washed away by Christ.

> "All praise to God, the Father of our Lord Jesus Christ. It is by his great mercy that we have been born again because God raised Jesus Christ from the dead. Now we live with great expectations."
>
> 1 PETER 1:3 NLT

Could our relationship with Christ be enhanced as simply as beginning to set our expectations on him instead of this world? That requires us to set our expectations then. Let us ask ourselves these three questions. The first is why is my new expectation going to Honor Christ? The second question is what will we do to achieve a new result? We include Jesus, yourself, and the church. The last question is how will I measure if I am doing my part? So, brothers and sisters, are we willing to create a launch? This launch might be the biggest growth phase of your faith journey. This launch could be the first step in repairing relationships of the world because there is no relationship that the Holy Spirit cannot impact. What possibilities are you keeping from happening because we do not have an expectation of ourselves to grow with Jesus? Are you willing to focus on a launch? Ready, three, two, one, launch!

Let us pray, Heavenly Father, it is time for a new dawn and a new day. Make the sunrise remind us daily of new expectations. May forgiveness occur when forgetfulness comes. Bring fascination where frustration might be the norm. Bring Christ when crisis might be the standard. In Jesus' name, we pray. Amen.

NOVEMBER 15: BATTERIES INCLUDED!

As leaders, we give many things in our roles. We give directions for what to do as well as for what not to do. Those directions take the form of instructions. But possibly the most important thing we give as leaders is appreciation and affirmation to our team members. There are two ways in which to give this AA duo that I know of. They are by using words and the other is by actions. The easier of the two is to use words. Saying please and thank you is the basic start. But even writing a bonus check is done by using words. The more difficult part of the AA duo is to use actions. How do you show your team members appreciation without using words? To do so requires some deep thinking to do it effectively. There is no better time to show these types of actions than during November that celebrates Thanksgiving.

What might you do for your team members during this time of year? I suspect your team does not gather on Thanksgiving. It is a day that many people gather with their families. But as a leader, who says you cannot impact your team's day off. If they are giving thanks, how might you show your thanks for them and all that they do to impact results for others? Consider that your team likely wants to be appreciated in their family as well. Sharing with our teams' families that our team members are important and valued might just be an energizing boost your team needs. It is common for leaders to gather and invite team family members to retirements. Who can you provide some energy to with your AA duo this week?

As Christians, the end of the year brings with it two interesting holidays, Thanksgiving and Christmas. The secular world has turned Thanksgiving into the start of the shopping season which delivers us to Christmas. But Christmas is about Christ, a gift to us from God.

"Thank God for this gift too wonderful for words!"

2 CORINTHIANS 9:15 NLT

If this gift of Christ is too wonderful for words, how are we showing our appreciation? You have probably heard the expression "words are cheap." If our words are cheap then it might be like giving away a battery powered toy with dead batteries. Maybe the emphasis this holiday season can be on our showing and sharing. There is power in the idea of showing and sharing to affirm and appreciate others. It is an AA duo, and it is fully charged by God. God's gift comes batteries included. Are we using the batteries? There is about half the month of November left and all of December. How much energy could you create in your team with the AA duo? Consider what would happen to your team if every day you were to genuinely show and share why you appreciate how your team members make a difference. What is the first thing you can do about it in the next seven days?

Let us pray.

Heavenly Father, we appreciate your efforts and your gifts. There is so much joy to be had through you. Let us pray, show you through our behaviors, through our kneeling, through our raised hands, and through our hands reaching out in your name. In Jesus' name, we pray. Amen.

NOVEMBER 16: LEANING, LISTING, AND LIMPING

As leaders of a company, group, or family it is one of our responsibilities to nurture the body of people we lead. But just like our physical bodies, parts get tired, worn out, and even broken or torn sometimes. When a body part is injured, the rest of the body is affected. The body compensates for the weakness by limping, leaning, and listing to one side or the other. The compensation our bodies do is part of the limiting process. The balance system is off when this occurs, and our brains get distracted. What are you doing to help those on your team to nurture them where they might be off a little or a lot? If we do not take care of nurturing the person back to wholeness, we might lose them.

Investing in those that need nurturing might be the best investment we can make. The cost of training a new team member is high in both productivity, time, and other resources. The investment of nurturing team members can remove the limits. The cost of nurturing can be as little as some of our genuinely spent time with those who need it. Stop and think about your team. Has anyone been limping along recently? Maybe you can provide a temporary brace or crutch to heal them. What is the first thing that you can do about it in the next seven days?

As brothers and sisters in Christ, we are called the body of the church. We are what Jesus died on the cross for. So how are we nurturing each other?

> "From him the whole body, joined and held together by every supporting ligament, grows and builds itself up in love, as each part does its work."
>
> EPHESIANS 4:16 NIV

Are we being supporting ligaments to one another? Am I supposed to be helping others even when I am the one who is hurting? That seems like it might be a difficult thing to do. But God's path for us is not necessarily supposed to be easy. Life is full of challenges which limit us physically and mentally. Many times, we need a crutch or brace to help hold us up or even support us. We as the body of the church can provide one another with that support. Now that is starting to sound like the church I want to be associated with. That sounds like the people that I want to be in a relationship with. Where are you hurting and limping along? Maybe there is someone near to you that has been put in your life for just such a moment. Where can you be the crutch someone else needs for just a six-week period? Crutches do not get used for the long term. People's broken legs heal, and the crutches are put away until they are needed again. What is the first thing that you can do to support someone in the next seven days?

Let us pray.

Heavenly Father, your creation is amazing. You give us amazing capacities to love but we can get trapped by fear and pain when we are broken. Find us now and help us to encourage one another in this place. Let your comfort be the compassion we give to one another. Find us broken and send your Holy Spirit to guide us to be the healing touch for one another in love and caring words. In Jesus' name, we pray. Amen.

NOVEMBER 17: A WELL-OILED SPIRIT

Leaders, I think this is a good time of year to do an audit. Think of your team and the processes you assemble as an electrically operated machine. You might have people that are called the operators of the machine. You might have maintenance people to keep the machine functional. You might have technological people to keep the machine running. You probably have people that sell your services or products. There are also accounting and management responsibilities and many others. Not every leader or team has all of the same functions as others. But we all have different parts to our machines. What is your role going to be as leader? In the next ninety days, does your role need to be the same as it has been in the past? I think that all of the team members have an equal part in keeping the machine producing value.

But having an equal part as a team member does not mean that they have the same duties, skills, or talents. We certainly do not want our machines breaking down. I like to believe that one of the major roles of the leader is to keep the team accountable. I recall an individual who had a conversation and told me he was going to achieve six significant improvements with himself and the team in just a week. It was a big commitment. I know that he provided a consequence if he did not keep the promise. Low and behold, would you believe he kept all six promises. Six small but potentially life altering adjustments were made, just because I asked. Where does your team need some attention? What can you do about it in the next ninety or maybe just seven days?

As a Christian, we are to be in relationship with Christ. But we can get isolated believing that we must do everything ourselves.

> "In the same way, you husbands must give honor to your wives. Treat your wife with understanding as you live together. She may be weaker than you are, but she is your equal partner in God's gift of new life. Treat her as you should so your prayers will not be hindered."
>
> 1 PETER 3:7 NLT

I like that this verse brings a husband and wife together as equal partners. But I envision that I am to be an equal partner with my brothers and sisters in Christ as well. We are called to love one another and to bring others to Christ together. It is our invitations to others, to know Christ, that allows the Holy Spirit to act as our partner as well. It is the Holy Spirit that warms the heart and puts people into action. How are you doing with going out and plugging into your relationship with Christ so that your machine is ready to run? If you have not got the power of Christ at the top of your mind and tip of your tongue, it might be time for a recharge. We are the ones who can be accountable for getting plugged in. If we are plugged in, may the Holy Spirit come today and turn us on and into action. What is the first thing you can do to get plugged in in the next seven days? Make a promise to do it this week and make it happen. If you do not have an accountability partner, feel free to send us your promise by email and tell us how it went.

Let us pray.

Jesus, we have heard your call, and we are so happy to be in a relationship with you. Help us to work together to honor you and our relationship with you. May our partners do their part as we do ours. Assemble us together to be productive in sharing your love with the world. In Jesus' name, we pray. Amen.

NOVEMBER 18: A COMPLETE TURNAROUND

As a leader of families, in your job or at your companies, I think one of our important roles is to embrace change. Our team will grow as we do a better job of defining our value. How will that change you if your team grows? Our sphere of influence will grow as our value proposition grows. How will that change your team and your competition? Our global leaders will transition and so do their powers. Your value proposition might go through a transition as well. It does not matter what geopolitical office you look at; it will change over time. Our leadership and systems might be critical at those transitions. Do you have systems in place to assist the transition process where you lead? It could be that a transition is when someone else can bring value to you and your team. Where do you see a possible transition in the next ninety days?

Transitions have traditionally been a place where collaborating with others can bring a new and different perspective. When we collaborate, we have new eyes that see the issues at hand. Things change when people are watching. This is true especially when you ask them to watch and comment. Can you prove this thinking about witnessing a bad breakup of a relationship? Breakups happen differently in a public place versus a private. A transition is a breakup, but it is a good break up because there is a need for the transition. What transition is about to happen in the next three years? How can you collaborate with others to make it the best transition you have ever experienced?

As brothers and sisters in Christ, forgiveness is a challenge to many of us. Our competitive and survival focus is not about forgiveness. But the joy we can obtain from forgiving makes opportunities ever present.

> "Now I, Nebuchadnezzar, praise and glorify and honor the King of heaven. All his acts are just and true, and he is able to humble the proud."
>
> DANIEL 4:37 NLT

Wow, this is the same King that is spoken about being so ruthless and strong. He was powerful and his armies terrifying but now we see that he praises God. If God can turn the heart and mind of a powerful king like Nebuchadnezzar, He can surely turn those people that have harmed us. To take hope in that tends to give us a lift emotionally. Imagine if our enemies would get right with the world and with us. But it should remind us of our hope in Christ. I hope that it is us that will be forgiven by our fellow man. In that forgiveness, we might be ready for the transitions and change. Withholding forgiveness weighs us down and stops a transition. Where in our unforgiving of others might we be stuck? How can getting unstuck in this area be accelerated by collaborating with others? I bet there is someone in your life that you can collaborate with without their judgment getting in the way. What is the first thing you can do about it in the next seven days?

Let us pray.

Heavenly Father, we thank you for giving us the opportunity to transition. Thank you for placing people in our lives that can help with those transitions. Send your Holy Spirit to us today to guide us. May the trees swaying in the wind remind us to stay rooted in our relationship with Christ. In Jesus' name, we pray. Amen.

NOVEMBER 19: NO COMPROMISE!

As leaders, there are times that it seems reasonable that we might compromise. We value the opinions, intelligence, and insights of our team members. That is why they are on our team. But each organization, whether it is a family or company, needs to have some nonnegotiable values. When is it all right to lie to your customers, your team, or their family? If you asked your team what are your top ten values, would they come up with ten? It is that time of year when we will start to see the top ten lists for this or that. Maybe we need to be confident with our own top ten list. How many can you think of? I wonder how your list might compare with your team's list. Our team members and the leadership need to be aligned.

If one member values safety and another does not put safety at the top of the value list there will likely be a gap in safety somewhere. Would you be willing to ride in a professional race car without proper equipment? Would you ride it if the pit crew of that car did not inspect the brakes at all? What if they did not provide a helmet? Once we have our values aligned, we can continuously make improvements to how we can live them out more intentionally. Head protection helmets today are not the same as they were ninety years ago. Is your team needing to wear helmets? If so, are they all the same and the most up to date pieces of equipment that your team needs? What is the first thing you can do in the next seven days? Perhaps you might find your list if you have one.

As brothers and sisters in Christ, we know that we live in a world of sin. We are not above sin but that does not mean we must like it. It is a worthwhile endeavor to rid our lives of sin where we can.

> "But Daniel was determined not to defile himself by eating the food and wine given to them by the king. He asked the chief of staff for permission not to eat these unacceptable foods."
>
> DANIEL 1:8 NLT

What a great story from the Old Testament. Daniel refused this one specific area of sin that was challenging his life. The king wanted him to eat what the king thought was correct. But Daniel refused. Daniel knew his body should be treated as a temple which was a gift from God. How are we doing in our modern world in regard to treating our bodies as the temple that God has gifted us? Are we merely accepting what others prepare for us like the king prepared for Daniel? Maybe it is time to be a little more intentional about what we put into the temple. Maybe that is an area unworthy of compromising our attention. Not putting a value on your physical health is like driving a race car without a helmet or safety belt. It can be done, but when you crash it will likely have a long-term effect. What are the top ten things you want to change about your mental and physical health in the coming year? Starting the new year with a well-constructed list is like having a launch pad ready for your rocket to rise up. What is the first thing you can do about it in the next seven days?

Let us pray.

Heavenly Father, thank you for the abundance that you place around the world when it comes to food. We ask that you guide us as you guided Daniel when it comes to fueling our bodies. Help us to distribute that food to feed your people. May food be used not only as fuel for the body but fuel for the mind and soul and spirit. Help us to draw near you with the food we eat, share, and discard because of our love for you. In Jesus' name, we pray. Amen.

NOVEMBER 20: IS THE HANDWRITING ON THE WALL?

"The handwriting is on the wall" is an expression that has been used throughout the ages to signify an impending doom. Does that bring up negative feelings? I have heard this used when someone felt that some season of life or some event was about to end. But the fact is, we can choose what is written on the wall. As a leader, our attitude about what we write on the wall for others to see, hear, and experience matters. Do you write down your goals and aspirations and share them with your team? The best teams that I know of have goals for the week, the quarter, and at least the calendar year. Once written down, we need to have them measured. The purpose of having them communicated is so that others can help us evaluate how we are doing. We then can decide to adopt new behaviors and actions to adjust for the success we want.

Who on your team is missing out, and how robust are your processes? I think we have kept it a secret if they do not know or are not engaged with an appropriate attitude. If the team believes that impending doom is coming, it is up to the leader to address it. It might be time to get out the no-doom broom and sweep out those negative attitudes. What is it that you choose to write on your wall today that might attract others to your team? What is the first thing that you can do about it in the next seven days?

As a Christian, I think that Jesus can write on our hearts. But He writes on the inside wall not the outside of it.

"This is the message that was written: MENE, MENE, TEKEL, and PARSIN."

Daniel was called upon to tell the king what the mysterious hand wrote on the King's wall. The answer was these words, "numbered, weighed, divided." God was not happy with the actions and attitudes of King Belteshazzar. He was being held accountable for his arrogance against God. But we have received Jesus and the grace of God through him. That means that we can use these words to draw nearer to Christ.

What are you doing to set goals in your faith journey? There is no more important place to set goals than in our faith. But following up with a habit of weighing your activity against your goal will probably take a new habit as well. Both making and weighing combined may be what is needed for us to make changes in our behaviors that honor Christ. But starting with writing them down may just give us another opportunity to let Jesus write them in our hearts. I like the idea of letting Christ write his goal for our journey together in my heart. It might start by you writing some down on paper. That is the challenge for today. Are you willing to spend some mental time and adjust your attitude with regards to goal setting? We do not set goals to earn God's grace. That has already been done. We set goals so that we might experience the love of Jesus in a more robust and meaningful way. What is the first thing you can do about it in the next seven days?

Let us pray.

Lord Jesus, thank you for taking us on a journey. We ask you to write in our hearts. Let us know where you might see that we can make a turn together. We want to weigh our own actions and draw nearer to you by following your example of love. But that requires change, change that is not always easy. Write on our walls so that we might know your love so confidently that our new behaviors honor you. So let it be written, so let it be done. In Jesus' name, we pray. Amen.

NOVEMBER 21: CAN THE DREAMER HELP YOU?

When a leader needs help leading, where do they turn to? Where do you turn to? I believe that it is a common perception that leaders' experience, education, and training will protect and guide them. But if our future is bigger than our past, one will surely run across a situation that has not been met by ourselves or our teams before.

What then? When we arrive at a new high or new low, our perception is not focused because we can be limited by our past. That is where a new perspective just might be the answer. The challenge is finding a person that is trustworthy, who can assimilate to your situation, and who may share perspective without judgment.

You are, after all, a leader, who can make judgments for your new direction. Who have you helped bring a new perspective to before? Are they worth reaching out to again? You have brought value to others and can remember the joy of helping others. Let that encourage you. Who can you reach out to, that you trust, to do the same for you? Allowing ourselves to place a focus on an outside perspective allows us to see things in a new way. There may be no better time than now to reach out to set the stage to do exactly that. What can you do with a focus like that this week?

Who are your Christian mentors or accountability partners? Many people do not have anyone. But there are times for many of us when we need others to help us.

> "So I approached one of those standing beside the throne and asked him what it all meant. He explained it to me like this."
>
> DANIEL 7:16 NLT

This is such an encouraging concept to me. Daniel, the master dream interpreter, had to get help to interpret his own dream. If Daniel, inspired by God with a spiritual talent, needed help then surely there are those that can help you and me. We are brothers and sisters together. Daniel was certainly in a unique ability zone as a dream interpreter. But even Daniel could place a focus on getting some help. When we are practicing in areas of our faith in the "doing just okay" zone, we can make improvements as well. Who do you know that might be able to assist you in your walk of faith? God has created each human being in his own likeness, and each is full of special gifts. Who might have a gift that can be used to help you reach your dreams? What is the first thing you can do about it in the next seven days?

Let us pray.

Heavenly Father, you have given us tools to use to complete your tasks of love on this earth. But often we find that our tools are not used in the correct manner, or we do not have the right ones for the job. Make obvious to us those that have the capabilities to assist us when we just cannot see the solution. Making the blind to see is the prayer we pray. In Jesus' name, we pray. Amen.

NOVEMBER 22: YOU CAN GET UP OR GET DOWN!

As a leader, are we ready to help pick people up? It seems reasonable to be ready because we know they will fall. We all fall. As leaders of companies, the results we attempt to deliver have probably seemed daunting to some of our team. This might be especially true of the newest members of the team. They might have fallen away from the idea, fainted at the mere idea, and started to doubt even before they started. When we start new projects, some of our team might get overwhelmed at just the thought. Our ability to pick them up and reset them on a solid foundation is critical. Part of being a leader is constructing the safety net and solid foundation so that when we fall, we do not damage the foundation.

We do not want our team members falling off and getting hurt either. Think about the crow's nest or a lookout deck high above on a sailing ship. Having a net to catch an accidental fall helps to protect the crew and the ship itself. When was the last time someone on your team fell? What can you do as a leader to lift them now and get them standing strong? Leadership can require us to be creative, powerful, and compassionate to help people get up. Which one do you think you can leverage to assist others to rise up?

We live in a broken world. But we also have Christ that renews our souls and accepts us. It is easy to get stuck in brokenness when we fail and fall. But our world is full of grace and love as well, so maybe there is a better way to fall.

> "As Gabriel approached the place where I was standing, I became so terrified that I fell with my face to the ground. 'Son of man,' he said, 'you must understand that the events you have seen in your vision relate to the time of the end.'"
>
> DANIEL 8:17 NLT

When was the last time you fell to your knees to pray? When was the last time you fell to your knees to honor the Father and give thanks? To take a knee requires leadership of ourselves. We must make a conscious decision to go to a knee and do it with intention or else we could get injured. If you ram your knee onto the hard floor or a stick, there will be pain. Taking a knee is done with thought. If you feel it is time to take a knee, you might consider if there are others to ask to join you. Be a leader and take a knee this week to honor God. You just might be surprised who might join you. There might not be a better time than today to do it.

Let us pray.

Heavenly Father, from the minute we come into being you want us. So much so, that you even sent your Son to pay the price for our brokenness. As we age, our joints and muscles grow old and wear out, but may we never forget to come to you occasionally on bended knees. May we bend now and ask you for guidance on what we might give today to Honor you. In Jesus' name, we pray. Amen.

NOVEMBER 23: MY MAP IS NOT TALKING

Those who have been leaders in the past do not say, "It is an easy road to be a leader." Regardless of whether you lead a family, an organization, a team or a company, there are going to be potholes, detours, and natural disasters along the road. So, what are you doing to prepare for them? When you drive, it might be wise to have a spare tire, a map, a navigator, and to know the weather forecast. As a leader, do you have an emergency readiness plan communicated? Technology allows for some work to be done remotely, are you allowing that on snow days? You have a team in place to deliver value and run the tasks you have established. But do you have a navigator to help coordinate the path that you have planned for the trip?

A computerized system on your phone or Garmin will only reflect what you put in. Its perspective is severely restricted. When the potholes, detours, and natural disasters occur, we again will have to face limits. But limits are themselves limited. They can be overcome. Prior to Jim Ryan breaking the four-minute mile in track, it was said that it could not be done. But now every Olympic competition of the event breaks that record because there has been coaching that has occurred. Being an entrepreneur or leader does not mean you have to do it by yourself. What limits would you like to eliminate? Who can come alongside you and help you to break them?

Just because we have faith does not mean that we are not going to get scared or overwhelmed.

"'Do not be afraid, you who are highly esteemed,' he said. 'Peace! Be strong now; be strong.' When he spoke to me, I was strengthened and said, 'Speak, my lord, since you have given me strength.'"

DANIEL 10:19 NIV

This intervention brought comfort from God to Daniel. As the hands and feet of the faith, we too can inspire each other to be strong. Think back to the times of your life where others, maybe even just one person, lifted you up. They emboldened you and at that minute you knew you were worth something. We are priceless in the sight of God, and we can be the outstretched hands to help each other up. Who in your sphere needs someone to lean on? We can be a pillar to help. Who is making a misjudgment and going down a wrong path which will limit them? How soon will you have a conversation to challenge their perspective so that they might see it for themselves? Who do you know that is using the wrong map to get somewhere? Maybe you can find a navigator or be one to help the situation. What is the first thing you can do about it in the next seven days?

Let us pray.

Heavenly Father, the road less traveled is curved and at times, a treacherous path. Thank you for sending Jesus to be our copilot. Guide us to be in relationship as His church to help one another. Send us navigators we can trust, like you have sent the angels we read about in the Bible. Guide us to be your hands and feet where you might be able to use us. In Jesus' name, we pray. Amen.

NOVEMBER 24: BATTER UP!

"Strike three, you are out," is something that an umpire says. If you are the batter, your current role has just changed, and you are living a temporary letdown. But the leaders of the team know that this is a transition point. If it is not the third out, then another batter is coming to the plate. No single out is the full expression of the team's efforts. No out defines the value of a team or the value they provide. As the leader of a family or organization, we sometimes have players that get stuck in that transition. We lead so that our team members do not get so stuck that they try to fight their way out of the transition by taking bats to coolers, helmets, and potentially other people. But you have probably seen that happen on the sports highlight reel. If that happens it becomes part of the full expression of your teams' values. A teams' value is determined not by the singular results of one but by the full delivery of the collaboration of the team.

As leader, when was the last time you looked at the full expression of your team? It changes over time and is especially vulnerable when the third strike is called. Where might someone on your team need assistance through a transition? If coolers are flying, it is too late to stop. If anyone is injured on strike two, you may be the only one who can send in a pinch batter. The full expression of you, as leader, and of your organization, starts with your call, not the umpires. The leader is accountable for how the team responds in the dugout and the damage done to coolers. What is the first thing that you can do about it in the next seven days?

As brothers and sisters in Christ, we live in a world where our perspective gets narrow and small. We all get attentive to ourselves at times when we are part of a much larger picture.

> "No one has ever seen God. But if we love each other, God lives in us, and his love is brought to full expression in us."
>
> 1 JOHN 4:12 NLT

Each of us have moments where we are part of the full expression of God. When we choose to love others, we are in those moments of transition. Those are the base hits and home runs I want to experience. I suspect you do as well. They make God smile and they warm our hearts, both the lover and the loved. When we are in a world without love, it is more than coolers and bats that get broken. Lives and families get shattered. Where are you and those around you in transition? Maybe it is time for some love. The only person that can be accountable for sharing your love with others is you. You will likely be at the plate, that is, to have an opportunity to love others this week. Are you willing to commit to share some love in a place that you have not been willing to do so? Maybe it is volunteering somewhere that makes you uncomfortable. On the other side of fear is freedom. In that freedom might be some love that you can bring. What is the first thing that you can do about it in the next seven days?

Let us pray.

Heavenly Father, it is a glorious day to be in relationship with one another. Guide us to remember that we are on your team, and we can never strike out. We will remember that our actions and attitudes reflect upon you. Make the words of our mouths and the actions of ourselves bring you honor. In Jesus' name, we pray. Amen.

NOVEMBER 25: POWER V OR C?

Discipline is one of the least favorite activities that leaders deal with. Whether you lead a family with young children or a company with thousands of employees, discipline is important. Without it, our value propositions will change from a team supporting one value to one team supporting separate, often competing, and distinct value propositions. Think for a minute about a flock of geese flying south for the winter. Discipline says, stay in the strategic V formation, reduce the drag, increase lift, and save energy to survive the thousands of miles of flight. The flock in power V formation can be successful.

Without discipline at all, the individual goose exhausts itself well before the destination and risks dying from exposure in the winter. But individual discipline within the group is even more productive as the geese alternate who leads the V, where the drag is the most difficult. They take turns allowing others to move forward to take the lead at the appropriate time. You are a leader. Where do you need to take a turn and when can you let others on your team fly the point for a while? Being the leader does not mean you have to do it alone. Collaborating and letting others fly up front for a while is tactical and strategic. Are you choosing to trust others to fly at the front or do you make everyone fly in formation behind you?

As followers of Christ, we get tired as well. The constant push and pull of our societies weigh on us. For many, it is a struggle from day to day just to survive the harshness of the environment of the earth. People die from disease and starvation daily. The temptation is great to do your own thing. Push your way to the front of the line. Steal in the darkness if you must. But that is flying solo. Even for successful folks, where needs are met, the battle can be to get even more. There is temptation there, just like the goose who goes solo might leave early to get to the best fields, seeking the best crops. But he will always fight the drag on his own. He is disciplined by the laws of nature.

> "'I will punish her for the days she burned incense to the Baals; she decked herself with rings and jewelry, and went after her lovers, but me she forgot,' declares the Lord."
>
> HOSEA 2:13 NIV

The Israelites suffered through persecutions, but God always came back with love. Who might you help to look up and see a flock passing by in formation and share the story of Jesus? Who do you know that is not connected to a church? It is totally possible that they have never understood or had explained to them the power V. Through Christ, we have power C. Will we ask them to join us? When we do, the lost may join us as we close the C of Christ into a circle and come into communion with Christ. Will you collaborate with them this week? What is the first thing that you can do about it in the next seven days?

Let us pray.

Heavenly Father, sometimes it is difficult to say thank you for your laws of discipline. We constantly test them with our words and actions. But when we love, we show our self-discipline. Guide us as we look for ways to draw near you. Let our hearts and minds be disciplined to look for you first. Help us to inspire those who have been grounded from flying alone to take flight with Christ. In Jesus' name, we pray. Amen.

NOVEMBER 26: FURROWED BROWS OR MUMBLED LIPS?

How do you say good job? Do you say it with a smile or with furrowed brows? When we do it, we could do so with our arms crossed and our body leaning forward in an aggressive manner. As a leader, how we say things to our team starts with why we say things. Those two components must match, or the message will have interference that keeps it from being clearly received. That should make us very careful with the use of technological communication. The likelihood of interference occurring can also heighten the importance of our spoken word and maybe even the pen and paper form as well. When was the last time that you gave a written note to someone on your team? A written note is an antiquated idea for many people. That is exactly why it might be the most valuable at this point in time.

The written note is something physical which requires care to be stored if you wish to keep it. It is not a virtual piece of data which can be tucked away and lost in all technology. I have a book so important to me that I have handwritten a copy of it for each of my children to have. I did not pay for those extra copies with money. I paid for them with my time and sacrifice to make it happen. Maybe that is why the handwritten note is so valuable. When was the last time you received a written note yourself? If you can recall the ones you received, then you have given them value in your mind. What is the first thing that you can do about it this week?

I cannot imagine what it was like to walk the earth with Jesus during His short time here among His family and His work with the disciples. But I am so grateful that people took the time to be inspired enough that they wrote down that history.

> "I have much more to say to you, but I do not want to do it with paper and ink. For I hope to visit you soon and talk with you face to face. Then our joy will be complete."
>
> 2 JOHN 1:12 NLT

We can get busy with our modern forms of communication like text, email, chatting on snapchat and so much more. It just might be that moving everyday communication to electronically transferred forms has heightened the value of the written word. I know that a pen and a piece of paper is certainly less expensive than the most recent phone that I acquired. Maybe we can save the best conversation for the face-to-face kind. Who among your sphere of influence might benefit from a written note from you? Could it be a pastor, a coworker, or maybe a family member? Maybe the most important note could be the one you write to those serving you who seem to be struggling. Who is the person in the world that you would value receiving a note from? Did you name someone? If you did, then know that you can make a difference in someone's life by giving a note to them. What is the first thing you can do about it in the next seven days?

Let us pray.

Heavenly Father, thank you for inspiring those that have come before us. They have left us a rich written history that we can share and pass on. Send your Holy Spirit to inspire us to share with others as well. May the pen and paper, as well as the keyboard, serve you. In Jesus' name, we pray. Amen.

NOVEMBER 27: TOAST OR BOAST?

There is always more than what meets the eye. Leaders know this. Family leaders often have spouses, children, and distant family members. Entrepreneurs have managers and departmental workers behind the scenes. There are also those external resources that contribute to what we do. So, who gets the credit? The fact is, we all want to be affirmed and acknowledged, and it is the leader's mindset that shows the way that it will be done in your organization. How are you recognizing your team's contributions? You can do it privately, or internally among your team. You can do it publicly as well. Three things all people psychologically want are money, affirmation, and appreciation. Two of the three do not drain a company or a family of cash. That allows financial resources to be used in other more purposeful ways. Where can you shift and make an attitude adjustment to share either of the AA's this week?

We do not have to celebrate Thanksgiving only on the fourth Thursday in

November. We can do it every day. Consider doing a quick audit of the last ninety days. What were the three things that you told someone that made a difference to their mindset? Can you come up with three or not? If you cannot, why might that be? I will grant that there are many people that have made giving appreciation to others a habit. Those people might be the exception to a rule. If we have not been taught to make it a habit, then it is likely that it has not become one yet. But the most important word in that last sentence is yet. What is the first thing that you can do about it in the next seven days?

Celebrating is an important part of our faith. We are not called to be sorrowful and mournful about all that we have lost or given up. Being a follower of Jesus Christ is something to celebrate. But celebrating can move to boasting and there can be a fine line between the two.

> "Israel boasts, 'I am rich! I've made a fortune all by myself! No one has caught me cheating! My record is spotless!'"
>
> HOSEA 12:8 NLT

This reading might teach us the difference between that fine line of toasting or boasting. Maybe boasting is about us and celebrating is about our team. Could a focus on celebrating be that simple? Then why is it that we do not see more of it? Where can we join in celebrating with others? It might be that celebrating comes from the heart first and we are using our heads instead. I am curious if we can start our appreciation of others in our hearts. If we can do that, we will have a great starting point. Who do you appreciate making a difference in your faith journey? Who do you appreciate for serving in your local community or church? Which writer in the Bible has made the largest difference in your life? If you have answered any of the questions with a name, then you have an opportunity to show appreciation in some way. You might share it with them directly. You can also share appreciation of people's work of the past with those of the present. What is the first thing you can do about it in the next seven days?

Let us pray.

Heavenly Father, we want to celebrate with you. We can only imagine how the heavens celebrate with us. May you bring heaven to earth when we find ways to celebrate with each other. Especially help us to find a way to celebrate your love with the lost. In Jesus' name, we pray. Amen.

NOVEMBER 28: HERE IS ONE OR MAYBE TWO

Every leader must deal with sets. There are always two. Two what? I would say that is what a leader must figure out. It is not that there is just one set, but there are multiple sets to decide what to give our attention and energy to. In a game of football, you have quarterbacks and receivers, kickers, and returners as well as offense and defense. The leader helps the team to focus and give energy to the right set at the right time. The result of putting a defense on the field when your team has four downs with possession of the ball is not going to deliver long-term value. But the sets we have as a leader deal with our teams, our family, our faith, our companies, and our communities. What are the most important sets that your team is working on? Do they see it as a set or something singular, or could you as leader find the other part? What is your most important objective today? When you decide what is most important today, you also select what is not the most important thing today. That is a set. Which sets will you put your focus on to finish out the remainder of this year? What is the first thing that you can do about it today?

As Christians, we also have sets. We do not think of them as offense and defense, however. We can be thinking of them as relationships of one thing with another.

> "Blow the ram's horn in Jerusalem! Announce a time of fasting; call the people together for a solemn meeting...Do not be afraid, O land. Be glad now and rejoice, for the LORD has done great things."
>
> JOEL 2:15 & 21 NLT

Did you catch the set? These passages show the relationship of repentance and rejoicing. What kind of life would we lead if all we did was repent or be sorry about everything from the past? I am excited about a future filled with joyous living. I know that I am going to fail, to falter, but God sent Christ to pay the price of my shortcomings. It is going to be okay. I will certainly repent when I sin and fall short but that does not mean that I will go and sin on purpose. But our faith journeys are about the sets as well. When the quarterback throws the ball, I want my team's receiver to catch the ball. Where might you be frustrated today with an issue? Maybe if we look for the set, Christ might be able to transform frustrations into fascination. That is a pretty cool set. With great sorrow great joy can follow. Where great tragedy occurs, great revival can happen. Are we willing to focus on finding the set when we get down? Finding the set allows us to find freedom on the other side of fear. What is the first thing that you can do about it in the next seven days?

Let us pray.

Heavenly Father, we recognize that there is only one God, but everything else might just be made of sets. Help us to see the side of love instead of the side of hate. Send your Holy Spirit among us to transform desires solely for ourselves to desires for our relationship with you. Thank you for Jesus Christ and the opportunity to transform frustration into fascination as easily as the quarterback says, ready, set, hike. In Jesus' name, we pray. Amen.

NOVEMBER 29: DEFEAT!

Defeat is a word that is probably best defined by the individual that uses it. As a leader, how do you define defeat? How you define it makes a difference for those on your team. We are creatures of habit as it allows our brain to conserve energy. There is not much thought required to follow your habits. Changing our habits takes energy, and in doing so we defeat the old habit. There is that word defeat again. It does not appear as such a negative thing when we look at it that way. When a leader of a team is battling the team in a manner to defeat them, you have a negative connotation. As a leader, if your definition of defeat is to help change habits, it has a positive connotation. Which leader are you today? It matters to your family, your company, and your team. Look to the leaders of the world powers. What would you like them to defeat today? A couple of ideas to consider would be to defeat hate and fear. What habits would you like your team and family to consider picking up? If you want new habits for your team or in your life, it is time to defeat the old ones. Both will take a conscious effort to achieve. That is one role of the leader. Will you exhibit leadership to help create new habits? What is the first step you can take in the next seven days?

As a people of faith, we are subject to the limits of our habits. Our habits assist us to grow and make progress, to a point. But those habits that get us to point A, are probably not the habits we need to get to point C.

"But the LORD is good; he has cut me free from the ropes of the ungodly."

PSALMS 129:4 NLT

If God has cut the bonds that restrict us, why are we holding on so tightly to our old habits? If we want to apply defeat anywhere, our faith is a great place to focus. Who can help you in your faith journey to challenge your perspective? Which old habits would you like to defeat for new ones? Are you reading the Bible as much as you want? Are you attending worship in a meaningful manner? Is your prayer life as strong as you wish? Be the leader that you want to become by thinking about your habits. Are you struggling to decide what habits to change? Perhaps you can start with being curious. What area do you believe you can grow the most in the next ninety days? Who do you believe might give you some ideas about some habits that are possible to create? Our journey of faith is not experienced by us but by those we are in relationship with. Consider habits that will have a positive impact on others as well. What is the first thing you can do about it in the next seven days?

Let us pray.

Heavenly Father, you have defeated many obstacles as we have read in the bible. You have shown us Jesus defeating blindness and disease. You showed us disciples defeating fear as they followed. You have shown us how you defeated law with love. Send your Holy Spirit to be among us and assist us in defeating anything that keeps us from drawing close to you. In Jesus' name, we pray. Amen.

NOVEMBER 30: DO YOU PREFER A BUZZER OR MUSIC?

As leaders, some of our work will be repetitious. We can find value in doing some things over and over. We want to find ways to strengthen our team and give more value. We want to reset the alarm clock to be a reminder for ourselves and the team. An alarm or reminder going off and saying, "Strengthening at nine, strengthening at nine" might be the routine to encourage others. Without the alarm clock, we might miss the opportunity to strengthen someone else. When we are not strengthening others, we have allowed some limits to stop our growth. Can a leader really expect to achieve growth without the interruption happening?

What repetitions for strengthening does your team have in place? Has someone hit the snooze button on the alarm clock and missed the limits? Maybe the leader or leadership team has not set the alarm. What alarm clock are you using as a leader to strengthen your value? Buzz! There is not just one way for the alarm to go off. Clocks vary with their alarms as some can use a buzzer, music, and others use digitally spoken words. Which will you choose to use to break some limits? What is the first thing that you can do about it in the next seven days?

As followers of Christ, we want to grow in our journey with him. But there might be times in our lives, in the ups and downs, that we are not as strong in our relationship as we wish. Some greet the trials of life by retreating in their faith, and others retreat in their faith while experiencing successes. It happens both ways. But it is never too late to reconnect.

> "Wake up! Strengthen what little remains, for even what is left is almost dead. I find that your actions do not meet the requirements of my God."
>
> REVELATION 3:2 NLT

Wake up, it says. I like that because regardless of the type of alarm clock or system you use to wake up, every day starts anew. We do not have to drag on from day to day, living in a world of decay. We can choose to reset, to search, and live life to the fullest. What system are you using to reset every day in your faith? Living with Christ is not about resetting only on Sunday or a day of worship. When we choose to reset only on a day of worship, we are limiting our ability to grow. An alarm clock limits the sleep mode of our body and calls us to action. We certainly need our sleep to re-energize our internal batteries. But even charging our internal batteries has limits. Where can you set the alarm and reset now to prepare for the end of the year? What is the first thing you can do about it in the next seven days?

Let us pray.

Jesus, you have no alarm clock that needs reset for us, as you are continually there for us. But as the Father chooses the color of the sunrise, let us reset daily. May we stop snoozing and choose our activities and attitudes to draw nearer to you. May we breathe deeply in the joy of life, and may we exhale our sins and stress. In Jesus' name, we pray. Amen.

DECEMBER 1: TURN THE TAP

Leaders, across the board you might have some exciting members with unique and even extreme skills and capabilities. If you are adding people to your team with those qualities, then I would like to see the results of your leadership. I think that might be a strong team. But think of our leadership as a faucet which adds hot or cold water to the mix. When we need hot water, there is not any need for lukewarm or cold. They do not deliver value at that point. And if it is cold water we need, adding hot water can be wasteful or even dangerous as well. The leader is the controller of the faucet. You decide which temperature to acquire, what quantity is needed, and when to stop. We do not waste resources by heating cold water to then transport it to an aircraft to put out a forest fire.

What would be the purpose of putting hot water on a forest fire? Not only does it waste our resources, but it can also endanger the team. Hot water can scald or even burn members in the process of heating it up. Think about a cast iron cooking pot beginning to boil over an open campfire. We need to be thoughtful about how to handle that pot as the pot will likely be hot like the water. Would you hand the pot to someone to carry without providing them oven mitts or some sort of protection or tool to carry it? Where do you need to add some cold or hot to your organization? What tools or equipment do they need to handle it? We as leaders are accountable to assist with the hot and cold. Who on your team can you help get back to their hot or cold?

Are you lukewarm in your faith right now? Have you ever been that way? If you have, you might have figured out how to get to the proper place by modifying your perception, attitude, or activities.

"I know all the things you do, that you are neither hot nor cold. I wish that you were one or the other!"

REVELATION 3:15 NLT

When we are lukewarm, it can be difficult to share and show the love Jesus taught. It can be challenging to accept that love as well. The cold tap is totally separated from the hot. The two taps do not put water into one another. They might be combined by the faucet that delivers the water to the sink, though. Where might you need to get cold or hot? Is your reading of the Bible hot or cold? How is your prayer life right now? Is it hot or cold? What area of your faith do you want to warm up? In the northern hemisphere, wintery conditions have arrived. If you live there, you can either accept that you will be cold because of the weather, or you can bundle up and dress for it. We are the first step for accountability in the growth we experience in our faith. What is the first thing you can do about it in the next seven days?

Let us pray.

Heavenly Father, our world attempts to move us to the average. But you have asked us to be more than average, more than lukewarm. Move us to warm up in our faith as easily as the faucet gets hot when the handle is turned. Send your living water, Lord. May the cold be cold and that which is to be hot, be hot. In Jesus' name, we pray. Amen.

DECEMBER 2: I HAVE BREAKING NEWS

As leaders of families and organizations, we can expect both the good times and the bad. But leadership is not about dread but about deliverance. It is about the value. Our value proposition does not have to go away when our feelings of happiness or success are absent. I remember seeing an interview with the losing pitcher for a World Series game. He chose not to be sad and live in "dread of defeat" but chose to see what they did accomplish. He did it regardless of the reporter's desire to hear the dread. He saw the value that his team provided to the fans, to the vendors, to their city with taxes, entertainment, and spirit. We can remember that when we have a value delivery system it never, never, never has to stop working. Who on your team might be derailed by life and be choosing dread over deliverance right now? As a leader, we can collaborate in ways that can help all of our team transition from dread into delivery.

It can be a difficult transition when we are alone. But bring another person or two that are the right fit people at the right time, and dread can disappear quickly. That is the power of collaboration at its best, and it can help us to grow exponentially. Just think how fast we can leave dread behind. Those moments will happen, but they will only represent a very short part of our lives if we choose it. There is no reason that your interviewer must have a camera crew to help to bring deliverance. Your interview may be the one that you lead with others on your team. What is the first thing that you can do about it in the next seven days?

As brothers and sisters in faith, we live in societies that challenge faithful living as Christians. Our lives are full of choices. We either choose Christ or we do not. We then choose daily just how well we will follow.

> "I know that you live in the city where Satan has his throne, yet you have remained loyal to me. You refused to deny me even when Antipas, my faithful witness, was martyred among you there in Satan's city."
>
> REVELATION 2:13 NLT

Loyalty, are we choosing to be loyal to Christ with our words, thoughts, and actions? No one told me it would be easy to do. Sometimes it is not, but I can look to those in my faith journey to lift me up. We can do our interviews with our friends, Sunday school participants, and our pastors. No television crew and no reporter needed. The value of our faith will not be measured by the news team. It is measured and delivered by Christ. Perhaps we might consider the news broken. Is the news and information that you are listening to or reading bringing you joy and happiness? If not, maybe the news sources you are using are to be considered broken. Where can you collaborate with others in your faith this week? There is no need to wait until the next worship service. Just reach out to someone as if you have a breaking news story and collaborate as Christ has called us to do. What is the first thing that you can do about it in the next seven days?

Let us pray.

Dear Jesus, there is nothing more valuable than you. Thank you for our brothers and sisters in Christ who help us live in a world where reporting on others is acceptable. May we live life today in a way that makes what you have shared with us the top story. I want my breaking news to be about you today. In Jesus' name, we pray. Amen.

DECEMBER 3: DIPPER OR DEEPER

Where does your team work deeper? As a leader, it often can be our responsibility to take our teams deeper into value. Our families are stronger when the relationships grow deeper. Our teams strengthen as we seek and grow the value proposition deeply. But when any of the teams fall, we become at risk. Falls do not hurt people; it is the landing that hurts. When falling, our minds get off track of the value and begin to think about the landing or the results of it. Fall into the ocean and you might begin to think about how long you can swim. You might even begin to wonder how long you could hold your breath. One might have seaweed entangling you and of course, sharks are always lurking it seems! Falling into the ocean will take your mind off of what it was on originally. As a leader, we want to seek those oceans of opportunity and when we do, we prepare. We get diving gear, training and if appropriate, equipment like shark cages and spear guns.

Could any of your team be tied up in the seaweed? Someone on the diving team should always have a diving knife. You may not think you are a leader. But if you can help someone grow deeper in ways that provide value, you are a leader. If you can bring the gear to help someone get into the water safely, you are a leader. When you show up and help someone cut loose the seaweed that has them wrapped up, you are a leader. What is the first thing you can do to be a leader in the next seven days? Sometimes the only permission you need is your own.

We find value in our faith when we dig deeper as well. Discussing a topic in a Sunday school, small group, or understanding a sermon can connect us deeper. We can take the seasons of our faith and commit them to spiritual practices like fasting, doing a prayer journal, or starting a devotion. But if we get caught up in falling, our perception jumps almost automatically to the landing. That is what fear does to us.

> "I sank beneath the waves, and the waters closed over me. Seaweed wrapped itself around my head."
>
> JONAH 2:5 NLT

That sounds scary to me, what about you? I am not in that ocean today, and it sounds scary. Sometimes fear and being scared is just a matter of perception. Where do you think it feels like the seaweed is getting to you? Maybe it is time to go deeper into prayer, reflection, or meditation in our relationship with Christ. Just because it seems like seaweed is wrapped around you does not mean that it is. Maybe it is just your scarf that the wind has blown around. In your faith, you are the leader and make the decisions about how to grow. On the other side of fear is freedom. Move the seaweed out of your way. Get the Bible out and dig deeper into it, and you may find that it provides the protection of a shark cage for your faith. What is the first thing you can do about it in the next seven days?

Let us pray.

Heavenly Father, thank you for our emotions as we might experience the mountain tops with you. But when we fall from those peaks it can be scary. Guide us and hold us in the comfort of the palms of your hands when that occurs. May we have the confidence and wisdom to remember the innocence of the prayers of children. We are your children. In Jesus' name, we pray. Amen.

DECEMBER 4: HERE COMES THE RAIN

How is your team doing with their workflow and attitudes? As a leader, you guide that process for their benefit and for the people that you are in relationship with. It is as if our team and relationships move like the clouds move over the earth. Where do you move them? If we help to move them, we can enhance where the rain falls from the clouds. The ground needs that moisture. Leaders are like the jet stream over the weather pattern influencing the temperature, the rainfall, and elements of the earth. Where do you need to bend and influence your team? The value and harvest to be received are at stake. If we fail to get the clouds and rain where we need it the crops will not get watered. Our attitudes can create deserts where orchards are supposed to be.

What attitudes are not acceptable for your team? A member who does not value safety will not be a valuable part of a team on a high-rise construction team. A member who does not have an attitude that values accuracy will not make a good surgeon for your team. Everyone has developed attitudes, but they are capable of changing just like the weather. If you change the amount of rain that the desert gets, the plant life and environment will transform the area. As a leader, what attitudes need influence on your team? What is the first thing that you can do about it in the next seven days?

As followers of Christ, we have read the stories of his love and examples of living. Oh, the joy we might experience daily with him as our value. We can endure so much with his joy.

> "Then the remnant left in Israel will take their place among the nations. They will be like dew sent by the LORD or like rain falling on the grass, which no one can hold back, and no one can restrain."
>
> MICAH 5:7 NLT

I am reminded how I am a remnant of Christ's love and so are you. This verse reminds me to be soaked. No attitude has to hold back the rain that soaks the grass, the garden, and fills the pond. Let Jesus love us and remind us that we do not need to run for shelter when it happens. We do not need an umbrella to protect us from His rain of love. We are challenged to run for protection though in our world. Maybe your attitude of forgiveness has created a drought in your faith walk recently. Maybe an attitude of fear might have yourself running for shelter unknowingly and is keeping yourself from the rain you need to grow. Our attitudes make a difference in our faith. Perhaps what we need to lead a strong journey in our faith is to check in with the weather report. For us, the weather report is an audit of our attitudes. What is the first thing that you can do about it in the next seven days?

Let us pray.

Heavenly Father, we thank you for the joy of your love. We thank you for the relationships that you bless us with today and ask that you touch them to grow. We ask that you soak those relationships with your rain of love and grow our ability to form new attitudes. Bring people and circumstances into our lives that encourage us. Let us change the attitudes we hold that make us run for shelter and keep us from you. In Jesus' name, we pray. Amen.

DECEMBER 5: SPRINKLES ON THE COUNTER

As leaders, one will inevitably have to discipline or correct a team member. It might be a family member, a coworker, or even an external resource. But why we do it is an important question that leads to how we do it. If you do not show concern and compassion for the member, then you might harm the situation instead of helping it. When we must correct, our focus is to continue to deliver value. It might be that our adjustments and corrections are best served by dealing directly with the source of the problem. How often do we work around the edges of the issue instead of facing them head on? That is not likely to enhance our value.

That would be like shaking ice cream sprinkles on the counter and expecting the taste of the ice cream to be enhanced. Where might you be shaking the sprinkles in the wrong place? Perhaps the focus begins with the ice cream which is the item to be enhanced. As a leader we are enhancing value somewhere. Maybe it can be on the sprinkles spread all over the place. Maybe it should be on the sprinkle container. What is the first thing you can do to get the focus on the most important value for your team this week?

As followers of Christ, we have so many great examples and stories that Jesus shared with us. Many of them were of Christ pointing right into people's own hearts for their pain and suffering. There was no work around, no sprinkles on the counter, as He went straight to the issue.

> "Never slander a worker to the employer, or the person will curse you, and you will pay for it."
>
> PROVERBS 30:10 NLT

Are we in relationship with Jesus first or our world first? I believe Jesus has taught us to choose Him first. We can work directly with one another to show our love and respect for one another. A problem is generally with a person, not a supervisor. If you have a problem with Christ, He is waiting for you with nothing in the way. We do not need some work around to go to Him. Where are we distracted and giving our attention to the wrong place? When we need love, the focus needs to change to love. Will we allow hunger, blame, or pain to get in the way? When we do that, it is like grabbing the sprinkles container and just shaking it all over the floor. Where are you missing the ice cream bowl? The sweet love of Jesus is worth us taking the time to focus. What is the first thing you can do about it in the next seven days?

Let us pray.

Heavenly Father, guide us as we prepare to rest. May we find you by the shortest route possible. Help us to show compassion and love with the correct mindset and appropriate action. Guide our hearts today to focus on the love that Jesus has for us. In Jesus' name, we pray. Amen.

DECEMBER 6: DO EAGLES HAVE HABITS?

There once was an old man who was invited by a youngster to have a cup of coffee at a local coffee shop by the river. As they chatted, the old man noticed two eagles, one who was always sitting in the treetops and one who always sat on the bank. He asked his young guest, "Why do you suppose one sits in the treetops and one is on the bank?" His young guest, unaware of the reason why and confident to show respect, simply asked the old man to tell him the reason. The old man replied, "I believe it is because the eagle on the bank never learned the power of habits. You see, the eagle in the treetops has learned that it is easier to take flight when you launch from the treetops. It allows the laws of nature to work with the eagle.

So, every time the eagle stops flying it always lands at a high point. The other eagle did not pay attention to its habits and did not establish new ones. It always lands safely on the bank, again and again. It will always have to exert the maximum energy to get itself flying versus the treetop eagle.

Treetop eagles soar at the start while bank eagles always flap hard." As leader, where are you landing and where is your team landing? Maybe it is time to consider choosing a higher point. As a leader, we can exhibit our role when we set new habits for ourselves and encourage others to do the same.

As brothers and sisters in Christ, we too will develop habits. New habits can be those that can empower us to change the old habits which restrict us. New habits can draw us nearer to God. We read,

> "But those who trust in the LORD will find new strength. They will soar high on wings like eagles. They will run and not grow weary. They will walk and not faint."
>
> ISAIAH 40:31 NLT

There is no time better than right now to begin thinking about where you are spending your energy. Where are you always flapping diligently to take off again and again? Are you willing to even consider the simple change of landing on a treetop? Yes, it will be a little different, it might even look dangerous. But remember this, the default is that one is strong enough to flap diligently to take off from the ground. So, if you miss your landing on a high point, you can always flap hard to right yourself. Where are you willing to commit to a new treetop? Is it a new small group, maybe to read a book of the Bible, or maybe the entire thing? Maybe attending worship regularly is your treetop. Is it time to serve in a ministry or mission? Can you help someone locally that you have not been willing to because you have been flapping too hard? Hey eagles, is it time for you to walk where we used to sit? It is time to run or maybe even to soar. Let the Holy Spirit assist you and spread your wings. Show your willingness to be a leader by setting some new habits. What is the first thing that you can do about it in the next seven days?

Let us pray.

Heavenly Father, help us to see with new eyes. Let our perspective be challenged and see where we are spending our time and our energy. Hold us in the comfort of the palms of your hands as we find a new high point. May we find our strength in you. In Jesus' name, we pray. Amen.

DECEMBER 7: MULTIPLIERS OR MAGNIFIERS UP!

Leaders impact the perceptions of our members. If our team members' attention is away from the value our team provides, the perception needs to be examined. If we want to focus on value, we must get close to it. In doing that, we might need to magnify it. Think about germs for a moment. When you clean a kitchen counter you must address the entire counter to get all the germs. The germs are too little to be seen with your eyes. There are mites and other items around that are too small to see also. If you could see where the germs were, one would not waste energy and resources cleaning things that were already clean. A magnifying glass makes everything bigger. It even seems to show more light as well. But unlike science class where the magnifying glass was used, leaders do not run around holding up the glass to their members. But we do not need to because leaders themselves can be magnifiers.

When was the last time you took a team member aside and thanked them under the magnifier of appreciation for what they have done? Our words of appreciation can break down limits. When leaders make sure that members are known, we break limits. What does it mean to be known? It might mean that you know your members' partners, their parents, or their children. It might mean you know their hobbies or what they like to do for entertainment. To know this level of detail might require the leader to look in deeper than they are currently. It is very much like holding up a magnifying glass. What is the first thing you can do to remove limits by using your tools?

As Christians, what are we trying to magnify? Could it be Santa Claus, presents under the tree, maybe the Christmas ham perhaps?

> "I will worship toward thy holy temple, and give thanks unto thy name for thy loving kindness and for thy truth: For thou hast magnified thy word above all thy name."
>
> PSALM 138:2 ASV

As we prepare to celebrate the birth of Jesus, what will we magnify in our celebrations? Maybe the word of God might be a great place to start. The holiday season can bring so many distractions which limit us from the reason for the season. Are you going to be engaged in the black Friday event?

Perhaps you are waiting for the cyber-Monday event. If these have your attention, then you might be experiencing a limit. How would you strengthen your relationship during either of these events? Would you be able to make sure that you are expressing love, patience, and generosity? Maybe a real magnifying glass could be a physical reminder for us to place our focus intentionally. I would bet that a magnifying glass would fit in a purse, pocket, or a picture of one could be a screensaver on your phone or computer. Will we break the limits that society has put on Jesus' birthday this year? How might you do it? What is the first thing that you can do about it in the next seven days?

Let us pray.

Heavenly Father, magnify your glory on this earth. Shine your light and love. May everything about you be visible to us. Make all other distractions be set aside. Open our eyes to your love and to those that are in need during this season. May love be the gift we offer one another. In Jesus' name, we pray. Together, Amen.

DECEMBER 8: WHEN SPARKS ARE GREAT

You have probably heard the phrase, "Where there is smoke, there is fire." But as a leader, our concern might be more for sparks than smoke. We can encourage our teams towards many things. We can take them to stronger relationships, to a better focus on value, and work with better collaboration. But we all need a little help, sometimes a lot of help. Leaders can provide that spark which might take resources and burst them into flame. Good flames are those that are in places where the heat is created on purpose. Once a fire is started, we can add coal and wood to maintain the heat like an entrepreneur might add capital, systems, team members and other resources to bring more value to the customers of the business.

Where might you spark something for the last of the year? What can you spark right now that might make a significant difference in the year to come? If the leader is not the one to create the spark, then it may be likely that no one is creating them. Imagine your team members and resources as a stack of kindling. That stack is surrounded by heaps of firewood to provide warmth to the world. Your value to others has amazing capacity. The question is, are you as a leader going to be responsible to be accountable for spreading some sparks on purpose this quarter?

As Christian brothers and sisters, we are called to be sparks for Christ. We are to encourage and love one another which can spark the church into action. We can share the word and message of Christ with the lost, which might even start a new flame. Can you recall someone who was on fire for Christ and their passion was obvious? It is possible that someone just like you provided a spark for that person.

> "So the LORD sparked the enthusiasm of Zerubbabel son of Shealtiel, governor of Judah, and the enthusiasm of Jeshua son of Jehozadak, the high priest, and the enthusiasm of the whole remnant of God's people. They began to work on the house of their God, the LORD of Heaven's Armies."
>
> HAGGAI 1:14 NLT

I think God likes the right kind of sparks. Who has been providing sparks for you in your faith journey? Maybe it would be appropriate to thank them and let them know of your fire. Are there others around you that might be able to be that spark? When love seems to be absent and hate seems to be the passion of the day, God's love is ready to transform the situation. Will we be accountable to bring the sparks of love where they are needed?

There is more than one way to create a spark. Consider using a lighter that is out of fuel which some might think of as trash. It still has a spark. One might possibly use a flint stone. Our faith has lots of tools that are available to us, including prayer, the Bible, and the people of the church. There may not be any better time of year than right now to be a spark. What is the first thing that you can do about it in the next seven days?

Let us pray.

Heavenly Father, you are so full of grace, and we thank you for the fire of the Holy Spirit. Let your love for us be the flint by which we might spark others. May the flames of compassion warm others as we share the sparks that you might create in us. In Jesus' name, we pray. Together, Amen.

DECEMBER 9: IS THE MESSAGE FOR MARY?

Leaders need instruction and guidance on their journeys just like the members of the team need them. I had a conversation recently with a woman named Betty. She talked about her work history and how her best leaders were the ones who had worked in her position as teller at the bank. The leader knew the challenges and the opportunities of the position. These good leaders are the ones that received instructions and guidance themselves of what to do and how to do it.

As leaders, what are you doing to grow in your leadership and capabilities? If instruction is crucial for our teams to complete their functions, it just might be as important for us as leaders as well. If one is not planning on receiving some direction of leadership, then they might be the limiting factor for the team. Getting instruction and ideas requires collaboration.

A leader might get involved with a leadership school. There are also some great books to read about levels of leadership. Many conferences happen yearly that are focused on leadership as well. Peer groups exist which will challenge leaders from the same industry to challenge one another. Mentorships shape both the mentor and the mentee. When there are so many options, it should be obvious to us that there is demand and that the options are valuable. What will you do to collaborate with others to shape your leadership this week?

In our faith journey, we need instruction and guidance as well.

> "And she will have a son, and you are to name him Jesus, for he will save his people from their sins."
>
> MATTHEW 1:21 NLT

That is pretty simple instruction. It is clear and obvious what Mary is to do. But this message is to Joseph! The in-control person has received her instructions and Joseph, acting in a leadership role, has a task to do also, which is to give the name to the child. We all need instruction, and we can thank God for the words of the Bible to do some of it. Where will you get instruction from this next year in your faith? You are a leader whether you think so or not. Our faith calls on us to spread the message with the lost. We are to love the unlovable. We are to forgive the unforgivable. We have these calls and therefore, we are leaders. Who have you seen that has exemplified any of these concepts? Perhaps the examples that you are aware of would be willing to answer questions that come from your curiosity to be a better leader. Collaborating with other leaders is one of the easiest ways to grow in our leadership. But our egos can get in the way. We can allow our focus to be on our teams instead of ourselves. There are times that we need to focus on our growth as well because if we are not growing, we are stagnant or worse, shrinking. Remember this, when the leader gets better, everyone can get better. How will you collaborate with others by the end of the year? What is the first thing that you can do about it in the next seven days?

Let us pray.

Father God, we thank you for Jesus and allowing Him to walk on the earth. Thank you for the words of the Bible as well. Turn our hearts towards those words so that we might receive instruction in our minds. Let us use our instructions from you to spread your word, share your love, and seek Jesus more. In Jesus' name, we pray. Amen.

DECEMBER 10: IS THAT GIFT WRAPPED?

What do you do when it comes to giving gifts to team members? As leaders, I think that our best gifts might require some explaining. Explaining a gift may show our understanding of the person's situation, that we know their passions, and even their concerns. A gift given that needs no explanation might mean that it is common, or it might mean that you have already discussed it so well that it was anticipated. But even if the gift was anticipated, there is the backstory about it. A leader can also discuss what will be done with the gift and talk about how it might be used. This is a season of gift giving, what will you be doing for your team members? One of the key items to avoid having a miserable job is to be known. We can express that we know our team members by the forms of the gifts that we might share with them. If you provide team members with a general gift, then you might expect general performance and loyalty. What team is going to reach their full potential by meeting the expectations of the general population? That seems to be unreasonable to think that full potential and general expectations will align. The leader who shows their team members that they are known by the words and gifts they share has exponential capability. How will you share gifts this year with your team? The holidays are great times for gift giving. What is the first thing that you are going to do about it in the next seven days?

As brothers and sisters of faith we have been given the gift of Jesus. What a powerful gift of love, but that gift must come with some explaining. To receive Christ, we have to accept his cleansing gift. We get to live a new life and way of being. We are no longer just human beings but human doers as well. Without the explanation and acceptance, it is like we have been offered a gift and it has never been unwrapped.

> "God showed how much he loved us by sending his one and only Son into the world so that we might have eternal life through him."
>
> 1 JOHN 4:9 NLT

Have you ever experienced a child that just ravaged and tore through the wrapping paper on a present? Have you ever seen someone who methodically and delicately unwrapped a package? Both achieved the unwrapping and might well be better off than those that still have their gifts unwrapped. What part of the gift of Christ is not unwrapped for you? Finding the gift of Jesus today and opening the present is up to us. Maybe we have left some wrapping paper on the gift and your instructions are under that part of the gift. I think that it is time to unwrap the gift. Go ahead and tear it open or do the delicate unwrap. Jesus is just glad that you are ready to open it. Once it is open, it is time to install the batteries and make the relationship work. I promise, it is likely to be one of the most energizing gifts you could ever receive. If you have it, are you willing to share it with others? What is the first thing that you can do about it in the next seven days?

Let us pray.

Jesus, thank you for the gift of the examples of your walk here on earth. Thank you for teaching us about love. Thank you for forgiving us and for paying the price for our trespasses. Guide the process of understanding these gifts. May we be overcome with joy and our hearts be warmed every time we touch the wrapping. In Jesus' name, we pray. Amen.

DECEMBER 11: THE MAYO, CHICKEN, AND MILK WAS BAD?

As we approach the end of the year, we can choose to see the best of the worst or the best of the best. There will be lots of top ten or even top one hundred programs put together. They will highlight the best or the worst. As leaders, what we highlight and work on with our team is important. It sets the standard and focus. Should we choose to think about the worst and how we were harmed? Shall we allow our minds to cower and run from fear? Maybe a better use of our time today is to focus on what is glorious or even wondrous. Where will you set the bar with your mindset? Where we place our mindset is very important. Our brains are wired to recognize and pay attention to the negative. We have many more receptors for the chemical cortisol. That chemical functions to heighten our stress capacities. Our breathing will quicken and so will our heartbeat when it is present. If our team is going to have our levels raised, one might desire that they be raised by the excitement of a bigger future. A bigger future is more aligned with the best of the best list and improving upon them. If you are going to share a top ten list with your team for the end of the year, which list will you present? Perhaps your focus on a best of the best list will serve as a launch pad for what is ahead. What is the first thing you can do to make that list?

In our faith walk, we have a choice as well. What will we give to honor our relationship with Jesus? Does our Savior want the best, just what is okay, or how about the least of what you have to give?

> "But you dishonor my name with your actions. By bringing contemptible food, you are saying it is all right to defile the Lord's table."
>
> MALACHI 1:12 NLT

Have you ever been offered a food that you suspected was not at its peak? I think that could be an easy definition of contemptible food. Do you stay clear of the mayonnaise bowl on the buffet line when the food has been out for hours? Why would we do anything less when we think about what we give to God? If we give to the food drive or food pantry, do we give expired food or give the best that we have? Do we keep for ourselves what is best or give the best as God has asked? In our relationship with God, we can plan to give the best. To do so will require our focus to monitor and change our attitudes. We can keep the concept fresh for the whole year by renewing our commitment at least weekly. Evaluating weekly keeps the idea at the top of our mind and hopefully at the tip of our tongues. What is the first thing you can do about it in the next seven days?

Let us pray.

Heavenly Father, thank you for so many gifts that are indescribable. You give us the best that you have to give. Help us to honor our relationship with you with the best of our worship, the best of our actions, and the best of our thoughts. In Jesus' name, we pray. Amen.

DECEMBER 12: FOCUSING TO LEARN

On teams, there are many things to avoid; harming teammates, holding grudges, and being siloed are a few examples. Some of the things we avoid are likely to allow us to want to escape when we encounter them in our businesses or families. If a business abandons value, the business suffers consequences. Some have the opinion that love might not be an appropriate attribute to encourage in a business. But value and love are in alignment with one another. We do not need to avoid love or value in the workplace. In fact, some of the world's most engaged and admired companies focus on embracing love in the workplace. These corporate examples have found a way to align love and value to the customers and the team members. The alignment of the two concepts can deliver to teams an attraction to new members that want love. The alignment delivers a new way to profits and a seemingly unfair competitive advantage. How will you embrace love on your teams, at your workplace, or with your family? There are likely areas on our teams, in our companies, and in the organizations that we serve with where the alignment has not occurred. The focus on alignment might be the easiest way to increase the value that you bring to the world. How much focus can you give it today, this week, or this quarter? What is the first thing that you can do about it in the next seven days?

When I think of Jonah, I think of someone who was trying to escape. He was running from his opinion and feelings of God's love.

> "But Jonah ran away from the Lord and headed for Tarshish. He went down to Joppa, where he found a ship bound for that port. After paying the fare, he went aboard and sailed for Tarshish to flee from the Lord."
>
> JONAH 1:3

If God was going to save the people of Nineveh, why would Jonah have to be embarrassed? Why would he have to be wrong? We have a basic human desire to be right. Our brains will even lie to ourselves when it feels stressed or pressured just to be right. It is easy to have an opinion which we might believe is right. But opinions are not necessarily right, and they certainly do not have to show love or value. Perhaps we can focus on being kind instead of being right today. The two are not always aligned. There is no need to run from love like Jonah did, but it might be very human to do so. This week our challenge is to observe where we are confident that we are right. Maybe we will find that we have left love out of our hearts and minds in doing so. If we can keep our focus on love, I suspect our desire to be right can be maintained at a healthy level for our faith. When we allow our focus to drift, it is like the tires of a vehicle which become misaligned. The tires in the case of misalignment will wear out early. They will experience needless friction and frustration. They will cost the owner in many ways. Is the alignment in your faith worth the energy this week? What is the first thing that you can do about it this week?

Let us pray.

Heavenly Father, you know what is in our hearts. Help our minds to be loving this week as much as it desires to be right. Send us courage to embrace love instead of correctness. Send us strength and learning from those with opinions different from ours and open our eyes to collaboration. In Jesus' name, we pray. Amen.

DECEMBER 13: CHANGE YOUR SOIL, CHANGE YOUR TREE

As a leader, I like to think we can always develop and grow. In that sense, we might use a comparison of the natural world. Let us consider a tree. I am not an expert about trees but think that they mostly have roots, trunks, branches, limbs, and leaves. Some trees are certainly shaped differently, and a set of leaves on one tree might be a set of needles on another. But the trees need soil to grow. As leaders, are we helping the members of our team grow by making better decisions? It might be that giving them authority to make decisions is a way to grow. Providing the necessary components to grow is as important as the soil is to the tree. Think about the elements of the tree as the levels of importance of a decision. If your team has authority to make a leaf decision, the tree or team is not threatened by a mistake made at this level.

But if a limb decision is made poorly, it will affect many leaves. The team can survive without a limb, but there will be costs. What if someone makes a bad decision and the tree loses a branch? The tree will likely be unbalanced and may appear changed forever. But the tree and team will survive it. But the trunk and root decisions are the ones that risk the entire operation. Is your soil providing the nutrients to help your team members grow to be able to make a more important level of decision? As leader, our plan to grow our team starts with the roots and soil. As a leader, do you have just okay soil with too many rocks and little water? You will have roots working hard to get nutrients to survive regardless of your soil, but the better your soil the better your team and tree will grow. What kind of soil are your roots growing in this week?

As brothers and sisters in Christ, we have two sides of the Bible. The Bible is made up of the Old Testament and the New Testament. The Old Testament is rooted in the law and commands of God. But the New Testament is rooted in Jesus.

> "So that Christ may dwell in your hearts through faith. And I pray that you, being rooted and established in love, may have power, together with all the Lord's holy people, to grasp how wide and long and high and deep is the love of Christ."
>
> EPHESIANS 3:17-18

It is like God changed the soil for us. It was not that the original soil was bad, but our growth and love was limited if we only lived in the soil of law. When we choose to live in new soil, it allows us to sprout new shoots. We grow differently. Our leaves can be brighter colors and our branches stronger to withstand the winds of time. But we must pay attention to putting away the old soil. We can no longer be dependent on the old source for nutrients. Where are we still living in worldly ways and old soil instead of a biblical way with Jesus? Perhaps we should begin to dig around the roots and get to some fertile soil of God. What is the first thing you are willing to dig up and shovel away? Is there junk or rocks that your roots have to battle with? Jesus has taught us that the Holy Spirit can fill the holes with his soil. Trust him and go digging with me this week. What is the first thing that you will do about your soil and roots this week?

Let us pray.

Heavenly Father, your bounty is endless. Guide our thoughts and hearts this week as we begin to dig and uncover where you have light for us. May we find light where there was darkness. Strengthen our roots by putting your soil and spirit near us. Send us living water to grow. In Jesus' name, we pray. Amen.

DECEMBER 14: WHERE IS YOUR WATER FOUNTAIN?

As leaders, we might have a responsibility to shape many benefits for our teams. Our members need many things to survive and thrive. Included could be water, food, and shelter. Some might come from incomes and assets that you influence. Members might also get compassion, confidence, and enhanced self-worth from the way you might value them. Like a fountain is built to provide a flow or water into a pool, leaders can structure their value to provide comfort, relief, and sustenance to their teams. Where might you be missing a fountain? If you have a pool, you have to maintain it to keep the water fresh.

How does your pool look if you have one? Are there leaks and cracks which are wasting the energy and structure of the fountain itself? As a leader, you are the one that places the limits on the benefits. They need our attention if we are going to provide them appropriately for the team.

Giving compassion when the team needs food will not keep our team connected at the deepest level. If our most important resource is our people, then we must pay attention to the benefits. What do you need to do this week to change or adjust the benefits for your team in the coming year? What is the first thing that you can do about it this week?

As Christians, we have the Bible to serve as a fountain. It provides a means by which the living water of Jesus might be shared with us and the lost.

> "On that day a fountain will be opened for the dynasty of David and for the people of Jerusalem, a fountain to cleanse them from all their sins and impurity."
>
> ZECHARIAH 13:1 NLT

We know the dynasty of David through the Savior, Jesus the Christ. How often do we go to the fountain to experience the living water? Are we sharing the living water from the fountain with those that are thirsty? The living water of Jesus is only limited by us. The fountain will never run dry. The water will never go stagnant or become impure. Water is a life-giving resource for the human body. The living water of Jesus is the resource for the heart and soul. It is a resource that we can constantly tap into.

Not only can we tap into it, but we can become the fountain that shares the water with others. How can you share it so that others can be refreshed by the pool? Perhaps you are tired, broken, and worn out by the world. If so, perhaps you might talk to someone to learn more about living water available through Jesus. What is the first thing that you want to do about the living water in the next seven days?

Let us pray.

Heavenly Father, thank you for the words of the Bible. Thank you for those that have shaped it and kept it intact for so many years. May its spray refresh and renew us. May the pools cleanse and cool us. May we drink deeply from the trickle of living water that you have designed for us. In Jesus' name, we pray. Amen.

DECEMBER 15: WALL OUTLETS ARE NOT NEEDED

Imagine it is 10 AM. The building that you and your team are in has lost power. As leader of the team, what will you do next? What will the members of the team do? One option is that some will begin the process to speculate what has occurred, of which they have no control. Another option is that the members might find a way to bring value to the team in a way not related to the use of the energy grid.

We can remember that as a leader or as a team member, that we do not have to plug into the wall circuitry to give energy. Thus, we are reminded that we might be the igniter or the spark that lights the candle so that people might be in action. Where might the power be gone, cut off, or interrupted on your team right now? Can you go light the candle?

Accountability, in our leaders and throughout the entire team, is itself a spark. Do you have protocols in place for emergencies? Do people know who the leader will be when the power goes out in different ways? As a leader, it is up to us to create or to ask others to create such a plan. We are accountable for its creation, deployment, and assignment. What is the first thing that you can do about it today?

As brothers and sisters, the birth of Christ brought the light into the world. We can often get disconnected or distracted and wind up in dark places. But we can always spark love and compassion.

> "Therefore, go and make disciples of all the nations, baptizing them in the name of the Father and the Son and the Holy Spirit."
>
> MATTHEW 28:19 NLT

This verse reminds me that we can share the light of Christ. This can occur regardless of the storms and their raging winds that they may bring. Our power line, our connection through Christ, is never broken or never cut off. If it is dark, then we are accountable to find a way to get the light shining. If our power outlets seem to be covered up, we are accountable to move the obstacles. We never have to move the obstacle alone as we can always ask for help. If the outlet is without power, we are accountable to check the breaker box to see if the fuse is blown. If we are shining the light of Christ, we can make our way to the box. If the fuse is fine, then it is up to us to call the power company. We can always send out a prayer to call on the power of God. What is the first thing you can do about it in the next seven days?

Let us pray.

Heavenly Father, at times it is easy to fall victim in the darkness. That might occur even if we fall victim to our own attitudes and behaviors. Guide us so that we might be the interruption to those situations. Warm our hearts so that we might be the spark that brings light to those periods of power outages. Use us as your extension cord to bring your power to those that are hurting. Make us a generator to bring your power and light to those that are lost. Let us be the match that starts a fire in someone's heart for love of you. In Jesus' name, we pray. Amen.

DECEMBER 16: GREATER THAN ONE TIMES TWENTY

Growing our team's knowledge and capacity to serve is a fundamental component of strong teams. Attending professional conventions, attending worship services on Sunday, and attending virtual conferences or training sessions might be ways to expand that capacity. But the debrief after the event with your team might be the most important part. The knowledge and information presented can multiply the results of your whole team when it is shared. It is the power of the debrief, where the mundane becomes insight for others. Perspectives get rotated, challenged, and activity and energy get accelerated with accountability. How does your team share the power of the debrief? How might you be leaving others out and restricting your capacity? Do you choose to multiply by one or by one hundred? When twenty people hold all the same information the multiplication is limited.

It only happens one time. But if we multiply four, many times, the results will be greater. Debrief lets the capacity and knowledge multiply by a greater number. All it takes is the willingness to collaborate. If your team is missing a high level of collaboration, then your team is adding instead of multiplying. As the leader, we are responsible to assure that the multiplication sign is going to be used. Which sign are you focused on right now? It might be the addition, the multiplication, or the equal sign. It's easy to use a multiplication sign, just start a debrief once a week. See how it works for your team to use it more often and let us know if it helped.

The birth of Jesus is shared in the gospels of the Bible. As a believer, our sins were washed away and our relationship with Christ became new. But the story has not stopped, it is not over yet, or at least it is not supposed to be.

> "The shepherds went back to their flocks, glorifying and praising God for all they had heard and seen. It was just as the angel had told them."
>
> LUKE 2:20 NLT

The debrief is occurring here. Can you envision it? One shepherd telling the other, confirming what they saw. I can imagine they were discussing how they were moved, how they were inspired. Two thousand years later the story of Jesus' birth, life and death is still being talked about. You do not have to be a Christian to know that the holiday of Christmas exists. It exists because others have been sharing the story, using a debrief, to let the generations know of Jesus' birth. What are you doing to share the idea of a debrief with others in regard to your faith? You do not have to stand on a curb and shout to the crowds that are passing by. You can if you think that is the best debrief you can provide. I suspect many of us have not really found the best way for us to create a debrief for others. What is the first thing that you can do about it in the next seven days?

Let us pray.

Heavenly Father, guide us as we continue with our own personal journey of faith. Transform one another's mundane into inspiration for others. Accelerate action through us that honors you. Guide us as we find a way to debrief others about our journey and about Jesus. Make our love grow and spread, like the story of Christ has continued throughout the ages. In Jesus' name, we pray. Amen.

DECEMBER 17: FREEDOM TO WHAT?

As leaders, we hold the responsibility of using the powerful word duet of "freedom to...". At all times throughout history, leaders have had the power of freedom to...do something specific. Leaders have used the freedom to subvert genocide, slavery, and conquerors. They have used the power to liberate, express love, and show compassion. When you can choose, you can exercise the two words like a melody. It is like bringing them together so that "freedom" and "to" become a musical duet. But the power of "freedom to" includes the power to avoid, abandon, and abstain, just as it has the power to engage, enmesh, and embrace. There have been societies that have erased freedom by illuminating the power of the freedom to phrase. As a leader, one can choose to be a leader that uses the phrase to build up, enhance value, and grow our team. Eliminating this power for those being led is not a road of aligned value. This is a tough lesson and challenge of leadership, as not everyone has a desire to be aligned. Where might you see examples in your community and culture right now that need the freedom to duet? Perhaps it is time for you to bring the phrase "freedom to" inside of your sphere of influence. You have the freedom to or not. Will you choose to be inspired to do so this week? What is the first thing that you can do about it in the next seven days?

As brothers and sisters in Christ, we have chosen to follow Jesus. We, therefore, have the use of this word duet as well. King Solomon had all the resources he needed to accomplish the building of the temple. But before he started, he prayed to God. He did not start without God. How often do we start anything without going to God first? I suspect it is the norm and not the exception for many. When Solomon prayed, God answered his prayer and granted him a request for anything he wished. Talk about an example of using the power of "freedom to". He could have asked for anything! But he asked for wisdom. He exercised his freedom to love others. He asked for the wisdom needed to act and think which is a God-honoring concept. We see in Romans 6 a passage that explains the freedom to love and live outside of the law of the Old Testament. This passage is all about the "freedom to" concept.

We have the freedom to continue to live a life of sin but are reminded that we died to the way of sin. We hung that "freedom to" up on the cross just as Jesus hung there. It was a choice. Now I ask you, my brothers and sisters and those that want to know and love Jesus, what "freedom to" are we exercising in our lives that we need to stop, abandon, and exit stage left? I am just as curious as to what "freedom to" you might put in its place. For me today, I will remember the theme of "freedom to" by starting every morning with a daily freedom to quest. If you wish, join me.

Let us pray.

Heavenly Father, everything in the existence of the universe is recognized as your freedom to do everything. You have created us and given us the ability to reason, have experiences, to study scripture, and examine tradition. Guide our hearts back this week when we begin to go down the destructive path of freedom which might not honor you. Awaken us with your Holy Spirit to choose to take a path of collaboration and love. We thank you for creating a world by which we can live with the freedom to draw nearer to you. In Jesus' name, we pray. Amen.

DECEMBER 18: FEAR, FERTILIZER, AND FASCINATION

Neil Sedaka made famous, "Breaking up is hard to do." As a leader, I am sure that we can attest to that. Whether a leader leaves or a team member leaves, our emotions are going to affect us. Specifically, it is fear that is probably going to rear its head at some point. But our ability to focus on value is an attitude that leaders can engage in at a moment's notice. It is our attitude of curiosity that might just be a way to transform fear into fascination. Just for a second, think about what fears you had when someone left or those that you had as you left as leader. Now, remember how valuable that person was, even if it was you. Did you remember how they helped your family, your team, your organization, and yourself individually? I would bet that you can remember at least three ways they helped in each of these categories.

Sometimes it is fear that keeps people's value from increasing. Fear stagnates us by sticking around too long, and our growth is restricted. Like a plant in the ground that does not get nutrients from the soil, people will not grow when they cannot get value from your team, your organization, or family. Who might need some nutrients, some value on your team right now? That person just might be experiencing some fear, and the value proposition will be affected if that is true. You might just transform fear to fascination by seeking or enhancing their value. What is the first thing that you can do in the next seven days?

Our faith does not eliminate the world's events or attitudes of fear that we will experience. But if our attitude of providing value transforms fear into fascination, we can remember our value proposition.

> "I have tried hard to find you—do not let me wander from your commands."
>
> PSALMS 119:10 NLT

Our value, Jesus Christ, does not leave us, ever. Never, never, never does He leave us. Sure, we might wander away, and we might go where the soil is not fertile. We mistakenly put roots down where the nutrients are weak, where the Son is not shining, and the living water does not fall around us. But if our focus is on His value in our lives, let's face the fear of our failures and rejoice. It is time to change! Pull up your roots and transplant somewhere else when this happens. Get some fertilizer brought in or cut down the trees to let the Son shine. You just might be the best forester, the best fertilizer, or transplant this week. What is the first thing that you can do about it in the next seven days?

Let us pray.

Heavenly Father, thank you for such wonderful gifts. Thank you for the fertile earth and refreshing water. And thank you for never ever taking your Son away from us. May we be inspired to transform fear into fascination. In Jesus' name, we pray. Amen.

DECEMBER 19: COIN FLIP, BACK FLIP, AND PERCEPTION FLIP

Do you flip? You might think I am speaking about gymnastics maneuvers. As leaders, one of our tasks is to help our team flip perceptions. It is not uncommon for team members to occasionally get off task. Like ourselves, we start to chase a shiny object and begin to do something that we might even be incompetent doing? You have probably heard that someone's perception is their reality. If a team member has a perception that is incongruent with your value delivery method, we need to change that perception. It is time for a flip if that is the case. Where might you need to consider a flip for yourself?

How about asking this from your team, "What is the most beneficial change for our team, that I as a leader, am in the way of accomplishing?" That might challenge us to flip a little bit or a lot. We all need to flip occasionally. Where can you put the focus this week on a flip for yourself? How might you challenge your team to achieve at least one flip? Flips of perception can be achieved when we bring curiosity to the top of mind and tip of our tongues. Where can you and your team focus to do a flip in your professional, personal, or faith areas? What is the first thing that you can do about it in the next seven days?

As Christians, we are subject to the flip as well. But there are things that God does not want us to flip about.

> "Sometimes it praises our Lord and Father, and sometimes it curses those who have been made in the image of God."
>
> JAMES 3:9 NLT

Do you wield the all-mighty power of the tongue? I do not know of any examples where God wants us to use the power of the tongue to harm others. He never wants us to flip our love for Jesus to hate. He does not want us to flip our love for our fellow man to hate either. But we can do that as our pain and suffering can draw our attention. What activity might be beneficial during the Christmas season to flip? We can allow our weaknesses to be the focus. We can allow ourselves to be the focus as well. The birth of Christ is the focus of Christmas, so we can ask ourselves if that is where our focus is at. Let us flip what society might put as the focus and bring it to the story of Jesus. There is no focus more important than this. Can you locate any distractions and eliminate them so that this will be the most loving celebration you can experience? What is the first thing you can do about it in the next seven days?

Let us pray.

Heavenly Father, we are about to celebrate the birth of Jesus. Help us to consider our behaviors that might be focused on presents and gifts instead of love and joy. Help us to flip and turn towards you. Be our guiding factor this week as we approach the day of Christmas. In Jesus' name, we pray. Amen.

DECEMBER 20: A JEWELER OR GEMOLOGIST?

Who is on your team? If you have team members, then you will have times that you will be the leader. This is true because you have your part of the value delivery system to provide. You lead that part at some time in the process. So, what are you doing to improve? Before we begin to learn and grow, we are like raw nuggets of gold. We have glimmers of hope that shine occasionally, but we are still in the rough. Then we begin to have our rough edges removed by a team of players. Gold nuggets are compressed as veins in the depths of mountains. They are shaped by other rocks as they move in streams that flow across those same mountains. The team of our parents and of educators begin our process of shaping, and our value begins to show like the gold that is separated from the rock and dirt.

The relationships we create and the work that we contribute begin to refine, bend us, and give us shape. Finally, we are resolved into some form, like a wedding band, that has value to others. But once we have our shape, we must continue to be shined or we begin to be lackluster. We need to be buffed and polished from the wear and tear of the world. What are you doing to improve and keep your shine? Who on your team needs a little buffing, and how might you help? The polisher is valuable to all that they touch, including themselves. How can you buff and shine as the leader this week? What is the first thing that you can do about it in the next seven days?

As a people of faith, when we accept Christ, we become like the wedding band. We are to be the band, which brings Christ and the lost together. We are to continue to become a better and better band through our relationship with Christ. But we also are to share our Lord with those that do not know him.

> "Many will be purified, made spotless and refined, but the wicked will continue to be wicked. None of the wicked will understand, but those who are wise will understand."
>
> DANIEL 12:10 NIV

Brothers and sisters, we get filled with blemishes from our sins. We get tarnished by the sins of others as well. So, let us be of one mind to continue to grow and be purified in Christ. Let us refine our relationship to shine and let the world know. Where do you need to do some polishing? The raw nuggets are ready for the harvest, but someone must start the process. Maybe that someone is you and your polishing may be just the shine that catches their eye. Christ will be the light and we can reflect it. Will we choose to share the light and polish others as well? When others are polished, they can reflect the light of Christ, and the world will be brightened as we do it. If the world is too dark where you are, then maybe it is time for you to be the leader and shine the light. What is the first thing that you can do about it in the next seven days?

Let us pray.

Heavenly Father, thank you for your gifts. Thank you for sending people into our lives who have knocked the chunks of dirt and rock from us. Thank you for Christ who washes us, accepts our raw shape and broken fissures, and gives us new life. Bless those that have given us shape. Thank you for sending the Holy Spirit to guide and inspire that process. May the process of polishing us bring others closer to a relationship with Christ. May the honor and glory be yours. In Jesus' name, we pray. Amen.

DECEMBER 21: IS THERE A TIME DOCTOR?

Are we stuck in transaction-oriented relationships? They are the ones where the focus is based on what you can do for me now. There are many examples of that in our everyday walks. But as leaders, we might be called to be more value-based. Value-based relationships, whether they are with our families or in our businesses, require patience. It might be that there are times that others are hurt or damaged by transactions. This can happen when the perspective of a win-lose proposition is chosen. When people lose, or are hurt, they can become patients because of our lack of patience.

Where might you consider uncrossing the letter T and bending it to make the letter C because of showing patience? Did you notice a change of the spelling of the two words? As a leader, we can transform others by using our patience. That transformation starts with us as leaders and gives us the power to impact time. Where is our team creating patients because of harm? If that happens, we are creating limits. When we inspire our team to use patience, we remove limits. What is the first thing that you can do about it in the next seven days?

In our faith, our actions sometimes get crossed up with our intentions. It might be that we are rushing into things and hitting limits when that occurs.

> "And remember, our Lord's patience gives people time to be saved. This is what our beloved brother Paul also wrote to you with the wisdom God gave him—"
>
> 2 PETER 3:15 NLT

God's patience, that phrase is something that should enhance our hope. I often get distracted and rush into what the world might ask me to do when I should be listening to the Holy Spirit to speak instead. Patience, just take a breath and wait a second. The world can surely wait. I think we might grow our relationship with Christ better by testing the patience of the world more and testing the patience of God less.

Where has your patience been weak this year? God's patiently waiting for us to forgive and find love. Jesus came to the earth and found love with actions that honored God. Where can we break the limits of our intentions and act this week? Will it be in the scriptures, in actions of love towards others, or perhaps a change of our attitude? Maybe this week we can consider how we can give three times more than we receive. With the help of The Holy Spirit, Jesus Christ, and The Father, anything seems possible. What is the first thing you can do about it in the next seven days?

Let us pray.

Heavenly Father, your love has no boundaries and neither does your clock. Let our love for one another be what marks time instead of the clock. Change our concept of time so that love is what makes us move. Guide us not to hurt one another but to have patience with each other. In Jesus' name, we pray. Amen.

DECEMBER 22: NO SHARKS HERE

Where does your team work deep? As a leader, it often can be our responsibility to take our teams deeper into value. Our families are stronger when the relationships grow deeper. Our teams strengthen as we seek and grow the value proposition deeply. But when any of the team falls deeper into anything, we are at risk. Falls do not hurt; it is the landing that hurts. When falling, our minds get off track of value and begin to think about the landing or the results of it. Fall into the ocean and you might begin to think about how long you can swim. When falling into its waves, you think how long you might hold your breath, or will seaweed entangle you. Falling into the ocean will also likely allow your mind to think about sharks! As a leader, we want to seek those oceans, and when we do, we prepare. We get diving gear, training, and if appropriate, equipment like shark cages and spear guns.

Where might any of your team be tied up in the seaweed? As a leader, who is accountable to help the team get rid of seaweed? Who is responsible for finding the shark cages if needed? We cannot keep our team from falling occasionally. We live in a fallen world which is not going to be perfect. But as the leader, we can be accountable to make sure to live deeply and provide our teams with value as well. What is the first thing that you can do in the next seven days to recognize where others are falling?

We find value in our faith when we dig deeper as well. Discussing a topic in a Sunday school, small group, and understanding a sermon can connect us deeper. We can take the seasons of our faith and commit them to spiritual practices like fasting, doing a prayer journal, or starting a devotion. But if we get caught up in falling, our perception jumps almost automatically to the landing. That is what fear does to us.

> "I sank beneath the waves, and the waters closed over me. Seaweed wrapped itself around my head."
>
> JONAH 2:5 NLT

That sounds scary to me, what about you? It sounds scary, and I am not even in that ocean. Sometimes our fear is just a matter of perception. Where do you think it feels like the seaweed is getting to you? Maybe it is time to go deeper into prayer in your relationship with Christ. We have tools like the church, our small groups, and scripture to assist us. How are you being accountable to grow deeper in your faith?

The only person that has the authority to hold you accountable in this world is you. What is the first thing you can do about it in the next seven days?

Let us pray.

Heavenly Father, thank you for our emotions as we might experience the mountain tops with you. But when we fall from those peaks it can be scary. Guide us and hold us in the comfort of the palms of your hands when that occurs. May we have the confidence and wisdom to remember the innocence of the prayers of children. We are your children. In Jesus' name, we pray. Amen.

DECEMBER 23: A LITTLE HEAT, PLEASE

Leaders, when was the last time you had a fire? It is easy to think that fires are dangerous, and that damage control is always required. But as leaders, we need to remember that fire produces heat and warmth. Are we leading in a way that acts like a thermostat to keep fires from raging out of control, or do we throw water on the embers as soon as they are seen? Our families and organizations might grow cold and become dormant for a long winter if we put out the embers. We might want to encourage and stoke the embers of productivity, creativity, and results.

When water is put on a fire, the heat begins to dissipate, and the flames go out. Putting water on the fire is not desired when the heat and light of the fire is needed. When leaders fail to collaborate with the team, it is like that water that gets put on the fire. Where is your team smoldering? How can you collaborate with someone so that the smoldering moves from smoke to flame? If you do not have any embers around, either the leader is not creating them, or someone is putting them out? As a leader, we can seek the answers to what is putting out the fire. If you cannot find the issue, then perhaps you need to find a collaborator to discover why the fire will not stay lit. What is the first thing that you can do about it in the next seven days?

Brothers and sisters in Christ, it is time to let the light of the fire come.

> "Dear friends, do not be surprised at the fiery trials you are going through, as if something strange were happening to you. Instead, be very glad—for these trials make you partners with Christ in his suffering, so that you will have the wonderful joy of seeing his glory when it is revealed to all the world."
>
> 1 PETER 4:12-13 NLT

Maybe we can turn the nozzle of fear off for a bit. Can we turn back our fear and let the living water be in control of the fire for a while? We are not called to be a firefighter daily when we have Christ. We are called to follow the living water. We do not have to be holding the fire hose, fearing that the fire will get out of control, when we trust Jesus. Our hands can be freed to do other things if the fear hose can be put down. If Jesus is putting out the fires, maybe we can hold people with compassion, care, and love. What is the first thing you can do about it in the next seven days?

Let us pray.

Heavenly Father, place inside of us embers for love, compassion, caring and sharing. Guide us to be comfortable with such embers, embers that bring us warmth of life. May we turn our fire extinguishers of fear to your control. Let our eyes see the sparks of your grace. Let our hearts feel the warmth of your love. Let us bask in the light of your forgiveness. Allow us to put away our fears, one fire at a time. In Jesus' name, we pray. Amen.

DECEMBER 24: LOVE, COMPETITORS, AND COMPETITION

As a leader, sometimes we can find our organization in competition with another organization. But how we lead our team and compete can be measured by love. Our role is to drive value. Our value does not need to be called the best value but needs to meet the value of those we serve. It seemingly comes down to what actions we will or will we not provide. Are we looking inward towards our service delivery with love, respect, and value? If so, our actions will probably bear witness to it. If we are not of this type of mindset, greed and cost are likely to be the most important characteristics. There are examples of companies and leaders who are willing to expend extreme costs that affect others for their own personal win. Think back to times that you might have witnessed greed in your journey. If you can identify some of those times, take a deeper look and evaluate how the impact of love was happening.

I suspect that love might not have been very present or possibly missing completely. How might you see a different way that the situation could have been handled? Sometimes all we must do to increase value is to find a way to make love present. Where do you have an unfair competitive advantage because of love being part of the value your team delivers? If you are missing the component of love, it might be that the growth of your team is dependent upon it. What is the first thing that you can do in the next seven days? As brothers and sisters in Christ, how do you love someone else and God? I believe that the feeling of love is different from the actions of love.

"But I say, love your enemies! Pray for those who persecute you!"

MATTHEW 5:44 NLT

To be in love with someone might be all about us. I remember the emergent love that occurred while I developed my relationship with my wife. She held my hand, and physically, I could feel she loved me. We even occupied space and time together which made me aware of her love because she was present with me. But could God love us this way? It may be that our love for God is not so much about ourselves as it may be about us. It is about action. It is about being in love with Jesus and acting to show others our love. We may not hold Jesus' hands, but we can hold the hand of our children as we walk them to school. We can hold the hand of the homeless and walk them to dinner. We can put our arms under others to support them when they are hurting and need assistance. A big part of our love of God is about actions, our actions. Where can you enhance your faith, your relationships, your love in the next ninety days? What is the first thing that you can do about it in the next seven days?

Let us pray.

Heavenly Father, we understand that we do not have your knowledge. We know that you love us because you sent your Son to us to show us how to relate to you through our roles in this world. Help us today to be in love with you, to have the confidence to share your love for all through our actions. May you send the Holy

Spirit to guide us today for an action step. For we fear a world that would be without you. In Jesus' name, we pray. Amen.

DECEMBER 25: DO NOT OPEN THAT

An attitude of excellence might include the belief that everyone has special gifts or a special set of aptitudes. As a leader, what are yours? A powerful exercise can be to reflect on what it is that you do that seems to come easy for you. We can ask what seems natural for you to do and give you energy when you do it. If the leader of a family or organization has not done this exercise for themselves, it might be likely that the people of the organization have not done it either. That sounds like an organization that has a huge untapped resource to me. Do you have an inventory or list of special gifts for your team? Think about it for a minute. Consider thinking about three gifts that give you energy. Does it give you energy just thinking about these activities? I suspect that it might put you in a mindset that is empowering and positive. If that is true, how do you think the exercise might make your team feel? It is liberating at some level to recognize that we have been created with unique gifts. How often do you as a leader adjust your attitude to seek out unique abilities of team members? What is the first thing you can do about it in the next seven days?

As brothers and sisters in Christ, we have been given special spiritual gifts by God. We were created in the image of God. This combination makes each one of us unique.

> "God gave these four young men an unusual aptitude for understanding every aspect of literature and wisdom. And God gave Daniel the special ability to interpret the meanings of visions and dreams."
>
> DANIEL 1:17 NLT

But a special gift sealed up and stored away serves no one. Imagine an anniversary, birthday, or Christmas celebration where gifts are presented and then put in the attic unwrapped. As the presenter of that gift, would you feel unappreciated and shorted somehow? Does a gift that is unwrapped really seem like a gift if it is unopened? It seems like the gift is incomplete if it stays in the package. What are your spiritual gifts and how are you using them? It may be that you have never been through a spiritual gifts inventory project. If that is true, then we will consider it a gift to let you know that there are classes and projects that are designed to help you discover them. Doing these exercises can be just like unwrapping a gift. A focus on these gifts is likely to be more rewarding than another necktie or fruitcake. Maybe the most important gifts of this holiday season are the ones that are God-given and are waiting to be opened by our hearts and minds. Instead of presents under a tree, or gifts given for a birthday, can we adjust our attitude to look for our spiritual gifts? What is the first thing you can do about it in the next seven days?

Let us pray.

Heavenly Father, you are the Creator. You have given us one another, love, spiritual gifts, and aptitudes. Open our eyes so that we might see these gifts. Inspire curiosity in us so that we might seek to know them. When found, grant us the courage and confidence to use them in honor of your holy name. In Jesus' name, we pray. Together, Amen.

DECEMBER 26: BREADCRUMBS ON THE TRAIL

As the leader of a family or an organization we can set the possibility of how we are followed. It can seem at times that some cultures promote entertainment, rest, and relaxation more than it promotes value and action. As a leader, are we promoting the culture or our value proposition? If our team spends excessive time getting ready, to get ready, and then needs a vacation, we miss the value delivery. Where are you or your team in the "get ready" zone? When our attitude is in "get ready" mode it can feel like there is momentum moving in the right direction. That is a great feeling when you believe that your team is working to provide value. But imagine a vehicle with low, medium, and high gear.

A multiple-geared vehicle has gears to achieve efficiency and maximize power which results in value. If our attitudes are allowed to get stuck in "getting ready" gear, we will not maximize that efficiency and power. When a set of gears moves through the progression, getting stuck brings stress and friction. I can hear the whining in my mind as I think about a transmission that has not shifted. It sounds uncomfortable when people hear it. It does not sound like a natural sound. I suspect that people can exhibit the same types of symptoms when they get stuck as well. Where do you think that members of your team might be stuck? As the leader, how will you go about helping to adjust the focus to make the old way uncomfortable? A new focus will help the team to become comfortable with a new level of success. Let us leave a trail for the team to see how to get unstuck. What is the first thing that you can do about it in the next seven days?

As brothers and sisters in Christ, we are to be called a people of action. But often we can be distracted by the ways of this world.

> "So prepare your minds for action and exercise self-control. Put all your hope in the gracious salvation that will come to you when Jesus Christ is revealed to the world."
>
> 1 PETER 1:13

If we have a great set of instructions, what is holding us back? Could it be that it is our mindset and reliance on something other than on God? Our attitudes are influenced by the world and the example that Jesus gave us. The example of the world is constantly in front of us. Perhaps we can challenge each attitude that we take with an alternative one. Instead of an attitude of being right this week, perhaps we can consider an attitude of being kind. Which might emulate Jesus more? If we focus on an attitude of kindness instead of being right, I believe we will be compelled to be in action more. Being right will not likely cause much to be in action about. Nor will it compel us to honor God and show love. If our attitude gets stuck with being right it will likely act to create that same friction and stress I wrote about earlier. If the leader refuses to make the shift, I suspect that they are also stuck. A trail of action will leave proof that others have been here before. What can you do this week to be in action to honor Jesus?

Let us pray.

Heavenly Father, you created this world as a place of action. There was one day of rest and the balance of the days were productive. Make a six-to-one ratio be the ratio that we ourselves begin to live. In Jesus' name, we pray. Amen.

DECEMBER 27: FEAR THIS

As a leader of a family, business, or group it might seem that we have more to fear because of more people being involved. But our fears are mostly of things that are not truly dangerous. Fears are relevant because we have a desire to survive. When team members work with us, we can begin to be fearful about the team members' survival also. But our survival needs today are not what they were thousands of years ago. As leaders, are we satisfied with something so small as simple survival or are we wanting more? I believe that as a leader our main fear should be of being less than our team is capable of being. Our best fear could be of being less than what our minds believe is the best of who we are. That is the kind of fear that will produce a great result instead of complacency or settling. Who on your team might be focused on too small of a fear? Where are you as a leader, fearing something too small?

I suspect the best things to be fearful of are the things that we are willing to address because of the risk. Here are two fears that a leader might have. One could fear a team member leaving. Another fear could be of the entire team leaving. Which fear would you address if both were to happen to you? I suspect it would be the entire team leaving. The best news about finding bigger fears and obstacles is that they likely represent bigger opportunities as well. Are you willing to think bigger this week for the future of your team? What is the first thing that you can do about it in the next seven days?

Being a Christian or a person of faith does not make us have less fears. As humans, our brains are designed to recognize fear. In fact, our brains pay five times the amount of attention to fears than to the positive things in our lives. But I do not think that is what Jesus wants in our relationship with Him.

> "How joyful are those who fear the Lord—all who follow his ways!"
>
> PSALMS 128:1

Should we fear the challenges of this world, or should we fear having to face them without Jesus? As people who know the Lord Jesus Christ, we can jump up from our comforts and claim the glory that is before us.

Where are you comfortable and fearing losing that comfortableness? If a robber were to come and take three things from you, what three things do you want to keep safe from their crime? Did your list include Jesus? Losing Jesus is the fear that is worthy of our attention. May our comfortableness be focused on that first. All other fears are secondary, they are real, but secondary. Where do you need to transform your fears as Jesus wants? Living without Christ restricts us to the expectations of this world. We can experience more love and less fear when we focus on following him. Leading in one's faith will help us to prioritize the fears, but it can be difficult to do. Who can you trust to assist you in doing an inventory to find a bigger life with Christ? What is the first thing you can do about it in the next seven days?

Let us pray.

Heavenly Father, Master of all, you know us. You know our hearts and minds which include our fears. Find us in our comfort and meet us today. Open our ears and eyes to see that our fears can keep us from you. Split the fog so that we see through the fears to see you on the other side. Make us know your presence as easily as we know when the clothes we wear are dripping with water. Bring your living water to soak our souls. In Jesus' name, we pray. Together, Amen.

DECEMBER 28: REFOCUSED

As a leader of an already established team, you have experienced success. Past goals have been met, new team members have been assigned roles, and new ways have been shaped. When external factors change, it can challenge us and the team. It is like a thunderstorm building in the pathway of your flight plan. The thunderstorm is viewed as a limiting factor. The extreme winds of the storm test the aerodynamics and the passengers will be required to remain seated with lap belts attached. The risks on the outside of the airplane even create limits on the interior of the plane. Completing the trip will require a decision to fly through, fly over, avoid the storm to the left or the right. It is possible that the flight would best be served by slowing down to let the storm pass or perhaps landing is the best choice. The storm requires an adjustment by the pilot to keep the plane and passengers safe.

When this occurs, it is now that the plane's navigator and its tools are extra valuable. The navigator will give the pilot the data it needs to make the decision for the protection of the people and the equipment. Acquiring the benefits of a navigator helps to identify and remove the limits that a leader faces. What challenges have arisen in the last ninety days? Who on your team can serve as a navigator? If you do not have one, perhaps now is the time to find one to finish strong and start something even stronger. What is the first thing that you can do about it in the next seven days?

As brothers and sisters, we too can have external factors that arise in our lives. They affect our journey with Christ as well as the team.

> "You issued a decree requiring all the people to bow down and worship the gold statue when they hear the sound of the horn, flute, zither, lyre, harp, pipes, and other musical instruments."
>
> DANIEL 3:10 NLT

Daniel and his associates refused to abandon their primary purpose. Worshiping only God as they knew him was their purpose. They did not have an alternative they were willing to consider. New regulations, new details, and new leadership affect our journey. But your destination does not have to be altered. It is our pathway that must alter. That can be uncomfortable. Maybe God wants us to get comfortable being a little bit uncomfortable. Where are you feeling a little anxious or uncomfortable? We have a navigator in Jesus that is willing to engage us. He has paid the price to give us a new path. He can help us to land where we are uncomfortable. He can guide us to slow down or speed up. And he can bring others who can help us to love when the thunderstorms of life come upon us. Are you ready to bust through the limits of your life with the help of Christ? What can you do daily in the next seven days to adjust your flight path of your faith?

Let us pray.

Heavenly Father, you are the Creator and the Great Comforter. You have sent Jesus Christ to comfort us. There is nothing that we can do or have done that can separate your comfort from us. When we find ourselves unstrung, unhinged, and undone, make us find you faster. Put our frustrations and distractions aside so that we might clearly have sight on our destination. Make our new path known. In Jesus' name, we pray. Amen.

DECEMBER 29: WHEN MUSIC MELTS?

As a leader of a family, a company, or team we have many tools available to us. How do you assist your team with growing their capacity? We might think of our team's value delivery capabilities as a funnel with your team at the top and the capacity at the bottom. Your team's capacity determines the width of that funnel. As a leader, we want our team to multiply the value by collaborating and expanding that delivery wider and wider to have an impact on the world and return profits of some kind to us. But if a team member gets stuck and stops growing it acts like a plug, restriction, or obstacle in the funnel. As leaders, we can help them get back to value delivery. What tools are you using?

Fear is not the most valuable tool that a servant leader needs to deploy. Where might fear have snuck into the funnel this past thirty days or maybe this year? Is it time for a different tool? Research shows that music has power over our mindset. Is music a tool that you are using? During this time of year, holiday music seems to abound. Music makes a difference. Many research studies have proven it. What is the first thing you can do to use music to replace fear? As a leader, another critical tool is accountability. Where can you put multiple tools to work to increase your capacity? What is the first thing that you can do about it in the next seven days?

As brothers and sisters in Christ, we are subject to the world and the fears that it casts. But many of our fears are based on our perception and experience, not reality. Many times, we struggle to get past the fears and spend way too much time behaving directly because of them. During the holiday season of Christmas, we hear special music that carries its message. Stop and list your favorite three holiday songs. Make a mental note of them. Is there any fear in them or do they help us focus on what is good and right with the world?

"Fearing people is a dangerous trap but trusting in the Lord means safety."

PROVERBS 29:25 NLT

During this joyous time of year, I find that displacing fear is a good thing. What fears would you relieve or displace if you could? Maybe it is time to focus on the music that has been created and inspired in us as brothers and sisters to celebrate the birth of Christ. If you find this an attractive idea, would you be willing to be accountable for it? Perhaps you could promise to listen to music to start off your day. Maybe you could listen to the songs in your cubicle, in your office, or in your vehicle. Some of the easiest ways to displace fear is to be accountable and to set a new habit when fear appears. Our capacity for God is larger than we will be able to comprehend. Are you willing to be accountable to experience more of his love? Maybe all it takes is a little music. What is the first thing that you can do about it in the next seven days?

Let us pray.

Heavenly Father, you are an inspiring force in our world. Open our hearts and ears to hear the still small voice that you might use to speak to us. Bring special clarity to us as we listen to the notes and melodies that have been shaped by human minds during this holiday season. Melt our fears away like the sun melts the ice cube on a sidewalk. Make them evaporate and let our hearts and minds be cleansed to worship and celebrate you. In Jesus' name, we pray. Amen.

DECEMBER 30: A DISAPPEARING TRICK

As a leader, there will be times that you will probably see people running from problems, the truth, or even responsibilities. Running from these issues is sometimes done out of fear. I think that we all likely do it, even leaders. We might think that running from issues is a sign of lack of resolve or weakness, or it could carry a negative connotation. Running away from the problems does not resolve them. But it could be that we can always look for the positive. Even in the worst of conditions, it is possible that a positive might exist. When disaster strikes your team, does your compassion step up? I would think that is a positive. When destruction happens to others, do you send some sort of relief? If so, I believe that is something positive as well. There is always the possibility of something positive, but many times we can get bogged down. Where might you be carrying a negative connotation about some run-away event? It just might be time for a perception check and that is where someone else can share a positive perspective. All we need to do is to be curious and look for it. It can start by asking someone to look for it on your team. Who is the someone on your team that you go to for a positive perspective? Maybe you can add a few other collaborators to bring a positive focus to some conditions that need improvement. What is the first thing that you can do about it in the next seven days?

As a person of faith, have you ever noticed people who have disappeared from your worship center, church, or group? Sometimes people just do a little magic trick and poof they are gone. It could be that they are running away because of something that they have done. But those that are left can notice the absence. When you do notice an absence, you have a license issued by Christ to take note and to change yourself.

> "Then the sailors picked Jonah up and threw him into the raging sea, and the storm stopped at once! The sailors were awestruck by the Lord's great power, and they offered him a sacrifice and vowed to serve him."
>
> JONAH 1:15-16 NLT

This passage shares about the sailors who did not know of our God. When they threw Jonah overboard, they were changed. It is Jonah who is doing the running here and avoiding God, but his actions brought these idol worshippers into relationships with the one true God. We can miss many opportunities in this world because we are looking out for ourselves. Where have you missed an opportunity this year? Maybe it is not too late to do something about it. There are a couple of days left. The short time frame might best be served if you could collaborate with others on it. Who is the one person, regardless of their position in life, their profession, or where they live, that you would trust to have a conversation with? What is the first thing that you can do about it? It is time to get it done.

Let us pray.

Heavenly Father, you are the knower of the unknown and the seer of the unseen. Open our eyes so that we might see the opportunities to bring others to a relationship with you. Find us when we run away, and show us your compassion. Search for us in the depths of our fears when we feel that we are being crushed by the pounding waves of this world. Make your Son and our Savior shine the light to brighten our paths. Place our hands together with those that are lost instead of gripping our own hands in fear. Move us to action. In Jesus' name, we pray. Amen.

DECEMBER 31: HEART OR GRAPES IN THE PRESS?

As a leader, one is subject to many pressures. But pressure is not good or bad, it just is. It is our perception that gives it meaning. If pressure is one step of the value delivery system of your team, then it is valuable. Imagine that your team produces fish aquarium pebbles for the bottom of the tank. If your team applies pressure to large rocks to create the pebbles, it is valuable. But if that same pressure used to break the rocks was used against the glass, the tank would be destroyed. Where on your team does it seem that there is inappropriate pressure? Inappropriate pressure can be pressure that is lacking, or it can be pressure put in the wrong place. Imagine the pressure of the wine press used to crush coconuts. The equipment is wrong for the project. There is no means by which to separate the husk of the coconut from the meat of the nut. The coconut juice is going to escape like grape juice. That is until the coconut meat begins to clog the drainage system. This is an example of pressure in the wrong place. What can you do as a leader to capture and redirect it? What is the first thing you can do about it in the next seven days?

As brothers and sisters in Christ, we might look back over the last year with reverence or maybe fear. But we also look forward and, in this world, there is pressure all around it seems. Our culture promotes and puts pressures on us to bend to its way of behaving.

> "So the angel swung his sickle over the earth and loaded the grapes into the great winepress of God's wrath."
>
> REVELATION 14:19 NLT

When grapes get harvested and turned into wine, they are pressed and trampled. The fruit, glorious and plump, even beautiful to look at, is destroyed, and the juice extracted. Sometimes it can feel that way for us. Our God knows our name regardless of how society wants to judge and separate us. God knows each of us and there is nothing that can be done to become unrecognizable to him. So let the grapes be picked. Let the skin be split, the fruit be exposed, and the juice to run. Whatever happens this year, know that our Savior is ready to forgive if we have done the splitting and exposing. Just because we know that some juice will run does not mean that we will be kept from enjoying its refreshing capabilities. Are you ready for the new year? Many are likely to make some New Year's resolutions tonight. Not many people will carry them through. What challenges are you willing to be inspired to put before you today in your faith? Will you read through the Bible or maybe just one of the books? Can you commit to praying hourly or perhaps it would be daily or weekly? Whatever you want to achieve is up to you to establish. Setting our mind to draw closer to God does not have to be done when we get put in that wine press by others. Are you willing to change where the pressure will be put this year in your faith? What is the first thing that you can do to redirect the pressure in the next seven days?

Let us pray.

Heavenly Father, we come to you in such a lowly state. We know there are those among us who feel crushed and beyond repair. Nothing, not one thing is beyond your sight. May we be the hands and feet of your Spirit this coming year. Empower us as we start a new calendar year. May our fruit be whole as we start and make known how you might use us to glorify your Son and our Savior. In Jesus' name, we pray. Amen,

Bonus Devotionals

When this project came to life, we asked the team to think about what would make it even more impactful or valuable. The idea was agreed upon to welcome our sphere of influence to share a devotional as well. We had nine people that agreed and submitted a piece. Different perspectives allow us to see an issue from a different angle. I hope you find each of them a unique experience to explore and to be curious about just as I have. We are indebted to them and thank them for having an impact on the Kingdom through their contribution.

Blessing in Disguise

BLESSING IN DISGUISE

We have been told many times throughout our lives—life is not so much what happens to us but how we respond to it! From my earliest childhood, I was taught there would be times, particularly times of disappointment, sadness, and defeat that I could not be able to control … things will happen that I must learn to accept! This is a very hard concept for anyone, but I learned it at a very young age when my Dad, who was a chronic alcoholic joined A.A. (Alcoholics Anonymous.) The prayer that was repeated before each and every meeting he attended and became a part of our family nightly prayers is well known to many as The Serenity Prayer.

"God, grant me the serenity to ACCEPT what I cannot change, the STRENGTH to change the things I can, and the WISDOM to know the difference"!

These words became imprinted in my brain and through my life I have come to the awareness that my Dad's addiction had become one of my greatest gifts and blessings.

In 1975 on a rainy spring day in April, my life changed forever. Our family was camping with friends at Lake Wilson, and there was a tragic rock slide. Donovan our oldest son age 14 and our youngest daughter Dana age 7, were instantly killed! Personally, I believe this to be any parent's greatest nightmare; but it was reality, and life had to go on, not only for ourselves, but for our other 3 surviving children. Diane age 15, Darren age 13, and Dave age 8.

We accomplished this most difficult task only through the GRACE of God as we were blessed with what we referred to as our 3 F's…Faith, Family and Friends.

It was during this incredibly sad time that the words of The Serenity Prayer comforted me, and I asked God many times to give me the strength to accept what I could not change but also the wisdom to trust Him in my time of sorrow. God heard the prayers of this grieving mother and much to our surprise and joy, in August, I realized I was pregnant! Dustin our son was due on April 27, exactly a year from the date of the accident! God doesn't make mistakes, and He always hear our prayers!

I wish I could tell you it was smooth sailing from then on but this was not to be the case, 10 years later on March 12, 1985 our son Darren age 23, had experienced a difficult marriage and divorce, became depressed and chose to commit suicide as his only way out of his pain!

Once again, these same words came back to visit/comfort me, and again God was faithful!

Life continued to be challenging as my husband of 50 years was diagnosed in 2008 with lung cancer and God called him home on September 7, 2009. My prayers and trust in God were my strength, courage and comfort! I also became aware of the fact that He would be blessed to see our children in their heavenly home before I would, but they will all be there to meet me when God calls my name!

I was widowed for 8 years, and it was so obvious during that time God never forsake me! On July 15, 2017 I married a beautiful Christian man who is a daily reminder of God's faithfulness and love!

Let us pray.

Heavenly Father, your love, your kindness, and your generosity go so far beyond my mind can possibly comprehend, but I do thank you from all that is within me! Jesus, you are the true Shepherd that has already laid down His life for His sheep. Thank you for counting me as one of your fold, as undeserving as I am! I am so thankful that through your death on the cross, you paid the price for my salvation, and I have joy in knowing I shall see my children again in Heaven!

Thankfully the Bible gives me a true path of hope in 1 Thessalonians 5:16-18 which says, "Be joyful always; pray continually; give thanks in all circumstances, for this is God's will for you in Christ Jesus". Amen.

— Carolyn Dreiling

COMPARISON IS THE THIEF OF JOY

Author John Acuff says this, "Don't compare your beginning to someone else's middle." The temptation to COMPARE is at every turn for fathers. Your next chat with a friend, trip to the store, or your next social media engagement. Trust me...I get it. Social media is filled with posts of fathers at their best. And when we look up at the comparison scoreboard, what do we see? Whether you come out on top or come up lacking, there is simply no win in comparison. There's never a finish line or sense of satisfaction. His game of comparison is a game with no winners.

If you are a father reading this, I challenge you not to fall into the comparison pitfall. Comparison is being caught in the trap of constantly asking, "Does he or she have more than me? Are they better off? Is he or she smarter, funnier, cooler?" We preoccupy ourselves with these questions, but God has a better plan. He desires that we be free from comparison.

When we don't measure up, envy and jealousy take root. For example, your mancave was perfectly fine until you saw your friend's newly renovated one. You were cool with your SUV until your neighbor pulled their new truck out of their garage. When comparison ends up in our favor, pride and arrogance can trap us. What's uglier is that comparison can trick us into delighting in the misfortune of others. Have you ever been just a *little bit happy* to hear about a friend's breakup? Or to see a colleague at work passed over for a promotion? There is simply no win in comparison. It brings envy, jealousy, pride, and arrogance. It leads us to make unwise financial decisions just to keep up with those around us. It stains our friendships with gossip and striving.

Don't fall for the Father Comparison Pitfall.

How has the comparison pitfall affected you? Are you exhausted or broke from trying to keep up with friends or neighbors? What is *your* greatest ambition in life right now? What are *you* doing to pursue it? Is that ambition motivated at all by comparing yourself to others? Let's decide today to stop playing the game of comparison—it's a game you simply can't win.

Try this:

See how many times you can catch yourself in the comparison pitfall today—maybe with co-workers, while on the subway, or while on social media.

Meditate on This:

Keep your lives free from the love of money, and be content with what you have because God has said,

"Never will I leave you; never will I forsake you."

HEBREWS 13:5

— Chauncey Julius

COMMITTED TO PURPOSE

As leaders, we are committed to purpose and are accountable for making progress toward that purpose. The reality is that we are often tempted to get off course. We can be tempted to stay "busy," convincing ourselves that we are doing good, but falling short in advancing the mission and purpose of our organizations. Many of us look and see needs to be addressed, and wanting to be helpful, we jump to act and accomplish a task at hand.

However, we may be missing the point of staying true and accountable to the larger purpose. I am guilty of this. I trust you are too. Often what I need is to reassess and to re-align myself more clearly with my purpose and that of my organization. Or to say it differently, I need to be accountable for my actions as they relate to the purpose of my organization, my own personal call and purpose. When I measure my actions as they relate to the larger purpose, I can then better act in ways that are most important. It allows me to do the work that only I can do, helping to advance mission through my best effort. What is your purpose? How can you put into place an accountability plan and practice to stay committed to purpose? What do you need: clearer scheduling, smarter goals, maybe even a transparent support network? When you do get off track, what will it take for you to get back to purpose? Create an accountability plan for the next three weeks and stay committed.

We are also accountable as disciples of Jesus Christ. We are accountable for how we live, how we serve, how we used the resources we have been entrusted. I have shared in my preaching that when we come to the end of our journey of life, I trust Jesus is going to ask us, "What did you do with what I gave you?"

I believe He will ask accountability questions related to multiple aspects of our lives: our time, our relationships, our calling, and our financial resources. We are called to live our lives accountable to Jesus' purposes for the world, for the church, and for our lives. To do this, we need clarity of our purpose and we need a plan to advance that purpose. I believe Jesus expects our best, and I pray that He will be gracious when we fall short.

For us to commit to Him and to the higher purpose to which we have been called, we will need an accountability process in place. It will lead us in our family lives, our vocational work, and in our faith. What accountability do you need to hold to your life purpose? What would you need so that when you stand before Jesus and make an account for your life, He will say, "Well done good and faithful servant, enter into the joy of your master?"

Let us pray.

Almighty God, we give you thanks for the purposes you have placed in our lives. Thank you for leading us and calling us to make a lasting difference through the gifts you have given us. Place within us the courage to measure ourselves, our efforts, and our lives against your vision. Give us the courage to make the greatest impact we can, not for our glory or benefit, but for your glory and your kingdom. We are honored to serve. Keep us accountable and committed. In your name we pray. Amen.

— Dustin Petz

PURPOSEFUL FOCUS

Successful leadership experiences will make a person a better leader. But time and experience can also tempt a strong leader to lose focus. King David won many victories on the battlefield and was a great leader of Israel. But David is also known for a terrible failure. Most are familiar with the story of David and Bathsheba. David forced another man's wife to sleep with him, got her pregnant, and then had her husband killed.

Even great leaders are vulnerable if they lose focus. The Bible says,

> "In the spring, at the time when kings march out to war, David sent out Joab and his servants with the whole army of Israel . . . but David remained in Jerusalem."
>
> 2 Samuel 11:1

Instead of leading his army, David stayed home. One evening, David got up from his bed and strolled around the roof of the palace. From the roof, he saw Bathsheba bathing below. She was very beautiful, and David sent for her. Bathsheba could not refuse the king. If David had been leading his army as he normally did, he would not have been bored in his palace. Leadership ability increases with success and experience. But it takes intentional effort and discipline to stay focused when victories become routine.

Let us pray.

Heavenly Father, we praise you and thank you for our leadership skills and opportunities. Help us stay focused by not taking the victories you give us for granted. Thank you for your grace when we fail and then repent like King David did. And give us the wisdom and faith to trust and obey you in our future endeavors. Amen.

— Rex Zenger

STRENGTH IN NUMBERS

Don Boggs wrote the below article about the effects of collaborating in worship towards the end of the pandemic of 2021. His message also applies conceptually to entrepreneurs and leaders regarding working with teams. As a leader, you can be the single stick which can provide a little smoke, heat and light and do it for a short period of time. But that same stick could be the source to ignite a roaring fire. Enjoy

If you try to light one stick with a match, you may get some smoke, a small, albeit short-lived flame, and some smoldering. If you put two sticks together and light them, you will get only a slightly larger flame, and a longer burn. But if you put hundreds of sticks together in a pile and light them, you can get a roaring fire that generates warmth and energy.

The COVID pandemic changed many things in our lives, including the way we worshipped. Churches quickly adapted to provide online services to their members. With many members now vaccinated, churches either have or are planning their reopening. I worry about the number of people who have become comfortable, and perhaps even complacent, with the ability to worship at home. At our house, my wife times the preparation of our Sunday brunch for us to sit down and eat as we watch the online service. It is comfortable, convenient, and efficient. But it begs the question, "is watching the same as worshipping?" I do believe a person can have a meaningful worship experience online, but what are we sacrificing when we worship alone, rather than gathering to worship with others in our congregation.

Beyond the congregational fellowship, I believe we lose the synergy that comes from gathering and worshipping together. What all do we lose by not having our "sticks" on the same fire as others in the congregation?

In Hebrews 10 we are told "And let us consider one another in order to stir up love and good works, not forsaking the assembling of ourselves together, as is the manner of some, but exhorting one another".

And in John 15 we hear, "No branch can bear fruit by itself; it must remain in the vine."

Our United Methodist symbol is the cross and the flame. I pray that as we re-open our church, everyone will return to help rekindle the flame of Christ in all of us.

— Don Boggs

GOD WANTS YOU TO BE RICH

Somewhere along the way, many Christians have been taught that money is the root of all evil; however, the LOVE of money is the root of all evil. People, often Christians, condemn those that have money, or repel it whenever it comes their way. Where does this come from? I think it stems from many things, but one idea that it might stem from is from the word meekness in the bible.

Sometimes meekness is interpreted as being poor and living in poverty. I've experienced being broke as a joke, and having wealth beyond anything I ever imagined. All I know is this-when we DIDN'T have money THAT'S when money became more of an idol than when we did have money. Why? Because when we didn't have it, every decision and thought were centered around money, or lack thereof.

God WANTS you to prosper in many ways, including your bank account. This became a revelation to me when I read the bible cover to cover as I was starting my online business many years ago. All throughout the scripture, there are stories of how God abundantly poured out His favor and riches to people. And yes, it included money and wealth.

This changed my thinking about money and gave me the green light to go out and be all that God called me to be. In my industry, the only way to succeed is by helping others to succeed. And it's okay to make millions doing it.

The more you make, the more you can give and make the world a better place right? If you can't afford to help yourself, how can you help others? You may be thinking, "Yeah, but money can't buy happiness." You are correct, money CAN'T buy happiness. But neither can poverty. I pray that any negative strongholds you have about poverty mentality and/or negative money mindsets to be lifted.

Humble beginnings-
A single wide trailer and snapping mousetraps.

When we were first married, we lived in a single wide used trailer. My husband

and I used to lay in bed at night and listen to the mousetraps go off. I'm so grateful for our humble beginnings.

People often ask me to share or speak on the one thing that led from being on the verge of financial disaster to becoming a multiple 7 figure earner. If I had to narrow it down to one, it would be vision.

The bible says, without a vision, the people will perish. I realized that the pain to stay the same was much greater than the pain to change. So I created a clear mental vision of exactly what I wanted to happen, and I played a videotape of that every day in my head. And when I say every day, I mean every day for years!

Without a mental picture in your head, you will be tempted to quit when the going gets tough. Lose the vision, lose the dream. Vision was the gas that fueled my action when the motivation was long gone.

You will never leave where you are until you see in your mind where you'd rather be. Control your vision, control your future. Create YOUR vision, and start pushing play on the videotape in your mind day after day, visualizing that which you desire. Once you are able to imagine and visualize it, you're one step closer to having it. Don't use your imagination / vision to escape reality, use it to create it instead.

May the Lord give you eyes to see, ears to hear, and a heart to understand what He planted inside your heart. And most importantly, the guts and grit to go after it.

— Jayna Dyer

DEVELOP YOU

I'll never forget one of my first experiences as a leader. I was a sophomore in High School and had just assumed the coveted position of Co-Chair of the Debate Team. After winning tournament after tournament and ranking third in the state of my division, I felt confident and ready to rule the world… well, as much as you could as a fouteen-year-old girl from Kansas City. In preparation for my first tournament as co-chair after the big win, my debate coach pulled me aside and said "it's time to ditch the skirts & dresses. In this world, you have to lead like a man, and so you have to dress like one." I took her words as Gospel and began to create a leadership style modeled after strong men I had witnessed in my life.

My next leadership position came when I was hired as a Waitress & Bar Manager at a Bar & Grill in college. Not knowing where to start I ordered the book "Management for Dummies." In my reading, I learned the first step would be to develop my leadership style. As the only female leader within the chain at that time, I heard the words of my debate coach in my head: "lead like a man." I observed the male peers around me lead with gruffness, masculine power and a no-nonsense attitude and adopted the same. I soon felt an angst within me grow as I felt distant from my team and unauthentic in my role.

It took years for me to realize that I needed to step away from my preconceived notions and bad lessons on what a leader looked and acted like. I needed to step away from those, so I could step into the leader that God uniquely made me to be – as a woman and as my unique self. Almost from birth, I've been a nurturer, a caregiver of anything… plants, bugs, pets, ailing friends. When I stopped trying to lead like a man, I realized I could use my nurturing tendencies as I led. I also noticed that leadership styles transcend the gender spectrum. When I stopped making leadership styles about gender, I realized it's a person's gifts that guides their styles. I've been able to look at all the ways in which God has made me and use my gifts to develop a leading style that best serves my authenticity and the people around me.

God made you unique. God has made just one of you in this world. What are your strengths? What are your weaknesses? How can you develop a style of leading God's creation that honors who you are and how you tick? When we lead from our heart and soul, we operate with transparency and strength about who we are and what we need from our team.

Let us pray.

Creator God, thank you for uniquely creating me just as I am. Help me to embrace the ways in which I lead and care for your people on this Earth. Help me to let go of the leadership expectations or lessons I've put onto myself that don't honor who I am and how you've created me to lead. Be with me in my leadership journey, so that I can always use the position I've been put in – whether it be boss, family member, neighbor or volunteer – to honor you and your Kingdom.

— Melanie Nord

UNLIKELY COLLABORATORS

Genesis 41 (verses 37-49) denotes a plan for an anticipated outcome, from a dream, that required an unlikely collaborator. Pharaoh needed someone to interpret a dream. Once that someone was identified, a partnership was formed for a mission to collect food in advance before a famine – the interpreted dream outcome.

Pharaoh had vivid dreams and needed an interpreter. He was trying to align everything to his dreams. The man with the ability to spiritually interpret dreams is the imprisoned Joseph. God's way of making himself known in a unique way to Joseph and Pharaoh is curious. Joseph's words are powerful to Pharaoh and it is the spiritual discipline of hearing from the Lord and listening to his commands that go unnoticed. Pharaoh gave Joseph the earthly kingdom power, but the Lord granted Joseph to be a heavenly kingdom worker.

The Holy Spirit guided Joseph. Pharaoh "dressed him up" and gave Joseph the best for the mission and execution of the plan. Typically when I think of going on mission, I think of "dressing down" to get dirty and ready for what might come. Pharaoh continued to be the known person in charge, but the shift was that people started listening to Joseph because of his leadership in the land of Egypt. Joseph was sent and therefore he went to lead the people amongst them.

While Joseph was young, Joseph had vision and provided stability for future leadership. A series of collections and stories become bigger than him and impacted generations to come. The abundance blessed people beyond measure and the Lord worked through the people in the present and into the future where uncertainty lurked. Through listening to God, and then interpreting the following of the Spirit, comes great (and even greater) responsibility than we, and our dreams, could ever imagine.

Let us pray

Father God, we praise you for the Holy Spirit who grants us wisdom, fills us with life, guards our hearts, and illuminates our minds to comprehend the good news of Jesus Christ. Let us settle for nothing less than the truth that you have revealed to us in your Holy Word.

— Shane Warta

DO NOT FEAR

As a recognized leader, I want people to think of me as calm and collected. I want new acquaintances to see me as a person in complete control of any and all situations. That is my expectation! The reality is that I'm a world champion worrier! I can get anxious several times a day. I worry about little things, such as, am I dressed warmly enough as I leave the house. Should I take an umbrella? I also worry about big things like will my dear friend be safe driving in bad weather from Kansas City to see me. I check the weather reports several times while waiting anxiously.

One of my more frequent fears (worry is much the same as fear) is that I have said or done something to offend someone. This happens if I'm expecting a call from a dear friend and that person doesn't call. After waiting for a short time, I start to worry that he or she is upset with me over something I have said or done. Or, perhaps something that I did not say or do! More than once, I have asked someone why they are unhappy with me. This preoccupation with worries sometime keeps me from being productive.

Most days, I have a long to-do list to start the day. Often, I go to work on an assigned task, moving efficiently through a project. There are days when I can finish a project without interruption. Those are days when I am free of worry. Or, more likely, my thought process takes a sharp turn as I remember that I haven't heard from my daughter today. She always calls in the morning to see how I'm doing. Oh, my! She must have had an accident while driving to work. I can't get back to work until I hastily call her to make certain she is all right. That important project lies unfinished. I cannot focus on my work.

As a Christian, I need only to turn to the scriptures to relieve myself of my worries. Worry is a waste of energy. I need to pause and tell myself to put my worries aside and place my trust in God.

> "Cast your cares on the LORD and he will sustain you; he will never let the righteous be shaken."
>
> PSALM 55:22

One interpretation of this passage is that God loves us beyond our wildest imaginations. We must trust that in our troubled times, He is showing us how to rely on Him for everything. One of my favorite passages is in Philippians 4:6-7.

> "Do not be anxious about anything, but in every situation, by prayer and petition, with thanksgiving, present your requests to God. And the peace of God, which surpasses all understanding, will guard your hearts and your minds in Christ Jesus."

Another relevant scripture is Matthew 11:28-30.

> "Come unto me, all you who are weary and burdened, and I will give you rest. Take my yoke upon you and learn from me, for I am gentle and humble in heart, and you will find rest for your souls. For my yoke is easy and my burden is light."

From Isaiah 41:10:

"So do not fear, for I am with you; do not be dismayed, for I am your God. I will strengthen you and help you; I will uphold you with my righteous right hand."

And from Proverbs 12:25:

"Anxiety in a person's heart weighs him down, but an encouraging word brings him joy."

Let us pray.

Lord, we come to you full of anxieties. Often, we are shackled with fear that something terrible has happened to a loved one. Or we have unknowingly offended someone with a careless remark. Please relieve my mind of such stressful thoughts and help me to focus on the everlasting love which comes from you. Amen

— C. Clyde Jones

Acknowledgments

This book would not be possible without several individuals. First, my savior Jesus Christ, who fills my life when I allow it. The Holy Spirit who has moved me many times during the writing and sharing of the work.

My wife Kayla. The rudder of my ship. The one who does her best to share her wisdom, opinion, and perspective to keep me on course. To our children, David, Bryan, and Kristen who have been the inspiration and witnesses to many of the occasions that inspired a devotion. To my parents, Paul and Kathy Queen who started the journey of faith for myself and my brother Lawrence.

The writers of each of the 66 books which make up the Bible cannot be overlooked. Next would be all those that have contributed to making the Bible what it is today by working through the process of what it's made of, what language it is in, and of course the Holy Spirit that guided them through the process.

I have to acknowledge all of those that have impacted my faith journey, including pastors, Sunday school classmates both young and old, and members of the body of Christ's church that have poured into me in some way. To the authors of books that I have studied and been impacted by. And to those that have shared their lives with us in some way.

I especially want to thank our guest authors, who may have thought that they were not writers. We all have capability, but sometimes it just takes someone to have the courage to believe in them. Others are people that I respect and believe that they have wisdom to share.

In no particular order, thank you to C. Clyde Jones (you and your wife Midge were examples of what I want our marriage to exhibit), Don Boggs (a committee chair who showed how to listen, lead and love), Jayna Dyer (having the courage to change and share with others to be courageous), Chancey Julius (showing the power of challenging us to stand tall), Shane Warta (a leader willing to grow others spiritually and in other ways), Melane Nord (for being courageous enough to make course corrections and change directions), Rex Zenger (for your time and talents to the kingdom and the stewardship of the resources in the word of Agriculture), Dustin Petz (for holding the principal of accountability as component of growth), and Carolyn Dreiling (a modern day woman whose life experiences could be part of a modern day Bible if it were written today).

And not lastly by any means, to Cynthia Anaya, who did the final edits, layout, and served as project manager to put it all together. We came together seemingly by a movement of the Holy Spirit. (She might think differently since she has now completed the project). Our connection in finding one another was a spark that moved the project forward. Thank you for your stewardship of this project.

About the Author

From a paper route at age seven to navigating complex business terrains for entrepreneurs, Mark's life is a compelling narrative of faith, family, and professional evolution. He's not just a man who crossed religious and business domains; he's a connector, a navigator, and above all, a man of faith who believes that ones foundation of faith doesn't need to be left at the worship center.

Mark is the founder of Core Score, a business consulting firm that specializes in building navigation teams to assist entrepreneurs in their pursuits both personally and entrepreneurially.

You can visit Mark's website at: https://www.corescore.net/

You can also listen to his podcast on TuneIn

facebook.com/corescore.net

linkedin.com/company/core-score

youtube.com/@corescore-business-navigators

Made in the USA
Monee, IL
25 April 2024

57517326R00203